ANNUAL EDITIONS

Marketing 12/13

Thirty-Fifth Edition

EDITORS

John E. Richardson
Pepperdine University

Dr. John E. Richardson is Professor of Marketing in The George L. Graziadio School of Business and Management at Pepperdine University. He is president of his own consulting firm and has consulted with organizations such as Bell and Howell, Dayton-Hudson, Epson, and the U.S. Navy, as well as with various service, nonprofit, and franchise organizations. Dr. Richardson is a member of the American Marketing Association, the American Management Association, the Society for Business Ethics, and Beta Gamma Sigma honorary business fraternity.

Nisreen N. Bahnan

Dr. Nisreen Bahnan is Associate Professor of Marketing at Salem State University's Bertolon School of Business. She has earned her PhD in Business Studies from Temple University in Philadelphia. She teaches several marketing courses at the undergraduate and graduate levels, including Principles of Marketing, Consumer Behavior and Nonprofit Marketing. She has presented at conferences and published articles in the fields of services marketing and consumer behavior.

ANNUAL EDITIONS: MARKETING, THIRTY-FIFTH EDITION

Published by McGraw-Hill, a business unit of The McGraw-Hill Companies, Inc., 1221 Avenue of the Americas, New York, NY 10020. Copyright © 2013 by The McGraw-Hill Companies, Inc. All rights reserved. Printed in the United States of America. Previous edition(s) 2012, 2011, 2009, and 2008. No part of this publication may be reproduced or distributed in any form or by any means, or stored in a database or retrieval system, without the prior written consent of The McGraw-Hill Companies, Inc., including, but not limited to, in any network or other electronic storage or transmission, or broadcast for distance learning.

Some ancillaries, including electronic and print components, may not be available to customers outside the United States.

This book is printed on acid-free paper.

Annual Editions® is a registered trademark of The McGraw-Hill Companies, Inc.

Annual Editions is published by the **Contemporary Learning Series** group within the McGraw-Hill Higher Education division.

1 2 3 4 5 6 7 8 9 0 QDB/QDB 1 0 9 8 7 6 5 4 3 2

ISBN 978-0-07-352870-0
MHID 0-07-352870-6
ISSN 0730-2606 (print)
ISSN 2159-0621 (online)

Managing Editor: *Larry Loeppke*
Developmental Editor: *Dave Welsh*
Permissions Supervisor: *Lenny J. Behnke*
Senior Marketing Communications Specialist: *Alice Link*
Project Manager: *Joyce Watters*
Design Coordinator: *Margarite Reynolds*
Cover Designer: *Studio Montage, St. Louis, Missouri*
Buyer: *Susan K. Culbertson*
Media Project Manager: *Sridevi Palani*

Compositor: Laserwords Private Limited
Cover Image Credits: Comstock Images/Getty Images (inset); Comstock Images/Getty Images (background)

Editors/Academic Advisory Board

Members of the Academic Advisory Board are instrumental in the final selection of articles for each edition of ANNUAL EDITIONS. Their review of articles for content, level, and appropriateness provides critical direction to the editors and staff. We think that you will find their careful consideration well reflected in this volume.

Preface

In publishing ANNUAL EDITIONS we recognize the enormous role played by the magazines, newspapers, and journals of the public press in providing current, first-rate educational information in a broad spectrum of interest areas. Many of these articles are appropriate for students, researchers, and professionals seeking accurate, current material to help bridge the gap between principles and theories and the real world. These articles, however, become more useful for study when those of lasting value are carefully collected, organized, indexed, and reproduced in a low-cost format, which provides easy and permanent access when the material is needed. That is the role played by ANNUAL EDITIONS.

The new millennium should prove to be an exciting and challenging time for the American business community. Recent dramatic social, economic, and technological changes have become an important part of the present marketplace. These changes—accompanied by increasing domestic and foreign competition—are leading a wide array of companies and industries toward the realization that better marketing must become a top priority now to assure their future success.

How does the marketing manager respond to this growing challenge? How does the marketing student apply marketing theory to the real-world practice? Many reach for the *Wall Street Journal, BusinessWeek, Fortune,* and other well-known sources of business information. There, specific industry and company strategies are discussed and analyzed, marketing principles are often reaffirmed by real occurrences, and textbook theories are supported or challenged by current events.

The articles reprinted in this edition of *Annual Editions: Marketing 12/13* have been carefully chosen from numerous public press sources to provide current information on marketing in the world today. Within these pages you will find articles that address marketing theory and application in a wide range of industries. In addition, the selections reveal how several firms interpret and utilize marketing principles in their daily operations and corporate planning.

The volume contains a number of features designed to make it useful for marketing students, researchers, and professionals. These include the *Topic Guide* to locate articles on specific marketing subjects; *Internet References* pages; the *Table of Contents* abstracts, which summarize each article and highlight key concepts; and a *Glossary* of key marketing terms. Also included are Learning Outcomes at the beginning of each Unit, as well Critical Thinking study questions after each article to help students better understand what they have read.

The articles are organized into four units. Selections that focus on similar issues are concentrated into subsections within the broader units. Each unit is preceded by a list of unit selections, as well as a list of key points to consider that focus on major themes running throughout the selections, web links that provide extra support for the unit's data, and an overview that provides background for informed reading of the articles and emphasizes critical issues.

This is the thirty-fifth edition of *Annual Editions: Marketing.* Since its first edition in the mid-1970s, the efforts of many individuals have contributed toward its success. We think this is by far the most useful collection of material available for the marketing student. We are anxious to know what you think. What are your opinions? What are your recommendations? Any book can be improved and this one will continue to be, annually.

John E. Richardson
Editor

Nisreen N. Bahnan
Editor

The Annual Editions Series

VOLUMES AVAILABLE

Adolescent Psychology

Aging

American Foreign Policy

American Government

Anthropology

Archaeology

Assessment and Evaluation

Business Ethics

Child Growth and Development

Comparative Politics

Criminal Justice

Developing World

Drugs, Society, and Behavior

Dying, Death, and Bereavement

Early Childhood Education

Economics

Educating Children with Exceptionalities

Education

Educational Psychology

Entrepreneurship

Environment

The Family

Gender

Geography

Global Issues

Health

Homeland Security

Human Development

Human Resources

Human Sexualities

International Business

Management

Marketing

Mass Media

Microbiology

Multicultural Education

Nursing

Nutrition

Physical Anthropology

Psychology

Race and Ethnic Relations

Social Problems

Sociology

State and Local Government

Sustainability

Technologies, Social Media, and Society

United States History, Volume 1

United States History, Volume 2

Urban Society

Violence and Terrorism

Western Civilization, Volume 1

World History, Volume 1

World History, Volume 2

World Politics

Contents

UNIT 1
Marketing in the 2000s and Beyond

The concepts in bold italics are developed in the article. For further expansion, please refer to the Topic Guide.

UNIT 2
Research, Markets, and Consumer Behavior

The concepts in bold italics are developed in the article. For further expansion, please refer to the Topic Guide.

UNIT 3
Developing and Implementing Marketing Strategies

The concepts in bold italics are developed in the article. For further expansion, please refer to the Topic Guide.

The concepts in bold italics are developed in the article. For further expansion, please refer to the Topic Guide.

UNIT 4
Global Marketing

The concepts in bold italics are developed in the article. For further expansion, please refer to the Topic Guide.

Correlation Guide

The *Annual Editions* series provides students with convenient, inexpensive access to current, carefully selected articles from the public press. **Annual Editions: Marketing 12/13** is an easy-to-use reader that presents articles on important topics such as *the future of marketing, developing marketing strategies,* and many more. For more information on *Annual Editions* and other *McGraw-Hill Contemporary Learning Series* titles, visit www.mhhe.com/cls.

This convenient guide matches the units in **Annual Editions: Marketing 12/13** with the corresponding chapters in three of our best-selling McGraw-Hill Marketing textbooks by Perreault et al., Kerin et al. and Grewal/Levy.

Annual Editions: Marketing 12/13	Essentials of Marketing, 13/e by Perreault et al.	Marketing, 11/e by Kerin et al.	Marketing, 3/e by Grewal/Levy
Unit 1: Marketing in the 2000s and Beyond	**Chapter 2:** Marketing Strategy Planning	**Chapter 3:** Scanning the Marketing Environment **Chapter 4:** Ethical and Social Responsibility in Marketing	**Chapter 3:** Marketing Ethics **Chapter 12:** Services: The Intangible Product
Unit 2: Research, Markets, and Consumer Behavior	**Chapter 2:** Marketing Strategy Planning **Chapter 5:** Final Consumers and Their Buying Behavior **Chapter 6:** Business and Organizational Customers and Their Buying Behavior	**Chapter 1:** Creating Customer Relationships and Value through Marketing **Chapter 5:** Understanding Consumer Behavior **Chapter 8:** Marketing Research: From Customer Insights to Actions	**Chapter 4:** Analyzing the Marketing Environment **Chapter 5:** Consumer Behavior **Chapter 9:** Marketing Research and Information Systems
Unit 3: Developing and Implementing Marketing Strategies	**Chapter 2:** Marketing Strategy Planning **Chapter 3:** Evaluating Opportunities in the Changing Marketing Environment **Chapter 4:** Focusing Marketing Strategy with Segmentation and Positioning **Chapter 13:** Promotion—Introduction to Integrated Marketing Communications **Chapter 15:** Advertising, Publicity, and Sales Promotion **Chapter 16:** Pricing Objectives and Policies **Chapter 17:** Price Setting in the Business World	**Chapter 2:** Developing Successful Marketing and Organizational Strategies **Chapter 3:** Scanning the Marketing Environment **Chapter 6:** Understanding Organizations as Customers **Chapter 13:** Building the Price Foundation **Chapter 14:** Arriving at the Final Price **Chapter 15:** Managing Marketing Channels and Wholesaling **Chapter 16:** Customer-Driven Supply Chain and Logistics Management **Chapter 17:** Retailing **Chapter 18:** Integrated Marketing Communications and Direct Marketing **Chapter 19:** Advertising, Sales Promotion, and Public Relations **Chapter 21:** Implementing Interactive and Multichannel Marketing **Chapter 22:** Pulling It All Together: The Strategic Marketing Process	**Chapter 2:** Developing Marketing Strategies and a Marketing Plan **Chapter 6:** Business-to- Business Marketing **Chapter 8:** Segmentation, Targeting, and Positioning **Chapter 10:** Product, Branding, and Package Decisions **Chapter 11:** Developing New Products **Chapter 13:** Pricing Concepts for Establishing Value **Chapter 14:** Supply Chain Management **Chapter 15:** Retailing and Multichannel Marketing **Chapter 16:** Integrated Marketing Communications **Chapter 17:** Advertising, Public Relations, and Sales Promotions
Unit 4: Global Marketing		**Chapter 7:** Understanding and Reaching Global Consumers and Markets	**Chapter 7:** Global Marketing

Topic Guide

This topic guide suggests how the selections in this book relate to the subjects covered in your course. You may want to use the topics listed on these pages to search the Web more easily.

On the following pages a number of websites have been gathered specifically for this book. They are arranged to reflect the units of this *Annual Editions* reader. You can link to these sites by going to www.mhhe.com/cls

All the articles that relate to each topic are listed below the bold-faced term.

Advertising
1. Hot Stuff: Make These Top Trends Part of Your Marketing Mix
25. Logoland: Why Consumers Balk at Companies' Efforts to Rebrand Themselves
38. Fellow Graduates, before We Greet the Future, a Word from My Sponsor
40. 20 Highlights in 20 Years: Making Super Bowl Ad History Is No Easy Feat
42. Three Dimensional

Branding
1. Hot Stuff: Make These Top Trends Part of Your Marketing Mix
3. The Unmarketables
6. The Branding Sweet Spot
16. Trust in the Marketplace
25. Logoland: Why Consumers Balk at Companies' Efforts to Rebrand Themselves
28. Brand Integrity
29. Brand Apathy Calls for New Methods: Turn Customer Preference from "No Brand" to "Some Brand"
30. Should You Launch a Fighter Brand?
42. Three Dimensional

Competition
26. The Very Model of a Modern Marketing Plan
30. Should You Launch a Fighter Brand?
33. Competing against Free

Consumer behavior
1. Hot Stuff: Make These Top Trends Part of Your Marketing Mix
8. Putting Customers First: Nine Surefire Ways to Increase Brand Loyalty
23. The Tyranny of Choice: You Choose
25. Logoland: Why Consumers Balk at Companies' Efforts to Rebrand Themselves
42. Three Dimensional

Consumer demographics
1. Hot Stuff: Make These Top Trends Part of Your Marketing Mix
20. Marketing to Kids Gets More Savvy with New Technologies
21. It's Cooler than Ever to Be a Tween
42. Three Dimensional

Direct marketing
16. Trust in the Marketplace

Distribution planning
34. The Devolution of Marketing: Is America's Marketing Model Fighting Hard Enough to Keep Up?
35. In Lean Times, Retailers Shop for Survival Strategies

Economic environment
33. Competing against Free

Event marketing
11. Become the Main Attraction

Focus groups
26. The Very Model of a Modern Marketing Plan
27. Surveyor of the Fittest

Franchising
42. Three Dimensional

Global marketing
2. Evolve
34. The Devolution of Marketing: Is America's Marketing Model Fighting Hard Enough to Keep Up?
41. Emerging Lessons
42. Three Dimensional
43. Cracking the Next Growth Market: Africa
44. What the West Doesn't Get about China

Innovation
2. Evolve
32. Rocket Plan
42. Three Dimensional

Internet commerce
5. The Secrets of Marketing in a Web 2.0 World
31. Everybody Loves Zappos

Internet marketing
1. Hot Stuff: Make These Top Trends Part of Your Marketing Mix
5. The Secrets of Marketing in a Web 2.0 World
39. What's Your Social Media Strategy?

Lifestyle marketing
24. A Shift in Meaning for 'Luxury'

Marketing and technology
2. Evolve
26. The Very Model of a Modern Marketing Plan
39. What's Your Social Media Strategy?

Marketing concept
7. Marketing Myopia (with Retrospective Commentary)
23. The Tyranny of Choice: You Choose

Marketing ethics
16. Trust in the Marketplace
20. Marketing to Kids Gets More Savvy with New Technologies
38. Fellow Graduates, before We Greet the Future, a Word from My Sponsor

Marketing mix
1. Hot Stuff: Make These Top Trends Part of Your Marketing Mix
26. The Very Model of a Modern Marketing Plan

Marketing plan
26. The Very Model of a Modern Marketing Plan

Internet References

The following Internet sites have been selected to support the articles found in this reader. These sites were available at the time of publication. However, because websites often change their structure and content, the information listed may no longer be available. We invite you to visit www.mhhe.com/cls for easy access to these sites.

Annual Editions: Marketing 12/13

General Sources

Baruch College BusinessWeek—Harris Poll Demographics
www.businessweek.com/1997/18/b352511.htm

The Baruch College–Harris poll commissioned by *BusinessWeek* is used at this site to show interested businesses that are on the Net in the United States.

General Social Survey
webapp.icpsr.umich.edu/cocoon/ICPSR-SERIES/00028.xml

The GSS (see DPLS Archive: http://DPLS.DACC.WISC.EDU/SAF/) is an almost annual personal interview survey of U.S. households that began in 1972. More than 35,000 respondents have answered 2,500 questions. It covers a broad range of variables, many of which relate to microeconomic issues.

BestOfAdvertising.net
www.bestofadvertising.net

This is a complete list of sites that include information on marketing research, marketing on the Internet, demographic sources, and organizations and associations. The site also features current books on the subject of marketing.

STAT-USA/Internet Site Economic, Trade, Business Information
www.stat-usa.gov

This site, from the U.S. Department of Commerce, contains Daily Economic News, Frequently Requested Statistical Releases, Information on Export and International Trade, Domestic Economic News and Statistical Series, and Databases.

U.S. Census Bureau Home Page
www.census.gov

This is a major source of social, demographic, and economic information, such as income/employment data and the latest indicators, income distribution, and poverty data.

UNIT 1: Marketing in the 2000s and Beyond

American Marketing Association Code of Ethics
www.marketingpower.com

At this American Marketing Association site, use the search mechanism to access the organization's Code of Ethics for marketers.

Futures Research Quarterly
www.wfs.org/frq.htm

Published by the World Future Society, this publication describes future research that encompasses both an evolving philosophy and a range of techniques, with the aim of assisting decision makers in all fields to understand better the potential consequences of decisions by developing images of alternative futures. From this page explore the current and back issues and What's Coming Up!

Center for Innovation in Product Development (CIPD)
web.mit.edu/cipd/research/prdctdevelop.htm

CIPD is one of the National Science Foundation's engineering research centers. It shares the goal of future product development with academia, industry, and government.

UNIT 2: Research, Markets, and Consumer Behavior

Canadian Innovation Centre
www.innovationcentre.ca

The Canadian Innovation Centre has developed a unique mix of innovation services that can help a company from idea to market launch. Their services are based on the review of 12,000 new product ideas through their technology and market assessment programs over the past 20 years.

BizMiner—Industry Analysis and Trends
www.bizminer.com/market_research.asp

The importance of using market research databases and pinpointing local and national trends, including details of industry and small business startups, is emphasized by this site of the Brandow Company that offers samples of market research profiles.

Small Business Center—Articles & Insights
www.bcentral.com/articles/krotz/123.asp

This article discusses five market intelligence blunders made by the giant retailer K-Mart. "There were warning signs that K-Mart management mishandled, downplayed or just plain ignored," Joanna L. Krotz says.

Maritz Marketing Research
www.maritzresearch.com

Maritz Marketing Research Inc. (MMRI) specializes in custom-designed research studies that link the consumer to the marketer through information. Go to Maritz Loyalty Marketing in the Maritz Companies menu to find resources to identify, retain, and grow your most valuable customers. Also visit Maritz Research for polls, stats, and archived research reports.

USADATA
www.usadata.com

This leading provider of marketing, company, advertising, and consumer behavior data offers national and local data covering the top 60 U.S. markets.

WWW Virtual Library: Demography & Population Studies
http://demography.anu.edu.au/VirtualLibrary

More than 150 links can be found at this major resource to keep track of information of value to researchers in the fields of demography and population studies.

UNIT 3: Developing and Implementing Marketing Strategies

American Marketing Association Homepage
www.marketingpower.com

This site of the American Marketing Association is geared to managers, educators, researchers, students, and global electronic members. It contains a search mechanism, definitions of marketing and market research, and links.

Internet References

Consumer Buying Behavior

www.courses.psu.edu/mktg/mktg220_rso3/sls_cons.htm

The Center for Academic Computing at Penn State posts this course data that includes a review of consumer buying behaviors; group, environment, and internal influences; problem-solving; and post-purchasing behavior.

UNIT 4: Global Marketing

International Trade Administration

www.ita.doc.gov

The U.S. Department of Commerce is dedicated to helping U.S. businesses compete in the global marketplace, and at this site it offers assistance through many web links under such headings as Trade Statistics, Cross-Cutting Programs, Regions and Countries, and Import Administration.

World Chambers Network

www.worldchambers.net

International trade at work is viewable at this site. For example, click on Global Business eXchange (GBX) for a list of active business opportunities worldwide or to submit your new business opportunity for validation.

World Trade Center Association OnLine

http://iserve.wtca.org

Data on world trade is available at this site that features information, services, a virtual trade fair, an exporter's encyclopedia, trade opportunities, and a resource center.

UNIT 1

Marketing in the 2000s and Beyond

Unit Selections

Learning Outcomes

After reading this Unit, you should be able to:

- Dramatic changes are occurring in the marketing of products and services. What social and economic trends do you believe are most significant today, and how do you think these will affect marketing in the future?

- Theodore Levitt suggests that as times change, the marketing concept must be reinterpreted. Given the varied perspectives of the other articles in this unit, what do you think this reinterpretation will entail?

- In the present competitive business arena, is it possible for marketers to behave ethically in the environment and both survive and prosper? What suggestions can you give that could be incorporated into the marketing strategy for firms that want to be both ethical and successful?

Student Website

www.mhhe.com/cls

Internet References

American Marketing Association Code of Ethics
 www.marketingpower.com
Futures Research Quarterly
 www.wfs.org/frq.htm
Center for Innovation in Product Development (CIPD)
 www.web.mit.edu/cipd/research/prdctdevelop.htm

"If we want to know what a business is we must start with its purpose. . . . There is only one valid definition of business purpose: to create a customer. What business thinks it produces is not of first importance—especially not to the future of the business or to its success. What the customer thinks he is buying, what he considers 'value' is decisive—it determines what a business is, what it produces, and whether it will prosper."
—Peter Drucker, *The Practice of Management*

© Hill Street Studios/Getty Images

When Peter Drucker penned these words in 1954, American industry was just awakening to the realization that marketing would play an important role in the future success of businesses. The ensuing years have seen an increasing number of firms in highly competitive areas—particularly in the consumer goods industry—adopt a more sophisticated customer orientation and an integrated marketing focus.

The dramatic economic and social changes of the last decade have stirred companies in an even broader range of industries—from banking and air travel to communications—to the realization that marketing will provide them with their cutting edge. Demographic and lifestyle changes have splintered mass, homogeneous markets into many markets, each with different needs and interests. Deregulation has made once-protected industries vulnerable to the vagaries of competition. Vast and rapid technological changes are making an increasing number of products and services obsolete. Intense international competition, rapid expansion of the Internet-based economy, and the growth of truly global markets have many firms looking well beyond their national boundaries.

Indeed, it appears that during the new millennium marketing will take on a unique significance—and not just within the industrial sector. Social institutions of all kinds, which had thought themselves exempt from the pressures of the marketplace, are also beginning to recognize the need for marketing in the management of their affairs. Colleges and universities, charities, museums, symphony orchestras, and even hospitals are beginning to give attention to the marketing concept—to secure funds and donations and to provide what the consumer wants to buy.

The selections in this unit are grouped into four areas. Their purposes are to provide current perspectives on marketing, discuss differing views of the marketing concept, analyze the use of marketing by social institutions and nonprofit organizations, and examine the ethical and social responsibilities of marketing.

The articles in the first subsection provide significant clues about salient approaches and issues that marketers need to address in the future in order to create, promote, and sell their products and services in ways that meet the expectations of consumers.

The selections that address the marketing concept include Levitt's now classic "Marketing Myopia," which first appeared in the *Harvard Business Review* in 1960. This version includes the author's retrospective commentary, written in 1975, in which he discusses how shortsightedness can make management unable to recognize that there is no such thing as a growth industry. Also in this area is "Putting Customers First," which suggests nine ways to increase customers' brand loyalty. The next two articles in this subsection reflect the importance of companies focusing on customer satisfaction and customer service. The last article in this subsection, "Become the Main Attraction," gives some practical suggestions for successful event marketing.

In the *Services and Social Marketing* subsection, the first article discusses why some manufacturers are branching out into the service business. The second article discloses the importance of delivering unique value and faster service to meet and exceed customer expectations. The final article in this subsection reveals how six marketers have positioned their companies' services to respond to consumers' changing behaviors.

In the final subsection, *Marketing Ethics and Social Responsibility,* a careful look is taken at the strategic process and practice of incorporating ethics and social responsibility into the marketplace. "Honest Innovation" reveals that ethical issues in new product development could be hampering innovation growth, and "Trust in the Marketplace" discusses the importance of gaining and maintaining customers' trust.

Hot Stuff

Make These Top Trends Part of Your Marketing Mix

GWEN MORAN

Still using the same marketing tactics you were using five years ago? Those won't work with today's shifting demographics and preferences. The U.S. population is older, more multicultural, more time-pressed and more jaded toward overt sales pitches than ever before. And your marketing strategy should be built accordingly.

So what's working? After consulting over a dozen experts in the field, we've uncovered the following hot trends in marketing.

Market on the Move

According to the Mobile Marketing Association, by 2008, 89 percent of brands will use text and multimedia messaging to reach their audiences, with nearly one-third planning to spend more than 10 percent of their marketing budgets on advertising in the medium. As phones with video capability become more prevalent, expect more rich media marketing options. Plus, now that mobile phone service providers are dipping their toes into the credit card pool—soon your phone or PDA may make plastic obsolete—customers will be relying on these devices more than ever.

"There are some low-cost mobile marketing onramps for small businesses," says Kim Bayne, author of *Marketing Without Wires.* "Businesses can implement opt-in text messaging services and coupons with their loyal customers. We've already seen local restaurants send the day's specials to nearby lunch patrons. The cost is fairly low, and it can be done from a PC, without involving a pricey service provider."

Go Online

"Think globally, act locally" is now the mantra for entrepreneurs advertising online. Online ad spending is up as much as 33 percent over last year, says David J. Moore, chairman and CEO of digital marketing firm 24/7 Real Media Inc. in New York City. Earlier this year, Google announced a new local advertising program linked to its map service and AdWords program, allowing businesses to drive some of Google's traffic to their brick-and-mortar locations.

"[Entrepreneurs] should pay attention to any targeting that allows them to increase advertising efficiency by reaching users in their particular geographic area," says Moore. Online ads are also migrating to podcasts and blogs, where advertisers can reach very specific niche audiences. And with increased access to broadband and the falling cost of video production, Moore foresees a rise in online video ads for businesses as well.

Court the Boom

A baby boomer turns 50 every 7 seconds—joining a population segment that will grow by 25 percent in the next decade while other segments remain flat.

Matt Thornhill, founder of consulting firm The Boomer Project, which helps businesses reach adults born between 1946 and 1964, says it's time for marketers to recalibrate their thinking about marketing to older adults. Boomers are a dynamic group that's much more open to new experiences and brands than previous generations of older adults have been.

Stephanie Lakhani found that to be true at her upscale Breathe Wellness Spas (www.breathetoheal.com) in Boise, Idaho. Catering primarily to boomers, the two spas bring in about $1.2 million per year. She says boomers are an excellent target, with disposable income and a tendency to refer business. "They expect perfect service," says Lakhani, 35, who adds, "They tend to travel and buy in groups, so giving them an incentive to refer a friend in the form of an upgrade or a thank you [gesture] works very well. They are also very responsive to direct mail."

Thornhill adds that marketers should target boomers by what they're doing instead of how old they are. "Boomers are living such cyclical lives. In their 40s or 50s, they could be going back to college, be empty nesters or be married a second time and raising a young family," he explains. "You wouldn't sell the same vacation package to all these people. So pick the lifestyle segment you're targeting, and focus on that."

Sindicate Simply

For something that's named Really Simple Syndication, few tools are more misunderstood or misused than RSS. Provided by such companies as Bloglines (www.bloglines.com) and News-Gator (www.newsgator.com), RSS lets you send and receive information without using e-mail. Instead, the information is sent directly to a subscriber, who receives it through an RSS reader. With browsers like Internet Explorer integrating such readers, we'll be seeing more information feeds. That could be a good thing—or not—depending on whether businesses use them properly.

"You don't need to blog to offer an RSS feed," says online marketing consultant Debbie Weil, author of *The Corporate Blogging Book.* "But you should have a blogging mind-set. Show the reader what's in it for them. Write clear and interesting headlines. There's a bit of an art to writing RSS [content]." She adds that you should break up your feeds by audience—customers, investors, media and the like—just as you would any other message distribution.

Jim Edwards, 38, uses a blog and RSS to promote his business, Guaranteed Response Marketing. "Whenever I publish an article, either through my blog [www.igottatellyou.com/blog] or through another site's RSS feeder, I expect to get 100 to 300 references back to me in a week," says Edwards, whose $2 million Lightfoot, Virginia, business provides electronic tutorials and publications. "It's a quick way to get links back to you, as well as to get on sites that people are actively looking at."

Use Social Networks

Customers are making friends online through social networking sites like MySpace.com. The massive site—boasting millions of users, all segmented by age, geography and interests—offers an unbridled opportunity for marketers, according to Libby Pigg, senior account manager at Edelman Interactive in New York City.

"You [can] launch a profile for your business and give it a personality," says Pigg, who has launched MySpace marketing campaigns for major consumer products companies. "It's simi-

lar to a dating site, where you tell people a bit about yourself. Then, you use the search function to find the group you want to target—maybe single people in New York [City] between 24 and 30—and contact them to become your 'friends.'"

A MySpace profile helped Taylor Bond generate interest in Egismoz.com, the electronics division of his $20 million retail company, Children's Orchard, in Ann Arbor, Michigan. Earlier this year, Bond sent invitations to some of the site's young, tech-savvy users. The key to maintaining their interest, he says, is to provide fresh content and special offers.

"We're seeing more people come into the store saying that they saw us on MySpace," says Bond, 44. "We're definitely seeing more traffic and feedback on the profile, and we're getting some incredible feedback about what's hot and what people want, so it's good for market research, too." Opportunities also exist on other networking sites like Friendster.com, LinkedIn.com, and even niche sites like Adholes.com, which focuses on the advertising community.

Advertise in Unusual Places

From valet tickets and hubcaps to T-shirts emblazoned with video displays, advertising is popping up in new places. A March survey of marketing executives by Blackfriars Communications entitled "Marketing 2006: 2006's Timid Start" found that business spending on traditional advertising continued its decline, and spending on nontraditional marketing methods—from online promotions to buzz marketing—rose 12 percent since late 2005.

Scott Montgomery, principal and creative director of Bradley and Montgomery, an advertising and branding firm in Indianapolis, says the shift in ad spending will continue as advertisers look to make their ad dollars more effective.

Make It Stick

Tap these marketing trends to get into customers' hearts and minds.

- **Multicultural Market:** By 2010, the buying power of American blacks and Hispanics is expected to exceed the gross domestic product of Canada, according to the Selig Center for Economic Growth at the University of Georgia in Athens. Make sure you're not overlooking this market. Rochelle Newman-Carrasco, CEO of Enlace Communications, a Los Angeles multicultural marketing firm, advises companies not only to translate materials when appropriate, but also to be conscious of cultural images: "In lifestyle shots, go beyond multicultural casting. Show scenes where the clothing, food and other backgrounds reflect different cultures."
- **Experiential Marketing:** Kathy Sherbrooke, president of Circles, an experiential marketing firm in Boston, says businesses must figure out the key messages of their brand and find ways for their staffs and locations to reflect that image—young and trendy, sophisticated and elegant, and so on. "Create an environment that's consistent with your brand," she says. She points to Apple Computer's retail stores, where clerks use handheld

checkout machines and pull product bags out of their back pockets to reinforce the ease-of-use and streamlined processes for which Apple is known.
- **Customer Evangelism:** From hiring word-of-mouth marketing companies to creating incentives for customer referrals, businesses are placing more importance on customer evangelism, says Andrew Pierce, senior partner at New York City branding firm Prophet. "Companies need to be customer-centric for this to happen," he explains. "If you're not finding ways to increase value and inspire loyalty, it won't work."

At the simplest level, Pierce advises using customer testimonials to add credibility to marketing efforts, including webinars where customers talk about your company. More extreme examples include buzz marketing campaigns where happy customers talk up the product, or inviting customers to trade shows or other events where they can show their enthusiasm in person.

Montgomery and his team were the first to develop advertising programs on electrical outlets in airports. Reasoning that business travelers—one of the holy grail audiences marketers love—power up portable technology while waiting for their planes, it seemed a natural place to reach them.

"Smart marketers are looking [for] places where people are engaged," says Montgomery. "You have to target your message in a way that makes sense for [how] people behave."

Premium-ize Your Brand

Brands like Coach and Grey Goose vodka have mastered the art of taking everyday items and introducing luxe versions at much higher price points. Now, growing businesses are also going upscale with their products or services.

Andrew Rohm, professor of marketing at Northeastern University's College of Business Administration in Boston, says smaller businesses can often "trickle up" more easily than large brands, which may find that customers are resistant to accepting their more expensive offerings. "A small brand can reinvent itself without having to swim upstream against its image," says Rohm.

To posh up your product, he advises the same best practices as with any new offering: Do your research, and make sure there's a market for the product or service before you make your brand go bling.

Blog On

With the blogosphere more than 43.1 million blogs strong, according to blog search engine Technorati, it appears everyone and his grandmother are blogging. Robert Scoble, technical evangelist at Microsoft and author of *Naked Conversations: How Blogs Are Changing the Way That Businesses Talk With Customers,* believes blogs are important for businesses that want direct customer feedback. And development blogs, where businesses get direct input about products and services from readers, will soon become even more important, he says.

Scoble predicts a rise in regional blogs linked to Google's new local advertising program and Mapquest.com for quick access to directions, giving people more insight into the local businesses they want to frequent. He also says we'll see more video blogs, which won't replace text blogs but will more effectively communicate with some audiences. "If I'm trying to explain to you what [video game] Halo 2 is, I can write 10,000 words and I'm not going to get it right, but you can see a 2-minute video and you'll understand," he says.

Take these trends into consideration as you plan for the coming year. Not every idea may apply to your company, but most are market forces you can't afford to ignore.

Critical Thinking

1. Discuss some recent shifts in the demographic and sociocultural environments in the United States.

2. Explain how technology impacts marketing strategies and decisions, namely promotional tactics.

GWEN MORAN is *Entrepreneur's* "Retail Register" and "Quick Pick" columnist.

Evolve

The old business methods won't work anymore. It's time to evolve.

CHRIS PENTTILA

For companies feeling their way through the worst recession since the 1930s, it's easiest to stay focused on next quarter's numbers, improving operations and lowering costs where possible. Just stick with the playbook and keep your head down, and things will be fine, right?

Wrong. This recession is different from other recessions in its scope and depth, and the worst thing you can do is more of the same. Staying the course with your current business model "might let you survive a little bit longer, but you're not going to create that competitive advantage necessary for the long term," says Scott Anthony, president of Innosight, an innovation consulting firm, and author of next month's new book *The Silver Lining: An Innovation Playbook for Uncertain Times.*

You've got to change your game. But how can you do it? Here are seven ways to be a game changer right now:

Get comfortable with chaos. Globalization and technology are leading to constant economic turbulence. Being a game changer begins with a recognition of this new normality, says John A. Caslione, founder of GCS Business Capital, an M&A advisory company with offices worldwide, and co-author of *Chaotics: The Business of Managing and Marketing in the Age of Turbulence.* "[There's] going to be continuous turbulence punctuated by spurts of prosperity and downturns," he explains. "Understand that you're not going to be able to count on uninterrupted periods of prosperity."

Reassess your customers' values. This recession is changing people's mind-sets, not just their spending habits. It's still too early to tell what long-term impact this recession will have on customer behavior, but a more cautious, anxiety-ridden consumer has arisen in the short term. People are reevaluating their values and their purchases. How have your customers' values changed in the past six months, and how have their needs changed? The answers could spark new product and service ideas aimed at value-conscious consumers. Your company's closeness to customers is a huge advantage, so talk to them or work up a simple survey. Says Caslione, "You've got to be talking to your customers more than ever before to be able to understand how their needs are changing."

The Dos and Don'ts of Game Changing

Do

- Look at your business through the lens of another industry to find new ways to operate. If you're in manufacturing, how would you operate as a retailer, or vice versa?
- Talk to your customers about what they need today. This will help you find new competitive advantages.
- Get employees on the front lines talking about how customer mind-sets have changed and how the company can better reach consumers.
- Reexamine your business model for products, processes, promotions and so on that are no longer effective.
- Constantly look for ways to add value to your company, product or service. This doesn't have to be expensive. A retailer, for example, might set up a small play area with secondhand toys to keep kids busy while parents shop. It's the small things that can boost a revenue line.

Don't

- Stay the course. Realize the economy has changed and your company must change with it.
- Stop marketing your product or service. You need to actually communicate with customers now more than ever.
- Assume your suppliers, vendors and distributors are doing fine. Go see them in person. Check in with their suppliers, too.
- Get complacent if margins are still good because rapid industry transformations rise to the surface in tough times. The newspaper industry, for example, saw trouble coming for years, but healthy sales kept it from making necessary changes.
- Stop being creative. Aim for discipline in your core business balanced with a willingness to try new things and create new markets.

Understand that a good product always sells. A startling number of companies and game-changing products were actually launched in very tough times. Campbell's Soup was introduced in the 1890s. IBM launched its personal computer in 1981. The first iPod came out in late 2001. These periods were economic low points and seemingly not the time to launch new products. Marketing research company Nielsen found customers' willingness to purchase innovative products in good times and bad times has stayed remarkably constant over the past 30 years. "Just because times get tough," says Anthony, "doesn't mean people aren't willing to pay for things that help them solve problems."

Think new markets, not just cost cutting. Trimming costs where you can (renegotiating prices with suppliers and distributors and lowering your overhead) is very important, but don't stop there. Game changers see levers they can pull (e.g., affordability, convenience, accessibility, location and cost) that change a market or create an entirely new one. When MinuteClinic, a timesaving one-stop shop for simple ailments, launched in 2000 inside select CVS pharmacies, its model changed the game-and consumers responded.

View scarcity as a good thing. When sales are good, there's no urgency or any real need to be innovative. Feeling like your back is against the wall actually forces you to try new things. Now's the time to ramp up a few low-cost experiments and reexamine your entire business model for weaknesses in light of the economy. What have you got to lose? Welcome the challenge.

Stop defending the status quo. An idea sounds great—until you realize the operating margin or some other metric will be lower than expected. Microsoft had all the tools to create Google's search advertising business but abandoned the idea when search produced a paltry (by Microsoft standards) $1 million in sales during its first few months. By the time Microsoft finally recognized the importance of search, Google had a commanding lead in the market. Bending a little bit could pay off big time.

Serve the customers you hate. Every company has customers it sees as undesirable from a cost or profit perspective. Consider Netflix, which started out with a traditional pay-per-rental model in which customers paid late fees. In early 2000, 45-employee Netflix switched to a subscription model without late fees, a move that appealed particularly to customers who have trouble returning movies on time. Today, Netflix has around 250 employees and its business model is thriving in the recession. "It's not just the customers you've learned to love but, in fact, customers you've learned to hate and figuring out ways to innovate to make them great customers," Anthony says.

Every game has winners and losers. Which side will you be on? "Continue to dream, continue to experiment, continue to think differently," Anthony says. "But you've got to prove your dream more quickly than you ever did before." Now hurry—your customers are waiting.

Critical Thinking

1. In your perspective, what recent economic forces require companies to transform their business approach?
2. List and summarize the seven changes that the author of the article recommends businesses make.

CHRIS PENTTILA is a freelance journalist in the Chapel Hill, North Carolina, area.

The Unmarketables

Tough times call for new marketing strategies and tactics. Here are five approaches that these practitioners hope will revitalize their images and put them on the road to business recovery.

PIET LEVY, JOHN N. FRANK, AND ALLISON ENRIGHT

Brands, products and business segments have their ups and downs. The downs challenge marketers to find new approaches to revitalize and rejuvenate images to reconnect with key audiences.

This feature looks at a cross-section of businesses and products that are down for a variety of reasons. Some, like restaurants, financial services companies, and business travel and meeting resources, have been pushed out of favor because of the recession. Others, like U.S. automakers GM and Chrysler, need to battle the negatives that come with filing for bankruptcy protection. And another, high fructose corn syrup, faces image and health issues.

The first lesson for any brand, company or business segment facing similar challenges is that adversity means it's time to find new approaches for marketing, says brand guru David Aaker, vice chairman of Prophet, a San Francisco-based branding and marketing consultancy.

"I just don't think you can do business as usual and continue to spend money the way you've been spending money; you just need to be really creative," he counsels. Look to connect with your key audiences in new ways, with approaches that help you stand out dramatically from competitors, he says. You'll find more advice from Aaker, who also is *Marketing News*' newest columnist, throughout this piece. Look for his first *Marketing News* column in our Aug. 30 issue.

Restaurants: Value Tops the Menu

When your stomach's growling but your wallet's whimpering, a restaurant meal isn't as appetizing as it may have been in better times.

As a result, restaurant chains are hurting. Fine dining and casual dining sales likely will drop 10 to 15% and 5 to 8% respectively this year, says Darren Tristano, executive vice president of Chicago-based food industry consulting firm Technomic Inc.

Trying to do better than those predictions, many restaurant groups are stressing value and unique experiences in their marketing efforts.

Denny's Corp., for example, grabbed attention with its Grand Slam giveaway advertised during the Super Bowl. It gave away nearly 2 million free meals on Feb. 3, introducing consumers to its recently revamped menu in the process. It also provided incentives for return trips, says Mark Chmiel, executive vice president and chief marketing and innovation officer for the Spartanburg, S.C.-based company. Sales dropped in the first quarter but beat analyst expectations. In a statement, Denny's CEO Nelson Marchioli said the promotion was an "overwhelming success" and that the company "made significant progress on our primary goal of improving sales and guest traffic trends." Denny's continues to offer free meals through Twitter.

Besides value, Denny's is targeting niche audiences with new items and campaigns. Health nuts finally have some Denny's options, including chicken sausage and granola, which debuted in June. The company also has been stepping up early morning, young adult business with a funky social media campaign involving emerging rock bands and a talking unicorn.

Like Denny's, The Cheesecake Factory Inc., based in Calabasas Hills, Calif., had better than expected sales in the first quarter. Mark Mears, the company's senior vice president and CMO, says one reason for that is the chain's "Small Plates & Snacks" menu, nationally released in March. Meanwhile, the 200-item main menu trumpets variety and sharable meals as value options, Mears says.

Cheesecake Factory's "Share the Love" and "Share the Celebration" campaigns offered dine-again incentives during select weeks; the former touted a design-a-cheesecake feature online, and the latter encouraged fans to post descriptions of events they celebrated at Cheesecake Factory for entry into a sweepstakes.

At the higher end of the dining price chain, Morton's Restaurant Group Inc. in Chicago experienced a 24.1% decrease in comparable restaurant revenues in the first quarter of its fiscal 2009 because of cutbacks in business-related dining.

Aaker Advice
Restaurants

Find True Points of Difference

"You really need to help generate really different ideas that will break out of the clutter. You always need to find new things, but these days [it's] the only way."

Aaker Advice
Financial Services

Target Consumer Education

"If they really want to educate, the problem becomes how do you do it effectively? You need to segment the population. You need to target people."

It's trying to turn things around with value messaging driven by social media. Morton's blog recently featured recipes for meals and details on a new Morton's cookbook being promoted on a national tour at Morton outlets. Roger J. Drake, the company's chief communications officer, says the book pushes brand awareness and the book events drive restaurant traffic.

The company's biggest social media success has been through Twitter, with 1,424 followers as of late June. Twitter was exclusively used to promote a networking event at the new Bar 1221 inside a Chicago Morton's restaurant; Drake says sales were so successful that the strategy will be used at other locations.

Morton's Facebook page showcases other events like an absinthe tasting experience and price promotions such as a $99.99 deal for a pair of three-course steak and seafood dinners.

Value messaging, to many consumers, equals lower prices. So offering value through too many price promotions carries its own problems for when the economy improves. "It's not something you want consumers to get used to," Technomic's Tristano says. "It's hard to go back to the regular price points."

The Problem	Consumers are less likely to eat out in a bad economy.
The Fix	Create value messaging via price promotions, lower-cost menus and new food offerings.
Potential Pitfall	Consumers will continue to demand lower prices even in a healthier economy.

Financial Services: Listen to Customers

Financial services firms have seen better days.

"Banking as a business and bankers in a generic sense have been getting bashed pretty badly," acknowledges long-time banking consultant Bert Ely, founder of Ely & Co. in Alexandria, Va.

Indeed, the credit card corner of the banking world became one of the first hit with new legislation this year when Congress passed a bill restricting a wide range of card issuer practices.

In the face of such negative perceptions, credit card companies are stressing their core brand values in marketing. They're also talking about responsible borrowing and financial education. Banks are trying a variety of approaches, including changing their names and their product offerings in response to consumer input.

Credit card companies such as Discover Financial Services "face a major challenge to their business models because now they have to invest an enormous amount of money changing all their systems to conform with new rules," Ely says. They need to do that while cutting overall spending in response to shareholder concerns. This recession is the first in which the major credit card companies—Discover, MasterCard and Visa—all are publicly traded companies. "The fact that they're public could change marketing spending. . . . You have to meet investor expectations," says Michael Kon, a senior analyst who follows credit cards at Morning-star Inc. in Chicago. Visa cut spending on marketing, advertising, sales and promotions by 8.8% in the first quarter of 2009 compared with the same period in 2008; MasterCard cut such spending 35%, Discover 21% and American Express Co. 42%, Kon notes.

Harit Talwar, CMO at Riverwoods, Ill.-based Discover, says he's using more online tools in his marketing mix and working to better integrate all his marketing efforts. Messaging stresses what he calls Discover's core brand mission, which is "helping consumers spend smarter, manage debt better, save more," he says. Discover in February introduced its Paydown Planner, Purchase Planner and Spend Analyzer on its website, three financial management tools that speak to its core mission, he says.

At rival MasterCard Worldwide, "we focus on what the Priceless campaign [MasterCard's ongoing advertising effort] has always been about; [it's] not about conspicuous consumption, it's about things that matter most," says Chris Jogis, vice president of U.S. consumer marketing for the Purchase, N.Y. company.

MasterCard's digital efforts center on financial education and the utility of using MasterCard. An iPhone application, for example, helps people find the nearest MasterCard-accepting ATM.

In an effort to get a more up-to-the-minute read on consumer sentiment, MasterCard has stepped up the frequency of economic focus groups to ask consumers how they're feeling financially.

Asking consumers what they want led to new products and a new name at what was known as GMAC Bank, an online banking operation owned by General Motors' financing arm, GMAC.

The newly named Ally kicked off its marketing campaign May 15, offering consumer-requested products like no withdrawal penalty CDs and less legalese in describing its offerings, notes Vinoo Vijay, product, brand and marketing executive at Ally. "Consumers are going to demand that banks do better by them, recession or not," Vijay says.

The Problem	Counter negative consumer and legislator perceptions.
The Fix	Stress responsible borrowing and spending, and offer financial education.
Potential Pitfall	Consumers will see new financial education efforts as disingenuous.

Business Travel: Go to Washington

As they boarded their luxury corporate jets last fall to testify before Congress about their incredibly, painfully red financial statements, the heads of GM, Ford and Chrysler probably couldn't fathom the storm they were flying into. Nor, perhaps, could the meeting planners for AIG, who hosted a $440,000 corporate retreat at a California luxury resort in September, less than a week after accepting $85 billion in bailout funds from taxpayers. Certainly, a large part of their collective actions were rooted in habit and pre-planning—albeit executed in a state of economic tone-deafness.

The resulting press coverage and 'can-you-believe-it' water cooler conversations produced a devastating effect on the related industries—private jet travel and the meeting planning and hotel industries—by default.

Faced with the enormous challenge of changing consumer sentiment and revving up business, the two industries quickly created separate integrated marketing efforts that shared similar messaging and intent. The National Business Aviation Association (NBAA) and the General Aviation Manufacturers Association jointly created "No Plane No Gain," while the U.S. Travel Association (USTA) tried to shore up its interests via a "Meetings Mean Business" campaign, coordinated with eight other travel-oriented association groups. The messages for both stressed the impact the negativity and related business losses had on frontline employment among employees serving these industries and the businesspeople that benefit from using those services. Both made a strong effort to change the tenor of statements coming from influential voices on Capitol Hill.

"We watched [the Meetings Mean Business] campaign with great interest because there is so much commonality there. . . . For us, it's 'how did you get there?' In [USTA's] case, it's 'where did you go?'" says Dan Hubbard, vice president of communications for NBAA and the in-house manager of the No Plane No Gain campaign in Washington, D.C.

"The tenor of the conversation had neglected a lot of facts. . . . [The campaign] helped frame it in the right terms, to help politicians understand that when you make off-the-cuff comments, you are putting people out of a job," says Chris Gaia, vice president of marketing for meetings, events and travel incentive planner Maritz Travel in St. Louis.

Maritz Travel's leadership worked with USTA to develop the Meetings Mean Business effort. Gaia estimates that Maritz Travel saw a 30% decline in the November time frame from 2007 to 2008. "A large portion of that was driven by [clients] not wanting to be targets of the media. They didn't want to get

+++

Aaker Advice **Business Travel**
Stress the Business Value of Conferences
"Make sure people remember why they're doing these things—the importance of building the team."

called out for excesses. There were genuine economic problems [and adding the] political thing was icing on the cake," he says.

Both marketing efforts included intense communication efforts in the Washington area—No Plane No Gain included ad buys on local cable and in *Roll Call, Politico, USA Today* and *The Wall Street Journal*—and culminated in separate meetings at the White House with President Obama.

Business is trickling back at Maritz Travel, Gaia says. "In the last 60 days, we've had clients who cancelled stuff scheduled two years out come back and say: 'We need to add a short-term incentive sprint. We need to do a CEO roadshow to increase communication,'" he says.

At NBAA, Hubbard is optimistic that the efforts are taking hold. "A lot of that has come together in recent weeks and we're hopeful. It seems to have had a helpful impact."

| The Problem | Condemned by the excesses of a few, the private aviation and corporate travel and meetings industries are hit hard by the economy. |
| The Fix | Industry groups installed intensive marketing initiatives to challenge and correct the public comments made by influencers. |

See more, www.NoPlaneNoGain.com and www.MeetingsMeanBusiness.com

Bankrupt Automakers: Come Back, Shoppers

To say that U.S. automakers are facing marketing challenges this year is a bit akin to saying the crew of the Titanic had some problems with ice—the scale involved dwarfs anything Detroit has faced before.

"This is not an auto recession, it's an auto depression. The challenge everyone is facing is just staying alive," says David Cole, chairman of the nonprofit Center for Automotive Research, an Ann Arbor, Mich.-based auto think tank. U.S. car and light truck sales had been between 16.5 million and 17 million units annually two years ago. They fell to 13.5 million in 2008 and this year have been hovering around the 9 to 10 million annual rate.

The market dive drove Chrysler and General Motors into bankruptcy court by the start of June.

The marketing battle for each company has become a two-front war. Each needs to convince consumers it will still be in business once the recession ends. They also need to get reluctant buyers back into showrooms.

Aaker Advice
U.S. Automakers

Regain Consumer Trust

"You need a branded program that packages the logic of why [consumers] should trust you and why it's going to be OK. Just to run ads that say 'we're trustworthy' [is] a complete waste of time. There needs to be substance."

Aaker Advice
HFCS

Combat Rumors with Facts

"Find out what the facts are [about HFCS] and find a way to communicate them."

Chrysler addressed the first challenge with an advertising campaign starting May 3 that included print ads in 50 large U.S. newspapers, including the *New York Times, Wall Street Journal* and *USA Today*. "The tagline is, 'We're building a new car company, come see what we're building for you,' " says Jodi Tinson, Chrysler's manager of marketing communications.

"The whole purpose of the campaign is to let people know, yes, we're still out there for you."

The "We Build" campaign also includes five TV ads, two discussing restructuring and three featuring Chrysler, Dodge and Jeep products. The product ads focus on various Chrysler products in efforts to distinguish them from the competition. The Auburn Hills, Mich.-based automaker continues to work with its ad agency of record, BBDO, on the campaign, which also will have some online elements, Tinson says.

General Motors has joined industry efforts to assure people they won't get stuck with a new car and no regular paycheck. It's offering a payment protection plan to pay up to $500 a month for nine months to any buyer who loses a job, explains John M. McDonald, GM's manager for pricing incentives and market trends. It's also touting a vehicle protection plan that addresses trade-in values by offering buyers up to $5,000 if they trade in a GM car in the next two-and-a-half years and find the trade-in value has fallen below the amount of their auto loan.

For its Cadillac and Hummer lines, marketing has focused on letting people know financing is available, McDonald says. GM partnered with credit unions earlier this year to get discounted financing for credit union members buying GM products.

Cole thinks automakers should be touting the fact that the deals being offered now won't last once the economy revives. "One of the things that gets Americans to move is a deal or the potential loss of a deal," he says.

McDonald agrees that deal messaging will help with anyone already thinking about buying, but adds that "the issue right now is getting people into the marketplace."

The Problem	Convince consumers the companies won't go out of business; get consumers into a buying mood again.
The Fix	Stress corporate staying power, product attributes and financial concerns.
Potential Pitfall	Only those already thinking about a purchase will care; the rest will stay on the sidelines.

Corn Syrup: Sticky Sweet Truths

Give me your gut reaction: Is high fructose corn syrup (HFCS) good or bad?

It is generally agreed that most consumers' first reactions fall somewhere on the scale from negative to neutral. And that's meant marketing troubles for the HFCS business. Indeed, 67% of consumers indicated they were trying to consume less HFCS last year, up from 60% in 2007 and 54% in 2006, found the Washington-based International Food Information Council's 2008 Food & Health Survey.

Turning negative perceptions around has become a major industry challenge. The marketing response from the Washington-based Corn Refiners Association (CRA), which represents the largest corn refiners in the United States including Archer Daniels Midland and Corn Products International, has been a consumer education campaign begun in June 2008. The Sweet Surprise integrated campaign produced with agency DDB Chicago presents the scientific data about HFCS via TV ads, print and online elements, and includes a PR media outreach effort coordinated by Weber Shandwick. The CRA won't disclose spending, but industry estimates put the campaign in the $20-$30 million range.

"The reason [for the campaign] is to correct the significant misinformation being given to consumers about our corn sweetener," says Audrae Erickson, the president of the CRA. "Most of that information was misleading and completely inaccurate. Our goal is to ensure that consumers have the facts [and] that they understand that these two sweeteners [sugar and HFCS] are essentially the same."

HFCS is a corn-derived sweetener that is nearly identical in chemical composition to sugar. It has the same calorie count per gram and numerous scientific studies have indicated that the human body processes the product the same way. And government subsidies made to U.S. corn farmers also makes it a cheaper ingredient for food and beverage makers to use than sugar, which is why it appears in food and beverage products that formerly contained natural sugar.

Since the ingredient is found in few products produced outside the United States—it is cheaper to use sugar elsewhere—and frequent news headlines at home alert us that we are turning into a nation of chunks, some health and dietary groups assert that a connection can be made between our obesity problem and the growth of HFCS consumption during the past 30 years. Those headlines appear to be having an impact on consumer consumption patterns.

The per capita delivery of HFCS for food and beverage use declined 16.4% from 1999 (HFCS's peak year) to 2008, according to U.S. Department of Agriculture statistics. Worried about a consumer backlash, food and beverage marketers have begun to try to distinguish their products as containing no HFCS; 146 products carried the claim in 2007, up from just six products in 2003, according to London-based Datamonitor.

The Sweet Surprise campaign's target market is mothers, says Don Hoffman, executive vice president and managing director of accounts with DDB Chicago. "The tone of the communications is simple and straightforward. It is targeted to women as decision makers and good communicators. . . . [Women] find the right facts and disseminate the right facts," he says.

Early returns are limited, but Erickson says the campaign is helping. "We have been very successful in making a difference in correcting the record. But based on the stories that continue, there is more work to be done to ensure that consumers get the truth."

The Problem	High fructose corn syrup is getting a bad rep in the media and among consumers.
The Fix	The Corn Refiners Association launched an integrated media blitz to disseminate scientifically backed facts about the ingredient. For more, see www.SweetSurprise.com.
Trivia	The average U.S. consumer consumed 40.1 pounds of HFCS and 44.2 pounds of refined sugar in 2007, according to the U.S.D.A. Economic Research Service.

Critical Thinking

1. Describe the effects of the current economic recession on various industries and sectors.

2. Explain how technology impacts marketing strategies and decisions, namely promotional tactics.

Six Strategies for Successful Niche Marketing

How to win big by thinking small.

ERIC K. CLEMONS, PAUL F. NUNES, AND MATT REILLY

There's been a lot of buzz about the long-tail phenomenon—the strategy of selling smaller quantities of a wider range of goods that are designed to resonate with consumers' preferences and earn higher margins. And a quick scan of everyday products seems to confirm the long tail's merit: Where once we wore jeans from Levi, Wrangler or Lee, we now have scores of options from design houses. If you're looking for a nutrition bar, there's one exactly right for you, whether you're a triathlete, a dieter or a weight lifter. Hundreds of brewers offer thousands of craft beers suited to every conceivable taste.

It's not surprising that so many companies have embraced this strategy. It allows them to avoid the intense competition found in mass markets. Look at the sales growth that has taken place in low-volume, high-margin products such as super-premium ice cream, noncarbonated beverages, heritage meats and heirloom vegetables.

But the case for the long tail has frequently been overstated. This strategy can be expensive to implement, and it doesn't work for all products or all categories. It's surely better to produce a blockbuster film, for instance, than a smattering of low-volume art films.

In other words, simply avoiding the clutter of mass markets isn't enough. Companies need to stake out unique market *sweet spots,* those areas that resonate so strongly with target consumers that they are willing to pay a premium price, which offsets the higher production and distribution costs associated with niche offerings. We call this approach resonance marketing.

The vast amount of information available on the Internet has made this kind of niche marketing more important than ever and easier to do. More important because all that information encourages comparison shopping, putting tremendous downward pressure on prices and profits in highly competitive mass markets. And easier because it eliminates much of consumers' uncertainty about new

Questions to Ask Yourself

1. As part of a strategy of selling a wider range of high-margin goods, are you being careful to distinguish potential future market sweet spots from valueless niches that produce needless complexity?
2. Are you listening carefully to what consumers are saying online about your products, not just to you but also to each other, and are you reacting quickly to make improvements that address any negative comments?
3. Are you standardizing design components as much as possible to limit the costs of producing an extensive product line?
4. Are you aggressively keeping inventory and distribution costs down with strategies that allow you to configure finished products quickly when orders arrive, swap inventory among outlets or share distribution with other producers?
5. Are you continually reviewing your product portfolio to weed out those products that aren't contributing to profits, while being careful not to dump products that aren't big sellers but still contribute to the portfolio's overall profitability?

If you answered no to any of these questions, you're not getting the most out of what we call resonance marketing—selling a variety of precisely targeted goods designed to resonate with consumers. Following the steps in this article will help you manage the complexity of this strategy and reap superior profitability.

For Further Reading

These related articles from MIT Sloan Management Review can be accessed online

From Niches to Riches: Anatomy of the Long Tail

Erik Brynjolfsson, Yu "Jeffrey" Hu and Michael D. Smith (Summer 2006)

The Internet marketplace allows companies to produce and sell a far wider range of products than ever before. This profoundly changes both consumer behavior and business strategy.

Harnessing the Power of the Oh-So-Social Web

Josh Bernoff and Charlene Li (Spring 2008)

People are connecting with one another in increasing numbers, thanks to blogs, social networking sites and countless communities across the Web. Some companies are learning to turn this growing groundswell to their advantage.

Cracking the Code of Mass Customization

Fabrizio Salvador, Pablo Martin de Holan and Frank Piller (Spring 2009)

Most companies can benefit from mass customization, yet few do. The key is to think of it as a process for aligning a business with its customers' needs.

niche products, since they can easily find reviews, ratings and comments on everything that hits the market. For decades consumer uncertainty blocked the launch of new offerings that were too focused to be supported by national ad campaigns; today's empowered consumer is truly listening to word-of-mouth.

Finding sweet spots in the market is especially important in these tough economic times, when so many consumers are strapped for cash. Many shoppers will compromise whenever possible by looking for cheaper alternatives to the things they usually buy—but keep buying products that don't have any direct substitutes.

With the right approach, resonance marketing can fulfill its promise. We have found that six marketing principles, taken together, will allow a company to manage the complexity of this strategy and reap superior profitability.

Target Carefully

Sweet-spot offerings aren't better than other products in any absolute sense; they simply have to be different from existing options and better for their target consumers. They have to resonate powerfully with them.

But that's not as easy as it might sound. Finding profitable new niches requires a set of skills different from those needed to build market share or to create variations of an existing product—you're looking for places where no offerings exist, not one where consumers are complaining about existing choices.

Consider the success of Toyota Motor Corp.'s Lexus line of luxury cars. Toyota's research indicated there was an untapped market in the U.S. for Mercedes-quality luxury cars at a lower price, rather than superior quality at a comparable price. The Lexus line was designed to offer quality at a price that indicated the owners could afford whatever they wanted but also were smart enough to get it at a great price. The brand fulfilled an unmet need in the market and enjoyed immediate success.

Simply identifying gaps in the market isn't enough, though. Plenty of unique consumer products have failed to capture the imagination of shoppers. There's no guaranteed way to avoid such failures, but extensive research is essential. Often an ethnologist can help. Many companies use these analysts to explore why consumers buy what they do and what they would buy if it were available.

Listen to Your Customers. Really Listen.

Traditional advertising campaigns don't make sense for most niche markets; they're too expensive and too difficult to target precisely enough. Indeed, there are entire product categories, including nutrition bars and craft beers, where most products are never advertised. Their producers have learned how to work with consumer-generated content online—reviews, ratings or just chatter about a product. They don't just listen when customers talk to them; they listen just as carefully when customers talk about them.

The beauty of consumer-generated content is that companies get immediate and continuous feedback about their products. The key here is to listen closely and react quickly. Marketing executives should watch for the first online comments about their wares with the same excitement and apprehension as Broadway producers waiting for opening-night reviews. Consumers will make it clear right away what they like about the product and what they don't.

Harsh reviews can have devastating consequences. We analyzed two years of data on hotel bookings and found that the length, specificity and detail of negative online reviews are the best predictors of a hotel's inability to sell itself online.

So what do you do if the product you so carefully crafted to appeal to a particular market segment is trashed by those very consumers? Fix it immediately.

If defects pointed out by consumers are fixed quickly, more-favorable comments will emerge just as quickly. But companies should never assume that they've gotten it right and can stop listening. Continuous monitoring of online comments will alert executives to any new issues that arise, any improvements consumers might like to see as they become more familiar with the product, and even the emergence of any competitors or alternatives that might siphon off buyers.

Some traditional marketing still has its place, and indeed has become more powerful thanks to the way word-of-mouth spreads so quickly over the Internet. Companies can generate positive buzz for niche products with events like the Great American Beer Festival that small, specialty brewers attend every year. The brewers make sure to attract both professional critics and passionate amateur bloggers alike.

Moreover, craft brewers have learned to work together to make these events successful; they understand that at this point in their industry's development, their greatest danger comes not from each other but from consumer acceptance of mass-produced, generic beers.

Control Production Costs

Selling a large number of narrowly targeted products may sound like a production nightmare, but it doesn't have to be. There are several ways to maintain economies of scale over a broad range of product offerings.

Variety and standardization can coexist. For instance, Callaway Golf Co. offers buyers of its drivers multiple options for a club's head, loft angle and shaft—several hundred different combinations in all. But the company doesn't manufacture every variety separately. Any configuration of the various components can be readily assembled, since the interconnections are standardized.

Manufacturing processes can also be standardized to a large extent. While pumpkin spice ice cream appeals to a very different group of consumers than vanilla does, the manufacturing process is nearly identical for both flavors and any others. Brewing involves cold-fermenting lagers in one set of tanks and warm-fermenting ales in another, but the two varieties share many other processes: mashing grains, adding hops, bottling.

It also pays for a company to have a high-volume product in its portfolio that will keep its manufacturing equipment and employees from sitting idle for stretches of time. The relatively low volume of sales in narrowly targeted markets means production plants might not need to work to their full capacity to meet demand. A high-volume, if less profitable, product can take up the slack.

Control Distribution Costs

It's not just production costs that will determine the profitability and ultimate success of resonance offerings. Distribution costs are also important. There are ways here, too, to keep costs under control.

It can be difficult to forecast demand for products with limited sales, but that doesn't necessarily mean a company needs to stockpile high levels of inventory to keep from getting caught short. Companies that offer many varieties of a product based on different combinations of components, as Callaway does with its golf clubs, can keep inventory low by postponing final assembly until a particular product is ordered—there's no need to keep a given number of every combination in stock.

Flexible inventory allocation is another way to keep from having to stockpile goods. Auto makers, for instance, often swap needed items. If a customer in New Jersey wants a copper-colored Infiniti FX35 and his dealer has the car in silver, while a customer in Pennsylvania wants the same car in silver and his dealer has the copper, the dealers can arrange an exchange.

Shared distribution is another option worth considering. Small brewers, for instance, cut costs this way.

Selling to customers directly from a company website can reduce costs by eliminating intermediaries. But companies should be aware that shoppers can be less forgiving online than they are offline. A consumer who visits a store to buy a product or orders it from a catalog may be miffed if it is temporarily out of stock. But frustration may rise to the level of anger if the same consumer orders the product online and isn't notified until three days later that the item is out of stock, because of a glitch in the site's inventory software.

Some Apparent Losers Are Worth Keeping

Even with the best research and the most careful marketing, production and distribution, some products will be unprofitable or only marginally profitable. But before discontinuing a product, a company should consider the product's value in broader terms.

Some products that don't generate significant profit directly still help make a company's other products more profitable. Feeder routes on airlines transport customers to more-profitable routes, such as trans-Atlantic flights. Likewise, niche books that don't account for a significant portion of Amazon.com Inc.'s sales are valuable to the company because they contribute to its reputation as a one-stop source for any book.

Prune Your Portfolio Ruthlessly

Companies must relentlessly drop niche offerings that don't contribute to profitability directly or indirectly. The scores of flavors discontinued over the years by Ben & Jerry's Homemade Inc., remembered fondly in the "flavor graveyard" on the company's website, serve as a reminder to all companies that the flip side of creative expansion of a product line is eliminating those that no longer resonate with consumers. And the success of Ben & Jerry's is a reminder of the power of resonance marketing done right.

Critical Thinking

1. List a possible seventh strategy and explain why you came up with it.
2. What questions would you ask in the pursuit of an additional niche market(s)?

Dr. Clemons is a professor of operations and information management at the Wharton School of the University of Pennsylvania. **Mr. Nunes** is executive director of research at the Accenture Institute for High Performance and is based in Boston. **Mr. Reilly** is a senior executive in Accenture's management-consulting business, global managing director of the firm's Process and Innovation Performance practice and global co-leader of its Operational Excellence service. They can be reached at reports@wsj.com.

The Secrets of Marketing in a Web 2.0 World

Consumers are flocking to blogs, social-networking sites, and virtual worlds. And they are leaving a lot of marketers behind.

SALVATORE PARISE, PATRICIA J. GUINAN, AND BRUCE D. WEINBERG

For marketers, Web 2.0 offers a remarkable new opportunity to engage consumers.

If only they knew how to do it.

That's where this article aims to help. We interviewed more than 30 executives and managers in both large and small organizations that are at the forefront of experimenting with Web 2.0 tools. From those conversations and further research, we identified a set of emerging principles for marketing.

But first, a more basic question: What is Web 2.0, anyway? Essentially, it encompasses the set of tools that allow people to build social and business connections, share information and collaborate on projects online. That includes blogs, wikis, social-networking sites and other online communities, and virtual worlds.

Millions of people have become familiar with these tools through sites like Facebook, Wikipedia and Second Life, or by writing their own blogs. And a growing number of marketers are using Web 2.0 tools to collaborate with consumers on product development, service enhancement and promotion. But most companies still don't appear to be well versed in this area.

So here's a look at the principles we arrived at—and how marketers can use them to get the best results.

Don't just talk at consumers—work with them throughout the marketing process.

Web 2.0 tools can be used to do what traditional advertising does: persuade consumers to buy a company's products or services. An executive can write a blog, for instance, that regularly talks up the company's goods. But that kind of approach misses the point of 2.0. Instead, companies should use these tools to get the consumers *involved,* inviting them to participate in marketing-related activities from product development to feedback to customer service.

Getting Sociable

- **A New Approach:** Marketing these days is more about building a two-way relationship with consumers. Web 2.0 tools are a powerful way to do that.

- **The Pioneers:** A growing number of companies are learning how to collaborate with consumers online on product development, service enhancement and promotion.

- **The Lessons:** From these early efforts, a set of marketing principles have emerged. Among them: get consumers involved in all aspects of marketing, listen to and join the online conversation about your products outside your site, and give the consumers you work with plenty of leeway to express their opinions.

How can you do that? A leading greeting-card and gift company that we spoke with is one of many that have set up an online community—a site where it can talk to consumers and the consumers can talk to each other. The company solicits opinions on various aspects of greeting-card design and on ideas for gifts and their pricing. It also asks the consumers to talk about their lifestyles and even upload photos of themselves, so that it can better understand its market.

A marketing manager at the company says that, as a way to obtain consumer feedback and ideas for product development, the online community is much faster and cheaper than the traditional focus groups and surveys used in the past. The conversations consumers have with each other, he adds, result in "some of the most interesting insights," including gift ideas for specific occasions, such as a college graduation, and the prices consumers are willing to pay for different gifts.

Similarly, a large technology company uses several Web 2.0 tools to improve collaboration with both its business partners and consumers. Among other things, company employees have created wikis—websites that allow users to add, delete and edit content—to list answers to frequently asked questions about each product, and consumers have added significant contributions. For instance, within days of the release of a new piece of software by the company, consumers spotted a problem with it and posted a way for users to deal with it. They later proposed a way to fix the problem, which the company adopted. Having those solutions available so quickly showed customers that the company was on top of problems with its products.

Give consumers a reason to participate.

Consumers have to have some incentive to share their thoughts, opinions and experiences on a company website.

One lure is to make sure consumers can use the online community to network among themselves on topics of their own choosing. That way the site isn't all about the company, it's also about them. For instance, a toy company that created a community of hundreds of mothers to solicit their opinions and ideas on toys also enables them to write their own blogs on the site, a feature that many use to discuss family issues.

Other companies provide more-direct incentives: cash rewards or products, some of which are available only to members of the online community. Still others offer consumers peer recognition by awarding points each time they post comments, answer questions or contribute to a wiki entry. Such recognition not only encourages participation, but also has the benefit of allowing both the company and the other members of the community to identify experts on various topics.

Many companies told us that a moderator plays a critical role in keeping conversations going, highlighting information that's important to a discussion and maintaining order. That's important because consumers are likely to drift away if conversations peter out or if they feel that their voices are lost in a chaotic flood of comments. The moderator can also see to it that consumer input is seen and responded to by the right people within the company.

And, of course, it's important to make a site as easy to use as possible. For instance, there should be clear, simple instructions for consumers to set up a blog or contribute to a wiki.

Consumers tend to trust one another's opinions more than a company's marketing pitch. And there is no shortage of opinions online.

The managers we interviewed accept that this type of content is here to stay and are aware of its potential impact—positive or negative—on consumers' buying decisions. So they monitor relevant online conversations among consumers and, when appropriate, look for opportunities to inject themselves into a conversation or initiate a potential collaboration.

For example, a marketing manager of a leading consumer-electronics company monitors blogs immediately after a new-product launch in order to understand "how customers are actually reacting to the product." Other managers keep an eye on sites like Digg.com and Del.icio.us that track the most popular topics on the Web, to see if there's any buzz around their new products, and whether they should be adjusting, say, features or prices.

In one case, a company found a popular blogger who had spoken highly of the company's brand. Just prior to launching a new product, the company sent the blogger a free sample, inviting him to review it with no strings attached. The end result: The blogger wrote a favorable review and generated a flood of comments. So the company got nearly free publicity and feedback.

Resist the temptation to sell, sell, sell.

Many marketers have been trained to bludgeon consumers with advertising—to sell, sell, sell anytime and anywhere consumers can be found. In an online community, it pays to resist that temptation.

When consumers are invited to participate in online communities, they expect marketers to listen and to consider their ideas. They don't want to feel like they're simply a captive audience for advertising, and if they do they're likely to abandon the community.

The head of consumer research for a leading consumer-electronics organization created an online community of nearly 50,000 consumers to discuss product-development and marketing issues. One of the key principles of the community, she says, was "not to do anything about marketing, because we weren't about selling; we were about conversing."

In short order, community members not only identified what it was they were looking for in the company's products, but also suggested innovations to satisfy those needs. The company quickly developed prototypes based on those suggestions, and got an enthusiastic response: Community members asked when they would be able to buy the products and if they would get the first opportunity to buy them. They didn't have to be sold on anything.

Don't control, let it go.

In an online community, every company needs to find an effective balance between trying to steer the conversation about its products and allowing the conversation to flow freely. In general, though, the managers we interviewed believe that companies are better off giving consumers the opportunity to say whatever is on their minds, positive or negative. Moderators can keep things running smoothly and coherently, but they shouldn't always keep the conversation on a predetermined track. The more that consumers talk freely, the more a company can learn about how it can improve its products and its marketing.

One marketing executive recalled the first time she let an online community created for a client interact with very little control or moderation, resulting in an animated discussion about the look of the company's product. The client, with great concern, asked. "Who told them [the consumers] they could do this, that they could go this far?" Of course, when this process resulted in totally new packaging that helped boost sales, the client was ecstatic.

As another executive of a company that creates online communities for clients told us: "You have to let the members drive. When community members feel controlled, told how to respond and how to act, the community shuts down."

Find a 'marketing technopologist.'

So who should direct a company's forays into Web 2.0 marketing? A number of managers identified an ideal set of skills for an executive that go beyond those of a typical M.B.A. holder or tech expert. We coined the term *marketing technopologist* for a person who brings together strengths in marketing, technology and social interaction. A manager said, "I'd want to see someone with the usual M.B.A. consultant's background, strong interest in psychology and sociology, and good social-networking skills throughout the organization."

Foot soldiers need to be carefully selected as well. One large technology company weighs employees' proven skills to choose writers for blogs that are read by consumers. The company has long used blogs internally to help employees discuss technical issues, products, and company and industry topics. When it decided to use blogs to raise its profile online, it recruited those who had shown the most skill at blogging within the company. The company currently has about 15 employees who blog publicly, mostly on technology trends, and is recruiting more the same way. Meanwhile, the bloggers plan to meet occasionally to share the lessons learned from their experiences.

Embrace experimentation.

One Web 2.0 strategy does not fit all, and sometimes the best way to find out what's best for a given company is to try some things out and see what happens.

Blogs, wikis and online communities are among the tools that companies are most commonly using for marketing, but there are other ways to reach consumers. Some of the companies we talked with have gotten their feet wet in the online virtual world Second Life, where millions of users interact with each other through avatars. Companies can sell their goods and services and sponsor events in Second Life just as they do in the real world; one sponsored a contest for the best avatar.

Others are considering new ways to use more-familiar tools. For instance, many companies have long used instant messaging on their websites to allow shoppers to chat with customer-service representatives. One executive we spoke with said he would like to experiment with allowing consumers to chat with each other as they shop on his company's site.

Critical Thinking

1. In your perspective, why are online communities more effective than traditional methods of exploratory research such as surveys and focus groups?

2. With a small group of peers from your class, list some possible incentives for consumers to become engaged and involved in online communities.

Dr. Parise is an assistant professor of technology, operations and information management at Babson College in Wellesley, Mass. **Dr. Guinan** is an associate professor of technology, operations and information management at Babson College. **Dr. Weinberg** is chairman of the marketing department and an associate professor of marketing and e-commerce at Bentley University in Waltham, Mass. They can be reached at reports@wsj.com.

The Branding Sweet Spot

Kevin Lane Keller and Frederick E. Webster, Jr.

One of the realities of modern brand marketing is that many of the decisions that marketers make with respect to their brands are seemingly characterized by conflicting goals, objectives and possible outcomes. Unfortunately, in our experience, too many marketers define their problems in "either/or" terms, creating situations where one idea, one individual or one option wins out. Opportunities are missed for finding an even better solution, a new idea that could have been discovered and developed by combining and refining conflicting points of view. As a result, resources may be squandered, consumers may be left unsatisfied or confused and the organization may find itself struggling with lingering internal conflict.

We submit that this is dangerously wrong, and there is a better way to approach such problems, one which we call "marketing balance." Achieving marketing balance requires understanding and addressing conflicting objectives and points of view, taking into account and resolving multiple interests. It is synonymous with moderation, and the opposite of self-indulgence or turbulence. It involves finding "win-wins"—the branding sweet spot—so that vulnerable extreme solutions and suboptimal compromises are avoided.

Marketing Trade-offs

Conflict and trade-offs are inherent in marketing decision making, and are the most fundamental challenge of marketing and brand management. Table 1 organizes these trade-offs or conflicts into four broad categories—strategic, tactical, financial or organizational decisions—which we briefly highlight here.

Strategy trade-offs. Marketing strategy trade-offs involve decisions related to targeting and positioning brands. Some involve trade-offs in growth strategies, such as concentrating marketing resources on expanding the brand into new product categories vs. fortifying the brand and further penetrating existing product categories. Another growth trade-off is emphasizing market retention and

targeting existing customers vs. emphasizing market expansion and targeting new customers.

Whether to use funds to build and retain existing customer relationships or spend resources to develop new customers is certainly a dilemma that many firms face.

Other marketing strategy trade-offs revolve around how brands are competitively positioned in the minds of customers—such as an emphasis on brand tangibles (product performance) vs. brand intangibles (user imagery); a classic vs. contemporary image; an independent vs. universal image; and so on. Some of the product-related performance trade-offs in brand positioning are between attributes and benefits—such as price and quality, convenience and quality, variety and simplicity, strength and sophistication, performance and luxury and efficacy and mildness.

One common trade-off is whether the marketing program should stress points of difference (i.e., how the brand is unique) or points of parity (i.e., how the brand is similar), with respect to competitors' offerings. Product development decisions are often defined in terms of whether to bring the next generation of products in line with a major competitor's level of performance, or to commit more research and development funds and time to achieving a technological breakthrough.

Tactics trade-offs. Marketing tactic trade-offs involve decisions related to the design and implementation of marketing program activities. Some of the more common trade-offs evident with marketing programs are push (intermediary-directed) vs. pull (end-consumer-related) strategies or how the program is updated over time (emphasizing continuity vs. change).

A real dilemma for many companies is whether to support existing channels or to develop new ones, which usually means creating competition for the companies' traditional outlets. The problem often comes down to a stark choice: Given evolution in customer buying patterns and preferences, and significant declines in the market position of our traditional dealers, do we create a whole new system for going to market or do we re-segment the market,

Table 1 Representative Marketing Trade-offs

Strategic (Targeting and Positioning)
- Retaining vs. acquiring customers
- Brand fortification vs. brand expansion
- Brand awareness vs. brand image
- Product performance vs. user imagery
- Points of parity vs. points of difference

Tactical (Design and Implementation)
- Push vs. pull
- Continuity vs. change
- Existing vs. new channels
- Direct market coverage vs. use of middlemen
- Selling systems vs. selling components
- Creative, attention-getting ads vs. informative, product-focused ads

Financial (Allocation and Accountability)
- Short-run vs. long-run objectives
- Revenue-generating vs. brand-building activities
- Easily measurable marketing activities vs. difficult to quantify marketing activities
- Quality maximization vs. cost minimization
- Social responsibility vs. profit maximizing

Organizational (Structure, Processes, and Responsibilities)
- Central vs. local control
- Top-down vs. bottom-up brand management
- Customized vs. standardized marketing plans and programs
- Internal vs. external focus

Executive Briefing

One of the challenges in modern brand marketing is the many strategic, tactical, financial and organizational trade-offs that seem to exist. Successfully developing and implementing marketing programs and activities, to build and maintain strong brands over time, often requires that marketers overcome conflicting objectives and realities in the marketplace. Guidelines and suggestions are offered on achieving marketing balance, to hit the branding sweet spot by arriving at "win-win" decisions that successfully reconcile marketing trade-offs.

---

refine our strategy and strengthen our position with our traditional distribution partners?

Financial trade-offs. Marketing financial trade-offs involve decisions related to the allocation and accountability of investments in marketing program activities. In arriving at marketing investment decisions, these are some common trade-offs:

- Invest in generating revenue vs. building brand equity.
- Go for clearly measurable effects vs. "softer" effects that are more difficult to measure.
- Maximize product or service quality vs. minimizing costs.

Perhaps the most common trade-off is the tension on long-term brand-building strategies created by pressure for short-term earnings results and "making the numbers." Marketing expenditures, especially for advertising and brand development, are among the most vulnerable when management is looking for ways to improve the bottom

line, because the long-term effects of most marketing expenditures are so hard to determine due to the problem of multiple causation.

Unfortunately, the paths of commerce are strewn with the debris of once-powerful brands that were milked for profit and cash, based on the mistaken belief that they were strong enough to sustain major spending cuts for improving the bottom line. As one example, Coors Brewing cut advertising spending in the 1990s for its flagship Coors beer brand—from $43 million annually to a meager $4 million. Not surprisingly, the brand's market share subsequently dropped in half.

Organization trade-offs. Finally, marketing organization trade-offs involve decisions in the structure, processes and responsibilities involved in marketing decision making. For large global organizations especially, trade-offs found in this area include centrally mandated vs. locally controlled authority and standardized vs. customized marketing approaches. As effective a marketer as Nike has been, the company has often lamented that it has not historically balanced global objectives with local realities as well as it would have liked. Walt Disney Co. has been even more blunt in its belief that it has needed to achieve more cultural relevance in its global pursuits.

In terms of brand management, trade-offs often emerge between top-down (corporate-level) vs. bottom-up (product/market level) and internal vs. external focus. Strong business-to-business brands, such as GE, often find themselves challenged with managing their corporate brand in the face of diverse business units with different competitive challenges and potentially different stages of brand development in the marketplace and in different countries.

Marketing Balance Levels

Although we discussed marketing trade-offs within our four main categories, trade-offs certainly exist across the categories too. Pressure to achieve certain earnings targets may lead to an emphasis on short-term tactical moves, for example. One response to these trade-offs is to adopt an "extreme" solution and maximize one of the two dimensions involved with the trade-off. Many management gurus advocate positions that, in effect, lead to such a singular, but clearly limited, focus. These approaches, however, obviously leave the brand vulnerable to the negative consequences of ignoring the other dimension.

The reality is that for marketing success, both dimensions in each of these different types of decision trade-offs must typically be adequately addressed. To do so involves achieving a more balanced marketing solution. Marketing balance occurs when marketers attempt to address the strategic, tactical, financial and organizational trade-offs as clearly as possible in organizing, planning and implementing their marketing programs.

There are three means or levels of achieving marketing balance—in increasing order of potential effectiveness as well as difficulty.

Alternate. The first means would be to identify and recognize the various trade-offs, but to emphasize one dimension at a time, alternating so that neither dimension is completely ignored. Although potentially effective, the downside with this approach is that the firm often experiences a "pendulum effect," as there can be a tendency to overreact to a perceived imbalance on one dimension leading to a subsequent imbalance on the other dimension. Too often, there is too much of the wrong thing at the wrong time.

Divide. The second means of achieving marketing balance would be to "split the difference" and do a little of both to "cover all the bases." The idea here is to mix and match marketing efforts, so that both dimensions are covered. For example, at one point, Dewar's Scotch ran two print ad campaigns simultaneously. "Portraits" offered descriptive "personals" type of information of young scotch drinkers in an attempt to make the brand more relevant to a younger audience. And "Authentics" focused on the heritage and quality of the scotch, appealing to an older audience that was already part of the brand franchise and presumably valued more intrinsic product qualities.

Clearly, such solutions can be expensive and difficult, as two distinct marketing programs have to be successfully designed, financed and implemented. They can also result in conflicting messages and customer confusion. Although potentially effective if properly executed, this approach may suffer if insufficient or inadequate resources are put against the two objectives, with critical mass not being

achieved. Attempting to do "a little of this and a little of that" may be too wishy-washy and lack sufficient impact.

Reconcile. Finally, perhaps the best way to achieve marketing balance is by reconciling the differences and achieving a positive synergy between the two dimensions. Marketing balance in this way occurs by shrewdly addressing the decision trade-offs head-on (i.e., by resolving the conflicting dimensions in some uniquely creative manner). Hitting the branding sweet spot in this way may involve some well thought out moderation and balance throughout the marketing organization and its activities. Top marketing organizations such as Procter & Gamble (P&G), Nike, LVMH, Virgin and Toyota differ in many ways, but they share one characteristic: They have been remarkably adept at balancing trade-offs in building and managing their brands.

Achieving Marketing Balance

A two-step approach can help in achieving marketing balance: First, the extent and nature of the marketing trade-offs faced by the organization must be defined. Then, appropriate solutions must be developed to address the trade-offs as carefully and completely as possible.

To understand the nature and extent of the marketing trade-offs, some key questions must be answered: How severe are they? Are they unavoidable, inherent in the nature of the decision problem and situation? How have they been dealt with before? Of particular importance is to recognize whether the trade-offs result from internal, organizational considerations or external, structural issues inherent in the marketing environment where management has less control.

Next, marketers must develop effective means for achieving marketing balance. Given the wide range of marketing trade-offs that exists, it is perhaps no surprise that a correspondingly wide range of solutions is also typically available. We briefly outline six different options that are available to marketers to achieve marketing balance in Table 2.

Breakthrough Product or Service

One compelling way to resolve potential marketing strategy trade-offs is through product or service innovations. For example, Miller Lite became the first successful nationally marketed light beer through an innovative brewing formulation that was able to retain more of the taste profile of a full-strength regular beer, while still having a lower calorie count. Breakthrough product or service innovations

Table 2   Achieving Marketing Balance

- Breakthrough product or service innovation
- Improved business models
- Expanded or leveraged resources
- Embellished marketing
- Perceptual framing
- Creativity and inspiration

may not necessarily always require such significant initial investments. Decades later, Miller Lite was able to re-assert its straddle "Tastes Great, Less Filling" brand promise through an intensive ad campaign that focused on its low carbohydrate levels. Miller Lite had always had a performance advantage on the basis of "low carbs," but it only became a positioning advantage when the company could tap into a growing consumer health trend.

As another example, when BMW first made a strong competitive push into the U.S. market in the early 1980s, it positioned the brand as being the only automobile that offered both luxury and performance. At that time, American luxury cars were seen by many as lacking performance, and American performance cars were seen as lacking luxury. By relying on the incomparable design of their car—and to some extent their German heritage too—BMW was able to simultaneously achieve (1) a point of difference on performance and a point of parity on luxury with respect to luxury cars and (2) a point of difference on luxury and a point of parity on performance with respect to performance cars. The clever slogan, "The Ultimate Driving Machine," effectively captured the newly created umbrella category: luxury performance cars. Product differentiation can occur through technological innovation or creative repositioning.

Improved Business Models

Sometimes the solution is broader than just the product itself, and encompasses other aspects of the business. For example, P&G's switch to every-day low prices (EDLP) necessitated that the company overcome the potential trade-offs between high-quality products vs. the high costs and prices that are typically involved in delivering high levels of quality. P&G knew it could not deliver everyday low prices without having low everyday costs.

To reduce costs, P&G implemented a number of changes, simplifying the distribution chain to make restocking more efficient through continuous product replenishment. The company also scaled back its product portfolio by eliminating 25 percent of its stock-keeping units. Importantly, all of these cost-reduction changes were done without sacrificing product quality, allowing P&G to maintain much of its market leadership.

Expanded or Leveraged Resources

Another means of achieving balance and overcoming the inherent trade-offs in marketing decision making is to find ways to expand or leverage existing resources to make them more productive. For example, one approach often employed in addressing positioning trade-offs—albeit not without some investment implications—is to use ingredient brands (e.g., "Intel Inside") or a celebrity spokesperson/endorser. Ingredient brands or celebrities can reinforce a potentially weak area of a brand image. For example, General Motors used the popular appeal of golfer Tiger Woods for a number of years, to give its aging Buick brand a potentially more youthful and contemporary image.

Skillfully expanding resources is another means to adequately address more dimensions in a trade-off. For example, taking the cue from Harley-Davidson, Apple and others, many firms are attempting to build online and/or off-line brand communities. Building brand communities allows firms to tap into the passions and dedication of existing customers, reinforcing their loyalty and motivating and empowering them to serve as brand ambassadors or even brand missionaries with other consumers. In this way, existing customers help to bring new customers into the fold. Brand communities can thus be an effective means to help a firm both acquire and retain customers for its brands.

Embellished Marketing

Another potentially productive strategy is to find ways to embellish existing marketing programs to encompass a neglected or even missing dimension. In what ways can a marketing decision or action that typically emphasizes one dimension be modified or augmented to also encompass another dimension at the same time?

For example, many sales promotions emphasize price or discounts at the expense of product or service advantages, and thus the equity of the brand. Bucking that trend, however, P&G ran a clever promotion for Ivory soap that reinforced its key attribute of "floating" and its key benefit of "purity" while also providing an incentive for purchase: A select number of bars of soap were weighted such that they sank in the bathtub, giving the purchaser the right to enter a contest to win $250,000. Equity-building promotions that introduce key selling points into traditionally price-focused sales promotions are thus one way to incorporate an important but underemphasized dimension into marketing decisions.

Perceptual Framing

Trade-offs vary in terms of whether they are based in reality, reflecting inherent "laws" of the marketplace or, instead, are based on perceptions—thus reflecting the potentially biased or maybe just idiosyncratic views of the parties involved. The more the latter is the case, the more opportunities there are for marketing efforts to overcome potentially inaccurate or incorrect perceptions.

Perceptual framing can be an especially powerful way to achieve robust brand positions and, thus, marketing balance. For example, when Apple Computer Inc. launched the Macintosh, its key point of difference was "user friendly." Many consumers valued ease of use—especially those who bought personal computers for the home, but customers who bought personal computers for business applications inferred that ease of use meant that the computer must not be very powerful—a key choice consideration in that market.

Recognizing this potential problem, Apple ran a clever ad campaign with the tag line "The power to be your best," to redefine what a powerful computer meant. The message behind the ads was that because Apple was easy to use, people in fact did just that—they used them! It was a simple, but important, indication of "power." From that point of view, there was a positive, not negative, correlation between the two choice criteria.

Creativity and Inspiration

One powerful solution to reconcile conflicts in marketing decision making is to find potentially overlooked synergies. Perhaps the common denominator to all the different advocated solutions reviewed in this article is marketing creativity and the ability to address seemingly insurmountable problems through imaginative marketing solutions. Achieving marketing balance requires penetrating insights, shrewd judgments and a knack for arriving at solutions that go beyond the obvious. Creativity, the combination of previously unrelated ideas into new forms, is often the inspiration to achieve marketing balance.

For example, in the early 1990s, the California Milk Processor Board (CMPB) uncovered an insight that had been overlooked by marketers of milk all over the world. Unlike traditional and increasingly ineffective marketing campaigns that emphasized the healthful benefits of milk (e.g., how it made people look and feel good), the CMPB recognized that one powerful advantage of milk was as an indispensable companion or even "ingredient" with certain foods (e.g., cookies, cakes, etc.). With their ad agency Goodby Silverstein, the CMPB took that insight and developed the highly creative Got Milk? ad campaign that entertained and engaged consumers and sold milk in the process. The amusing and beloved ads ensured that its humor did not detract from its fundamental message: Running out of milk is a pain!

The Implications of Marketing Balance

One of the challenges in modern brand marketing is the many strategic, tactical, financial and organizational trade-offs that seem to exist. Successfully developing and implementing marketing programs and activities to build and maintain strong brands over time often requires that marketers overcome conflicting objectives and realities in the marketplace. After reviewing the nature of these trade-offs, a set of guidelines and suggestions was offered toward achieving marketing balance and hitting the branding sweet spot—by arriving at "win-win" decisions that successfully reconcile marketing trade-offs.

Marketing balance can actually be more difficult to achieve than more extreme solutions that only emphasize one option, involving greater discipline, care and thought. To use a golf analogy, the golfer with the smoothest swing is often the one who hits the ball farther and straighter. Marketing balance may not be as exciting as more radical proposed solutions, but it can actually turn out to be much more challenging and productive.

It is all about making marketing work harder, be more versatile and achieve more objectives. To realize marketing balance, it is necessary to create multiple meanings, multiple responses and multiple effects with marketing activities. Marketing balance does not imply that marketers not take chances, not do different things or not do things differently. It just emphasizes the importance of recognizing the potential downside of failing to reconcile marketing trade-offs.

That said, there certainly may be times that given extreme circumstances, dire straits or an overwhelming need to achieve one objective at all costs, radical solutions are warranted. But even in these cases, marketers would be well-served to recognize exactly the extent and nature of the decision trade-offs they face, and the consequences of ignoring other options. Radical solutions should be thoroughly vetted and contrasted to more balanced solutions that offer more robust and complete solutions.

Marketing balance implies an acceptance of the fact that marketing is multi-faceted and involves multiple objectives, markets and activities. Marketing balance recognizes the importance of avoiding over-simplification: Marketers must do many things, and do them right. Fundamentally, to achieve marketing balance and truly hit the branding sweet spot, marketers must understand and fully address important marketing trade-offs.

Critical Thinking

1. Define marketing balance.
2. According to the article, why is maintaining marketing balance superior to the existence of strategic, tactical, financial, and organizational trade-offs?

KEVIN LANE KELLER has served as brand confidant for some of the world's successful brands, including Accenture, American Express, Disney, Intel, Levi-Strauss, Procter & Gamble, Samsung and Starbucks. His textbook, *Strategic Brand Management,* is in its 3rd edition and has been adopted at top business schools and firms around the world. He may be reached at kevin.keller@dartmouth.edu **FREDERICK E. WEBSTER,** Jr. is widely recognized for his extensive research, writing, teaching and consulting in the field of marketing strategy and organization. Author of 15 books and more than 75 academic and management journal articles, his executive program teaching and consulting clients have included Ford, Mobil, IBM, DuPont, Monsanto, Praxair, General Electric, ABB, Chase Manhattan, Volvo and Phillips. He may be reached at fred.webster@dartmouth.edu.

Marketing Myopia
(with Retrospective Commentary)

Shortsighted managements often fail to recognize that in fact there is no such thing as a growth industry.

THEODORE LEVITT

How can a company ensure its continued growth? In 1960 "Marketing Myopia" answered that question in a new and challenging way by urging organizations to define their industries broadly to take advantage of growth opportunities. Using the archetype of the railroads, Mr. Levitt showed how they declined inevitably as technology advanced because they defined themselves too narrowly. To continue growing, companies must ascertain and act on their customers' needs and desires, not bank on the presumptive longevity of their products. The success of the article testifies to the validity of its message. It has been widely quoted and anthologized, and HBR has sold more than 265,000 reprints of it. The author of 14 subsequent articles in HBR, Mr. Levitt is one of the magazine's most prolific contributors. In a retrospective commentary, he considers the use and misuse that have been made of "Marketing Myopia," describing its many interpretations and hypothesizing about its success.

Every major industry was once a growth industry. But some that are now riding a wave of growth enthusiasm are very much in the shadow of decline. Others which are thought of as seasoned growth industries have actually stopped growing. In every case the reason growth is threatened, slowed, or stopped is *not* because the market is saturated. It is because there has been a failure of management.

Fateful purposes: The failure is at the top. The executives responsible for it, in the last analysis, are those who deal with broad aims and policies. Thus:

- The railroads did not stop growing because the need for passenger and freight transportation declined. That grew. The railroads are in trouble today not because the need was filled by others (cars, trucks, airplanes, even telephones), but because it was *not* filled by the railroads themselves. They let others take customers away from them because they assumed themselves to be in the railroad business rather than in the transportation business. The reason they defined their industry wrong was because they were railroad-oriented instead of transportation-oriented; they were product-oriented instead of customer-oriented.

- Hollywood barely escaped being totally ravished by television. Actually, all the established film companies went through drastic reorganizations. Some simply disappeared. All of them got into trouble not because of TV's inroads but because of their own myopia. As with the railroads, Hollywood defined its business incorrectly. It thought it was in the movie business when it was actually in the entertainment business. "Movies" implied a specific, limited product. This produced a fatuous contentment which from the beginning led producers to view TV as a threat. Hollywood scorned and rejected TV when it should have welcomed it as an opportunity—an opportunity to expand the entertainment business.

Today TV is a bigger business than the old narrowly defined movie business ever was. Had Hollywood been customer-oriented (providing entertainment), rather then product-oriented (making movies), would it have gone through the fiscal purgatory that it did? I doubt it. What ultimately saved Hollywood and accounted for its recent resurgence was the wave of new young writers, producers, and directors whose previous successes in television had decimated the old movie companies and toppled the big movie moguls.

There are other less obvious examples of industries that have been and are now endangering their futures by improperly defining their purposes. I shall discuss some in detail later and analyze the kind of policies that lead to trouble. Right now it may help to show what a thoroughly customer-oriented management can do to keep a growth industry growing, even after the obvious opportunities have been exhausted; and here there are two examples that have been around for a long time. They are nylon and glass—specifically, E. I. duPont de Nemours & Company and Corning Glass Works.

Both companies have great technical competence. Their product orientation is unquestioned. But this alone does not explain their success. After all, who was more pridefully product-oriented and product-conscious than the erstwhile New England textile companies that have been so thoroughly massacred? The DuPonts and the Cornings have succeeded not primarily because of their product or research orientation but because they have been thoroughly customer-oriented also. It is constant watchfulness for opportunities to apply their technical know-how to the creation of customer-satisfying uses which accounts for their prodigious output of successful new products. Without a very sophisticated eye on the customer, most of their new products might have been wrong, their sales methods useless.

Aluminum has also continued to be a growth industry, thanks to the efforts of two wartime-created companies which deliberately set about creating new customer-satisfying uses. Without Kaiser Aluminum & Chemical Corporation and Reynolds Metals Company, the total demand for aluminum today would be vastly less.

Error of analysis: Some may argue that it is foolish to set the railroads off against aluminum or the movies off against glass. Are not aluminum and glass naturally so versatile that the industries are bound to have more growth opportunities than the railroads and movies? This view commits precisely the error I have been talking about. It defines an industry, or a product, or a cluster of know-how so narrowly as to guarantee its premature senescence. When we mention "railroads," we should make sure we mean "transportation." As transporters, the railroads still have a good chance for very considerable growth. They are not limited to the railroad business as such (though in my opinion rail transportation is potentially a much stronger transportation medium than is generally believed).

What the railroads lack is not opportunity, but some of the same managerial imaginativeness and audacity that made them great. Even an amateur like Jacques Barzun can see what is lacking when he says:

"I grieve to see the most advanced physical and social organization of the last century go down in shabby disgrace for lack of the same comprehensive imagination that built it up. [What is lacking is] the will of the companies to survive and to satisfy the public by inventiveness and skill."[1]

Shadow of Obsolescence

It is impossible to mention a single major industry that did not at one time qualify for the magic appellation of "growth industry." In each case its assumed strength lay in the apparently unchallenged superiority of its product. There appeared to be no effective substitute for it. It was itself a runaway substitute for the product it so triumphantly replaced. Yet one after another of these celebrated industries has come under a shadow. Let us look briefly at a few more of them, this time taking examples that have so far received a little less attention:

- *Dry cleaning*—This was once a growth industry with lavish prospects. In an age of wool garments, imagine being finally able to get them safely and easily clean. The boom was on.

  Yet here we are 30 years after the boom started and the industry is in trouble. Where has the competition

come from? From a better way of cleaning? No. It has come from synthetic fibers and chemical additives that have cut the need for dry cleaning. But this is only the beginning. Lurking in the wings and ready to make chemical dry cleaning totally obsolescent is that powerful magician, ultrasonics.

- *Electric utilities*—This is another one of those supposedly "no-substitute" products that has been enthroned on a pedestal of invincible growth. When the incandescent lamp came along, kerosene lights were finished. Later the water wheel and the steam engine were cut to ribbons by the flexibility, reliability, simplicity, and just plain easy availability of electric motors. The prosperity of electric utilities continues to wax extravagant as the home is converted into a museum of electric gadgetry. How can anybody miss by investing in utilities, with no competition, nothing but growth ahead?

  But a second look is not quite so comforting. A score of nonutility companies are well advanced toward developing a powerful chemical fuel cell which could sit in some hidden closet of every home silently ticking off electric power. The electric lines that vulgarize so many neighborhoods will be eliminated. So will the endless demolition of streets and service interruptions during storms. Also on the horizon is solar energy, again pioneered by nonutility companies.

  Who says that the utilities have no competition? They may be natural monopolies now, but tomorrow they may be natural deaths. To avoid this prospect, they too will have to develop fuel cells, solar energy, and other power sources. To survive, they themselves will have to plot the obsolescence of what now produces their livelihood.

- *Grocery stores*—Many people find it hard to realize that there ever was a thriving establishment known as the "corner grocery store." The supermarket has taken over with a powerful effectiveness. Yet the big food chains of the 1930s narrowly escaped being completely wiped out by the aggressive expansion of independent supermarkets. The first genuine supermarket was opened in 1930, in Jamaica, Long Island. By 1933 supermarkets were thriving in California, Ohio, Pennsylvania, and elsewhere. Yet the established chains pompously ignored them. When they chose to notice them, it was with such derisive descriptions as "cheapy," "horse-and-buggy," "cracker-barrel storekeeping," and "unethical opportunists."

The executive of one big chain announced at the time that he found it "hard to believe that people will drive for miles to shop for foods and sacrifice the personal service chains have perfected and to which Mrs. Consumer is accustomed."[2] As late as 1936, the National Wholesale Grocers convention and the New Jersey Retail Grocers Association said there was nothing to fear. They said that the supers' narrow appeal to the price buyer limited the size of their market. They had to draw from miles around. When imitators came, there would be wholesale liquidations as volume fell. The current high sales of the supers was said to be partly due to their novelty. Basically people wanted convenient neighborhood grocers. If the neighborhood stores "cooperate with their suppliers, pay attention to their costs, and improve their service," they would be able to weather the competition until it blew over.[3]

It never blew over. The chains discovered that survival required going into the supermarket business. This meant the wholesale destruction of their huge investments in corner store sites and in established distribution and merchandising methods. The companies with "the courage of their convictions" resolutely stuck to the corner store philosophy. They kept their pride but lost their shirts.

Self-deceiving cycle: But memories are short. For example, it is hard for people who today confidently hail the twin messiahs of electronics and chemicals to see how things could possibly go wrong with these galloping industries. They probably also cannot see how a reasonably sensible businessman could have been as myopic as the famous Boston millionaire who 50 years ago unintentionally sentenced his heirs to poverty by stipulating that his entire estate be forever invested exclusively in electric streetcar securities. His posthumous declaration, "There will always be a big demand for efficient urban transportation," is no consolation to his heirs who sustain life by pumping gasoline at automobile filling stations.

Yet, in a casual survey I recently took among a group of intelligent business executives, nearly half agreed that it would be hard to hurt their heirs by tying their estates forever to the electronics industry. When I then confronted them with the Boston streetcar example, they chorused unanimously, "That's different!" But is it? Is not the basic situation identical?

In truth, *there is no such thing* as a growth industry, I believe. There are only companies organized and operated to create and capitalize on growth opportunities. Industries that assume themselves to be riding some automatic growth escalator invariably descend into stagnation. The history of every dead and dying "growth" industry shows a self-deceiving cycle of bountiful expansion and undetected decay. There are four conditions which usually guarantee this cycle:

1. The belief that growth is assured by an expanding and more affluent population.
2. The belief that there is no competitive substitute for the industry's major product.
3. Too much faith in mass production and in the advantages of rapidly declining unit costs as output rises.
4. Preoccupation with a product that lends itself to carefully controlled scientific experimentation, improvement, and manufacturing cost reduction.

I should like now to begin examining each of these conditions in some detail. To build my case as boldly as possible, I shall illustrate the points with reference to three industries—petroleum, automobiles, and electronics—particularly petroleum, because it spans more years and more vicissitudes. Not only do these three have excellent reputations with the general public and also enjoy the confidence of sophisticated investors, but their managements have become known for progressive thinking in areas like financial control, product research, and management training. If obsolescence can cripple even these industries, it can happen anywhere.

Population Myth

The belief that profits are assured by an expanding and more affluent population is dear to the heart of every industry. It takes the edge off the apprehensions everybody understandably feels about the future. If consumers are multiplying and also buying more of your product or service, you can face the future with considerably more comfort than if the market is shrinking. An expanding market keeps the manufacturer from having to think very hard or imaginatively. If thinking is an intellectual response to a problem, then the absence of a problem leads to the absence of thinking. If your product has an automatically expanding market, then you will not give much thought to how to expand it.

One of the most interesting examples of this is provided by the petroleum industry. Probably our oldest growth industry, it has an enviable record. While there are some current apprehensions about its growth rate, the industry itself tends to be optimistic.

But I believe it can be demonstrated that it is undergoing a fundamental yet typical change. It is not only ceasing to be a growth industry, but may actually be a declining one, relative to other business. Although there is widespread unawareness of it, I believe that within 25 years the oil industry may find itself in much the same position of retrospective glory that the railroads are now in. Despite its pioneering work in developing and applying the present-value method of investment evaluation, in employee relations, and in working with backward countries, the petroleum business is a distressing example of how complacency and wrongheadedness can stubbornly convert opportunity into near disaster.

One of the characteristics of this and other industries that have believed very strongly in the beneficial consequences of an expanding population, while at the same time being industries with a generic product for which there has appeared to be no competitive substitute, is that the individual companies have sought to outdo their competitors by improving on what they are already doing. This makes sense, of course, if one assumes that sales are tied to the country's population strings, because the customer can compare products only on a feature-by-feature basis. I believe it is significant, for example, that not since John D. Rockefeller sent free kerosene lamps to China has the oil industry done anything really outstanding to create a demand for its product. Not even in product improvement has it showered itself with eminence. The greatest single improvement—namely, the development of tetraethyl lead—came from outside the industry, specifically from General Motors and DuPont. The big contributions made by the industry itself are confined to the technology of oil exploration, production, and refining.

Asking for trouble: In other words, the industry's efforts have focused on improving the *efficiency* of getting and making its product, not really on improving the generic product or its marketing. Moreover, its chief product has continuously been defined in the narrowest possible terms, namely, gasoline, not energy, fuel, or transportation. This attitude has helped assure that:

• Major improvements in gasoline quality tend not to originate in the oil industry. Also, the development of superior alternative fuels comes from outside the oil industry, as will be shown later.

- Major innovations in automobile fuel marketing are originated by small new oil companies that are not primarily preoccupied with production or refining. These are the companies that have been responsible for the rapidly expanding multipump gasoline stations, with their successful emphasis on large and clean layouts, rapid and efficient driveway service, and quality gasoline at low prices.

Thus, the oil industry is asking for trouble from outsiders. Sooner or later, in this land of hungry inventors and entrepreneurs, a threat is sure to come. The possibilities of this will become more apparent when we turn to the next dangerous belief of many managements. For the sake of continuity, because this second belief is tied closely to the first, I shall continue with the same example.

Idea of indispensability: The petroleum industry is pretty much persuaded that there is no competitive substitute for its major product, gasoline—or if there is, that it will continue to be a derivative of crude oil, such as diesel fuel or kerosene jet fuel.

There is a lot of automatic wishful thinking in this assumption. The trouble is that most refining companies own huge amounts of crude oil reserves. These have value only if there is a market for products into which oil can be converted—hence the tenacious belief in the continuing competitive superiority of automobile fuels made from crude oil.

This idea persists despite all historic evidence against it. The evidence not only shows that oil has never been a superior product for any purpose for very long, but it also shows that the oil industry has never really been a growth industry. It has been a succession of different businesses that have gone through the usual historic cycles of growth, maturity, and decay. Its overall survival is owed to a series of miraculous escapes from total obsolescence, of last-minute and unexpected reprieves from total disaster reminiscent of the Perils of Pauline.

Perils of petroleum: I shall sketch in only the main episodes.

First, crude oil was largely a patent medicine. But even before that fad ran out, demand was greatly expanded by the use of oil in kerosene lamps. The prospect of lighting the world's lamps gave rise to an extravagant promise of growth. The prospects were similar to those the industry now holds for gasoline in other parts of the world. It can hardly wait for the underdeveloped nations to get a car in every garage.

In the days of the kerosene lamp, the oil companies competed with each other and against gaslight by trying to improve the illuminating characteristics of kerosene. Then suddenly the impossible happened. Edison invented a light which was totally nondependent on crude oil. Had it not been for the growing use of kerosene in space heaters, the incandescent lamp would have completely finished oil as a growth industry at that time. Oil would have been good for little else than axle grease.

Then disaster and reprieve struck again. Two great innovations occurred, neither originating in the oil industry. The successful development of coal-burning domestic central-heating systems made the space heater obsolescent. While the industry reeled, along came its most magnificent boost yet—the internal combustion engine, also invented by outsiders. Then when the prodigious expansion for gasoline finally began to level off in the 1920s, along came the miraculous escape of a central oil heater. Once again, the escape was provided by an outsider's invention and development. And when that market weakened, wartime demand for aviation fuel came to the rescue. After the war the expansion of civilian aviation, the dieselization of railroads, and the explosive demand for cars and trucks kept the industry's growth in high gear.

Meanwhile, centralized oil heating—whose boom potential had only recently been proclaimed—ran into severe competition from natural gas. While the oil companies themselves owned the gas that now competed with their oil, the industry did not originate the natural gas revolution, nor has it to this day greatly profited from its gas ownership. The gas revolution was made by newly formed transmission companies that marketed the product with an aggressive ardor. They started a magnificent new industry, first against the advice and then against the resistance of the oil companies.

By all the logic of the situation, the oil companies themselves should have made the gas revolution. They not only owned the gas; they also were the only people experienced in handling, scrubbing, and using it, the only people experienced in pipeline technology and transmission, and they understood heating problems. But, partly because they knew that natural gas would compete with their own sale of heating oil, the oil companies pooh-poohed the potentials of gas.

The revolution was finally started by oil pipeline executives who, unable to persuade their own companies to go into gas, quit and organized the spectacularly successful gas transmission companies. Even after their success became painfully evident to the oil companies, the latter did not go into gas transmission. The multibillion dollar business which should have been theirs went to others. As in the past, the industry was blinded by its narrow preoccupation with a specific product and the value of its reserves. It paid little or no attention to its customers' basic needs and preferences.

The postwar years have not witnessed any change. Immediately after World War II the oil industry was greatly encouraged about its future by the rapid expansion of demand for its traditional line of products. In 1950 most companies projected annual rates of domestic expansion of around 6% through at least 1975. Though the ratio of crude oil reserves to demand in the Free World was about 20 to 1, with 10 to 1 being usually considered a reasonable working ratio in the United States, booming demand sent oil men searching for more without sufficient regard to what the future really promised. In 1952 they "hit" in the Middle East; the ratio skyrocketed to 42 to 1. If gross additions to reserves continue at the average rate of the past five years (37 billion barrels annually), then by 1970 the reserve ratio will be up to 45 to 1. This abundance of oil has weakened crude and product prices all over the world.

Uncertain future: Management cannot find much consolation today in the rapidly expanding petrochemical industry, another oil-using idea that did not originate in the leading firms. The total United States production of petrochemicals is equivalent to about 2% (by volume) of the demand for all petroleum products. Although the petrochemical industry is now expected to grow by about 10% per year, this will not offset other drains on the growth of crude oil consumption. Furthermore, while petrochemical products are many and growing, it is well to remember that there are nonpetroleum sources of the basic raw material, such as coal. Besides, a lot of plastics can be produced with relatively little oil. A 5,000-barrel-per-day oil refinery is now considered the absolute minimum size for efficiency. But a 5,000-barrel-per-day chemical plant is a giant operation.

Oil has never been a continuously strong growth industry. It has grown by fits and starts, always miraculously saved by innovations and developments not of its own making. The reason it has not grown in a smooth progression is that each time it thought it had a superior product safe from the possibility of competitive substitutes, the product turned out to be inferior and notoriously subject to obsolescence. Until now, gasoline (for motor fuel, anyhow) has escaped this fate. But, as we shall see later, it too may be on its last legs.

The point of all this is that there is no guarantee against product obsolescence. If a company's own research does not make it obsolete, another's will. Unless an industry is especially lucky, as oil has been until now, it can easily go down in a sea of red figures—just as the railroads have, as the buggy whip manufacturers have, as the corner grocery chains have, as most of the big movie companies have, and indeed as many other industries have.

The best way for a firm to be lucky is to make its own luck. That requires knowing what makes a business successful. One of the greatest enemies of this knowledge is mass production.

Production Pressures

Mass-production industries are impelled by a great drive to produce all they can. The prospect of steeply declining unit costs as output rises is more than most companies can usually resist. The profit possibilities look spectacular. All effort focuses on production. The result is that marketing gets neglected.

John Kenneth Galbraith contends that just the opposite occurs.[4] Output is so prodigious that all effort concentrates on trying to get rid of it. He says this accounts for singing commercials, desecration of the countryside with advertising signs, and other wasteful and vulgar practices. Galbraith has a finger on something real, but he misses the strategic point. Mass production does indeed generate great pressure to "move" the product. But what usually gets emphasized is selling, not marketing. Marketing, being a more sophisticated and complex process, gets ignored.

The difference between marketing and selling is more than semantic. Selling focuses on the needs of the seller, marketing on the needs of the buyer. Selling is preoccupied with the seller's need to convert his product into cash, marketing with the idea of satisfying the needs of the customer by means of the product and the whole cluster of things associated with creating, delivering, and finally consuming it.

In some industries the enticements of full mass production have been so powerful that for many years top management in effect has told the sales departments, "You get rid of it; we'll worry about profits." By contrast, a truly marketing-minded firm tries to create value-satisfying goods and services that consumers will want to buy. What it offers for sale includes not only the generic product or service, but also how it is made available to the customer, in what form, when, under what conditions, and at what terms of trade. Most important, what it offers for sale is determined not by the seller but by the buyer. The seller takes his cues from the buyer in such a way that the product becomes a consequence of the marketing effort, not vice versa.

Lag in Detroit: This may sound like an elementary rule of business, but that does not keep it from being violated wholesale. It is certainly more violated than honored. Take the automobile industry.

Here mass production is most famous, most honored, and has the greatest impact on the entire society. The industry has hitched its fortune to the relentless requirements of the annual model change, a policy that makes customer orientation an especially urgent necessity. Consequently the auto companies annually spend millions of dollars on consumer research. But the fact that the new compact cars are selling so well in their first year indicates that Detroit's vast researches have for a long time failed to reveal what the customer really wanted. Detroit was not persuaded that he wanted anything different from what he had been getting until it lost millions of customers to other small car manufacturers.

How could this unbelievable lag behind consumer wants have been perpetuated so long? Why did not research reveal consumer preferences before consumers' buying decisions themselves revealed the facts? Is that not what consumer research is for—to find out before the fact what is going to happen? The answer is that Detroit never really researched the customer's wants. It only researched his preferences between the kinds of things which it had already decided to offer him. For Detroit is mainly product-oriented, not customer-oriented. To the extent that the customer is recognized as having needs that the manufacturer should try to satisfy, Detroit usually acts as if the job can be done entirely by product changes. Occasionally attention gets paid to financing, too, but that is done more in order to sell than to enable the customer to buy.

As for taking care of other customer needs, there is not enough being done to write about. The areas of the greatest unsatisfied needs are ignored, or at best get stepchild attention. These are at the point of sale and on the matter of automotive repair and maintenance. Detroit views these problem areas as being of secondary importance. That is underscored by the fact that the retailing and servicing ends of this industry are neither owned and operated nor controlled by the manufacturers. Once the car is produced, things are pretty much in the dealer's inadequate hands. Illustrative of Detroit's arm's-length attitude is the fact that, while servicing holds enormous sales-stimulating, profit-building opportunities, only 57 of Chevrolet's 7,000 dealers provide night maintenance service.

Motorists repeatedly express their dissatisfaction with servicing and their apprehensions about buying cars under the present selling setup. The anxieties and problems they encounter during the auto buying and maintenance processes are probably more intense and widespread today than 30 years ago. Yet the automobile companies do not *seem* to listen to or take their cues from the anguished consumer. If they do listen, it must be through the filter of their own preoccupation with production.

The marketing effort is still viewed as a necessary consequence of the product, not vice versa, as it should be. That is the legacy of mass production, with its parochial view that profit resides essentially in low-cost full production.

What Ford put first: The profit lure of mass production obviously has a place in the plans and strategy of business management, but it must always *follow* hard thinking about the customer. This is one of the most important lessons that we can learn from the contradictory behavior of Henry Ford. In a sense, Ford was both the most brilliant and the most senseless marketer in American history. He was senseless because he refused to give the customer anything but a black car. He was brilliant because he fashioned a production system designed to fit market needs. We habitually celebrate him for the wrong reason, his production genius. His real genius was marketing. We think he was able to cut his selling price and therefore sell millions of $500 cars because his invention of the assembly line had reduced the costs. Actually he invented the assembly line because he had concluded that at $500 he could sell millions of cars. Mass production was the *result* not the cause of his low prices.

Ford repeatedly emphasized this point, but a nation of production-oriented business managers refuses to hear the great lesson he taught. Here is his operating philosophy as he expressed it succinctly:

"Our policy is to reduce the price, extend the operations, and improve the article. You will notice that the reduction of price comes first. We have never considered any costs as fixed. Therefore we first reduce the price to the point where we believe more sales will result. Then we go ahead and try to make the prices. We do not bother about the costs. The new price forces the costs down. The more usual way is to take the costs and then determine the price; and although that method may be scientific in the narrow sense, it is not scientific in the broad sense, because what earthly use is it to know the cost if it tells you that you cannot manufacture at a price at which the article can be sold? But more to the point is the fact that, although one may calculate what a cost is, and of course all of our costs are carefully calculated, no one knows what a cost ought to be. One of the ways of discovering . . . is to name a price so low as to force everybody in the place to the highest point of efficiency. The low price makes everybody dig for profits. We make more discoveries concerning manufacturing and selling under this forced method than by any method of leisurely investigation."[5]

Product provincialism: The tantalizing profit possibilities of low unit production costs may be the most seriously self-deceiving attitude that can afflict a company, particularly a "growth" company where an apparently assured expansion of demand already tends to undermine a proper concern for the importance of marketing and the customer.

The usual result of this narrow preoccupation with so-called concrete matters is that instead of growing, the industry declines. It usually means that the product fails to adapt to the constantly changing patterns of consumer needs and tastes, to new and modified marketing institutions and practices, or to product developments in competing or complementary industries. The industry has its eyes so firmly on its own specific product that it does not see how it is being made obsolete.

The classical example of this is the buggy whip industry. No amount of product improvement could stave off its death sentence. But had the industry defined itself as being in the transportation business rather than the buggy whip business, it might have survived. It would have done what survival always entails, that is, changing. Even if it had only defined its business as providing a stimulant or catalyst to an energy source, it might have survived by becoming a manufacturer of, say, fanbelts or air cleaners.

What may some day be a still more classical example is, again, the oil industry. Having let others steal marvelous opportunities from it (e.g., natural gas, as already mentioned, missile fuels, and jet engine lubricants), one would expect it to have taken steps never to let that happen again. But this is not the case. We are now getting extraordinary new developments in fuel systems specifically designed to power automobiles. Not only are these developments concentrated in firms outside the petroleum industry, but petroleum is almost systematically ignoring them, securely content in its wedded bliss to oil. It is the story of the kerosene lamp versus the incandescent lamp all over again. Oil is trying to improve hydrocarbon fuels rather than develop *any* fuels best suited to the needs of their users, whether or not made in different ways and with different raw materials from oil.

Here are some things which nonpetroleum companies are working on:

- Over a dozen such firms now have advanced working models of energy systems which, when perfected, will replace the internal combustion engine and eliminate the demand for gasoline. The superior merit of each of these systems is their elimination of frequent, time-consuming, and irritating refueling stops. Most of these systems are fuel cells designed to create electrical energy directly from chemicals without combustion. Most of them use chemicals that are not derived from oil, generally hydrogen and oxygen.

- Several other companies have advanced models of electric storage batteries designed to power automobiles. One of these is an aircraft producer that is working jointly with several electric utility companies. The latter hope to use off-peak generating capacity to supply overnight plug-in battery regeneration. Another company, also using the battery approach, is a medium-size electronics firm with extensive small-battery experience that it developed in connection with its work on hearing aids. It is collaborating with an automobile manufacturer. Recent improvements arising from the need for high-powered miniature power storage plants in rockets have put us within reach of a relatively small battery capable of withstanding great overloads or surges of power. Germanium diode applications and batteries using sintered-plate and nickel-cadmium techniques promise to make a revolution in our energy sources.

- Solar energy conversion systems are also getting increasing attention. One usually cautious Detroit auto executive recently ventured that solar-powered cars might be common by 1980.

As for the oil companies, they are more or less "watching developments," as one research director put it to me. A few are doing a bit of research on fuel cells, but almost always confined to developing cells powered by hydrocarbon chemicals. None of them are enthusiastically researching fuel cells, batteries, or solar power plants. None of them are spending a fraction as much on research in these profoundly important areas as they are on the usual run-of-the-mill things like reducing combustion chamber deposit in gasoline engines. One major integrated petroleum company recently took a tentative look at the fuel cell and concluded that although "the companies actively working on it indicate a belief in ultimate success . . . the timing and magnitude of its impact are too remote to warrant recognition in our forecasts."

One might, of course, ask: Why should the oil companies do anything different? Would not chemical fuel cells, batteries, or solar energy kill the present product lines? The answer is that they would indeed, and that is precisely the reason for the oil firms having to develop these power units before their competitors, so they will not be companies without an industry.

Management might be more likely to do what is needed for its own preservation if it thought of itself as being in the energy business. But even that would not be enough if it persists in imprisoning itself in the narrow grip of its tight product orientation. It has to think of itself as taking care of customer needs, not finding, refining, or even selling oil. Once it genuinely thinks of its business as taking care of people's transportation needs, nothing can stop it from creating its own extravagantly profitable growth.

'Creative destruction': Since words are cheap and deeds are dear, it may be appropriate to indicate what this kind of thinking involves and leads to. Let us start at the beginning—the customer. It can be shown that motorists strongly dislike the bother, delay, and experience of buying gasoline. People actually do not buy gasoline. They cannot see it, taste it, feel it, appreciate it, or really test it. What they buy is the right to continue driving their cars. The gas station is like a tax collector to whom people are compelled to pay a periodic toll as the price of using their cars. This makes the gas station a basically unpopular institution. It can never be made popular or pleasant, only less unpopular, less unpleasant.

To reduce its unpopularity completely means eliminating it. Nobody likes a tax collector, not even a pleasantly cheerful one. Nobody likes to interrupt a trip to buy a phantom product, not even from a handsome Adonis or a seductive Venus. Hence, companies that are working on exotic fuel substitutes which will eliminate the need for frequent refueling are heading directly into the outstretched arms of the irritated motorist. They are riding a wave of inevitability, not because they are creating something which is technologically superior or more sophisticated, but because they are satisfying a powerful customer need. They are also eliminating noxious odors and air pollution.

Once the petroleum companies recognize the customer-satisfying logic of what another power system can do they will see that they have no more choice about working on an efficient, long-lasting fuel (or some way of delivering present fuels without bothering the motorist) than the big food chains

had a choice about going into the supermarket business, or the vacuum tube companies had a choice about making semiconductors. For their own good the oil firms will have to destroy their own highly profitable assets. No amount of wishful thinking can save them from the necessity of engaging in this form of "creative destruction."

I phrase the need as strongly as this because I think management must make quite an effort to break itself loose from conventional ways. It is all too easy in this day and age for a company or industry to let its sense of purpose become dominated by the economies of full production and to develop a dangerously lopsided product orientation. In short, if management lets itself drift, it invariably drifts in the direction of thinking of itself as producing goods and services, not customer satisfactions. While it probably will not descend to the depths of telling its salesmen, "You get rid of it; we'll worry about profits," it can, without knowing it, be practicing precisely that formula for withering decay. The historic fate of one growth industry after another has been its suicidal product provincialism.

Dangers of R&D

Another big danger to a firm's continued growth arises when top management is wholly transfixed by the profit possibilities of technical research and development. To illustrate I shall turn first to a new industry—electronics—and then return once more to the oil companies. By comparing a fresh example with a familiar one, I hope to emphasize the prevalence and insidiousness of a hazardous way of thinking.

Marketing shortchanged: In the case of electronics, the greatest danger which faces the glamorous new companies in this field is not that they do not pay enough attention to research and development, but that they pay *too much* attention to it. And the fact that the fastest growing electronics firms owe their eminence to their heavy emphasis on technical research is completely beside the point. They have vaulted to affluence on a sudden crest of unusually strong general receptiveness to new technical ideas. Also, their success has been shaped in the virtually guaranteed market of military subsidies and by military orders that in many cases actually preceded the existence of facilities to make the products. Their expansion has, in other words, been almost totally devoid of marketing effort.

Thus, they are growing up under conditions that come dangerously close to creating the illusion that a superior product will sell itself. Having created a successful company by making a superior product, it is not surprising that management continues to be oriented toward the product rather than the people who consume it. It develops the philosophy that continued growth is a matter of continued product innovation and improvement.

A number of other factors tend to strengthen and sustain this belief:

1. Because electronic products are highly complex and sophisticated, managements become top-heavy with engineers and scientists. This creates a selective bias in favor of research and production at the expense of marketing. The organization tends to view itself as

making things rather than satisfying customer needs. Marketing gets treated as a residual activity, "something else" that must be done once the vital job of product creation and production is completed.

2. To this bias in favor of product research, development, and production is added the bias in favor of dealing with controllable variables. Engineers and scientists are at home in the world of concrete things like machines, test tubes, production lines, and even balance sheets. The abstractions to which they feel kindly are those which are testable or manipulatable in the laboratory, or, if not testable, then functional, such as Euclid's axioms. In short, the managements of the new glamour-growth companies tend to favor those business activities which lend themselves to careful study, experimentation, and control—the hard, practical realities of the lab, the shop, the books.

What gets shortchanged are the realities of the *market.* Consumers are unpredictable, varied, fickle, stupid, shortsighted, stubborn, and generally bothersome. This is not what the engineer-managers say, but deep down in their consciousness it is what they believe. And this accounts for their concentrating on what they know and what they can control, namely, product research, engineering, and production. The emphasis on production becomes particularly attractive when the product can be made at declining unit costs. There is no more inviting way of making money than by running the plant full blast.

Today the top-heavy science-engineering-production orientation of so many electronics companies works reasonably well because they are pushing into new frontiers in which the armed services have pioneered virtually assured markets. The companies are in the felicitous position of having to fill, not find markets; of not having to discover what the customer needs and wants, but of having the customer voluntarily come forward with specific new product demands. If a team of consultants had been assigned specifically to design a business situation calculated to prevent the emergence and development of a customer-oriented marketing viewpoint, it could not have produced anything better than the conditions just described.

Stepchild treatment: The oil industry is a stunning example of how science, technology, and mass production can divert an entire group of companies from their main task. To the extent the consumer is studied at all (which is not much), the focus is forever on getting information which is designed to help the oil companies improve what they are now doing. They try to discover more convincing advertising themes, more effective sales promotional drives, what the market shares of the various companies are, what people like or dislike about service station dealers and oil companies, and so forth. Nobody seems as interested in probing deeply into the basic human needs that the industry might be trying to satisfy as in probing into the basic properties of the raw material that the companies work with in trying to deliver customer satisfactions.

Basic questions about customers and markets seldom get asked. The latter occupy a stepchild status. They are recognized as existing, as having to be taken care of, but not worth very much real thought or dedicated attention. Nobody gets as excited about the customers in his own backyard as about the oil in the Sahara Desert. Nothing illustrates better the neglect of marketing than its treatment in the industry press.

The centennial issue of the *American Petroleum Institute Quarterly,* published in 1959 to celebrate the discovery of oil in Titusville, Pennsylvania, contained 21 feature articles proclaiming the industry's greatness. Only one of these talked about its achievements in marketing, and that was only a pictorial record of how service station architecture has changed. The issue also contained a special section on "New Horizons," which was devoted to showing the magnificent role oil would play in America's future. Every reference was ebulliently optimistic, never implying once that oil might have some hard competition. Even the reference to atomic energy was a cheerful catalogue of how oil would help make atomic energy a success. There was not a single apprehension that the oil industry's affluence might be threatened or a suggestion that one "new horizon" might include new and better ways of serving oil's present customers.

But the most revealing example of the stepchild treatment that marketing gets was still another special series of short articles on "The Revolutionary Potential of Electronics." Under that heading this list of articles appeared in the table of contents:

- "In the Search for Oil"
- "In Production Operations"
- "In Refinery Processes"
- "In Pipeline Operations"

Significantly, every one of the industry's major functional areas is listed, *except* marketing. Why? Either it is believed that electronics holds no revolutionary potential for petroleum marketing (which is palpably wrong), or the editors forgot to discuss marketing (which is more likely, and illustrates its stepchild status).

The order in which the four functional areas are listed also betrays the alienation of the oil industry from the consumer. The industry is implicitly defined as beginning with the search for oil and ending with its distribution from the refinery. But the truth is, it seems to me, that the industry begins with the needs of the customer for its products. From that primal position its definition moves steadily back-stream to areas of progressively lesser importance, until it finally comes to rest at the "search for oil."

Beginning & end: The view that an industry is a customer-satisfying process, not a goods-producing process, is vital for all businessmen to understand. An industry begins with the customer and his needs, not with a patent, a raw material, or a selling skill. Given the customer's needs, the industry develops backwards, first concerning itself with the physical *delivery* of customer satisfactions. Then it moves back further to *creating* the things by which these satisfactions are in part achieved. How these materials are created is a matter of indifference to the customer, hence the particular form of manufacturing, processing, or what-have-you cannot be considered as a vital aspect of the industry. Finally, the industry moves back still further to *finding* the raw materials necessary for making its products.

The irony of some industries oriented toward technical research and development is that the scientists who occupy the high executive positions are totally unscientific when it comes to defining their companies' overall needs and purposes. They violate the first two rules of the scientific method—being aware of and defining their companies' problems, and then developing testable hypotheses about solving them. They are scientific only about the convenient things, such as laboratory and product experiments.

The reason that the customer (and the satisfaction of his deepest needs) is not considered as being "the problem" is not because there is any certain belief that no such problem exists, but because an organizational lifetime has conditioned management to look in the opposite direction. Marketing is a stepchild.

I do not mean that selling is ignored. Far from it. But selling, again, is not marketing. As already pointed out, selling concerns itself with the tricks and techniques of getting people to exchange their cash for your product. It is not concerned with the values that the exchange is all about. And it does not, as marketing invariably does, view the entire business process as consisting of a tightly integrated effort to discover, create, arouse, and satisfy customer needs. The customer is somebody "out there" who, with proper cunning, can be separated from his loose change.

Actually, not even selling gets much attention in some technologically minded firms. Because there is a virtually guaranteed market for the abundant flow of their new products, they do not actually know what a real market is. It is as if they lived in a planned economy, moving their products routinely from factory to retail outlet. Their successful concentration on products tends to convince them of the soundness of what they have been doing, and they fail to see the gathering clouds over the market.

Conclusion

Less than 75 years ago American railroads enjoyed a fierce loyalty among astute Wall Streeters. European monarchs invested in them heavily. Eternal wealth was thought to be the benediction for anybody who could scrape a few thousand dollars together to put into rail stocks. No other form of transportation could compete with the railroads in speed, flexibility, durability, economy, and growth potentials.

As Jacques Barzun put it, "By the turn of the century it was an institution, an image of man, a tradition, a code of honor, a source of poetry, a nursery of boyhood desires, a sublimest of toys, and the most solemn machine—next to the funeral hearse—that marks the epochs in man's life."[6]

Even after the advent of automobiles, trucks, and airplanes, the railroad tycoons remained imperturbably self-confident. If you had told them 30 years ago that in 30 years they would be flat on their backs, broke, and pleading for government subsidies, they would have thought you totally demented. Such a future was simply not considered possible. It was not even a discussable subject, or an askable question, or a matter which any sane person would consider worth speculating about. The very thought was insane. Yet a lot of insane notions now have matter-of-fact acceptance—for example, the idea of 100-ton tubes of metal moving smoothly through the air 20,000 feet above the earth, loaded with 100 sane and solid citizens casu-

ally drinking martinis—and they have dealt cruel blows to the railroads.

What specifically must other companies do to avoid this fate? What does customer orientation involve? These questions have in part been answered by the preceding examples and analysis. It would take another article to show in detail what is required for specific industries. In any case, it should be obvious that building an effective customer-oriented company involves far more than good intentions or promotional tricks; it involves profound matters of human organization and leadership. For the present, let me merely suggest what appear to be some general requirements.

Visceral feel of greatness: Obviously the company has to do what survival demands. It has to adapt to the requirements of the market, and it has to do it sooner rather than later. But mere survival is a so-so aspiration. Anybody can survive in some way or other, even the skid-row bum. The trick is to survive gallantly, to feel the surging impulse of commercial mastery; not just to experience the sweet smell of success, but to have the visceral feel of entrepreneurial greatness.

No organization can achieve greatness without a vigorous leader who is driven onward by his own pulsating *will to succeed.* He has to have a vision of grandeur, a vision that can produce eager followers in vast numbers. In business, the followers are the customers.

In order to produce these customers, the entire corporation must be viewed as a customer-creating and customer-satisfying organism. Management must think of itself not as producing products but as providing customer-creating value satisfactions. It must push this idea (and everything it means and requires) into every nook and cranny of the organization. It has to do this continuously and with the kind of flair that excites and stimulates the people in it. Otherwise, the company will be merely a series of pigeonholed parts, with no consolidating sense of purpose or direction.

In short, the organization must learn to think of itself not as producing goods or services but as *buying customers,* as doing the things that will make people *want* to do business with it. And the chief executive himself has the inescapable responsibility for creating this environment, this viewpoint, this attitude, this aspiration. He himself must set the company's style, its direction, and its goals. This means he has to know precisely where he himself wants to go, and to make sure the whole organization is enthusiastically aware of where that is. This is a first requisite of leadership, for *unless he knows where he is going, any road will take him there.*

If any road is okay, the chief executive might as well pack his attaché case and go fishing. If an organization does not know or care where it is going, it does not need to advertise that fact with a ceremonial figurehead. Everybody will notice it soon enough.

Retrospective Commentary

Amazed, finally, by his literary success, Isaac Bashevis Singer reconciled an attendant problem: "I think the moment you have published a book, it's not any more your private property. . . . If it has value, everybody can find in it what he finds, and I cannot tell the man I did not intend it to be so." Over the past 15 years,

"Marketing Myopia" has become a case in point. Remarkably, the article spawned a legion of loyal partisans—not to mention a host of unlikely bedfellows.

Its most common and, I believe, most influential consequence is the way certain companies for the first time gave serious thought to the question of what businesses they are really in.

The strategic consequences of this have in many cases been dramatic. The best-known case, of course, is the shift in thinking of oneself as being in the "oil business" to being in the "energy business." In some instances the payoff has been spectacular (getting into coal, for example) and in others dreadful (in terms of the time and money spent so far on fuel cell research). Another successful example is a company with a large chain of retail shoe stores that redefined itself as a retailer of moderately priced, frequently purchased, widely assorted consumer specialty products. The result was a dramatic growth in volume, earnings, and return on assets.

Some companies, again for the first time, asked themselves whether they wished to be masters of certain technologies for which they would seek markets, or be masters of markets for which they would seek customer-satisfying products and services.

Choosing the former, one company has declared, in effect, "We are experts in glass technology. We intend to improve and expand that expertise with the object of creating products that will attract customers." This decision has forced the company into a much more systematic and customer-sensitive look at possible markets and users, even though its stated strategic object has been to capitalize on glass technology.

Deciding to concentrate on markets, another company has determined that "we want to help people (primarily women) enhance their beauty and sense of youthfulness." This company has expanded its line of cosmetic products, but has also entered the fields of proprietary drugs and vitamin supplements.

All these examples illustrate the "policy" results of "Marketing Myopia." On the operating level, there has been, I think, an extraordinary heightening of sensitivity to customers and consumers. R&D departments have cultivated a greater "external" orientation toward uses, users, and markets—balancing thereby the previously one-sided "internal" focus on materials and methods; upper management has realized that marketing and sales departments should be somewhat more willingly accommodated than before, finance departments have become more receptive to the legitimacy of budgets for market research and experimentation in marketing, and salesmen have been better trained to listen to and understand customer needs and problems, rather than merely to "push" the product.

A Mirror, Not a Window

My impression is that the article has had more impact in industrial-products companies than in consumer-products companies—perhaps because the former had lagged most in customer orientation. There are at least two reasons for this lag: (1) industrial-products companies tend to be more capital intensive, and (2) in the past, at least, they have had to rely heavily on communicating face-to-face the technical character of what they made and sold. These points are worth explaining.

Capital-intensive businesses are understandably preoccupied with magnitudes, especially where the capital, once invested, cannot be easily moved, manipulated, or modified for the production of a variety of products—e.g., chemical plants, steel mills, airlines, and railroads. Understandably, they seek big volumes and operating efficiencies to pay off the equipment and meet the carrying costs.

At least one problem results: corporate power becomes disproportionately lodged with operating or financial executives. If you read the charter of one of the nation's largest companies, you will see that the chairman of the finance committee, not the chief executive officer, is the "chief." Executives with such backgrounds have an almost trained incapacity to see that getting "volume" may require understanding and serving many discrete and sometimes small market segments, rather than going after a perhaps mythical batch of big or homogeneous customers.

These executives also often fail to appreciate the competitive changes going on around them. They observe the changes, all right, but devalue their significance or underestimate their ability to nibble away at the company's markets.

Once dramatically alerted to the concept of segments, sectors, and customers, though, managers of capital-intensive businesses have become more responsive to the necessity of balancing their inescapable preoccupation with "paying the bills" or breaking even with the fact that the best way to accomplish this may be to pay more attention to segments, sectors, and customers.

The second reason industrial products companies have probably been more influenced by the article is that, in the case of the more technical industrial products or services, the necessity of clearly communicating product and service characteristics to prospects results in a lot of face-to-face "selling" effort. But precisely because the product is so complex, the situation produces salesmen who know the product more than they know the customer, who are more adept at explaining what they have and what it can do than learning what the customer's needs and problems are. The result has been a narrow product orientation rather than a liberating customer orientation, and "service" often suffered. To be sure, sellers said, "We have to provide service," but they tended to define service by looking into the mirror rather than out the window. They *thought* they were looking out the window at the customer, but it was actually a mirror—a reflection of their own product-oriented biases rather than a reflection of their customers' situations.

A Manifesto, Not a Prescription

Not everything has been rosy. A lot of bizarre things have happened as a result of the article:

- Some companies have developed what I call "marketing mania"—they've become obsessively responsive to every fleeting whim of the customer. Mass production operations have been converted to approximations of job shops, with cost and price consequences far exceeding the willingness of customers to buy the product.
- Management has expanded product lines and added new lines of business without first establishing adequate control systems to run more complex operations.

- Marketing staffs have suddenly and rapidly expanded themselves and their research budgets without either getting sufficient prior organizational support or, thereafter, producing sufficient results.

- Companies that are functionally organized have converted to product, brand, or market-based organizations with the expectation of instant and miraculous results. The outcome has been ambiguity, frustration, confusion, corporate infighting, losses, and finally a reversion to functional arrangements that only worsened the situation.

- Companies have attempted to "serve" customers by creating complex and beautifully efficient products or services that buyers are either too risk-averse to adopt or incapable of learning how to employ—in effect, there are now steam shovels for people who haven't yet learned to use spades. This problem has happened repeatedly in the so-called service industries (financial services, insurance, computer-based services) and with American companies selling in less-developed economies.

"Marketing Myopia" was not intended as analysis or even prescription; it was intended as manifesto. It did not pretend to take a balanced position. Nor was it a new idea—Peter F. Drucker, J. B. McKitterick, Wroe Alderson, John Howard, and Neil Borden had each done more original and balanced work on "the marketing concept." My scheme, however, tied marketing more closely to the inner orbit of business policy. Drucker—especially in *The Concept of the Corporation* and *The Practice of Management*—originally provided me with a great deal of insight.

My contribution, therefore, appears merely to have been a simple, brief, and useful way of communicating an existing way of thinking. I tried to do it in a very direct, but responsible fashion, knowing that few readers (customers), especially managers and leaders, could stand much equivocation or hesitation. I also knew that the colorful and lightly documented affirmation works better than the tortuously reasoned explanation.

But why the enormous popularity of what was actually such a simple preexisting idea? Why its appeal throughout the world to resolutely restrained scholars, implacably temperate managers, and high government officials, all accustomed to balanced and thoughtful calculation? Is it that concrete examples, joined to illustrate a simple idea and presented with some attention to literacy, communicate better than massive analytical reasoning that reads as though it were translated from the German? Is it that provocative assertions are more memorable and persuasive than restrained and balanced explanations, no matter who the audience? Is it that the character of the message is as much the message as its content? Or was mine not simply a different tune, but a new symphony? I don't know.

Of course, I'd do it again and in the same way, given my purposes, even with what more I now know—the good and the bad, the power of facts and the limits of rhetoric. If your mission is the moon, you don't use a car. Don Marquis's cockroach, Archy, provides some final consolation: "an idea is not responsible for who believes in it."

Notes

1. Jacques Barzun, "Trains and the Mind of Man," *Holiday*, February 1960, p. 21.

2. For more details see M. M. Zimmerman, *The Super Market: A Revolution in Distribution* (New York, McGraw-Hill Book Company, Inc., 1955), p. 48.

3. Ibid., pp. 45–47.

4. *The Affluent Society* (Boston, Houghton Mifflin Company, 1958), pp. 152–160.

5. Henry Ford, *My Life and Work* (New York, Doubleday, Page & Company, 1923), pp. 146–147.

6. Jacques Barzun, "Trains and the Mind of Man," *Holiday*, February 1960, p. 20.

At the time of the article's publication, **THEODORE LEVITT** was lecturer in business administration at the Harvard Business School. He is the author of several books, including *The Third Sector: New Tactics for a Responsive Society* (1973) and *Marketing for Business Growth* (1974).

Putting Customers First
Nine Surefire Ways to Increase Brand Loyalty

KYLE LaMALFA

"Customers first." It's the mantra of businesses everywhere. Yet the average company still loses 10% to 15% of customers each year. Most of them leave due to poor service or a disappointing product experience, yet only 4% of them will tell you about it. And once they've left, it's difficult (not to mention expensive) to get them back.

Fostering true loyalty and engagement with customers starts at a basic level, but here are nine techniques you can employ to make customer loyalty a powerful competitive advantage for your company. They can be broken down into three categories: loyalty basics (one through four), loyalty technologies (five through seven) and loyalty measurement (eight and nine).

1. Give Customers What They Expect

Knowing your customer's expectations and making sure your product or service meets them is Business 101, yet often ignored. At the basic level, business needs to be a balanced transaction where someone pays for something and expects a fair trade in return.

Expectations of product quality come from many sources, including previous quality levels set by your organization, what competitors are saying about you, and the media. Marketing and sales should work together to monitor customer expectations through feedback and surveys.

2. Go Beyond Simple Reward Programs

Points and rewards encourage repeat purchases, but don't actually build loyalty. This is demonstrated by a drop in sales when the rewards are no longer offered. True loyalty comes when customers purchase products without being bribed.

3. Turn Complaints into Opportunities

Managing questions, comments and concerns benefits your business in two important ways. First, research indicates that an upset customer whose problem is addressed with swiftness and certainty can be turned into a highly loyal customer. Second, unstructured feedback, gathered and managed appropriately, can be a rich source of ideas. To that end:

- Establish channels (electronic, phone and written) to build engagement, one customer at a time.
- Encourage customers to voice their thoughts.
- Create metrics to improve response to concerns (i.e., "time to first response," "time to resolution," etc.).
- Create metrics to measure loyalty before and after the problem.
- Use technology to help you centralize the information, create reports and structure drill-downs.

4. Build Opportunities for Repeat Business

Give your customers a chance to be loyal by offering products for repeat business. Monitor what customers request most and offer products or services that compliment other purchases. In addition, exceed expectations by driving product development to offer more value for less cost. Use technology to track, classify and categorize open-ended feedback.

5. Engage Customers in a Two-Way Dialogue

An engaged customer is more than satisfied and more than loyal. They support you during both good and bad times because they believe what you have to offer is superior to others.

Engagement takes your customer beyond passive loyalty to become an active participant and promoter of your product. Engaged customers will give you more feedback so you should be ready to handle it! All this translates into a customer who will spend more money with you over time. Accordingly:

- Listen to customer feedback from comment cards, letters, phone calls and surveys.
- Respond quickly and personally to concerns of high interest to your customers.
- Organize unstructured feedback for tracking and trending over time.
- Trust your customers to tell you what the problem is.
- Use statistical techniques to discover which action items will have the most impact on your business.

6. Survey Customers and Solicit Feedback

Actively soliciting information from a population of customers is a time-tested technique pioneered by Arthur Nielsen (creator of the Nielsen ratings) in the 1920s. Survey research can be used for problem identification or solving. Questions with simple scales such as "agree/disagree" deliver quantitative insight for problem identification. Open-ended follow-up questions can provide rich insight for solving problems. Some tips:

- Make sure your surveys are short, bias-free and well structured.
- Use random sampling to gather feedback continuously without over-surveying.
- Create summary survey indices that can be displayed graphically and tracked over time.

7. Create a Centralized System for Managing Feedback throughout the Enterprise

Technology such as enterprise feedback management (EFM) helps to centralize surveys and customer feedback and track both qualitative and quantitative information. EFM involves more than just collecting data, though; it adopts a strategic approach to building dialogs with your customers. Follow these steps:

- Empower customers to give feedback through common advertised channels.

- Centralize reporting for proactive surveys and complaint management solutions.
- Structure quantitative feedback into a drill-down or rollup report.
- Make open-ended feedback intuitively searchable.

8. Tie Customer Loyalty and Engagement to Business Outcomes

Orienting your organization to focus on satisfaction, loyalty and engagement is no panacea. But researchers have clearly documented evidence of short-term benefits to customer/employee retention and long-term benefits to profitability. Hence:

- Determine whether to measure your engagement outcome by satisfaction, likelihood to purchase again, likelihood to recommend, or another voice of the customer (VOC) metric.
- If necessary, create hybrid VOC measurements using more than one metric.
- Link your VOC metrics with business outcomes like shareholder returns, annual sales growth, gross margin, market share, cash flows, Tobin's Q or customer churn.
- Be aware that changes in loyalty/engagement scores generally precede changes in business outcomes.

9. Use Analysis to Predict Future Loyalty

Businesses use a variety of statistical techniques to make predictions about the potential for future events. Furthermore, predictive analytics may be used to ascertain the degree to which answers from a survey relate to particular goals (such as loyalty and engagement). Tactical knowledge of how action items impact an outcome discourages the wasting of resources on ineffective programs, and competent statistical modeling reveals which tactical options work. Consequently:

- Analyze data using a statistical technique to reveal the most important areas of focus.
- Ask your analyst about common statistical methods, including correlation and logit models.
- Recognize that the major areas of focus may change in response to changes in your economic, competitive and demographic environments.

Following these steps may not be the easiest process, but stay focused. Increasing your engagement and loyalty equals increasing profits and a competitive edge.

Critical Thinking

1. Discuss the importance of establishing two-way dialogue with customers and effectively responding to customer feedback.

2. With a small group of peers from your class, develop some ways that companies can achieve effective two-way dialogue with customers.

KYLE LAMALFA is the best practices manager and loyalty expert for Allegiance, Inc. He can be reached at kyle.lamalfa@allegiance.com. For more information about how to increase your loyalty and engagement, visit www.allegiance.com.

From *Sales & Marketing Management,* January/February 2008, pp. 12–13. Copyright © 2008 by Sales & Marketing Management. Reprinted by permission of Lakewood Media Group.

Making the Most of Customer Complaints

Dealing with service failures means a lot more than just fixing the immediate problem. Here's how to do it right.

STEFAN MICHEL, DAVID BOWEN, AND ROBERT JOHNSTON

Nobody's perfect. That's a fact, not an excuse.

Which is why it's crucial for companies to realize that the way they handle customer complaints is every bit as important as trying to provide great service in the first place. Because things happen.

Customers are constantly judging companies for service failures large and small, from a glitch-ridden business-software program to a hamburger served cold. They judge the company first on how it handles the problem, then on its willingness to make sure similar problems don't happen in the future. And they are far less forgiving when it comes to the latter. Fixing breakdowns in service—we call this service recovery—has enormous impact on customer satisfaction, repeat business, and, ultimately, profits and growth.

But unfortunately, most companies limit service recovery to the staff who deal directly with customers. All too often, companies have customer service sort out the immediate problem, offer an apology or some compensation, and then assume all is well. This approach is particularly damaging because it does nothing to address the underlying problem, practically guaranteeing similar failures and complaints.

What businesses should be doing is looking at service recovery as a mission that involves three stakeholders: customers who want their complaints resolved; managers in charge of the process of addressing those concerns; and the frontline employees who deal with the customers. All three need to be integrated into addressing and fixing service problems.

Tensions naturally arise in and among the groups. For example, customers can be left feeling that their problem wasn't addressed seriously, even when they've received some form of compensation. Service reps can start seeing complaining customers as the enemy, even though they point out flaws that need fixing.

Managers in charge of service recovery, meanwhile, can feel pressure to limit flows of critical customer comments, even though acting on the information will improve efficiency and profits.

However, successfully integrating these three perspectives is something that fewer than 8% of the 60 organizations in our study did well.

Based on our research and our own years of work in service management, here is a look at the three stakeholders in service recovery, focusing on their different perspectives and the tensions that arise among them. We then make recommendations on how to address these tensions and integrate the aims of all three to achieve better—if not perfect—service.

The Customer

Fairness is typically the biggest concern of customers who have lodged a service complaint. Because a service failure implies unfair treatment of the customer, service recovery has to re-establish justice from the customer's perspective.

Say a bank customer requests a deposit receipt from an ATM but the machine fails to print one. The customer becomes worried and goes to one of the bank tellers. The teller checks the account, and assures the customer that there is no problem, that the deposit was made. But if the teller only focuses on the fact that the account was credited, he or she has ignored what in the customer's view was the most severe and critical aspect of the service failure: the worry initially felt, and the extra time it took to verify the deposit.

Customers often want to know—within a reasonable time—not only that their problem has been resolved, but how the failure occurred and what the company is doing to make sure it doesn't happen again.

A customer's faith can be restored using this kind of approach—once. We have even noted something referred to as a "recovery paradox," in which customers can be more delighted by a skillful service recovery than they are by service that was failure-free to start with.

But there is a flip side to this as well: Customers have more tolerance for poor service than for poor service recovery. And if a customer experiences a second failure of the same service, there is no recovery strategy that can work well. In all likelihood, that customer will be lost forever.

Our research suggests that after a failed service recovery, what annoys—and even angers—customers is not that they weren't satisfied, but that they believe the system remains unchanged and likely to fail again.

The Manager

The chief aim of managers in service recovery is to help the company learn from service failures so it doesn't repeat them. Learning from failures is more important than simply fixing problems for individual customers, because process improvements increase overall customer satisfaction and thus have a direct impact on the bottom line.

But companies generally obtain and study only a fraction of the service-failure data that could be gathered from customers, employees and managers. Even when managers agree that customer feedback is essential, there is often poor information flow between the division that collects and deals with customer problems and the rest of the organization.

In some cases, one study revealed, the more negative feedback a customer-service department collects, the more isolated that department becomes, because it doesn't want to be seen by the company at large as a source of friction. Some companies even create specialist units that can soak up customer complaints and problems with no expectation of feeding this information back to the organization. Others actually impede service recovery by rewarding low complaint rates, and then assuming that a decline in the number of reports indicates customer satisfaction is improving.

Some managers in our study saw conflicts between providing great customer satisfaction and achieving high productivity. For instance, incentive structures sometimes placed equal values on sales and on customer service. But as one manager noted: "If you want to achieve 100% [satisfaction], you don't have time for selling. It's questionable whether you can score 100% on service quality and 100% on [sales] objectives."

In any kind of business, there comes a point at which a service recovery can become excessive in the company's eyes, and be seen as giving away the store. However, many customers don't want a payoff. They simply want to have their problem fixed and to be reassured that it won't happen to other people in the future.

The Employee

Frontline service employees have the greatest job satisfaction when they believe they can give customers what they expect.

These workers have the difficult task of dealing with customers who hold them responsible even when the failures in question are completely out of their control. The attitudes of customer-service workers, positive and negative, spill over onto customers.

Yet companies do surprisingly little to support them.

To be successful, these workers need to feel that management is providing the means to deliver successful service recovery on a continuing basis. Alternatively, when employees believe management doesn't support them, they tend to feel they are being unfairly treated and so treat customers unfairly. They display passive, maladaptive behaviors and can even sabotage service.

This alienation is compounded when the workers believe that management is not improving the service-delivery process, which keeps employees in recurring failure situations. Even though complaining customers represent an opportunity to fix problems and improve satisfaction, alienated employees often see them as the enemy. In a study of a major European bank, employees in Switzerland consistently indicated that they did not consider reports of missing account statements to be complaints. As one said: "These things happen. There is nothing we can do about that."

At companies that reward low complaint rates, frontline employees become tempted to send dissatisfied customers away instead of admitting a failure has occurred.

Resolving the Tensions

Our experience with managers interested in improving service recovery indicates that most hope for a quick fix of some specific tensions. But quick fixes only treat the symptoms of underlying problems. Real resolutions should involve closer integration among the three stakeholders, such as gathering more information from customers and sharing it throughout the company, and adopting new structures and practices that make it easier to spot problems and fix them.

We suggest the following five strategies:

- **Create a "service logic" that explains how everything fits together.** This should be a kind of mission statement or summary of how and why the business provides its services. It should integrate the perspectives of all three groups:

  What is the customer trying to accomplish, and why?
  How is the service produced, and why?
  What are employees doing to provide the service, and why?

The results should serve as a guide both for delivering service and for help with service recovery. It should include a detailed study of internal operations; map out how the company responds to customer complaints; and describe how the company uses that information to improve service-recovery processes. Similar mapping should detail every step of customer experiences, including those of real customers with complaints, highlighting their thoughts, reactions and emotions along the way. Highly skilled managers and employees who can think outside the box are a must.

TNT NV, a Netherlands-based global delivery company, developed a service logic to help it grow in a mature market.

Using a small, high-powered management team backed up by customer discussion forums, the company mapped its processes from a customer point of view, including a map of customer emotions during both regular processes and service recovery. The mapping exercise and the service logic that it produced led to a redesign of processes by managers and field staff that cut across traditional functional boundaries.

For example, previously a driver running late for a scheduled delivery had to call into the control center, which would then contact customer services, which would then contact the customer. Such calls often arrived after the delivery already had been made, thus further annoying the customer and embarrassing the driver. Since the process redesign, however, a driver running late is allowed to contact the customer directly. TNT drivers frequently visit the same customers almost every day, so their customers know them and appreciate the personal contact. The drivers also appreciate being able to make the calls directly.

- **Draw attention to the successes of customer-service groups.** Companies use in-house publications, intranets and training programs to share stories that emphasize their values and culture. Employees who come up with cost-saving ideas, for example, are often singled out for praise. But rewards and recognition also should flow to heroes in service-recovery stories. Such heroes can be on the operations side, helping to develop cost-efficient systems for handling complaints, and on the marketing side, giving a customer extraordinarily helpful treatment after a service failure.

Singapore Airlines Ltd., in its in-house magazines, frequently tells stories about employees who have provided not only outstanding service, but exceptional service recoveries. Senior managers, too, will not hesitate to swoop in anywhere there is an issue, creating more stories about internal vigilance.

Recovery Mode

The Issue: Every business can expect complaints from customers. It's how a business handles the complaints that matters most, and many do so poorly.

The Problem: When companies don't give upset customers a fair hearing or some assurance that the problem won't happen again, they are putting repeat business, profits and growth at risk.

The Solution: The key is to address tensions that arise among front-line employees who handle complaints, the managers of those employees, and the customers themselves. Steps include starting a complaints database that managers can analyze and use to improve service, and rewarding service employees not for reductions in complaints but for providing exceptional solutions to problems.

When customer-service employees believe that their goals are in line with the organization's values, they are more willing to exert the extra effort required in a failure-and-recovery situation.

- **Give customer-service staff as much freedom as your business strategy allows.** When a business has very few routines and its ties to customers are based on individual relations, service representatives should have more autonomy in resolving complaints. For such businesses, spending more time on service recovery—and retaining customers—has a clear effect on the bottom line. By contrast, in a highly standardized business with purely transactional customer relationships, such as a fast-food restaurant, employees should adhere to procedures in resolving complaints. Customer satisfaction in such businesses is closely aligned with high productivity, so there is less to be gained by customizing resolutions of complaints.

Ritz-Carlton, for example, the luxury brand of Marriott International Inc., authorizes personnel at the front desks of its hotels to credit unhappy customers up to $2,000 without asking a supervisor's approval. On the other hand, in one of our consulting projects, a client reacted very negatively to this approach, claiming that such a policy would be too expensive for his company. We replied that the high cost of poor service is exactly what makes this system work so well: It forces management to eliminate service failures in the first place.

- **Collect as much data as you can, and share it widely.** Companies must gather more feedback about poor service, record it and make it accessible. Managers and other employees have to be armed with strong information to be effective at resolving disputes.

It should be easy for customers to file complaints. One way to achieve this is by offering many communication channels. A regional airline in Asia, for example, uses annual passenger surveys, interviews with frequent fliers, focus-group discussions, customer hot lines, critical-incident surveys, onboard suggestion leaflets and even live call-in radio shows.

Software should be used that serves as a database for both positive and negative communications with customers. Employees and managers should be trained to mine the data and put it to use easily and quickly.

- **Use meaningful measures of employee performance—rewards and demerits.** Positive reinforcement and incentives should be offered for solving problems and pleasing customers. A system for measuring customer satisfaction should be devised to help rate employee performance. Salary increases and promotions then should be linked to an employee's achieving certain levels. There also should be disincentives or demerits for poor handling of customer complaints. Performance reviews thus may include a balanced scorecard—one that recognizes the need for both productivity and customer satisfaction.

Critical Thinking

1. Summarize the perspectives of the three stakeholders involved in service recovery.

2. In your opinion, why is it important to empower customer-service employees?

DR. MICHEL is associate professor of marketing at Thunderbird School of Global Management, Glendale, Ariz. **DR. BOWEN** is the Robert and Katherine Herberger chair in global management and a professor at Thunderbird. **DR. JOHNSTON** is professor of operations management at Warwick Business School, University of Warwick, Coventry, England. They can be reached at reports@wsj.com.

When Service Means Survival

Keeping customers happy is more critical than ever. Service champs economize on everything but TLC.

Jena McGregor

Hertz couldn't ask for a better customer than Richard M. Garber. The Cleveland-based business development manager typically rents cars from the chain 20 to 40 times a year when traveling on business for materials manufacturer FLEXcon. But now Garber is rethinking that loyalty. In the past month he has returned Hertz cars to the Boston and Minneapolis airports only to find nobody waiting with a handheld check-in device. In Minneapolis, Garber had to drag his bags to the counter to return his car; in Boston, he finally tracked down an employee who came out and explained that some colleagues had just been laid off. "When you're rushing for an airplane, every minute counts," says Garber. "The less convenient they are, the more likely I am to try someone else."

As the economy plunges deeper into recession, many companies are confronting the same brutal choices Hertz faced when it announced layoffs of some 4,000 people on Jan. 16. While businesses may feel forced to trim costs, cutting too deeply can drive away customers. Hertz spokesman Richard Broome says the company has reduced "instant return" hours at some smaller airports but is making adjustments to restore that service in locations where it "might have gone too far." Says Broome: "You try to create the right balance."

Across the business world, managers are trying to pull off the same perilous high-wire act. Just as companies are dealing with plummeting sales and sinking employee morale, skittish customers want more attention, better quality, and greater value for their money. Those same customers are also acutely aware that their patronage is of growing importance to companies as others decrease their spending. BMW Vice-President Alan Harris argues that in the current environment, consumers expect "that anyone who is in the market with money to spend is going to get treated like a king."

Keep the Front Lines Strong

The reality, of course, is that the opposite is often true. From retailers such as Talbots, which have stiffened their rules on returns, to airlines that now charge for checked bags, companies are stretching budgets in ways that can make things tougher for customers.

But the best performers are actually doing more to safeguard service in this recession. Bruce D. Temkin, principal analyst for customer experience at Forrester Research, says about half of the 90 large companies he recently surveyed are trying to avoid cuts to their customer service budgets. "There's some real resilience in spending," says Temkin.

That's especially true for many of the winners of our third annual ranking of Customer Service Champs. Top performers are treating their best customers better than ever, even if that means doing less to wow new ones. While cutting back-office expenses, they're trying to preserve front-line jobs and investing in cheap technology to improve service.

If anything, the tough economy has made starker the difference between companies that put customers first and those that sacrifice loyalty for short-term gain. In this year's ranking, based on data from J.D. Power & Associates, which, like *BusinessWeek,* is owned by The McGraw-Hill Companies, more than half of the top 25 brands showed improved customer service scores over last year. Among the bottom 25 of the more than 200 brands surveyed, scores mostly fell.

Cutting just four reps at a call center of three dozen can send the number of customers put on hold for four minutes from zero to 80.

Smart players have learned from previous downturns. Companies used to go after customer reps with the same blunt ax used elsewhere. Now managers are starting to understand the long-term damage created by such moves, from eroded market share to diminished brand value. The International Customer Management Institute, a call center consultant, has done studies that show eliminating just four reps in a call center of about three dozen agents can increase the number of customers put on hold for four minutes from zero to 80.

A better strategy is to get more out of the people you have. USAA, the insurance and financial services giant that caters to military families and ranks at No. 2 on our list, started cross-training its call center reps in 2007. Some 60% of the agents who answer investment queries can now respond to insurance-related calls. Not only did such training curb call transfers between agents, which drive up the cost of running a call center, but it also improved productivity. Even with Hurricane Ike and the stock market's financial crisis prompting a flood of calls to USAA's contact centers last year, the cross-training meant the company didn't have to expand its call center staff. Existing reps are more empowered to deal with customers, even if they may also have to do more work. No. 25 JW Marriott is training administrative assistants to step in as banquet servers when needed. And in November, brokerage Charles Schwab, No. 21 on our ranking, launched a "Flex Force" team of employees such as finance specialists and marketing managers at its San Francisco headquarters to handle calls on days of, say, rapid market fluctuations.

For those that slash costs, the challenge is keeping customers from noticing. Putting call center reps under one roof, for example, can eventually save as much as 35%, says Scott Casson, director of technology services at consultant Customer Operations Performance Center. On Feb. 12, USAA announced it will combine its six call centers into four; companies such as No. 11 KeyBank and Ace Hardware, No. 10, have also consolidated operations in the past year. Ace plowed the savings from that move into longer evening and weekend hours for customer calls. "During tough times there are plenty of other pressures customers face," says Ace Vice-President John Venhuizen. "We don't want a customer service issue to be what makes them blow their cork."

Pleasing Repeat Buyers

Hoteliers also are trying to trim in ways customers are unlikely to detect. They're increasingly combining purchasing power to get better deals across properties that are within the same chain but may have different owners. Some hotels in the Four Seasons chain, No. 12, are joining

---

Safeguarding Service

Times are unquestionably tough. But cutting too deeply may only make things worse. Here are four ideas for keeping costs down and customer service solid:

Flex Your Workforce

Cutbacks in staffing levels may be necessary as sales slow. But to keep service quality high, make the most of the workers you have. Cross-train employees so they can step up to fill a variety of needs—and you can avoid making new hires.

Spoil Surviving Staff

Slashing jobs and benefits can wreak havoc on morale. If you must cut back, keep the front lines happy with flexibility and other rewards. American Express, for example, now lets call center reps choose their own hours and swap shifts without supervisors' approval.

Invest in Simple Technology

It may not be the best time to upgrade your call center with pricey software. But easy self-serve solutions such as in-store Web cams that link customers with remote tech experts can serve multiple locations at minimal cost.

Baby Your Best Customers

Now is not the time for equal treatment. Keep your most active buyers coming back with faster service, extra attention, and flexible rules. As business travel slows, Marriott, for instance, is extending elite status to its best guests even if they don't qualify under normal rules.

---

up to buy goods and services such as coffee, valet parking agreements, and overnight cleaning contracts that each hotel once bought on its own. JW Marriott hotels are teaming up to buy landscaping services that would be costlier if contracted for separately. The Ritz-Carlton, No. 5, is doing laundry at night to save electricity and replacing fresh flowers at posh properties with potted plants. With occupancy rates falling, notes Ritz COO Simon F. Cooper, "you have to get better because you're forced to."

As the game changes from acquiring new customers to keeping old ones, companies are shifting more resources to their steady patrons. They're the ones who pay the bills. And while first-time guests may not miss the absence of fresh flowers, repeat customers probably will. "It's the little things that often got you in the crook of those loyal customers' arms," says Jeanne Bliss, a former Lands' End service chief who now coaches customer service execs. That has led to a renewed emphasis on "tiering"—routing elite-level customers to better agents, nicer surroundings, or faster service.

A Road Warrior's Story: Four Stars for the Four Seasons

Last April, I was visiting top tech companies in Austin, Tex., while working for the World Economic Forum. On the flight in, after the attendant said: "Please put your laptop away. This is the fifth time I've told you," I closed my laptop and put it down beside me. I was jet-lagged and super tired.

The next thing I know, I'm in my room unzipping my bag, thinking "Where's my laptop?" I was at the Four Seasons, so I call the concierge, Steven Beasley, and tell him what happened. Two seconds later, he calls back and says he has American Airlines on the phone. I explain the problem, and they say nothing has come up on the system. About five minutes later, the concierge phones me back and says he's called the San Francisco airport to alert them to check the plane when it arrives there.

By that time I've given up. I go down to have dinner, and I'm having a predinner drink when the concierge turns up at my table and says: "Mr. Mulcahy? I've got your laptop," and hands it to me. "Would you like me to take it to your room?" I'm like "what the—what?" He'd taken it upon himself to keep badgering American. They did another check, and in fact they still had the laptop in Austin.

The concierge could have just left a message. I was so grateful to him for having gone this obscenely extra mile.

A Social Networker's Story: The Zappos CEO and UPS Step In

I usually get packages sent to the office, but in December I ordered a big 110-pound storage unit from Target and needed it delivered to my house. I called UPS to check on it, and the rep said that sometimes during the Christmas season packages don't arrive until 9 P.M.

Getting agitated, I posted on Twitter about waiting for UPS and mentioned how I couldn't take my dog, Ridley, for a walk. After 9 P.M., I got a message from Tony Hsieh, CEO of Zappos, who started following my Tweets [comments on Twitter] after we met last year. He was having dinner with UPS's president for the Western region and sent a message saying the guy would call me. I got a call in the next five minutes. The UPS exec got me in touch with an operations manager to arrange for a delivery the next morning so I could make a scheduled client meeting.

At 9 A.M. on the dot, the doorbell rings. Not only do they have the package, but there's a UPS guy with flowers and chocolates and another with treats and toys for Ridley. They even offered to assemble the unit and listened to my suggestions for improving service. I now go out of my way to use UPS—and I bought shoes the next day at Zappos.

Consider No. 7, Zappos.com, the online shoe retailer whose devoted fans rave about its free shipping on both orders and returns. The retailer had typically upgraded both first-time and repeat customers to overnight shipping even though it wasn't advertising that perk. But starting in 2009, Zappos will no longer offer overnight upgrades to first-time visitors. Instead, CEO Tony Hsieh is moving those dollars into a new VIP service for Zappos' most loyal shoppers. Launched in December, the site, which for now can only be accessed by loyal customers who receive an invitation, promises overnight shipping and plans to offer earlier access to sales and new merchandise than the plain-vanilla site. (Repeat customers who aren't yet asked to join the VIP service will continue getting the overnight upgrade for now.) "We decided we wanted to invest more in repeat customers," says Hsieh. "We're shifting some of the costs that would have gone into new customers."

Some are also getting tougher on suppliers who serve their most frequent customers. No. 24 L.L. Bean dropped Bank of America as its vendor of store-branded credit cards in July 2008. The outdoor outfitter says the bank wasn't measuring up in terms of its vaunted customer support. Complaints about long hold times and call transfers between the bank's customer service agents were "endless," says Terry Sutton, L.L. Bean's vice-president for customer satisfaction. (Bank of America says it doesn't comment on specific relationships but is "focused on providing competitive products and exceptional customer service.") L.L. Bean switched to Barclays, which meant customers had to reapply. The risk that some might not take the time was high. "From a service standpoint, it was loaded with land mines," says Sutton. But she felt the move was worth it, especially since Barclays gave them a say on agents' scripts and set up its call center in the retailer's home state of Maine. Over 60% of cardholders have already switched.

Some companies are experimenting more with cheap technology, such as responding to customers via Twitter after they broadcast their complaints to the world. Other tech upgrades for customers can deliver unexpected cost savings. When No. 22 BMW rolled out Wi-Fi service at its dealerships last year, the move was intended to give customers a cheap way to pass the time while their cars were serviced. The cost was next to nothing since BMW just expanded the broadband dealers already used to run their businesses. But now that customers can use their waiting time productively, fewer are opting for free loaner cars, which are pricey for dealers to maintain. BMW's Alan

Harris says Wi-Fi, along with software that helps dealers better estimate loaner needs, has helped BMW cut its monthly loaner expenses by 10% to 15%.

When companies come up with simple, low-cost ways to trim costs while improving life for customers, they're likely to win in good times and bad. "I have a saying: 'Fix the customer before you fix the car,' " says Harris. "If you focus on fixing the customer's problem first, the rest is easy."

Critical Thinking

1. According to this article, why is it vital, in today's economy, for businesses to avoid cutting front-line service employees?

2. Describe some high and low satisfaction interactions you have personally had with service providers.

With Aili McConnon in New York and David Kiley in Detroit.

Become the Main Attraction

People go to summer events for music, food and fun—not for marketing materials.

Here's how you get them to pay attention to you.

PIET LEVY

There are hundreds, maybe thousands of people here. Many of them are just the types of customers you are looking for. But odds are that none of them are here to see you. Instead, the masses have gathered at this event to hear music, watch sports, eat food or, in the case of conferences, network and listen to keynote presentations.

The consumers are there for their reasons and you're there for yours: to market your brand and increase awareness and sales. In a sea of noise, surrounded by hordes of talking people, distracting attractions and numerous marketing booths and street teams competing for consumers' attention, you have to stand out. But in addition to turning heads, you have to open minds. Beyond handing out coupons or samples or tchotchkes, you must showcase the value of your product or service in an interactive and engaging way, which also means training the right people to serve as brand messengers. If you make sure you're memorable, when the event ends and the consumers go about their daily lives, they'll remember you, tell others about you and pay to experience your product or service.

Step Right Up

Event marketing is important because it "places your product or service face to face with your target audience," argues Brad Horowitz, vice president of marketing for Elite Marketing Group, an experiential agency with headquarters in New Hyde Park, N.Y. "Brands can have a conversation with consumers rather than delivering a monologue. Conversations allow for customized learning, which fosters purchasing behavior. Additionally, it allows for valuable feedback from consumers about the product or service and the perception out there in the real world."

To be the most effective event marketer, you have to go beyond just being at a popular event and set up shop in a premium position. "Juxtaposing your footprint to a high-traffic location at an event such as the entry or the food court will allow for the greatest reach and greatest amount of impressions," Horowitz says.

That's also where a lot of other marketing booths or street teams will be hanging out. But don't worry about them; worry about yourself, and calm those concerns by establishing a physical presence that pops.

Overland Park, Kan.-based Sprint Nextel Corp., which sponsors the National Association for Stock Car Auto Racing's (NASCAR) Sprint Cup Series, incorporates a jumbotron, trophy replica and NASCAR driver appearances at its display at races, says Tim Considine, general manager of the sponsorship. To attract mechanics to its travelling display last year, the U.S. Air Force showcased customized vehicles that incorporated Air Force technology, says Kristin Krajecki, director of experiential marketing at the Air Force's experiential agency, GSD&M Idea City in Austin, Texas. For its presence at the National Religious Broadcasters Convention and Exposition earlier this year, TV Magic Inc., a San Diego-based broadcast solutions provider, presented a cross designed out of televisions at its booth, the sort of visual element that conference-attending pastors may want at their churches, says Stephen Rosen, president and CEO of the company. "You've got to make an impressive impression and let [consumers] feel that spending a few minutes with you of their very precious time is worth it," Sprint's Considine says.

You may not have the budget to bring your own jumbotron, super car, or elaborate TV display to an event, but you can find creative ways to cut costs. TV Magic actually reduced its trade show budget by 50% this year and was still able to replace its "worse than blah" booth from last year with one featuring the TV display, Rosen says. Savings came from two areas: TV Magic reduced the number of company representatives at the booth from seven to three, and the company partnered with electronic suppliers such as Sony and Panasonic to provide equipment at no cost, says Jeff Symon, President and CEO of San Diego-based Aim Agency, TV Magic's agency. In some cases, you may even be able to find a company partner to participate with you at the event and subsidize expenses, he also suggests.

Whatever you put together, make sure the element is relevant to the audience and reflective of your brand. The cars at the Air Force display appealed to gear heads, but given the Air Force-inspired modifications, including an ejection seat, vertical doors, and aircraft style controls, the brand was even more reinforced. In addition to the church-friendly TV display at its convention booth, TV Magic put together a system where pastors could be filmed and the video edited and broadcast to a TV, online, and mobile device on the spot as a way to demonstrate the type of service the company provides, Symon says.

It's also a good idea to make your display interactive to increase the odds and length of time that consumers will stick around. Incentives are another way to draw people in. Sprint stages racing video games on its jumbotron that people can participate in and offers free gifts to customers, Considine says.

You should also try to design the space to allow for easier traffic flow. Symon suggests removing any table separating consumers from brand messengers to allow greater interactivity and openness. Considine says the Sprint layout features no walls or interiors to better increase impressions and interaction, and the jumbotron is in place to increase the possibility of engaging people from the periphery.

Razzle-Dazzle Them

The wow factor and selling points are crucial event marketing criteria, but Considine argues that "the hand you shake, the kindness that you show to someone in an [event] marketing environment, may be more powerful than the information you present."

In addition to head-turning displays, you have to rely on your brand representatives to present the brand properly, yet oftentimes marketers may have to outsource for those services, as Sprint does for its NASCAR display.

To find the right people for the job, Aim Agency first profiles what the brand stands for and the type of people who would best represent it. Then comes an online evaluation process that serves as a screener to see if candidates match brand objectives, Symon says.

If you don't have the budget to recruit an agency to help you with staffing, use the interview process to determine which candidates are extroverted, upbeat, articulate, and professional, Considine and Symon say. Jessica Fisher, Senior Manager of events for athletic apparel company Reebok International Ltd. in Canton, Mass., says that before an interview begins it's important to have a casual conversation about the candidate's perspective of the brand to gauge his enthusiasm and understanding. It also helps to recruit people who can relate to the target audience. For its M&M's supporting street team at NASCAR races, Mars Chocolate North America utilizes two employees from the company's PR agency, Weber Shandwick, who are actual fans of NASCAR so their interaction with fans will be authentic, says Suzanne Beaudoin, Vice President of sponsorship and sports marketing for the Hackettstown, N.J.-based company.

Once your team is in place, make sure staff members dress the part to not only physically represent the brand but also attract consumers. The M&M's street team stands out with NASCAR-style jumpsuits, Beaudoin argues, to help

By the Numbers

The Norwalk, Conn.-based Event Marketing Institute and Auburn Hills, Mich.-based experiential agency George P. Johnson Co. interviewed 108 sales and marketing management leaders for its EventView report, an annual study assessing the relevance of event marketing. Some key findings:

62% of respondents say their marketing budget for events has either remained constant or increased in 2010.

32% consider event marketing a "vital component" of their marketing plan.

64% cited event marketing as one of the top three elements for accelerating and deepening relationships, followed by social marketing (55%) and online marketing (54%).

Want a Ticket to Ride?

Follow These 10 Instructions for Successful Event Marketing:

1. Set up your booth or street team in highly trafficked areas.
2. Have a visual element that turns heads but connects back to your brand.
3. Find participating partners to subsidize costs.
4. Present an interactive element, like a game, so consumers stick around for a while.
5. Make your space as open as possible to maximize traffic and engagement.
6. Entice visitors with incentives like coupons or samples.
7. Find upbeat, extroverted, professional, articulate people to act as brand representatives.
8. Cast people who can relate with the target demographic, like employing NASCAR fans for booths at NASCAR events.
9. Train representatives with quizzes and run-throughs, but don't overwhelm them with details.
10. Dress your staff so they stand out, but make sure they look approachable.

communicate the brand's Most Colorful Fan website and Facebook page, which encourage NASCAR fans to submit photos displaying their love of the sport for a cash prize. Similarly, the Air Force tries to place its brand representatives in the most appropriate attire based on the event, says Captain Homero Martinez, the former chief of event marketing for the Air Force Recruiting Service. For a recent Memorial Day race, Martinez says, formal dress was appropriate given the holiday weekend's correlation with the Air Force. For more casual events like music festivals, staff wear more relaxed uniforms to reduce any consumer concern that they will be pressured to sign up.

The U.S. Air Force paraded customized cars equipped with jet-inspired technology at events last year in an effort to attract mechanics for the Air Force on the spot, he says.

Beyond looking the part, training must be done so that brand representatives can act the part. Training should include quizzing participants about the brand and business objectives in addition to on-site run-throughs, Symon says, and participants should be encouraged to ask questions for clarification's sake. Fisher recommends giving representatives the product when applicable, so that when they are on site, "they are not just giving out words, but talking from their own experiences." It's ideal to have people who work for the company on hand to help address consumer questions, but for those assigned with attracting people with their presence and interaction, it's important not to overwhelm them with instructions during the training process. Considine says his advice boils down to one simple philosophy: Treat passing consumers like guests at your home. If they feel welcome, there's a greater chance they'll welcome your product or service into their lives.

Critical Thinking

1. What makes event marketing an attractive promotion option for businesses?

2. With a small group of peers from your class, design an event marketing plan for any business of your choice.

Beyond Products

More manufacturers are branching out into the service business. Here's how to make the move successfully.

STEPHEN W. BROWN, ANDERS GUSTAFSSON, AND LARS WITELL

For many manufacturers looking to boost their business, simply selling products doesn't cut it anymore.

Companies in a range of fields—from pulp and paper to telecommunications—have decided that they have to branch out into services to stay competitive. Some truck manufacturers, for instance, don't just offer vehicles; they also sell maintenance and service packages, as well as driver-training programs. In some cases, they even sell services that go well beyond caring for trucks, such as advising clients on ways to improve their logistics operation.

Why the push into services? In part, necessity. In the fiercely competitive global market, companies must do whatever they can to stand out. But companies that have successfully made the move say there are substantial benefits, too.

For one thing, unlike products, services often deliver a regular stream of income. They also require a lower fixed capital investment, and frequently bring higher margins, than products do. What's more, they can be tougher for rivals to copy—which can bring big competitive advantages.

Then there's marketing. Companies say they can build on their existing products, brand image and customer base when pitching a line of services. And when an existing customer buys services as well as products, it builds loyalty, since the two companies work together much more closely.

For all of that promise, though, making services work isn't easy, and success is far from assured. Many companies are unprepared when they make the move into new territory, and fall into a number of traps, such as introducing services the wrong way and focusing on the wrong points when pitching them to customers.

To learn the best way to do things, we surveyed hundreds of business-to-business manufacturers in a range of industries, interviewed many executives and developed several in-depth case studies. We looked at what made the unsuccessful firms stumble—and what helped the successful firms rise to the top.

Here's what we found, starting with what can go wrong.

Better Served

- **The Big Step:** Many manufacturers are starting to offer for-pay services in an effort to stand out in a competitive market and open up new streams of revenue.

- **The Pitfalls:** For all the promise that services hold, success is far from assured. Companies can fall into plenty of traps when entering this new territory—such as thinking the same strategies that worked for introducing new products will work for services.

- **The Road Map:** Successful companies use a number of common strategies, such as creating a separate division to handle services and devising generic service packages that customers can modify.

A Host of Hurdles

Many manufacturers in our research moved into the new territory without any clear strategy. For many years, they offered discounted or even free services to secure sales for their products, such as maintenance plans or training courses for the people who would be using the products. But later, when the companies tried to start charging for those services, they found that customers often weren't prepared to pay for something they used to get free.

Many companies also met internal resistance to their service plans. Sales forces were a particular challenge. For instance, sales teams often had incentive programs tied to meeting targets for product sales, and it was hard to incorporate services into that structure.

What's more, selling services is often more challenging than selling products. Aside from the fact that customers sometimes were used to getting the services free, it was much harder to show the value of an intangible offering and figure out how

Challenges and Payoffs

How surveyed manufacturing companies rated the severity of the hurdles to overcome in expanding their profitable service offerings (7 = most severe, 0 = not severe)

Organization not ready	4.2
Lack of experience	4.1
Pricing	4.0
Resistance from customers	4.0
Resistance from sales force	3.8
Lack of channels	3.6
Services are a cost driver	3.6
Economic potential	3.5

How the companies rated the benefits of making the transition to services (7 = high, 0 = low)

Improved customer relationships	6.6
Capturing a large share of the value life cycle	5.8
Meet the needs of customers to outsource	5.6
Response to changing customer needs	5.4
Achievement of competitive differentiation	5.0
Greater income stability	5.0
Profit margin for services	4.7
Response to decreased profit margin for hardware	4.3

Source: Stephen W. Brown, Anders Gustafsson, and Lars Witell.

to price it. And when the price finally got hammered out, it often led to disappointment. For people who are used to selling million-dollar equipment, it's tough to get excited about selling $50,000 maintenance contracts, even if they represent a recurring stream of income.

Meanwhile, moving into services often meant building up new sales connections within the customer's organization, often higher up the decision-making chain—and far removed from anyone who would actually be using the service.

The sales-force problem was just part of a larger issue: Many companies attempted to market new services the same way they sold new products—by giving employees new responsibilities while keeping the current structures, practices and incentives in place.

Different Knowledge Base

But people who have been focused on developing and selling products usually don't have the deep knowledge of a customer's operation they need to create and market services. To come up with an idea for a new product, for instance, you might only need to have a general knowledge of the industry and the problems that companies often face. But if you're trying to, say, take

over a customer's maintenance operation or offer advice on improving logistics, you must know specifics about how companies do their job.

That wasn't the only big organizational mistake. Some manufacturers tried to get their whole operation behind the service effort, letting every department help in developing and delivering the new offerings. It seemed to be the best way to use the company's limited resources and ensure that products and services would work well together.

But this approach leads to lots of practical problems. When multiple departments are responsible for delivering services, it's tough to ensure a consistent level of quality—which could potentially lead to lots of grumbling from customers. It also can be tough to get managers from across the company to agree on standards for pricing and other factors.

The result of all this? Manufacturing employees often ended up focusing on developing new products—and then rushing out new services to complement them almost as an afterthought.

Keep Services Separate

Many of the successful companies in our study addressed these issues by taking one big step: They kept services separate from the rest of the operation, creating separate units to develop and deliver their new offerings.

Telecom giant Telefon AB L.M. Ericsson, for instance, gathered its various service businesses into a single unit, Global Services. The division, which now accounts for nearly a third of the total employees at Ericsson, offers services such as managing the networks that mobile-phone companies use.

Some companies took the idea of a separate services unit a step further, partnering with outside firms to help them develop and deliver services.

Why wall off services this way? Culture. As we've seen, in a manufacturing company, all of the processes and habits are geared toward making and selling physical goods. Changing the focus of an entire organization is extremely difficult—and usually only marginally successful.

As a senior executive at Ericsson observed: "Culture wins over strategy each time."

New Mindset

Consider how much has to change to make services work. One auto executive described how his company added services to the mix:

"If you go back to even a very short while ago, our whole idea of a customer was that we would wholesale a car to a dealer, the dealer would then sell the car to the customer, and we hoped we never heard from the customer—because if we did, it meant something was wrong. Today, we want to establish a dialogue with the customer throughout the entire ownership experience. We want to talk to and touch our customers at every step of the way. We want to be a consumer-products and services company that just happens to be in the automotive business."

Not many companies can pull off that kind of a makeover—retraining hosts of employees and getting them not only to learn new skills but also to change the way they approach their job. So, it's usually easier to build a service operation from the ground up, one that works far more closely with customers than the rest of the business does, and charge it with creating and executing the strategy.

> **Many successful companies kept services separate from the rest of the operation, forming separate units to develop and deliver their new offerings.**

Beyond that, we found that successful companies tended to use similar strategies in developing and marketing their services.

Standardize—and Customize

Many companies often plunged into services by closely tailoring their offerings to each customer. Companies would come up with plans that fit the particulars of a customer's processes but couldn't be easily applied to another customer. And those kinds of services took a great deal of effort and significant costs to develop.

The more successful firms moved beyond this initial strategy and came up with generic service packages. These deals offer a standard set of services that clients can customize by adding or removing options. This lets the manufacturers balance customization and standardization—and keep costs down.

For instance, one truck maker offers a maintenance and repair package with standardized prices for spare parts and scheduling for service. But let's say a customer wants to use another company's replacement parts in the trucks. The service plan would let the client customize the plan by dropping the replacement-parts feature.

Look Beyond Costs

The successful firms in our research used another key strategy in crafting their services: They focused on more than helping customers cut costs.

Many companies in our work took a basic approach, pitching their services simply as a way for customers to save money. They might argue, for instance, that customers could lower overhead by outsourcing their maintenance operation.

The more successful companies found they did better by adding another dimension to their offerings. They looked for services that would help their customers provide benefits to their *own* customers—and thus boost business.

One truck company, for instance, sells its customers fleet-management services, such as monitoring fuel consumption and teaching drivers how to drive more fuel-efficiently. This, in turn, helps the company's customers sell themselves as environmentally friendly to potential clients. And that's often a crucial factor for many clients, such as government agencies.

Or consider Ericsson. When one of its phone-company clients wants to offer a new option to its subscribers—such as Internet connectivity over mobile phones—Ericsson can help develop the program and provide behind-the-scenes support.

Critical Thinking

1. In your perspective, how can services be used as a means for brand differentiation and competitive advantage?
2. Explain the phrase '*standardize and customize.*'

Dr. Brown is the Edward M. Carson chair in services marketing and executive director of the Center for Services Leadership at Arizona State University's W.P. Carey School of Business. **Dr. Gustafsson** is a professor of business administration at Karlstad University's Service Research Center in Karlstad, Sweden. **Dr. Witell** is an associate professor of marketing at the Karlstad Service Research Center. They can be reached at reports@wsj.com.

Imaginative Service

You need it more in tough times.

CHIP R. BELL AND JOHN R. PATTERSON

Take the Hertz shuttle bus at the Atlanta Airport, and you might meet *Archie Bostick.* Archie greets you with a welcoming grin. Instead of a tip jar, Archie paperclips dollar bills across the front of his shirt. Nothing subtle about that ploy—it's an attention-getter that announces *this is a unique experience.* Once on the bus, Archie delivers a comedy routine and uses any excuse to break into song. As Archie pulls up to the terminal, he announces, "Now, I may never see you again, so I want us all to say together, 'I love Hertz!'" And everyone hollers, "I love Hertz!" You witness a service innovator at work—he takes your breath away.

Value-added has been the service solution for many service exemplars—take what the customer expects and add a little more. Nordstrom sales clerk escorts you to another department. Southwest Airlines gives you free peanuts with slapstick humor. And Rosie's Diner refills your ice tea glass without you being charged.

But value-added extras have gotten more expensive. That free snack on a flight is now $8, and service charges are standard fare on most bills. Pursuing the extras can also send a mixed message. What do employees think when told to "wow" customers in the morning and are later informed of staff cutbacks and expense reductions? Challenging financial times call for a new approach: *value-unique service.*

Value-unique is different than value-added. For most customers, value-added means taking the expected to a higher-level: "They gave me *more* than I anticipated." But, value-unique is not about addition—it's about an imaginative creation.

When service people are asked to *give more,* they think, "I'm already doing the best I can." But, if asked to *pleasantly surprise* more customers, they feel less like worker bees and more like fireflies. If employees are asked to create a big customer smile instead of work harder, they feel a part of an adventure. And, when they get to create, not just perform, they feel prized. Just ask a Southwest, Disney, or Lexus dealership employee what they think of their job, and you will get a smiling "It's awesome," not a shrugging "It's all right."

Imaginative service is sourced in joy and fun. It comes from the same part of the soul that plans a prank, organizes a party, or helps a friend. When that part is used regularly, it raises self-esteem, increases resilience, and improves morale. Take a look at *Fortune Magazine's* annual *100 Best Companies in America to Work For*—Nordstrom, Container Store, Marriott, eBay, Zappos.com, and FedEx—and you see the great service-high morale link. They boast the lowest turnover (a cost saver), the best recruits (an investment), the highest productivity (another positive) and the greatest profits.

Five Ways to Deliver Unique Value

Here are five ways to foster service that takes your customers' breath away:

1. *Project realness.* Imaginative service is about *realness,* not *roleness.* The stereotypical leader gets caught up with looking, sounding, and "acting" executive, and employees get a message of "plastic power"—which may engender *compliance* but never *commitment.* Great leaders are unimpressed with the trappings of supremacy and more interested in communicating an authentic spirit and egalitarian style.

Imaginative service leaders know they get from employees the attitude they project. Employees do not watch the leader's mouth; they watch the leader's moves. As all leaders move in the floodlight of employee observation, their actions can telegraph either optimism or gloom; excitement or despair. An animated attitude is contagious. When we are around happy, upbeat people, we more easily join in the spirit—especially if the invitation comes from someone who prefers we enroll. An unbridled spirit has magnetic power on both customers and employees.

2. *Protect customers.* Tasks are important; rules are essential. But, revenue comes from customers. Imaginative service leaders encourage and empower employees to put customers (not procedures) first. This is not about deliberately violating rules or putting anybody at risk.

Zappos.com was founded in 1999 with goal of doing to on-line shoe apparel what Amazon.com did to online books. In 2000 they had $1.6 million in sales; in 2008 their sales exceeded $1 billion! CEO *Tony Hsieh* explains their growth this way: "We're aligned around one mission—to provide the best customer service possible. Rather than focus on maximizing short-term profits, we focus on how we can maximize the service to our customers. We are a service company that happens to sell shoes." They protect customers from being taken for granted or subjected to discomfort.

3. *Proclaim joy.* In times of frugality, staff reductions, cost controls, and cutbacks, employees tend to be somber. Optimism is replaced with anxiety; hope is overshadowed by fear. The receiving end of such dower dispositions are customers with money to spend. When customers most need a shot of enthusiasm, they are served by sleepwalking employees who seem indifferent and bored. The antidote to such melancholy is a leader with unmistakable passion and irresistible joy. "The ultimate measure of a man," said Martin Luther King, "is not where he stands in moments of comfort and convenience, but where he stands at times of challenge and controversy."

"To succeed," says *Scott Cook,* founder of Intuit, "you need people with passion. You can't just order someone to be passionate about a business direction." Passion comes from a deep sense of purpose—not the "ought to" sense of obligation that drives duty, but the "can't wait to" enthusiasm that sets an employee on fire. As Federal Signal President *Alan Shaffer* said: "Our goal is not merely to get buy-in. I want to put a lump in their throats and a tear in their eyes. I want to take their breath away."

The number one impact on customer relations is employee relations—happy employees create happy customers.

4. *Provide trust.* Imaginative service happens in a climate of trust—where people are considerate and supportive. If people are given license to criticize colleagues behind their back, the setting turns to suspicion. If manipulative or unfair behavior is tolerated, the climate turns to protection. It requires leaders disciplined to model thoughtfulness and hold others accountable.

Trustful cultures nurture appropriate risk-taking that leads to novel solutions and refreshing customer experiences. Trusting leaders view *error* as a chance to learn and *failure* as an invitation to try another approach. They treat employees as valued gifts, not indentured slaves. They empower and encourage. They are open about their own foibles and upfront when they make mistakes. The word embedded in *trust* is *us*. Trustful leaders care for their employees with the same humanity they give their family. *Family-like* doesn't mean entitlement, paternalism, or nepotism. It means attention to fairness, justice, and compassionate conduct.

5. *Preserve integrity. S. Truett Cathy,* founder of Chick-Fil-A, has elected to remain closed on Sunday and gained favor for courageously remaining true and faithful to his values.

"I like dealing with an organization whose leaders stand for something!" comment customers when asked what they like most. Chick-Fil-A, Southwest Airlines, USAA, and The Container Store receive high marks. Stand-for-something leaders aren't the loud, flamboyant, publicity-seeking types. Instead, they are clear, focused, courageous, and committed to stay their course and stand their ground.

Imaginative service leaders are grounded in complete, no-exceptions integrity. They reek of integrity. As *Tom Peters* says, "There is no such thing as a *minor lapse of integrity.*" They show their nobility when they courageously tell the truth, relentlessly do what they say they will do, and gallantly turn their backs on all shady actions. They send signals through their character.

Customers seek more value for their money. As you scramble to shore up value, the time is ripe for service with inventiveness—not just service with generosity. Leaders must ensure that the elements they add to their leadership advance service innovation.

Critical Thinking

1. What do the authors of the article mean by a *value-unique* service?
2. With a small group of peers from your class, come up with a list of other imaginative services based on your own experiences and observations.

Chip R. Bell and **John R. Patterson** are customer loyalty consultants and authors of *Take Their Breath Away: How Imaginative Service Creates Devoted Customers.* www.taketheirbreathaway.com.

From *Leadership Excellence,* May 2009, pp. 10–11. Copyright © 2009 by Leadership Excellence. Reprinted by permission.

Marketers, Come on Down!

Let's play the grand-prize game.

Some people know how to play the marketing game like chess; they play so well that they can accurately predict—and prepare for—the marketplace's next move. Some people happen to come up with the right idea at the right time (we're looking at you, Mark Zuckerberg!), and some people are just plain lucky.

These six marketers and marketing researchers have won that trifecta—they're smart, timely *and* lucky. They've positioned their companies' services to respond to consumers' changing behaviors and marketers' needs (a real double-whammy!). They're the marketing minds behind the tools that other marketers want, and they deliver on what marketers and consumers need: value.

Read on to find out who's behind some of the most talked-about marketing and marketing research tools that are helping marketers and consumers win big.

ALLISON ENRIGHT AND ELISABETH A. SULLIVAN

Vicki Lins
CMO of Canoe Ventures — SelecTV

If all goes as planned, 2011 will be a big year for SelecTV. Never heard of SelecTV? Don't worry, you will. Vicki Lins, CMO of New York-based Canoe Ventures and a veteran telecom marketer, is tackling the launch of the brand. Developed by Canoe Ventures with the support of a consortium of the nation's leading cable providers like Comcast and Cox Communications, the SelecTV brand is not a product but an industry-wide, consumer-facing brand that will appear on TV screens as an indication that the ad or program being viewed is interactive. It will be a "generic moniker for interactivity," Lins says.

The actual interactive elements will be managed by the viewer's respective cable provider or station programmer, but the education element for consumers needs to be equal among providers, Lins says. "We don't want to confuse the marketplace by sending mixed messages. If their interactive experience varies network by network and it is called something different, how confusing would that be? It benefits the industry, too, to align," Lins says.

"We are all moving forward in unison in 2011. It will be the year that interactivity hits scale and becomes significantly relevant in viewers' and advertisers' and marketers' lives," Lins says.

With the "brought to you by SelecTV" flag up and running, cable operators will be able to unify already-developed and to-be-developed interactive marketing platforms in a way that consumers will be able to recognize. For marketers, this means adding measurability and interaction to TV advertising and in-program product placements. Comcast Corp., for

example, is already testing interactive TV advertisements in select markets whereby a viewer can click "OK" on his remote to request that information about the advertiser be mailed to him.

Lins is pretty familiar with Comcast. She worked there for seven years and led the rebranding of Comcast Spotlight, the company's ad sales division, as its senior vice president. During her last year there, she was tasked to work on "project Canoe," which then developed into Canoe Ventures. She ran between offices for that year as Canoe Ventures developed as an initiative that spans the entire cable community.

Despite the hard work it takes to get everyone moving in lockstep to develop the SelecTV standards and implement them, Lins is hopeful that the life of the SelecTV moniker is short-lived. She compares the purpose of its development to that of the HD label that was used to educate consumers about the difference between HD viewing and regular viewing. "If we do a good job and generate a lot of awareness and equity, it will go away very quickly," she says. Stay tuned.

Allison Enright

Alexander Muse
Co-Founder of Big in Japan — ShopSavvy

Sometimes a marketing ploy can turn into big business. Just ask Alexander Muse, co-founder of Big in Japan, a Dallas-based mobile app developer.

When it launched in 2008, Big in Japan specialized in social Web development. But when mobile applications became all the

Survey Says!

87% of U.S. Internet users subscribe to cable or satellite TV. Of those, 26% say they have seen an interactive TV advertisement, while one in four in this group has actually tried it.

Source: Marketing News's exclusive research conducted by research partner Lightspeed Research, Basking Ridge, N.J. The survey of 1,085 Internet users was completed using Lightspeed's U.S. omnibus panel in June 2010.

rage that year, Muse and his colleagues realized that they had to prove their worth as app developers. "We thought we better build something—a demo app—to show people that we have good skills and that they should hire us," Muse says. Nearly two years later, that demo app has become Big in Japan's "primary business," he says.

Big in Japan designed an app that would leverage all of the tools that mobile has to offer—a camera, access to the Internet and GPS capabilities. Called ShopSavvy, the app allows users to research products and compare retailers' prices while shopping in-store. "The idea is really simple: Point your phone's camera at a barcode and we'll tell you where you can buy it and for how much," Muse says. ShopSavvy also gives users access to consumer reviews and allows them to compile shopping wish lists.

What sets ShopSavvy apart from other price-comparison apps is that it gives users access to retailers' and manufacturers' own product and pricing data, rather than relying on third-party data aggregators, Muse says. ShopSavvy offers data from 20,000 retailers on 20 million products.

Marketers can use ShopSavvy to their advantage, Muse says. "We're strange bedfellows in many ways; we're creating price transparency," which could make marketers nervous. But "retailers want to manage how consumers see them," he says. Plus, ShopSavvy functions much like a loyalty card program in that consumers are willing to divulge data about themselves in exchange for value at the register, which means that marketers have access to real-time data on consumers' shopping behaviors.

ShopSavvy now offers marketers the chance to advertise through the app with "AdOns": ads that pop up on users' mobile phones when a product's barcode is scanned promoting relevant information, or a related product or service. For example, if a consumer scans a DVD's barcode, a Netflix ad might pop up offering him a chance to watch the movie's trailer, Muse says.

Big in Japan also recently signed a deal with Cellfire Inc., a San Jose, Calif.-based mobile coupon provider, to add grocery coupons to ShopSavvy.

ShopSavvy currently is used by about 5.5 million mobile phone users. Android is the most dominant platform for ShopSavvy, with 10,000 to 20,000 new Android users signing up each day, compared with 5,000 to 10,000 new iPhone users daily, Muse says.

ShopSavvy now is preloaded onto many LG and Samsung models, and featured in marketing messaging for carriers such as T-Mobile and Sprint. Primarily, though, Big in Japan has relied on word of mouth to generate awareness, Muse says. "We're free and we work pretty well. We're not perfect. We suck on groceries . . . but we rock on everything else."

Elisabeth A. Sullivan

Jamie Myers
Director of Marketing and Sales for Radius Global Market Research—PriceDeveloper

Setting the price point for your product or service is a marketing function, and it's not just a measure of cost plus a markup. Uncovering the optimal price point that reflects the value of the product or service matched with what consumers will pay for it is a way to maximize your investment and not leave any money on the table. Enter PriceDeveloper, a research service launched this April by New York-based Radius Global Market Research, which was ranked No. 31 in *Marketing News'* Honomichl Top 50 Report last month.

"Pricing is a strategic decision. A lot of marketers on the brand side of things see it as a separate issue and treat it tactically [to their detriment]," says Jamie Myers, director of marketing and sales at Radius. Myers has been with Radius (formerly Data Development Worldwide) for 11 years and developed his marketing know-how on the job. His background is in constructing and conducting research.

What's happening now in light of the recession is companies are taking second (and third and fourth) looks at their bottom lines and seeing where costs can be cut or reallocated for better use. It's also made PriceDeveloper one of Radius' top three most-requested services by clients. "It's a matter of the environment we are in. People are asking a lot more questions about this approach and how they can use it," Myers says. For example, a membership-based retailer used the PriceDeveloper service to research the value proposition of its annual membership fee relative to savings it provides to members among other member benefits. "Clients are wanting to position [their services] in a compelling way and justify the price that they are offering," Myers says.

While Radius has offered price research services to clients for several years, Myers has been learning a lot more about marketing because of the push behind the launch of PriceDeveloper and the general rebranding of Radius from DDW, which occurred in January but was in the making for about five years. Marketing doesn't always come easily to small market research forms, he says, but "today we are much more intelligent about having a marketing plan and adhering to touchpoints. We have

Survey Says!

More than one-third of U.S. Internet users say they use online/mobile price comparison tools to check prices elsewhere when shopping in a retail store—that percentage leaps to 49% among shoppers aged 18 to 34.

Source: *Marketing News*/Lightspeed Research survey, June 2010.

a strict calendar [we follow] to connect to customers and prospects in different ways." Presumably, all his marketing elements are priced accordingly.

A. E.

Bari Harlam
Senior Vice President of Member Engagement for CVS Caremark Corp.—CVS Coupon Centers

Familiarity doesn't breed contempt when it comes to taking care of your clients or customers; it's called good customer service. By listening and knowing its customer base as well as it can, CVS Caremark Corp., the Woonsocket, R.I.-based operator of more than 7,000 drug stores, is constantly launching new marketing initiatives to satisfy customers and keep them loyal. Well-known already is its CVS/pharmacy's ExtraCare loyalty program, which boasts more than 50 million members. An add-on service to the ExtraCare program launched nationally in April that encourages loyalty-card carriers to scan their cards before they shop at an in-store "coupon center" kiosk and print coupons that can be redeemed immediately. With consumers paying even more attention to value, the scan rate at the coupon centers was more than double CVS' goal by June, says Bari Harlam, senior vice president of member engagement for CVS Caremark.

Harlam has been integral in the research, development and launch of the initiatives since she came to CVS in 2000 from a career in academia that included faculty positions at Columbia University and the University of Rhode Island. In her academic career, her research interest areas centered on loyalty programs and methods by which research processes that were developed in the academic arena could be applied in corporate settings. Harlam discovered her "awesome match" with CVS during a sabbatical year and then went to work for them full time. "CVS is a very metric-driven, data-driven, get-to-the-facts kind of company where that is possible. I didn't come in needing to convince them that we should use this [loyalty and customer] data; there was already a hunger and thirst to do that better," she says.

The coupon center initiative was first tested in 2007, and the initiative was in direct response to what CVS' customer service and research staff was hearing from ExtraCare card holders. "The message was: 'How come I get these offers on the bottom of my receipt when I've already checked out? How about I get them before instead of after?'" Harlam says.

Survey Says!

73% of U.S. Internet users report using loyalty discount cards when shopping and the average consumer uses two to three different store cards regularly. 28% of respondents have encountered a coupon kiosk in the store. When a coupon kiosk is available, 32% always scan before they shop and 57% sometimes scan, while only 11% report never using it.

Source: *Marketing News*/Lightspeed Research survey, June 2010.

The customer intelligence area at CVS is prioritized in a way that research can lead or move in lockstep with what customers want, rather than be reactionary. "We very much think of it as an ongoing effort. We understand where [customers] are and where their heads are. We know their pulse all the time," Harlam says.

A. E.

Christina Norsig
Founder and CEO of Pop-Up Insider—Pop-Up Insider

You've seen the Halloween costume stores that suddenly appear in formerly vacant retail spaces in time for the holiday and then close just as quickly. Target, too, has given the temporary leasing tactic a try. This March the mega-retailer opened a temporary shop in New York's Times Square to preview new clothes and home goods from British brand Liberty of London. The shop reportedly sold out of inventory before its short-term lease expired.

In response to the evolving marketplace and recent economic pressures, many marketers are experimenting with pop-up shops: purposefully short-lived retail locations that are open for a matter of days, weeks or months. Pop-up shops can help marketers test out new business ideas or product lines, test new retail locations, promote vendors, liquidate overstock, learn more about target markets or connect with customers in person. They can help landlords, too, by generating buzz for a retail location, says Christina Norsig, founder and CEO of Pop-Up Insider, a temporary real estate resource and consultancy based in New York.

Norsig speaks from firsthand experience. A retail expert who has helped highend tabletop companies market their fine china, glass and silver, Norsig launched her own website, eTableTop.com, in 2003 to give retailers an online distribution platform. During her first year of operation, she decided to open a pop-up shop in New York to build awareness and loyalty for her online business. She leased a deli on Broadway in Manhattan, displayed fine china and crystal in the funky glass meat cases, and sent an e-mail to her customer base alerting them to the temporary discounts on offer. She liked the experience so much that she decided to incorporate pop-up shops into her ongoing marketing strategy.

In the midst of the recession in 2009, companies began calling Norsig and asking to be included in her next pop-up shop. Landlords contacted her, too, to offer vacant spaces. "That got me thinking," Norsig says. "What I really need to do is start putting these people together." Last year Norsig formed Pop-Up Insider. In February, she launched a website, PopUpInsider.com—a "portal for all things pop-up," she says—giving landlords with vacant retail space the opportunity to list it for $499 per insertion. Norsig helps connect those landlords with retailers interested in opening a pop-up shop. While she and her small team don't negotiate leases, they do offer consulting services on what kind of location would suit a specific business. Pop-Up Insider also offers a range of "concierge services" including marketing, staffing, legal, insurance and design resources. "Our role is to put the pieces together," Norsig says.

"This is the next evolution of retail," she says. "This is the new way to market products. . . . Bricks, clicks and 'quicks' make a lot of sense to me."

E. A. S.

Jean Davis

*Co-Founder of Conversation
Strategies—Evolisten*

In many ways, consumers who use social media are a marketing researcher's dream: Not only do they talk openly and unprompted about products, stores and restaurants, but also they discuss their purchase behaviors and emotional responses. "These people are telling you what they're ordering, what they're drinking, where they're doing it and how they feel about it. . . . They just tell you. You don't have to go through 16 questions for that type of thing." Best of all? That data is ready and waiting for marketers to put to good use.

So says Jean Davis, co-founder of Conversition Strategies, a Toronto-based boutique social media marketing research firm. Together with her business partners, Tessie Ting and Annie Pettit, Davis founded Conversition in late 2009 to apply traditional research methodology to information compiled from social media. (The company is called Conversition rather than Conversation because "we put the 'i' where the 'a' was for intuition," Davis says.) She and her colleagues bring years of marketing research experience to their new venture; for example, most recently Davis served as president of Ipsos Online in North America. They wanted to get out in front of the trend toward deeper dives into social-media-mined data because they knew that 2010 would bring more interest in such online research.

Conversition's research offerings differ from other social media research services in that they go beyond tallying up brand mentions or counting keywords—which, for many companies, had been the norm until very recently, Davis says. "They were all about buzz counting," but such numbers "didn't mean anything" because they often don't account for meaningless brand mentions or irrelevant data.

The company now offers a social media research tool called Evolisten, which acts as a "refinery" to sort through data compiled by online data collection services. It incorporates sampling and weighting methodologies, traditional scoring

Survey Says!

Two-thirds of social media users talk about their experiences with brands and products. 56% of them do so at least once a week.

Source: *Marketing News*/Lightspeed Research survey, June 2010.

methods, filters that help determine consumer sentiment, and a set of constructs that enable marketers to compare social-media-mined data across industry verticals.

Conversition also offers Tweetfeel, which allows marketers to get "quick and dirty feedback" on who's Tweeting about their brands and what the general consumer sentiment is; and Tweetfeel Biz, which is a subscription-based Twitter-reading research tool that allows users to chart the Twitter buzz over time and build their own constructs to categorize it. Recently, Conversition partnered with Peanut Labs Inc., a San Francisco-based social media sample provider, to offer Peanut Labs' clients the chance to pair their social media-based survey research with Evolisten's data refinement capabilities.

Applying traditional marketing research methods to consumer data culled from social media is an important step, but such online research will get better and better as marketers start to leverage the Internet's data power, Davis says. "I think we're just at the real tip of the iceberg as far as the type of information that this data holds."

A. E. S

Critical Thinking

1. In your opinion, what traits and qualifications make a successful entrepreneur or a visionary?

2. You have been assigned to interview a successful entrepreneur; list the questions you would ask during the interview.

Honest Innovation

Ethics issues in new product development could be stalling innovation growth.

Calvin L. Hodock

Product innovation is the fuel for America's growth. Two Harvard economists described its importance as follows: "Innovation is no mere vanity plate on the nation's economic engine. It trumps capital accumulation and allocation of resources as the most important contributor to growth."

Innovative initiatives are a high risk game; failures widely outnumber successes. While enthusiasm, conviction and creativity should flourish in the hearts and minds of the innovation team, judgments must remain totally, even brutally, objective. But unconscious and conscious marketing dishonesty may make this easier said than done.

Unconscious Marketing Dishonesty

People fall in love with what they create, including movies, television pilots, novels, art and new products. And all too often that love is blind: As objectivity eludes the creator, normally rational people become evangelical rather than practical, rational marketing executives.

The Coca-Cola executive suite was convinced that New Coke was the right thing to do. Procter & Gamble's research and development (R&D) believed that Citrus Hill was a better-tasting orange juice than Tropicana and Minute Maid. The spirited Pepsi Blue team overlooked the obvious knowledge that colas should be brown. Ford's MBA crowd believed in a "cheap Jag" strategy. And Motorola's engineers were misguided in their devotion to the Iridium satellite telephone system.

Crest Rejuvenating Effects was fake innovation: It basically was just regular Crest with a great cinnamon vanilla flavor and feminine packaging, positioned for the "nip and tuck" generation of women aged 30 to 45. Similar to Rice Krispies' famous "snap, crackle, and pop" campaign, it encountered a tepid reception, but the brand's custodians believed that America was ready for "his and hers" tubes of toothpaste in their medicine cabinets.

These were well-meaning people who wandered off course because they became enamored with what they created. But let's face it, optimism has limits. The marketplace disagreed, and that's the only vote that counts in any innovation effort.

Conscious Marketing Dishonesty

Conscious marketing dishonesty is more insidious. Blinded passion may still be part of the equation, but in this case the innovation team consciously pushes the envelope across the line of propriety. Before long, there are disquieting signs or signals that all is not well with the new product.

Unfavorable data or information might be ignored, perhaps even suppressed. There might be the blithe assumption that some miracle will surface, and make it all right. Successful innovation initiatives are not products of miracles, but simply take a good idea and execute all the basic steps that are part of the discovery process. The reward goes to those who excel in executing the thousands of details associated with the dirt of doing.

Either way, conscious or unconscious, marketing dishonesty means resources are wasted, valuable time and energy are lost forever and shareholder value may be diminished (depending on the magnitude of the mistake). Often, nobody takes the blame—and many get promoted, because activity gets rewarded over achievement.

There's often no accountability, even though the new product blueprint is peppered with the fingerprints of many. New product assignments are similar to a NASCAR pit stop. The players are constantly moved around the chess board. The brand manager working on a new product for six to nine months moves to mouthwash. The mouthwash brand manager moves to shampoos. And what we have is a game of musical chairs, with no accountability. It is understandable why innovation teams are willing to "run bad ideas up the flag pole" in lassiez-faire-type innovation environments.

While there are supposed to be security checkpoints in the development process, the marketing "id" finds ways to maneuver around them. When important marketing research findings are ignored or rationalized away, because the innovation team is racing toward a launch date promised to management, the spigot of objectivity is turned off because reality might get in the way. Innovation initiatives build momentum to the point where nothing will stop the new product from being launched—not even dire news.

Marketing Dishonesty

There are eight recurring errors associated with flawed innovation. The most disingenuous is marketing dishonesty, where the innovation team consciously engages in deception—even though there is a red flag flapping in the breeze, indicating that a new product is ill. Six marketing dishonesty scenarios are outlined here.

Campbell's Souper Combo

Souper Combo was a combination frozen soup and sandwich for microwave heating; it tested extremely well as a concept. The product was test marketed, and national introduction was recommended.

Two forecasts surfaced. The new product team estimated that Souper Combo would be a $68 million business. The marketing research department viewed it differently: It would be a $40 million to $45 million business, due to weak repeat purchase rates. Nobody challenged the optimistic forecast. Senior management trusted what they heard, while being fed a bouillabaisse of marketing dishonesty. The national introduction was a disaster, and Souper Combo died on the altar of blemished innovation in nine months.

Crystal Pepsi

Pepsi's innovation team ignored focus group participants who hated the taste of this clear cola. It was forced through the Pepsi distribution system on its journey to failure. When was the last time you saw Crystal Pepsi on the store shelves?

Apple Newton

The Newton was the first (but flawed) PDA rushed to market, because then-CEO John Scully viewed it as his signature product—knowing that Apple loyalists were dismayed that a "Pepsi guy" was running the company. Scully wanted to establish a technical legacy that endured long after he left the Apple campus.

The first Newtons were shipped to market with more than a thousand documented bugs. Nobody had the courage to tell Scully and the Apple board about this.

Arthritis Foundation Pain Relievers

This was a line of parity analgesics, involving a licensing agreement where the company paid the Atlanta-based Arthritis Foundation $1 million annually for trademark use. This analgesic line was a positioning gimmick destined for a law and order encounter, and that doesn't mean the NBC television program. Nineteen states attorney generals said the proposition was deceptive. The drugs contained analgesics common to other pain relievers, and were developed without assistance from the Arthritis Foundation. The Foundation was paid handsomely for the use of its name.

Although McNeil Consumer Healthcare admitted no wrong doing, the case was settled for close to $2 million.

Pontiac Aztek

This was considered the ugliest car ever, and the research verified this. While the research predicted that the Aztek was a hopeless cause, the project team sanitized the research sent to senior management to make the situation look better than it was. Decisions about the Aztek's fate were based on intelligence that was heavily modified and edited. Get it out became more important than "get it right."

Aztek-type decisions became regrettably common in the General Motors culture. John Scully never heard the bad news about the Newton, and the General Motors executive suite didn't want to hear any bad news about their cars. It is a heck of way to run one of America's largest corporations and a bad deal for General Motors shareholders, when a culture of intimidation fuels marketing dishonesty. No wonder things are grim at GM these days.

Polaroid Captiva

This camera was similar to Polaroid's original goldmine product the SX 70, but with a smaller film format. It was priced at $120, although marketing research indicated it would not sell if priced over $60. In this scenario, marketing sold a bad idea supported with a specious assumption; marketing research couldn't sell the truth.

Captiva's potential sales were inflated with an assumption about high levels of repeat purchases after introduction. Selling cameras is different than selling cookies or shampoo, products that need replacement. Captiva perished in the marketplace, as the company violated its cardinal principle: Make the cash register ring selling film, while offering the cameras at cost.

Ethics Issues

While these new products had varied product deficiencies, they all share a common denominator: an optimistic sales forecast. An innovation team can manipulate the numbers to get any sales level it wants. It's easy to do, use optimistic assumptions. New product teams can, and do, cook the books with creative number crunching.

Most new product failures are heavily researched. It is used to justify moving a bad new product forward. In a recent *Advertising Age* article, Bob Barocci, the CEO of the Advertising Research Foundation, remarked, "There is a general belief

---

Executive Briefing

Jeffery Garten, former dean of the Yale School of Management and *BusinessWeek* columnist, graded briefing business schools with a C+ in teaching ethics. Sweeping bad news about new product initiatives under the rug can be more costly than embezzlement, and it is just as unethical. A *USA Today* survey says that 52% of students working on their master's of business administration degrees would buy stock illegally on inside information. Business schools need to emphasize ethics training far more than they do now, particularly since unethical behavior can be an underlying dynamic in new product failures.

that over 50% of the research done at companies is wasted." He attributed this to the desire to "support decisions already made." All too often, innovation teams push questionable new products through the pipeline with the support of "justification research."

Another ethical issue is targeting. It is difficult to imagine that ad agencies and their clients did not know Vioxx and Celebrex were overprescribed drugs, sold to consumers with minor aches and pains who could have used less expensive alternatives like Advil and Aleve. Both clients and agencies mutually formulated target strategies with Celebrex and Vioxx as examples. These drugs were developed for senior citizens with chronic pain. But the target segment was too small, so the focus shifted to aging baby boomers with clients and agencies in agreement on the reconfiguration.

Prescriptives

Here are seven recommendations:

1. **Innovation committee.** Boards have finance, audit, nominating and compensation committees. Why not an innovation committee composed of outsiders who are not board members? Their role is to assist the board in assessing innovation initiatives. The board can then decide what action should be taken, including pressing the "kill button."

   Companies sometimes do postmortems after failure. The innovation committee should perform pre-mortems early in the development process, before bad ideas soak up lots of money. There is a rich reservoir of people resources to serve on innovation committees (e.g., academics, retired senior executives, industrial designers, and product and industry specialists). But one thing that they should not be is cronies of professional management.

2. **Find a value-added marketing research department.** The prior case histories illustrate that bad research news often is ignored or rationalized away. Hire a research director who knows how to develop and steward a value-added research department, and that has senior management's respect. The respect factor will protect the function from retribution, should the news be bad. Such a person will not be easy to find. One company's solution was to hire a consultant from McKinsey & Company to steward their research department.

   In the early days, pioneer researchers such as Alfred Politz and Ernest Dichter presented their findings to boards of directors. Marketing research lost it status on its journey from infancy to maturity. Today's market research is frequently unseen by the board. The right person in the function—think one with management respect—gives marketing research an influential voice in the innovation process that it currently does not have.

3. **Reinforce the unvarnished truth.** Senior management needs to embrace skeptics, rather than surround themselves with "yes people." Before management

reviews a new product plan, key players—manufacturing, finance, marketing, and marketing research—should sign off that the plan's assumptions, the underlying source for rosy sales forecasts, are truthful.

4. **Ethics boot camp.** Corporations spend millions on employee training, but how much is focused on ethics to help marketers navigate through gray areas? The innovation team should attend an ethics boot camp early in the development process. This should include everybody, including the ad agencies. Manipulating the forecast for a new product is unethical. It cheats the shareholders even more than it cheats the public.

5. **Teaching new product development.** In academia, new product courses are taught with a focus on best practices; a different perspective is required. The abysmal failure rate is due to worst practices. Classroom discussions of best practices aren't doing much to reduce failure. Class lectures should focus on ethics issues, like manipulating forecasts and justification research used to keep bad ideas afloat.

6. **Ethics test.** Business schools screen candidates based on their graduate management admission test (GMAT) scores. But there is another much-needed test that business schools should implement: an ethics test. Ethics scores should carry equal weight with GMATs. This demonstrates to candidates that ethics are important, and represent a significant prerequisite for admission. As evidenced in new product cases, ethics is more than simply the despicable acts of WorldCom's Bernie Ebbers and Enron Corporation's Andrew Fastow. And, most important, this should help business schools turn out students with a stronger moral compass—ones who don't feed management a duplicitous forecast for a flawed new product.

7. **Corporate endowments.** Corporations interact with business schools on many different levels. They make sizable donations, fund basic research and send their executives to workshops and seminars. They also need to endow ethics chairs with dedicated academics who are interested in ethics scholarship. Corporations should not hesitate to open up their vaults of information to these academics. What are the ethical patterns that underscore an endless stream of new product failures?

Final Thoughts

Failure is inevitable in product innovation. Perfect success is impossible, even undesirable, because it impedes reaching for the stars like Apple did with iPhone or Toyota with the Prius. Perfect success would be a dull agenda of safe bets like a new fragrance or a new flavor. This means the company has elected to play small ball.

This was the trap that Procter & Gamble fell into for close to three decades, despite having 1,250 PhD scientists churning out a treasure chest of patents—leading to 250 proprietary technologies. Despite all this patent activity, very few marketplace hits that made the company famous—think Tide or Pampers as examples—had surfaced from this scientific capability. The innovation focus had drifted to minor product improvements, until the newly anointed CEO A. G. Lafley came along to change all that.

Lafley mandated that P&G be more aggressive, expect failures, and shoot for an innovation success rate in the range of 50% to 60%. And that means having only 4 out of 10 new products fail at Procter & Gamble, well below the industry norm.

The statistic—nine out of 10 new products fail—has hovered over the marketing landscape for six decades. It is estimated that the food industry loses $20 billion to $30 billion annually on failed new products. Would it not be refreshing to attempt to scale this back with a healthy dose of marketing honesty?

Critical Thinking

1. Define *unconscious marketing dishonesty*. Do you agree with the author's distinction between unconscious and conscious marketing dishonesty?

2. List some additional examples, beyond what's in the articles, of conscious and unconscious marketing dishonesty.

CALVIN L. HODOCK is former chairperson of the American Marketing Association board, author of *Why Smart Companies Do Dumb Things* (Prometheus Books, 2007), and professor of marketing at Berkeley College, based in West Paterson, N.J. He may be reached at calhodock@hotmail.com.

Trust in the Marketplace

JOHN E. RICHARDSON AND LINNEA BERNARD MCCORD

Traditionally, ethics is defined as a set of moral values or principles or a code of conduct.

. . . Ethics, as an expression of reality, is predicated upon the assumption that there are right and wrong motives, attitudes, traits of character, and actions that are exhibited in interpersonal relationships. Respectful social interaction is considered a norm by almost everyone.

. . . the overwhelming majority of people perceive others to be ethical when they observe what is considered to be their genuine kindness, consideration, politeness, empathy, and fairness in their interpersonal relationships. When these are absent, and unkindness, inconsideration, rudeness, hardness, and injustice are present, the people exhibiting such conduct are considered unethical. A genuine consideration of others is essential to an ethical life. (Chewning, pp. 175–176)

An essential concomitant of ethics is of trust. Webster's Dictionary defines trust as "assured reliance on the character, ability, strength or truth of someone or something." Businesses are built on a foundation of trust in our free-enterprise system. When there are violations of this trust between competitors, between employer and employees, or between businesses and consumers, our economic system ceases to run smoothly. From a moral viewpoint, ethical behavior should not exist because of economic pragmatism, governmental edict, or contemporary fashionability—it should exist because it is morally appropriate and right. From an economic point of view, ethical behavior should exist because it just makes good business sense to be ethical and operate in a manner that demonstrates trustworthiness.

Robert Bruce Shaw, in *Trust in the Balance,* makes some thoughtful observations about trust within an organization. Paraphrasing his observations and applying his ideas to the marketplace as a whole:

1. Trust requires consumers have confidence in organizational promises or claims made to them. This means that a consumer should be able to believe that a commitment made will be met.
2. Trust requires integrity and consistency in following a known set of values, beliefs, and practices.
3. Trust requires concern for the well-being of others. This does not mean that organizational needs are not given appropriate emphasis—but it suggests the importance of understanding the impact of decisions and actions on others—i.e. consumers. (Shaw, pp. 39–40)

Companies can lose the trust of their customers by portraying their products in a deceptive or inaccurate manner. In one recent example, a Nike advertisement exhorted golfers to buy the same golf balls used by Tiger Woods. However, since Tiger Woods was using custom-made Nike golf balls not yet available to the general golfing public, the ad was, in fact, deceptive. In one of its ads, Volvo represented that Volvo cars could withstand a physical impact that, in fact, was not possible. Once a company is "caught" giving inaccurate information, even if done innocently, trust in that company is eroded.

Companies can also lose the trust of their customers when they fail to act promptly and notify their customers of problems that the company has discovered, especially where deaths may be involved. This occurred when Chrysler dragged its feet in replacing a safety latch on its Minivan (Geyelin, pp. A1, A10). More recently, Firestone and Ford had been publicly brought to task for failing to expeditiously notify American consumers of tire defects in SUVs even though the problem had occurred years earlier in other countries. In cases like these, trust might not just be eroded, it might be destroyed. It could take years of painstaking effort to rebuild trust under these circumstances, and some companies might not have the economic ability to withstand such a rebuilding process with their consumers.

A *20/20* and *New York Times* investigation on a recent *ABC 20/20* program, entitled "The Car Dealer's Secret" revealed a sad example of the violation of trust in the marketplace. The investigation divulged that many unsuspecting consumers have had hidden charges tacked on by some car dealers when purchasing a new car. According to consumer attorney Gary Klein, "It's a dirty little secret that the auto lending industry has not owned up to." (*ABC News 20/20*)

The scheme worked in the following manner. Car dealers would send a prospective buyer's application to a number of lenders, who would report to the car dealer what interest rate the lender would give to the buyer for his or her car loan. This interest rate is referred to as the "buy rate." Legally a car dealer is not required to tell the buyer what the "buy rate" is or how much the dealer is marking up the loan. If dealers did most of the loans at the buy rate, they only get a small fee. However, if they were able to convince the buyer to pay a higher rate, they made considerably more money. Lenders encouraged car dealers to charge the buyer a higher rate than the "buy rate" by agreeing to split the extra income with the dealer.

David Robertson, head of the Association of Finance and Insurance Professionals—a trade group representing finance managers—defended the practice, reflecting that it was akin to a retail markup on loans. "The dealership provides a valuable service on behalf of the customer in negotiating these loans," he said. "Because of that, the dealership should be compensated for that work." (*ABC News 20/20*)

Careful examination of the entire report, however, makes one seriously question this apologetic. Even if this practice is deemed to be legal, the critical issue is what happens to trust when the buyers discover that they have been charged an additional 1–3% of the loan without their knowledge? In some cases, consumers were led to believe that they were getting the dealer's bank rate, and in other cases, they were told that the dealer had shopped around at several banks to secure the best loan rate they could get for the buyer. While this practice may be questionable from a legal standpoint, it is clearly in ethical breach of trust with the consumer. Once discovered, the companies doing this will have the same credibility and trustworthiness problems as the other examples mentioned above.

The untrustworthiness problems of the car companies was compounded by the fact that the investigation appeared to reveal statistics showing that black customers were twice as likely as whites to have their rate marked up—and at a higher level. That evidence—included in thousands of pages of confidential documents which *20/20* and *The New York Times* obtained from a Tennessee court—revealed that some Nissan and GM dealers in Tennessee routinely marked up rates for blacks, forcing them to pay between $300 and $400 more than whites. (*ABC News 20/20*)

This is a tragic example for everyone who was affected by this markup and was the victim of this secret policy. Not only is trust destroyed, there is a huge economic cost to the general public. It is estimated that in the last four years or so, Texas car dealers have received approximately $9 billion of kickbacks from lenders, affecting 5.2 million consumers. (*ABC News 20/20*)

Let's compare these unfortunate examples of untrustworthy corporate behavior with the landmark example of Johnson & Johnson which ultimately increased its trustworthiness with consumers by the way it handled the Tylenol incident. After seven individuals, who had consumed Tylenol capsules contaminated by a third party died, Johnson & Johnson instituted a total product recall within a week costing an estimated $50 million after taxes. The company did this, not because it was responsible for causing the problem, but because it was the right thing to do. In addition, Johnson & Johnson spearheaded the development of more effective tamper-proof containers for their industry. Because of the company's swift response, consumers once again were able to trust in the Johnson & Johnson name. Although Johnson & Johnson suffered a decrease in market share at the time because of the scare, over the long term it has maintained its profitability in a highly competitive market. Certainly part of this profit success is attributable to consumers believing that Johnson & Johnson is a trustworthy company. (Robin and Reidenbach)

The e-commerce arena presents another example of the importance of marketers building a mutually valuable relationship with customers through a trust-based collaboration process. Recent research with 50 e-businesses reflects that companies which create and nurture trust find customers return to their sites repeatedly. (Dayal . . . p. 64)

In the e-commerce world, six components of trust were found to be critical in developing trusting, satisfied customers:

- State-of-art reliable security measures on one's site
- Merchant legitimacy (e.g., ally one's product or service with an established brand)
- Order fulfillment (i.e. placing orders and getting merchandise efficiently and with minimal hassles)
- Tone and ambiance—handling consumers' personal information with sensitivity and iron-clad confidentiality
- Customers feeling that they are in control of the buying process
- Consumer collaboration—e.g., having chat groups to let consumers query each other about their purchases and experiences (Dayal . . . , pp. 64–67)

Additionally, one author noted recently that in the e-commerce world we've moved beyond brands and trademarks to "trustmarks." This author defined a trustmark as a

. . . (D)istinctive name or symbol that emotionally binds a company with the desires and aspirations of its customers. It's an emotional connection—and it's much bigger and more powerful than the uses that we traditionally associate with a trademark. . . . (Webber, p. 214)

Certainly if this is the case, trust—being an emotional link—is of supreme importance for a company that wants to succeed in doing business on the Internet.

It's unfortunate that while a plethora of examples of violation of trust easily come to mind, a paucity of examples "pop up" as noteworthy paradigms of organizational courage and trust in their relationship with consumers.

In conclusion, some key areas for companies to scrutinize and practice with regard to decisions that may affect trustworthiness in the marketplace might include:

- Does a company practice the Golden Rule with its customers? As a company insider, knowing what you know about the product, how willing would you be to purchase it for yourself or for a family member?
- How proud would you be if your marketing practices were made public. . . . shared with your friends. . . . or family? (Blanchard and Peale, p. 27)
- Are bottom-line concerns the sole component of your organizational decision-making process? What about human rights, the ecological/environmental impact, and other areas of social responsibility?
- Can a firm which engages in unethical business practices with customers be trusted to deal with its employees any differently? Unfortunately, frequently a willingness to violate standards of ethics is not an isolated phenomenon but permeates the culture. The result is erosion of integrity throughout a company. In such cases, trust is elusive at best. (Shaw, p. 75)
- Is your organization not only market driven, but also value-oriented? (Peters and Levering, Moskowitz, and Katz)
- Is there a strong commitment to a positive corporate culture and a clearly defined mission which is frequently and unambiguously voiced by upper-management?
- Does your organization exemplify trust by practicing a genuine relationship partnership with your customers—*before, during, and after* the initial purchase? (Strout, p. 69)

Companies which exemplify treating customers ethically are founded on a covenant of trust. There is a shared belief, confidence, and faith that the company and its people will be fair, reliable, and ethical in all its dealings. *Total trust is the belief that a company and its people will never take opportunistic advantage of customer vulnerabilities.* (Hart and Johnson, pp. 11–13)

References

ABC News 20/20, "The Car Dealer's Secret," October 27, 2000.

Blanchard, Kenneth, and Norman Vincent Peale, *The Power of Ethical Management,* New York: William Morrow and Company, Inc., 1988.

Chewning, Richard C., *Business Ethics in a Changing Culture* (Reston, Virginia: Reston Publishing, 1984).

Dayal, Sandeep, Landesberg, Helen, and Michael Zeissner, "How to Build Trust Online," *Marketing Management,* Fall 1999, pp. 64–69.

Geyelin, Milo, "Why One Jury Dealt a Big Blow to Chrysler in Minivan-Latch Case," *Wall Street Journal,* November 19, 1997, pp. A1, A10.

Hart, Christopher W. and Michael D. Johnson, "Growing the Trust Relationship," *Marketing Management,* Spring 1999, pp. 9–19.

Hosmer, La Rue Tone, *The Ethics of Management,* second edition (Homewood, Illinois: Irwin, 1991).

Kaydo, Chad, "A Position of Power," *Sales & Marketing Management,* June 2000, pp. 104–106, 108ff.

Levering, Robert; Moskowitz, Milton; and Michael Katz, *The 100 Best Companies to Work for in America* (Reading, Mass.: Addison-Wesley, 1984).

Magnet, Myron, "Meet the New Revolutionaries," *Fortune,* February 24, 1992, pp. 94–101.

Muoio, Anna, "The Experienced Customer," *Net Company,* Fall 1999, pp. 25–27.

Peters, Thomas J. and Robert H. Waterman Jr., *In Search of Excellence* (New York: Harper & Row, 1982).

Richardson, John (ed.), *Annual Editions: Business Ethics 00/01* (Guilford, CT: McGraw-Hill/Dushkin, 2000).

————, *Annual Editions: Marketing 00/01* (Guilford, CT: McGraw-Hill/Dushkin, 2000).

Robin, Donald P., and Erich Reidenbach, "Social Responsibility, Ethics, and Marketing Strategy: Closing the Gap Between Concept and Application," *Journal of Marketing,* Vol. 51 (January 1987), pp. 44–58.

Shaw, Robert Bruce, *Trust in the Balance,* (San Francisco: Jossey-Bass Publishers, 1997).

Strout, Erin, "Tough Customers," *Sales Marketing Management,* January 2000, pp. 63–69.

Webber, Alan M., "Trust in the Future," *Fast Company,* September 2000, pp. 209–212ff.

Critical Thinking

1. Formulate your own definition for ethics in business.
2. With the prevalence of e-commerce, do business ethics take on new meaning or dimensions?

DR. JOHN E. RICHARDSON is Professor of Marketing in the Graziadio School of Business and Management at Pepperdine University, Malibu, California. **DR. LINNEA BERNARD MCCORD** is Associate Professor of Business Law in the Graziadio School of Business and Management at Pepperdine University, Malibu, California.

UNIT 2

Research, Markets, and Consumer Behavior

Unit Selections

Learning Outcomes

After reading this Unit, you should be able to:

- As marketing research techniques become more and more advanced, and as psychographic analysis leads to more and more sophisticated models of consumer behavior, do you believe marketing will become more capable of predicting consumer behavior? Explain.

- Where the target population lives, its age, and its ethnicity are demographic factors of importance to marketers. What other demographic factors must be taken into account in long-range market planning?

- Psychographic segmentation is the process whereby consumer markets are divided up into segments based upon similarities in lifestyles, attitudes, personality type, social class, and buying behavior. In what specific ways do you envision psychographic research and findings helping marketing planning and strategy in the next decade?

Student Website

www.mhhe.com/cls

Internet References

Canadian Innovation Centre
www.innovationcentre.ca
BizMiner—Industry Analysis and Trends
www.bizminer.com/market_research.asp
Small Business Center—Articles & Insights
www.bcentral.com/articles/krotz/123.asp
Maritz Marketing Research
www.maritzresearch.com
USADATA
www.usadata.com
WWW Virtual Library: Demography & Population Studies
http://demography.anu.edu.au/VirtualLibrary

"It's hard to target a message to a generic 35-year-old middle-class working mother of two. It's much easier to target a message to Jennifer, who has two children under four, works as a paralegal, and is always looking for quick but healthy dinners and ways to spend more time with her kids and less time on housework."

—Elizabeth Gardner, Internet Retailer

If marketing activities were all we knew about an individual, we would know a great deal. By tracing these daily activities over only a short period of time, we could probably guess rather accurately that person's tastes, understand much of his or her system of personal values, and learn quite a bit about how he or she deals with the world.

In a sense, this is a key to successful marketing management: tracing a market's activities and understanding its behavior. However, in spite of the increasing sophistication of market research techniques, this task is not easy. Today, a new society is evolving out of the changing lifestyles of Americans, and these divergent lifestyles have put great pressure on the marketer who hopes to identify and profitably reach a target market. At the same time, however, each change in consumer behavior leads to new marketing opportunities.

The writings in this unit were selected to provide information and insight into the effect that lifestyle changes and demographic trends are having on American industry.

The first unit article in the *Market Research* subsection describes how as more companies are refocusing more squarely on the consumer, ethnography and its proponents have become star players. The second article, "Bertolli's Big Bite," presents a case where Unilever's brand underwent marketing research resulting in a significant increase in its market share. The articles in the *Markets and Demographics* subsection examine the

© McGraw-Hill Companies, Inc./Gary He, photographer

importance of demographic and psychographic data, economic forces, and age considerations in making marketing decisions. In "Marketing to Kids Gets More Savvy with New Technologies," Bruce Horovitz tackles the controversial issue of the increased practice of targeted advertising to tech-savvy children.

The articles in the final subsection analyze how consumer behavior, social attitudes, cues, and quality considerations will have an impact on the evaluation and purchase of various products and services for different consumers. *The Economist* presents an entertaining look at how variety in choices can hinder the consumer decision-making process. "Logoland: Why Consumers Balk at Companies' Efforts to Rebrand Themselves" questions the increased consumer involvement with, and attachment to, brand logos.

What Post-Recession Behavior Means for Marketers Today

New Research Predicts How We Will Spend

Michael Francesco Alioto

Given the magnitude of the current recession, there continues to be ongoing discussion about what the post-recession consumer will look like. Will consumers return to pre-recession spending and continue to stimulate new growth in the near-future economy? Or will they fundamentally change their habits, ultimately altering the next stage of national and global economic development?

A majority of economic analysts and futurists perceive that we are in the midst of a fundamental paradigm shift in our economic behavior. They suggest that similar to the Great Depression of the 1930s, the current mentality and habits of consumers will indeed change, resulting in long term attitude and behavior modifications that likely will give rise to an economy less dependent on consumer purchasing as a stimulus or economic growth.

The Consumer-Purchasing Model

It has long been thought that consumer spending, and the purchasing of both common disposable and durable goods, was a main driver of economic growth and business development. Many manufacturers and retail outlets have depended on robust consumer spending as a main impetus for economic growth.

The current recession, however, has placed us on a different path—one that is more global in nature. At the same time it also has exposed major weaknesses in the domestic economy as it relates to consumer purchasing habits and lifestyles. Massive governmental intervention has become a critical tool in the stimulation of future economic growth, both in the United States and global markets. However the real question is whether the global economy can depend on consumer spending to drive economic growth. This was a fundamental condition of the pre-recession economy, but will it return and to what extent?

The Grounding of Consumers

In conjunction with macro-level lifestyle changes (e.g., the severity of unemployment, particularly among Boomers and educated sectors, as well as in security about global economic

performance), it is the "new" consumer that will challenge manufacturers and retail stores alike as we move into the post-recession period. This may be the difference between a more robust economic recovery and a prolonged economic down turn.

Several key shifts in the mindset of the consumer have already begun to take place:

- **Consumers are purchasing less in terms of goods and services:** The idea of "less is more" is now in vogue.
- **Brands will be required to offer "proof of value":** Brands must add value to the products and services they represent. Many consumers will not purchase products and services based solely on brand reputation.
- **Consumers are conducting their own research:** The Internet and other information sources enable pre-shopping research and decision-making. Often, the targeted product consideration set has been narrowed or even decided upon before the customer has physically entered the store or the purchase decision stage of the shopping cycle.
- **Consumers are consistently becoming "value-driven" buyers:** They are looking more critically at bundled products and services, as well as deep-discount pricing.
- **Values are shifting:** From the more egocentric "me," to group and family "we," or even to the community "us."
- **Many consumers are becoming procrastinators:** Consumers are delaying the purchase of durables, technology and other high-ticket items.
- **Concern about the U.S. middle class:** The current recession has threatened the very existence of the middle class. Will it survive or, more importantly, will it continue to be a major driver of the domestic and global economies?

While we cannot change consumer purchasing habits or predict the post-recession economy, a number of analysts—ourselves included—offer the following recommendations for marketers as we all move toward post-recession strategic planning:

- **Know your customer:** This is even more critical in a post-recession market. We need to get close to customers and be prepared for both micro and macro attitudes and behavioral changes. We need to continue to research customers and understand their lifestyles and values. Organizations that are flexible and nimble will be able to survive and prosper in the next-generation economy, and a realistic view of the customer will enable this.
- **Embrace innovation and ideation:** We will need to do more "co-creation" and develop other consumer-centric approaches for the development of new products and services. It will be critical to get it right the first time, as consumers will have less tolerance for missteps or missed opportunities.
- **Continue to build and reinforce your brands:** Leverage emotional connections to create psychological attachment, while enhancing your brand's promise. Iconic brands are "top of mind" with customers. One should always strive for iconic status.
- **Accelerate new projects to "now":** This is the time to come to market with innovative concepts—before somebody else does or the market passes you by.
- **Do not necessarily reduce prices:** Rather, add value.
- **Think globally:** Both European and North American markets have become saturated in terms of products and services. The next hot markets will most likely continue to rise from the developing, not the developed, world.

While the next wave of economic activity associated with the post-recession consumer may be fundamentally different from current realties, manufacturers and retailers should not just strive to stay alive, but with pioneering planning and thought, they can actually flourish.

While the next wave of economic activity associated with the post-recession consumer may be fundamentally different from current realties, manufacturers and retailers should not just strive to stay alive, but with pioneering planning and thought, they can actually flourish.

This will be both the challenge and opportunity in the way we conduct business in a post-recession environment. One day as we look back on this era, we may say that we didn't just survive the next great depression, but that we forged the next great opportunity.

Critical Thinking

1. Summarize the post-recession consumer attitudinal and behavioral shifts outlined in this article.
2. In your perspective as a consumer, are these shifts short-term or long-term ones? Justify your answer.

MICHAEL FRANCESCO ALIOTO is vice president of analytics at Gongos Research in Auburn Hills, Mich. He can be reached at malioto@gongos.com.

Bertolli's Big Bite

How a Good Meal Fed a Brand's Fortunes

High-quality ingredients make for a satisfying meal, and for more than 100 years the Bertolli brand delivered this through its lines of olive oils and sauces. But as time-pressed consumers shifted away from home cooking and toward convenience options, Bertolli's marketing team saw a gap in the frozen meal landscape it knew it could fill, now Bertolli commands 38.6% of the market.

JEFF BORDEN

Baby boomers and Gen X-ers have been cocooning and nesting since the '90s—fueling, among other trends, a voracious appetite for savory meals prepared at home that are as convenient as take-out.

Bertolli Brand North America has had a name in the U.S. market since the 1890s with its pasta sauces and olive oils. But scanning sales figures for prepared meals, Bertolli executives saw a fast-growing segment where the company had zero presence.

"It was very clear to us that we were not playing in an area that was really growing," says Lori Zoppel, brand development director of marketing for Bertolli Brand North America, based in Englewood Cliffs, N.J. "All the food trends were toward convenience and serving working-couple homes. Here was an area that fit consumer desires, but there was no brand with an upscale name."

As the average number of hours worked each year grows— by 26% to 2,300 hours in 2006, compared to the workload in 1992—the number of frozen meals that Americans eat has also risen, by more than 47% to 82 meals a year, according to Chicago-based market research company Mintel. The huge $5.7 billion market already was dominated by several brand heavyweights, including Nestlé's Stouffer's lines, ConAgra's Banquet brand and Birds Eye.

The largest segment of the overall frozen meal category is single-serve options, with about 75% of the category. Multi-serve frozen entrées and dinner—the market eyed by Bertolli—represents about 20% of the category, but is the fastest-growing segment, Mintel reports. Clocking 16% growth between 2003 and 2005, the lure for Bertolli was irresistible.

"Whenever we're looking at a new product, we always look for the category drivers," Zoppel explains. "Is it a big space or a growing space, or both? Do we have a brand that can play and compete in that space? And, if so, what difference can we make? We saw a chance to leverage our brands into a new area. We needed to compete in complete meal solutions."

Bertolli's new product, Dinner for Two, offers frozen dinners for home preparation with such tasty titles as Shrimp, Asparagus & Penne and Spicy Shrimp Fra Diavolo & Penne.

Once the decision to enter the frozen entrée fray was made, Bertolli turned to ethnographic research in 2000 to help design meals that would stand out from competitors—that would mark its products as an upscale, luxurious end to a busy day, not just a convenience.

Zoppel worked closely with Debbie Weiss Clark, a research manager at Unilever, Bertolli's parent company. Clark has since joined GfK Market Measures in East Hanover, N.H.

"There is no substitute, when you want to learn about how people eat and cook, than going and observing them and talking to them while they are eating and cooking and experiencing things," Clark says. "It's so much better than a laboratory setting, where it's all so artificial and you cannot capture what is turning them on and turning them off."

Teams of Bertolli researchers hired subcontractors to identify families willing to participate in the research; participants were paid about $150. Researchers accompanied them to grocery stores to observe their shopping habits, and watched them cook and eat traditional frozen meals to learn areas of complaint and dissatisfaction.

Anatomy of a Package

As it prepared to introduce products nationally, Bertolli researchers paid considerable attention to packaging as it sought to cast its products as fresher and upscale.

An appetizing photo of the product and a glass of wine is meant to convey that the product quality is on par with that of a restaurant. The on-pack "Ready in 10 Minutes" tag emphasizes convenience.

What Bertolli heard was that polybag meals already on the market had mushy pasta and didn't taste fresh. Participants also complained that the packaging was unappealing and seemed downscale.

While ethnographic marketing research was not the "make or break" factor in the success of the polybag meals, Zoppel doesn't discount its importance. "The ethnographic issue was critical to combine the product and the consumer," she explains. "It helped us gain some insights and sell it internally. Not starting out with words on paper and asking people, but actually giving people food in their mouths and having different members of the team there to observe . . . added a lot of power to our plan."

Meanwhile, other researchers visited traditional Italian restaurants in Manhattan's Little Italy and the Bronx's Arthur Avenue, to see what kinds of ingredients chefs used in their dishes. Researchers also visited popular Italian chain restaurants, including Romano's Macaroni Grill and Olive Garden.

"We were looking for trends and the little things, the key ingredients, that add something," Clark says. "For example, using portabello mushrooms instead of standard mushrooms, or pecorino Romano instead of Parmesan cheese."

Even without the results of the research, Bertolli enjoyed a significant advantage when entering the frozen food arena: A popular Unilever brand in Italy, Quattra Salti En Padella, already had proprietary technology that produced fresher-tasting entrees. Furthermore, the Italian firm had a way to freeze the pasta in a ball-shaped form, a detail that differentiates Bertolli from its competitors.

"There's nothing better than a proposition where you can come in and differentiate your brand as a higher-quality brand," Zoppel says.

With the market research complete, the Bertolli team decided to bring the Dinner for Two concept to market. The product's initial offerings—such as Chicken Parmigiana & Penne—were test-marketed in New England for two years, beginning in January 2003. While under development Bertolli's marketing team made sure it paid equal attention to the packaging of the meals as was paid to the recipes. Designers placed a photograph of the cooked entrée against a sepia-toned background of the hills of Tuscany. There's also a glass of wine on the package, meant to

What's for Dinner?

Despite the choices available to consumers to make the task of putting dinner on the table quick and easy, most continue to take the time to cook up meals from scratch. An online survey of 2,000 adults asked: "How often do you do the following for your evening meal in a typical week?"

	Mean number per week
Cook a meal from scratch	2.6
Bring home carry-out	0.8
Eat at a full-service restaurant	0.7
Leftovers	0.6
Make a frozen entrée	0.5
Make a salad	0.5
Make dinner using a meal kit	0.4
Call for delivery	0.4
Eat canned soup	0.2
Skip dinner	0.2
Other	0.1
Total	7.0

Source: Mintel International Evening Meals (July 2006) report.

underscore the idea that the food inside is on par with a restaurant meal.

"The message is that this product is worth paying more for because there is better quality inside," Clark says.

The message is that this product is worth paying more for because there is better quality inside.

Consumers and food experts alike raved about the taste and the convenience, even as they cringed at the products' nutritional information in nearly the same breath. Since the Bertolli meals are made with richer ingredients—part of the effort to make them more indulgent and position them as an at-home version of a restaurant Italian meal—the original versions of Grilled Chicken Alfredo and other meals have more fat and sodium than some competitors in the category.

Bertolli recently launched a second-generation Mediterranean-style line featuring lighter sauces using more olive oil and wine. Among the four new offerings launched in 2007 are Shrimp &

Penne Primavera and Rosemary Chicken Linguine & Cherry Tomatoes.

"We took a look at how we could reduce fat from the Alfredo meals without sacrificing quality by adding a little less cream and a little less butter," Clark says.

All those efforts have produced a significant success story for Unilever.

Since launching nationwide in January 2005, Bertolli-brand frozen entrees have carved out a 38.6% share of the multi-serve polybag market, besting both Stouffer's and Birds Eye. In U.S. grocery stores, Bertolli accounts for eight of the top 11 best-selling polybag dinners, according to AC Nielsen.

Meanwhile, the line has become a new growth driver for Unilever with sales rising more than 185%, from $70 million in its first year to a projected $200 million plus in 2007.

There've been other benefits, too.

"This product has revolutionized our relationships with retailers," Zoppel says. "We were really able to come in and say we were participating in this segment, which was so important to consumers. We put together a marketing plan and delivered. We're leveraging our global footprint."

Critical Thinking

1. With a small group of peers from your class, outline the new product development process undertaken by Bertolli when it introduced *Dinner for Two*.

2. In your opinion, what demographic, psychographic, and lifestyle shifts in the United States attribute to Bertolli's *Dinner for Two success?*

Youth Marketing, Galvanized

Media & Marketers Diversify to Reach a Mercurial Market

Daniel B. Honigman

Ten years ago, marketers looking to target the youth segment didn't need to look much further than one channel: MTV. But changing media consumption habits are splintering media buys, shards of which are being claimed by other networks, experiential promotions and social networks. The fight to claim the bleeding edge of youth marketing is fierce and is forcing marketers to innovate beyond the pale.

"People live and breathe advertising and marketing in a different way now; they relate to it individually," says John Koller, senior marketing manager in charge of Sony's PlayStation Portable (PSP) video game console.

In 1998, the multimillion-dollar PlayStation marketing budget allocation was 75% broadcast, 20% print, and 5% events and online. "It's splintered significantly since then," Koller says, reporting that the allocation is now closer to 55% broadcast and 20%–25% online. The last quarter is split across mobile, outdoor and retail channels.

"Broadcast is great for awareness, but it's not a 100% driver to the retail environment. Working with PR and great editorial or being able to have a PSP truck outside a Wal-Mart, those are some of our drivers [now]," Koller says.

This splintering of media budgets is common across all segments, but figuring out how to balance these spinning plates is essential to brand survival, says Andrew Frank, research vice president of New York-based Gartner Research. "Anyone who's trying to reach the youth market can't put their eggs in one basket," he says. "Fragmentation has led to a situation in which there's not one seller of ad services that can reach it all. The most successful brands are using a variety of techniques to reach young consumers, but the challenge is keeping them all integrated and complementary."

One such innovator is Cartoon Network, a cable network created in 1992 by Atlanta-based Turner Broadcasting System Inc. Its heavy-hitting, late-night Adult Swim block of programming is the largest draw for men aged 18–34, according to Nielsen Media Research. Despite being a single cable outlet, it offers a mixed bag of marketing touch points for media buyers to choose among.

John O'Hara, senior vice president and general sales manager for Cartoon Network, attributes Adult Swim's success to the network's overall wackiness quotient. But even more, he says, is its pickiness when selecting and integrating an advertiser—and its campaign—into its lineup. This, he says, helps Adult Swim maintain credibility in the youth segment. "You can become uncool with this segment quickly," he says. "We want to make sure we do things with a partner that makes sense and [with whom] we can work something . . . that maintains that 'cool' element."

To do this, Adult Swim takes alternative paths for its ads. For example, in December 2007 its program *Aqua Teen Hunger Force* featured an in-show ad for XM Satellite Radio. The show's plot featured the main characters hijacking the signal of a fictitious hard-rock satellite radio station. During the program, viewers could tune in to the XM channel for a "live" broadcast, and XM posted a fake complaint letter against the program's characters on its website.

For an experiential promotion, Adult Swim teamed up with Virgin Mobile and video game developer Activision Inc. to sponsor a 12-show college tour featuring faux-hard rock band Dethklok from the program *Metalocalpyse*. At the band's stage shows, students—who received free tickets—got a chance to play the video game *GuitarHero III: Legends of Rock* and use Virgin cell phones to text messages that were viewable on the stage's video screen.

When it comes to engaging the youth segment, Adult Swim usually incorporates humor and music, but creativity is what advertisers look for most. "Adult Swim [shows have] some off-the-wall characters, and the sky's the limit for us," O'Hara says. "So creativity, in terms of what we can do with an advertiser across our platforms, will lead to engagement. If you start out with an audience that's so engaged with the network, you'll find a way to engage them with your product."

Utilizing the Web is no different. Simply measuring eyeballs, MTV.com drew 7.5 million unique viewers in October 2007, which pales in comparison with social networks MySpace and Facebook, which drew 123.4 million and 40.1 million unique visitors, respectively, according to Nielsen

Online. MTV.com traffic also trails music giants like Yahoo! Music and Project Playlist. MTV declined to comment for this story.

> **"You can become uncool with this segment quickly," he says. "We want to make sure we do things with a partner that makes sense and [with whom] we can work something . . . that maintains that 'cool' element."**

Anastasia Goodstein, founder and editor of Ypulse.com and author of *Totally Wired: What Teens And Tweens Are Really Doing Online,* says a big reason why MTV is trailing online is because it missed the boat with social networking. "You have the long-tail effect of people going to smaller sites or checking out their friends' blogs, all of which nibble away at MTV's Web properties," Goodstein says. "[And] MTV also [can't compete with] some of the authentic grassroots sites that are created by people within specific subcultures. [For marketers] trying to reach influencers in the snowboarding community, for example, they should find out what site or publication is embraced by the core group within that subculture."

This is not to say that MTV and its Web properties haven't responded to the more segmented markets. "From a youth marketing perspective, is MTV still the place to go? Of course it is," says Josh Weil, partner at Ramsey, N.J.-based youth marketing research firm Youth Trends. "They've made great inroads in the college market with mtvU, they're launching a ton of vertical websites against different music genres and, at some point, they're going to launch a social network. They consistently reach, through their TV channels, mobile and online, more people than any other platform." For MTV, it's just a matter of figuring out a combination that works for its audience and its advertisers. "On the digital end, like everyone else, MTV is trying to figure out how to best leverage its digital assets. Right now, its strategy is to throw a bunch of [stuff] up there and see what sticks," Weil says.

Peter Gardiner, partner and chief media officer with New York-based ad agency Deutsch, agrees. "It would be a bit over-blown to say MTV doesn't work anymore," he says. "Ten years ago, youth marketing started and ended with MTV, but while MTV isn't what it used to be in terms of its dominance over the youth market, it's still an incredibly powerful part of the mix."

In the end, however, whether marketers use MTV, Adult Swim, online or targeted verticals, media channels are only a part of what marketers need to do to effectively reach the youth market. "You hear a lot from marketing executives about the fracturing of media," says Sony's Koller. If you can parse the youth demographic into the smallest segment and can market to [each segment accordingly], you'll be ahead of the game."

Critical Thinking

1. How homogeneous is the youth (18–34) consumer segment?
2. In your opinion, what promotional appeals or themes appeal to today's youth segment?

From *Marketing News,* April 1, 2008, pp. 16–19. Copyright © 2008 by American Marketing Association. Reprinted by permission.

Marketing to Kids Gets More Savvy with New Technologies

Ads come in tricky, fun-loving new forms.

BRUCE HOROVITZ

Isabella Sweet doesn't wear a target on her chest. But kid marketers covet this 9-year-old as if she does. Perhaps it's because she's a techie. The fourth-grader from Davis, Calif., spends almost an hour a day on the Webkinz website. The site charms kids by linking Webkinz plush animals—of which she owns 18—with online games that encourage kids to earn and spend virtual money so they can create elaborate rooms for virtual versions of their Webkinz pets.

The site does one more thing: It posts ads that reward kids with virtual currency when they click. Every time a kid clicks on an ad, there's a virtual ka-ching at the other end for Ganz, which owns Webkinz.

At issue: With the use of new, kid-enchanting technologies, are savvy marketers gaining the upper hand on parents? Are toy marketers such as Ganz, food marketers such as McDonald's and kid-coddling apparel retailers such as 77kids by American Eagle too eager to target kids?

At stake: $1.12 trillion. That's the amount that kids influenced last year in overall family spending, says James McNeal, a kid marketing consultant and author of *Kids as Consumers: A Handbook of Marketing to Children*. "Up to age 16, kids are determining most expenditures in the household," he says. "This is very attractive to marketers."

It used to be so simple. A well-placed TV spot on a Saturday-morning cartoon show or a kid-friendly image on a cereal box was all it took. No longer. The world of marketing to kids has grown extremely complex and tech-heavy. Marketers that seek new ways to target kids are aware of new calls for federal action—including voluntary marketing guidelines that would affect food marketers. Kids, who are spending less time watching TV and more time on computers or smartphones, are becoming targets online.

"Marketers are getting more and more devious," says Susan Linn, director of Campaign for a Commercial-Free Childhood, a watchdog group. With the growing use of smartphones and social media, she says, "They have new avenues for targeting children" that parents might miss.

Even ad-savvy parents are sometimes unaware how marketers are reaching out to their children.

Getting around Ad Blockers

While on the Webkinz site, Sweet recently clicked once a day for seven days on an ad for a film trailer that was posted for *Judy Moody and the NOT Bummer Summer*. She says that she wasn't really interested in the movie. But each day that she clicked it and answered three questions, she earned a virtual lime-green dresser and bulletin board for the rooms she created online for her Webkinz.

"I've got five dressers and seven bulletin boards," says the girl. "I don't have enough rooms to fit them all in."

This kind of marketing to kids drives Isabella's mother crazy. "They're doing this right under the noses of parents," says Elizabeth Sweet, a doctoral student at University of California-Davis doing her dissertation on the marketing of kids' toys. Even so, she says, she had no idea about the video ads on Webkinz until her daughter told her.

"This whole planting of movie videos in the online game experience is new to me," Sweet says. "What bothers me most is that when she first signed up for the site, I thought it was OK."

Sweet has an ad-blocker app on her browser. These movie ads are woven into the site content in such a way that her daughter sees—and responds to them—anyway, she says.

"We occasionally introduce limited-time promotions so that our Webkinz World members can enjoy fun, unique activities and events," says Susan McVeigh, a Ganz spokeswoman, in an e-mail.

But Elizabeth Sweet isn't the only parent who's unhappy with how and what Webkinz markets to kids.

Last month, Christina Cunningham, a full-time mother from Port St. Lucie, Fla., happened to look over as two of her daughters—ages 9 and 7—were signing onto the Webkinz website. On the log-in screen, an ad flashed for BabyPictureMaker.com, which nudges consumers to download pictures of two people—promising to send back a picture of what a baby they might have together would look like.

"This is not acceptable," says Cunningham, who shooed her kids away from the site and fired off an e-mail to Webkinz. When she didn't hear back, she sent another. Again, she says, she received no response. But McVeigh says Webkinz e-mailed Cunningham responses, twice. A frustrated Cunningham contacted Campaign for a Commercial-Free Childhood. The group contacted Webkinz, which removed the ad. "We will make sure to open an investigation into the matter and take the appropriate steps," spokeswoman McVeigh assured the group in a letter.

The Fast-Food Connection

Webkinz declined to share the outcome of this investigation with *USA TODAY*—nor would it explain how the ad got on the site. "We're fully committed to a responsible approach regarding advertising and the advertisers we allow on the site," says McVeigh, in an e-mail.

But in the eyes of some parents, no one goes more over the top in marketing to kids than the big food sellers—particularly sellers of high-sugar cereals and high-fat, high-calorie fast food.

That's one reason the Obama administration is proposing that food-makers adopt voluntary limits on the way they market to kids.

These proposed voluntary guidelines, to be written by a team from four federal agencies, have set the food and ad industries howling—even before they've been completed.

"I can't imagine any mom in America who thinks stripping tigers and toucans off cereal boxes will do anything to address obesity," said Scott Faber, a spokesman for the Grocery Manufacturers Association, at a May hearing.

But Wayne Altman thinks the voluntary guidelines are critical.

He's a family physician in the Boston area who has three sons ages 13, 5 and 4. He's particularly concerned about Ronald McDonald. "We know that children under 8 have no ability to establish between truth and advertising," he says. "So, to have this clown get a new generation hooked on a bad product just isn't right."

Because of the obesity, heart disease and food-related illnesses fed partly by savvy food marketers such as McDonald's, Altman says, "We have a generation of children that is the first to have a life expectancy less than its parents."

Plenty of others think as Altman does, even though Ronald is regularly used to promote Ronald McDonald House Charities. Ronald also shows up in schools. He's got his own website, Ronald.com, where the clown promises that kids can "learn, play and create while having fun." And he's the focal point of a new social-media campaign that nudges kids to download their own photos with images of Ronald and share them with friends.

More than 1,000 doctors, including Altman, recently signed a petition that asked McDonald's to stop using Ronald to market to kids. "People have a right to sell and advertise," he says. "But where do we draw the line?"

McDonald's—which recently announced it will modify its Happy Meals in September by reducing the number of fries and adding apple slices—has no plans to dump Ronald. "Ronald McDonald is an ambassador for McDonald's and an ambassador for good," CEO Jim Skinner told shareholders in May at the company's annual meeting. "Ronald McDonald is going nowhere."

77kids Entertains Shoppers

But American Eagle is going somewhere. And if any retailer exemplifies the techie new world of marketing to kids, it may be 77kids by American Eagle.

The outside-the-box store that it just opened at New York's Times Square sells midpriced clothing targeting boys and girls from toddler to 12. But the heart of the target is the 10-year-old.

Getting a 10-year-old's attention is all about whiz-bang technology—like the chain's virtual ticket to rock stardom.

In the center of the Times Square store sits a "Be a Rock Star" photo booth. It's all about music and tech. The booth has a big-screen TV that shows a video of a rock band composed of 10- to 12-year-old kids singing *I Wanna Rock* by Twisted Sister. Any tween, with parental permission, can download his or her photo and substitute it on the screen for one of the rock stars.

"Our brand ideology is: Think like a mom, see like a kid," explains Betsy Schumacher, chief merchandising officer at 77kids. "It made sense to us to have technology in the store that speaks to a kid's experience—and how they play."

Each 77kids store also has two iPad-like touch-screens that allow kids to virtually try on most of the clothing in the store. Who needs a dressing room when you can download your own photo and have it instantly matched online with that cool motorcycle vest or hip pair of distressed jeans? The same touch-screen also allows kids to play instant DJ, where they can mess online with the very same music that's being played in the store—slowing it down, speeding it up or even voting it off the playlist.

Nearly nine in 10 kids who shop at 77kids try one of these technologies while visiting the store, Schumacher estimates.

The company makes no bones about laser-targeting 10-year-olds. "The point is to keep a kid engaged so that shopping is enjoyable," Schumacher says. "Kids are looking for entertainment when they come to the mall."

Ex-adman Wants Change

Marketers, in turn, are looking for kids. And profits.

It isn't just advertising watchdogs who think it's time for a change. So does the guy who two years ago was arguably the ad world's top creative executive, Alex Bogusky. The agency that he has since left, Crispin Porter + Bogusky, has created campaigns for such kid-craving companies as Burger King and Domino's. Now, with the ad biz in his rearview mirror, Bogusky suggests it may be time for marketers to rethink.

"So what if we stopped it?" he recently posed on his personal blog. "What if we decided that advertising to children was something none of us would engage in anymore? What would happen? A lot of things would happen, and almost all seem to be for the good of society."

Babies as young as 6 months old can form mental images of logos and mascots—and brand loyalties can be established as early as 2, says the watchdog group Center for a New American Dream. McNeal, the kids marketing guru, says he consults with companies that are constantly trying to figure out how to get inside day care centers and bore their images inside the minds of preschoolers.

Back at Isabella Sweet's Webkinz-filled home, she's still saving her weekly $1 allowance to buy yet more. She can't help it, she says, even though each one costs $5 to $13. Even the family cats drag out her Webkinz to play.

"I wish I had a favorite Webkinz, but I don't," says Isabella. "I love them all."

Critical Thinking

1. With a small group of peers from your class, debate the ethical implications of marketing directly to children and teens.

2. The article states that "Marketers are getting more and more devious . . . . They have new avenues for targeting children." Present current marketing examples that support this premise. Do you agree with this statement?

It's Cooler than Ever to Be a Tween

They're a hot market, they're complicated, and there are two in the White House.

SHARON JAYSON

The prepubescent children of days gone by have given way to a cooler kid—the tween—who aspires to teenhood but is not quite there yet.

Tweens are in-between—generally the 8-to-12 set. The U.S. Census estimates that in 2009, tweens are about 20 million strong and projected to hit almost 23 million by 2020.

Among them now are Malia Obama, at 10 already a tween, and sister Sasha, who turns 8 this year. With the Obama daughters in the White House, the nation's attention will focus even more on this emerging group—and the new "first tweens" will likely be high-profile representatives of their generation.

"My daughter is really excited that there's a girl in the White House the same age she is," says Courtney Pineau, 31, of Bellingham, Wash., mother of fifth-grader Sophia, age 10.

Retailers know tweens are a hot market for clothes, music and entertainment. But now psychologists and behavioral researchers are beginning to study tweens, too. They say tweens are a complicated lot, still forming their personalities, and are torn between family and BFFs, between fitting in and learning how to be an individual.

Tweens have "their own sense of fashion in a way we didn't have before and their own parts of the popular culture targeted toward them," says child and adolescent psychologist Dave Verhaagen of Charlotte. How will this shape their personalities? "Time will tell. We don't know."

Research has shown that middle school is where some troubles, particularly academic, first appear. Also, a 2007 review of surveys in the journal *Prevention Science* found that the percentage of children who use alcohol doubles between grades four and six; the largest jump comes between fifth and sixth grades.

"They're kids for a shorter period of time," adds psychologist Frank Gaskill, who also works with tweens

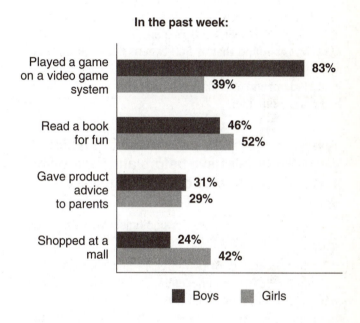

In the past week:

Played a game on a video game system: Boys 83%, Girls 39%

Read a book for fun: Boys 46%, Girls 52%

Gave product advice to parents: Boys 31%, Girls 29%

Shopped at a mall: Boys 24%, Girls 42%

■ Boys ■ Girls

What tweens are doing.
Source: Youth Trends (based on in-person interviews with 1,223 8-12-year-olds in December. Margin of error ±2.8 percentage points).

in Charlotte. "More is expected of them academically, responsibility-wise."

Many parents, including Beth Harpaz, 48, of Brooklyn, are well aware of this short-lived time. Her older son is 16 and a high school junior; her younger son is 11 and in fifth grade.

"I'm trying really hard to save his childhood. I want him to enjoy little-boy things and don't want him to feel that he has to put on that big hoodie and wear the $100 sneakers and have that iPod in his ear listening to what somebody has told him is cool music," says Harpaz, author of *13 is the New 18.*

Gender Differences

Boys haven't been the main target of marketers hawking all things tween, from clothes and makeup to TV shows and music. But Disney wants to change that with its launch Feb. 13 of Disney XD, a "boy-focused" cable brand that includes TV and a website with themes of adventure, accomplishment, gaming, music and sports.

Until now, Disney has been "a tween-girl machine," Verhaagen says. "It may be that teen idols and celebrities are more inherently appealing to girls because it's all about personality and music and relational things that girls are more interested in. Boys at that age are more interested in sports and adventure and are not as easily marketed to by personalities and pop stars."

The Disney Channel and Nickelodeon are favorites, according to an online survey this summer for the 2008–09 GfK Roper Youth Report. The data, released to *USA Today,* found that of 500 tweens ages 8 to 12 asked about activities within the past week, 82% had watched Nickelodeon and 69% had watched Disney; 92% said they had played outside.

Tweens have "their own sense of fashion in a way we didn't have before and their own parts of the popular culture targeted toward them."

—Psychologist Dave Verhaagen

Verhaagen, father of two girls, 11 and 13, says tweens are "immersed in consumer culture" and seek connections and identity through social networking and shared entertainment experiences, but they're still "aligned with their parents."

New data from in-person interviews in December by Youth Trends, a marketing services company based in Ramsey, N.J., found 85% of the 1,223 respondents ages 8–12 agreed that "my family is the most important part of my life" and 70% said "I consider my Mom and/or Dad to be one of my best friends."

Elizabeth Hartley-Brewer, a parenting expert in London and author of *Talking to Tweens,* says the tween years are when young people begin to realize the wider world, and to see themselves as separate from their families. That's why the peer group is so crucial, she says.

Jade Jacobs, 12, of North Potomac, Md., is active in soccer, basketball, gymnastics and two cheerleading teams. "The main reason I do most of my sports is to hang out with my friends and to get exercise," she says.

She also loves to shop with friends. "It's not always about buy, buy, buy," she says. But, "if we have a little money, we'll find a cute accessory."

Her mother, Christina Jacobs, 43, says the idea of "mean girls" is part of the tween years, which is one reason girls worry about clothes. "Girls are looking at each other and seeing who is wearing what. They're harder on each other," she says. "Girls are looking at each other at 9 and 10, and boys are in la-la land."

Music Is Cool

Eleven-year-old Campbell Shelhoss, a fifth-grader in Towson, Md., says he's not in a hurry to be a teenager, even though he says he has outgrown some childhood pastimes.

"I feel like Pokémon is a little young," he says, and he puts cartoon toys and handheld video games in the same category.

He plays baseball and golf. He wanted a cellphone "for a few weeks" and then decided it wasn't that important to him.

Almost two-thirds (63%) of kids 8 to 12 do not have a cellphone, the Youth Trends study finds. It also finds that tweens spend 12.1 hours a week watching TV and 7.3 hours online.

The Roper report also asked tweens to rate 17 items as "cool or not cool." Music was at the top of the cool list, followed by going to the movies. "Being smart" ranked third—tied with video games—followed by electronics, sports, fashion and protecting the environment.

The "First Tweens"

"Right now, their friends and their status is everything to them," says Marissa Aranki, 41, of Fullerton, Calif. She is a fifth-grade teacher and has two daughters, 18 and 12.

"It's universal for the age, but they show it in different ways. For boys, the whole friendship thing is through technology and through sports," she says. "Girls like to talk, either about other girls or about boys. A lot of the girls are really boy-crazy. And some of the boys are not really girl-crazy yet. They're really out of the loop in that case. They've got their little guy friends and they're trying to be athletic, and that's what they care about."

Tweens are part of the larger generational group sometimes called Millennials or Generation Y. Those in their late teens through mid-20s are "first-wave" Millennials because they're the ones who set the trends that this later wave (born between the early 1990s and about 2003 or 2004) continues to follow, suggests historian and demographer Neil Howe, co-author of several books on the generations.

Verhaagen, author of *Parenting the Millennial Generation,* says older and younger Millennials share certain traits, such as comfort with technology and diversity, and being family-oriented.

He believes the struggling economy also will leave an imprint on both groups of Millennials; the younger ones could become less materialistic and consumer-driven.

Howe says tweens are even more interested in being protected and sheltered than their older Millennial siblings; he says this is because the parents of older Millennials tend to be Baby Boomers while parents of the younger group are often part of Generation X, in their 30s to mid-40s.

"These Xers are concerned about such things as safety and protection," he says. "They're not as worried as Boomers were about making their children paragons of perfection. Xers care less about that and try to do less. They're more pragmatic."

Howe counts Barack and Michelle Obama as Gen Xers, those born between 1961 and 1981. But many view the president and first lady as post-Boomers who are part of "Generation Jones," a term coined by cultural historian Jonathan Pontell for people born between 1954 and 1965.

Either way, it may be tough for the Obama girls to stay out of the spotlight, suggests Denise Restauri, founder of a research and consulting firm called AK Tweens and the tween social networking site AllyKatzz.com.

"They're in nirvana," she says. "Right now, (Malia and Sasha) are the most popular girls in school. It doesn't get much better than that when you're a tween."

Critical Thinking

1. Summarize the purchasing attitudes and habits of Tweens in the United States.

2. In your opinion, what current lifestyle shifts explain Tweens' purchasing patterns?

Sowing the Seeds

A deeper understanding of the customer buying process can drive organic growth.

MARK POCHARSKI AND SHERYL JACOBSON

Marketers love to talk about getting closer to customers. But the reality today for most companies is that they aren't very close at all to the people or companies that purchase their products or services. The problem: It's a complicated world out there. What was once a fairly straightforward buying process that consumers followed—comprising one or two channels and an orderly progression of steps from awareness to purchase—has now morphed into a complex and constantly changing ecosystem made up of multiple channels, more competition, and less-attentive and increasingly empowered customers.

As a result, traditional sales and marketing tools that have worked for decades are no longer adequate. Consider how the scope and complexity of the buying process has grown for a product as simple as a doorknob. Not so long ago, a homeowner would go to a local hardware store or a big-box retailer such as Sears, maybe speak with an associate and choose from perhaps a half-dozen different types of doorknobs.

Now the consumer might start with a Google search of "new doorknob," which would turn up literally thousands of information sources on buying and replacing doorknobs (home improvement sites such as HGTV or This Old House) along with myriad purchase options, ranging among the following:

- retail giants such as The Home Depot, Lowe's, Wal-Mart, and Target
- regional hardware stores such as Ace, Aubuchon, and True Value
- for-sale-by-owner sites such as eBay and Craigslist
- numerous e-retailers such as doorknobdiscountcenter.com and knobsandhardware.com

It's safe to say, however, that none of those retailers has deep insight about that potential consumer other than his perceived need for a new doorknob. Is he building a house

Executive Briefing

With the increasing complexity of business today, many marketers have forgotten the fundamental principal that growth occurs only when you're able to change specific behaviors in customers during their buying process. That's harder today because the typical buying process is a complex ecosystem of channels, information sources, and marketing mix options—but it's absolutely essential. This article outlines specific ways companies can develop insights from the customer buying process and then focus their marketing efforts on the things that really matter.

or replacing a door? Does he want more security or is the new knob strictly for looks? How much of a factor is price? Did someone refer him to this brand? Beyond offering basic price information and product descriptions, most retailers are not likely to take any action to lead the consumer through a detailed buying process. And yet if companies don't invest in understanding where they can win or lose that customer in the buying process, then how can they invest in the marketing programs that matter most?

The irony is that marketers are being asked with increasing urgency to help drive organic business growth by acquiring and retaining customers—and by convincing them to buy more products or services. In many cases, however, their methods have yet to catch up with the madness of the current marketplace, in which consumers are less attentive to traditional messaging and just as likely to follow advice on a new product from a Web log (blog) or third-party website. Although most companies have a very good understanding of the transactions that a customer has historically engaged in, they have very little understanding of why an individual behaves in the way he does and what they could do to alter that behavior to their advantage.

Marketers need new tools that will help them develop deeper insights into customer behavior and identify key points in which they can influence purchase decisions. Conducting an in-depth analysis of the buying process to uncover these "leverage points" can help marketers define the best tactics to alter (or reinforce)—to increase sales and ultimately drive profitable growth.

New Buying Process

The proliferation of product choices, information sources, distribution channels, and marketing platforms has made the world a complex place for both buyers and sellers of goods and services. For marketers, it's the equivalent of moving from a simple game of checkers to trying to solve a Rubik's Cube and Sudoku puzzle simultaneously. Unfortunately, existing models for understanding the buying process—particularly the specificity of how a customer is motivated and influenced at each step along the way—are constrained by two significant flaws in conventional wisdom.

The buying process is nonlinear. The first flaw is viewing the buying process as a linear progression. Many marketing and sales teams still group the customer life cycle into orderly and discrete stages: awareness, trial, consideration, purchase, and repeat. They have systems in place to monitor what happens at each stage (e.g., customer relationship management, sales-force automation, loyalty analysis), but those systems don't show the numerous paths customers use to navigate throughout the process. That used to matter less when there were one or two ways of creating awareness or purchasing a product; the linkages then were fairly obvious. Now, however, the paths are so varied that companies cannot effectively track them. A customer might enter a store ready to buy a specific make and model of a computer after researching the product online, or he might be a novice looking for information and guidance. Those are two customers with very different purchase contexts that require two separate marketing approaches. Marketing tactics for the computer-savvy shopper might include word-of-mouth strategies, blogs, and third-party endorsements, whereas the computer-novice shopper might require aggressive sales promotions, in-store purchase displays, and endorsements from well-known media outlets such as *Consumer Reports.*

Compounding the problem: Marketing and sales personnel who treat the buying-process stages as a straight line (awareness leads to consideration, which leads to a purchase, which leads to repeat purchases) incorrectly assume that all buying processes begin with awareness and that success in one stage will naturally lead to success in the next. That attitude ignores other influences at various points in the buying process, which can lead a customer down an entirely different path.

Take, for example, a technology distributor that grew successfully over the years by following a simple marketing premise: that high-quality technical support was good for business, especially during the consideration phase. The company developed an unrivaled (online and offline) pre-sales technical support group to help customers configure complex technology solutions to meet their needs. Although this approach allowed the company to win customers and build share for a number of years, it also created a bloated cost structure that ate into margins. More alarmingly, the company was not aware of the increasing number of prospects—including some long-term customers—that were (1) using the distributor's best-in-class support to configure solutions but then (2) purchasing the solution from one of several new and lower-cost competitors that didn't offer technical support.

Acquisition and retention are interrelated. The second flaw involves treating customer acquisition and customer retention as independent processes. In too many companies, an artificial wall exists between the two. Sales and marketing will focus on the former (if sales are down) or the latter (if defection rates are high), but rarely does it examine the interdependencies between them. Viewing acquisition and retention separately ignores the fact that customers today may make frequent and often overlapping trips through the buying process and therefore cannot be categorized as either a prospect or an existing customer—they are often both.

How frequently do you see promotions from cell phone providers or credit card companies offering low rates or giveaways for new customers—deals for which long-term and loyal customers are not eligible? Companies spend billions on advertising and promotion to entice new customers while saddling existing customers with inferior prices, even when those current customers come with zero acquisition costs. Consumers are fighting back, either by canceling their subscriptions and re-engaging as new customers (to get the better prices) or by canceling their service altogether and purchasing a competitive offering.

A more subtle example comes from the pharmaceuticals industry. Many drug companies have developed a marketing approach of investing significant dollars into direct-to-consumer advertising—to convince patients to inquire about certain branded drugs with their physicians. In doing so, however, drug companies often overlook other, higher-potential growth opportunities. For example, recent research we conducted in the pharmaceutical industry showed that in some sectors, lack of patient compliance (e.g., taking less than the prescribed medication or stopping the medication early) was in fact the biggest barrier to long-term, profitable growth. By viewing acquisition and retention as interrelated processes we were able to demonstrate that focusing marketing and sales activities on compliance issues (targeted at doctors and patients to ensure patients took their full regimen of medication) rather than direct-to-consumer advertising would make certain drug classes grow faster and more profitably. The resulting marketing programs helped turn a negative-growth product into a 30% growth rate in just one year.

Understanding Buying Behaviors

As the examples here demonstrate, organic growth is driven by behavioral change in customers. A company can control and accelerate its growth rate only if it knows the specific customer behaviors it wants to change and focuses its marketing and sales teams on influencing the behaviors that have the highest potential for return.

How to begin the process of understanding customer behavior? The first step is developing a comprehensive understanding of where the leverage points exist in the buying process. Leverage points represent the place in the buying process where customers or prospects either enter or drop out of your process. By influencing prospects to move to the next stage instead of leaving, marketers can directly increase the purchase or usage of a product.

In many cases, leverage points are not obvious; they might even conflict with accepted beliefs about the business. Management teams often guess wrong about customer behavior because they neither see changes occurring in the marketplace quickly enough, nor have the data to challenge their operating assumptions. The following examples show how uncovering leverage points led to changes in marketing activities that provided a big payback.

The men's high-end fashion industry. For years, the prevailing wisdom was that men buy high-end clothing and accessories because they want to dress like Tiger Woods, George Clooney, or some other handsome and successful personality. One fashion retailer played this aspirational card to the hilt: investing heavily in celebrity-endorsed print ads in men's magazines and TV spots during sporting events, hoping to influence its target audience. However, after careful examination of the buying process, that retailer found that many of its targeted segments didn't buy fashion and accessories that way at all.

For many segments, purchase decisions were made in the racks of high-end specialty stores. The retailer's primary target group was gathering only 5% of its information from television and 7% from magazines. Its main influence was word of mouth; 68% of all information was gathered from the subject's wife, girlfriend, or mother. And at the point of sale, more than two-thirds based their purchase decision on the fit and feel of the product. If the consumer tried on the product, then he disproportionally bought it over competitors' brands. To address those behaviors, the company shifted a significant amount of its marketing spend from celebrity sponsorship to point-of-purchase promotion designed to

experience the product. It has since tripled the annual growth rate of its core business.

A watch manufacturer. Not all companies should move their marketing dollars downstream to the point of sale; sometimes the best move is in the opposite direction. Another example is of a watch manufacturer that historically had invested heavily with retailers to create attractive in-store promotional displays and signage. The marketing team spent a robust 85% of its budget on point-of-sale tactics. However, as younger consumers (a critical segment for this company) started using cell phones instead of watches to tell time, the watchmaker was experiencing significantly lower growth rates. Yet a closer examination of customer behaviors revealed that (1) younger shoppers didn't see the value of using a watch to keep time and (2) the point-of-purchase displays were having little impact on them. After examining the data, the watchmaker realized that the key leverage point—the opportunity to influence the youth segment's buying decisions and change its behavior—came well before they entered the store. The company shifted more than 60% of its marketing resources toward a broad-based campaign to promote the benefits and style of wearing a watch. The shift of marketing tactics had a significant impact in turning the brand around and driving new growth.

As the clothing retailer and watchmaker both discovered, focusing on the leverage points in the buying process can help you understand where you are winning and losing your customers. An in-depth analysis of the buying process provides specificity around the behavior that a company seeks to change among its target audience. Those insights include how and why people make decisions leading to purchase—and ultimately usage—of the product or where and why people drop out of the process. They can illuminate (1) where competition is really happening and (2) its impact on winning or losing customers. Importantly, they identify the role of influencers—any word-of-mouth advocacy manifested in blogs, chat rooms, or other venues—on the customer's behavior.

Most companies are swimming in the wrong kind of data, or they're analyzing the right data the wrong way.

The spirits world. Such outputs convinced one spirits maker to change its in-store promotional tactics. The marketing team knew that most of the company's customers were men, and it knew that the segment bought spirits roughly once a month. It didn't know much more than that, so it performed a deeper analysis to uncover the motivations behind the monthly visits. It uncovered two main scenarios. The first was the "special-occasions run," made when friends were coming over at the last minute. The second was the "stock-up," done monthly to replenish the customer's inventory. The last-minute shoppers cared more about packaging: opting for specialized glass bottles, often in smaller quantities. And in that segment of customers, the spirits maker was losing ground to new competitors. With that insight in hand, the spirits maker changed its in-store packaging to reinforce special-occasions buying behaviors. The change resulted in close to doubling the growth and profit from its primary spirits brand.

Turning Insights into Action

A key point to remember is you need the data to act. It's incredibly tempting to think you already know how consumers behave and to simply assume that you can rely on your intuition, years of experience, and macro-trend analysis to come up with the best approach. That's a tempting and sometimes fatal mistake. Most companies are swimming in the wrong kind of data, or they're analyzing the right data the wrong way. As we've highlighted, typical models for understanding buying and usage behaviors are not rich enough; you must go deeper where it really matters. There are two points to bear in mind.

Be broader in scope when you start analyzing the situation. Look at multiple buying processes in all corners of the market. Think more broadly about competitors/substitutes, consumers, geographies, and occasions. Have an unconstrained view of the opportunity first; then use feasibility and economics to highlight the best leverage points.

Don't get lost in the woods. At the end of the day, data must be actionable to have value (e.g., there are too many customer segmentations out there in which sales can't find the target). It's important to use interactive, hypothesis-driven processes combined with managerial insight to cut through the data clutter. Translate those data into holistic, living and breathing representations of your customers. To find the best opportunities, it's important to keep three questions in mind:

- Would the desired behavioral change drive significant profitable growth for the company? Does it provide a large-enough opportunity? (Unless the desired behavioral change tilts customers to your brand and results in profitable growth, there is limited upside to focusing on it.)
- Are the required skills and capabilities resident in the organization to execute on this opportunity? (If you don't have the marketing capabilities to affect this behavior, then it is not feasible in the short term.)
- Will it be cost-prohibitive to obtain the expected gains? (If you cannot overcome barriers through appropriate and affordable marketing tactics, then you won't achieve the desired behavioral change.)

With the leverage points identified in the buying process, a marketing team can then define a few critical "behavioral objectives" that will form the foundation of a sustainable growth strategy. These behavioral objectives help reinforce or change a customer's behavior to increase purchase and usage of a product. It's what you want the customer to do differently or more frequently. A behavioral objective is more actionable than a traditional marketing campaign goal.

For a financial services company, "attract new customers to the category" is a broad objective that is difficult to build a campaign around. A more important and valuable behavioral objective, such as "convert automatic teller machine users to debit cards," will allow for greater precision in marketing programs. The same lesson applies for a telecommunications company: Refining the behavioral objective from "initiate new cell phone usage" to "make personal calls with cell phone instead of home phone" provides enough specificity for a more targeted—and ultimately more successful—campaign. The point is that you can't be specific enough in targeting what customer behavior to change or reinforce without knowing where the leverage point is in the first place.

Focusing on What Matters

Leverage points and behavioral objectives are important elements of a detailed buying-process analysis. Done right, that type of analysis will move marketing's collective mind-set away from assumptions, estimates, and "spread-your-bet" marketing plans—toward a focus on the customer behaviors it needs to change (and where). A buying-process analysis is particularly helpful in multichannel industries such as pharmaceuticals, technology, and financial services. In such industries, the multiple constituencies involved in decision making make it even more critical to understand the behaviors and opportunities at each stage.

Buying-process analysis can also help a management team pinpoint the greatest achievable economic opportunities instead of spending too much time on broad-based ideas such as customer loyalty, awareness, and satisfaction. It also enables a company to see the marketplace in a way that's different from competitors, which will open up new opportunities upstream or downstream—and away from a head-to-head battle over market share.

Think about the elements that drive top-line growth: getting customers to buy more frequently, buy more products, buy instead of browse, or purchase from you instead of your competitor. Changing or reinforcing behaviors that affect any of those drivers in a positive way will directly contribute to increased revenue. Although it's easy for a company to state that it is focused on understanding its customers better, executing on that mission is the true challenge. The most successful companies have made a real commitment to developing deep insights into customer behavior—and they are taking steps to influence that behavior. Only by understanding the different dimensions of the buying process can companies solve the puzzle of sustainable organic growth.

Critical Thinking

1. What developments account for the increasing complexity of business in today's "complicated world"?

2. In your perspective, what new sources of information do consumers turn to and rely on when making purchasing decisions?

MARK POCHARSKI is a partner of Monitor Group (which helps organizations grow by working with leading corporations, governments, and social sector organizations around the world on the growth issues that are most important to them) and leader of Monitor's marketing strategy unit, Market2Customer (M2C), in Cambridge, Mass. He may be reached at mark_pocharski@monitor.com. **SHERYL JACOBSON** is a global account manager of M2C and may be reached at sheryl_jacobson@monitor.com. To join the discussion about this article, please visit www.marketingpower.com/marketingmanagementblog.

From *Marketing Management,* September/October 2007, pp. 26–31. Copyright © 2007 by American Marketing Association. Reprinted by permission.

The Tyranny of Choice

You Choose

If you can have everything in 57 varieties, making decisions becomes hard work.

THE ECONOMIST

These are momentous times for the British potato crisp. Little over a generation ago the humble snack came in just a trio of flavours: ready salted, cheese and onion, or salt and vinegar. Today the choice is tongue-tingling: Thai sweet chilli, balsamic vinegar and caramelised onion, Oriental red curry, lime and coriander chutney, vintage cheddar and onion chutney, buffalo mozzarella and herbs, chicken tikka masala. And those are merely the varieties confected by a single crispmaker, Walkers, a division of PepsiCo, which turns out 10m bags of crisps every day for the British market alone. Venture towards the gourmet fringes of the crisp offering, and the choice and exoticism multiply: jalapeño pepper, roast ox, horseradish and sour cream, Ludlow sausage with wholegrain mustard. Crisps these days can be crinkle-cut, thick-cut, ridge-cut, square-cut, hand-fried, reduced fat, sold in six-packs, grab bags, party size or family packs.

Wheel a trolley down the aisle of any modern Western hypermarket, and the choice of all sorts is dazzling. The average American supermarket now carries 48,750 items, according to the Food Marketing Institute, more than five times the number in 1975. Britain's Tesco stocks 91 different shampoos, 93 varieties of toothpaste and 115 of household cleaner. Carrefour's hypermarket in the Paris suburb of Montesson, a hangar-like place filled with everything from mountain bikes to foie gras, is so vast that staff circulate on rollerblades.

Choice seduces the modern consumer at every turn. Lattes come tall, short, skinny, decaf, flavoured, iced, spiced or frappé. Jeans come flared, bootlegged, skinny, cropped, straight, low-rise, bleach-rinsed, dark-washed or distressed. Moisturiser nourishes, lifts, smooths, revitalises, conditions, firms, refreshes and rejuvenates. Tropicana, another part of PepsiCo, turns out freshly pulped juice in more than 20 different varieties, up from just six in 2004; it says there could be as many as 30 in the next decade.

Thanks to a mix of modern medicine, technology and social change, choice has expanded from the grocery shelf to areas that once had few or none. Faces, noses, wrinkles, breasts and bellies can be remodelled, plumped or tucked. America in 2008 alone saw 2.5m Botox injections, 355,671 breast implants, 341,144 liposuction treatments, 195,104 eyelid lifts and 147,392 stomach tucks, according to the American Society for Aesthetic Plastic Surgery.

Teenagers can choose to surf, chat, tweet, zap or poke in ways that their parents can barely fathom. Moving pictures and music can be viewed, recorded, downloaded or streamed on all manner of screens or devices. The internet has handed huge power to the consumer to research options, whether of medical procedures or weekend breaks. Even the choice of price-comparison sites to help people choose is expanding.

Offline choices have multiplied too. European Union citizens can move, study, work and live wherever they like within the union. Vouchers and other school reforms in many countries give parents increasing choice over where to send their children. Modular university courses offer students endless combinations. The University of California, Berkeley, has over 350 degree programmes, including Buddhist Studies and Lesbian, Gay, Bisexual and Transgender Studies, each made up of scores of courses.

Choice has come to some of life's biggest personal decisions as well. In many countries couples can decide whether and where to marry, cohabit, divorce or remarry. Internet dating promises to find a match from a database of potential partners. Women in the rich world can choose when, and whether, to reproduce. "Do I want a baby? Will I find love again? Is this it?" screams the front cover of one recent women's magazine. Mothers (and sometimes fathers) can choose to work, or not, or take time off to raise children and then go back to their jobs. New life can be created against the odds. For sufferers from many chronic illnesses, life in old age can be prolonged—or ended.

Too Much of a Good Thing

Many of these options have improved life immeasurably in the rich world, and to a lesser extent in poorer parts. They are testimony to human ingenuity and innovation. Free choice is the basis on which markets work, driving competition and generating economic growth. It is the cornerstone of liberal democracy. The 20th century bears the scars of too many failed experiments in which people had no choice. But amid all the dizzying possibilities, a nagging question lurks: is so much extra choice unambiguously a good thing?

Over the past decade behavioural scientists have come up with some intriguing insights. In one landmark experiment, conducted in an upmarket grocery store in California, researchers set up a sampling table with a display of jams. In the first test they offered a tempting array of 24 different jams to taste; on a different day they displayed just six. Shoppers who took part in the sampling were rewarded with a discount voucher to buy any jam of the same brand in the store. It turned out that more shoppers stopped at the display when there were 24 jams. But when it came to buying afterwards, fully 30% of those who stopped at the six-jam table went on to purchase a pot, against merely 3% of those who were faced with the selection of 24.

The researchers repeated the experiment with chocolate as well as student essay topics and found similar results. Too much choice, concluded Sheena Iyengar of Columbia University and Mark Lepper of Stanford, is demotivating. Others have since come up with similar results from experiments with writing pens, gift boxes, coffee and even American 401(k) pension plans. (It is not all that way: German researchers, by contrast, found that shoppers were not put off by too much choice, whether of jams, chocolates or jelly beans—though this may be down to Germany's price-conscious shoppers and the sheer dreariness of the country's supermarkets.)

Expectations have been inflated to such an extent that people think the perfect choice exists.

As options multiply, there may be a point at which the effort required to obtain enough information to be able to distinguish sensibly between alternatives outweighs the benefit to the consumer of the extra choice. "At this point," writes Barry Schwartz in "The Paradox of Choice," "choice no longer liberates, but debilitates. It might even be said to tyrannise." In other words, as Mr Schwartz puts it, "the fact that *some* choice is good doesn't necessarily mean that *more* choice is better."

Daniel McFadden, an economist at the University of California, Berkeley, says that consumers find too many options troubling because of the "risk of misperception and miscalculation, of misunderstanding the available alternatives, of misreading one's own tastes, of yielding to a moment's whim and regretting it afterwards," combined with "the stress of information acquisition." Indeed, the expectation of indecision can prompt panic and a failure to choose at all. Too many options means too much effort to make a sensible decision: better to bury your head under a pillow, or have somebody else pick for you. The vast majority of shoppers in the Californian grocery store faced

with 24 jam varieties simply chose not to buy any. The more expensive an item—a car, say—the more daunting the decision. As the French saying has it: "Trop de choix tue le choix" (too much choice kills the choice).

Surely, though, knowing that lots of choice is out there still feels good? The thrill is in the anticipation of falling upon the perfect Tuscan hotel, or shade of duck-egg blue with which to repaint the kitchen. Or the reassurance that competition to supply all that choice of electricity or telephony is keeping prices down and pushing service up. But not, according to psychologists, if more choice raises expectations too high, which may make even a good decision feel bad. The potential for regret about the options not taken—the faster car, the hotel with the better view—seems to be greater in the face of multiple choices.

Expectations have been inflated to such an extent that people think the perfect choice exists, argues Renata Salecl in her book "Choice." Consider seduction. Bookshops are crowded with self-help guides and self-improvement manuals with titles such as "How to Choose & Keep Your Partner" or "Love is a Choice." Internet dating sites promise to find the perfect match with just a few clicks of the mouse. This nourishes the hope of making the ideal choice, she says, as well as the fanciful idea that there are "quick, rational solutions to the complicated question of seduction."

Confusion, indecision, panic, regret, anxiety: choice seems to come at a price. In one episode of "The Simpsons," Marge takes Apu shopping in a new supermarket, Monstromart, whose cheery advertising slogan is "where shopping is a baffling ordeal." "How is it," muses Ms Salecl, "that in the developed world this increase in choice, through which we can supposedly customise our lives and make them perfect leads not to more satisfaction but rather to greater anxiety, and greater feelings of inadequacy and guilt?" A 2010 study by researchers at the University of Bristol found that 47% of respondents thought life was more confusing than it was ten years ago, and 42% reported lying awake at night trying to resolve problems.

It could be that today's children, growing up in a world of abundant choice, will find decisions even harder to make when they grow up. Their lives may be packed with instant choices as they zap from one site to another while texting a friend and listening to music on YouTube. But much of this is reflexive activity. The digital generation is doing what Mr Schwartz calls "picking," not "choosing:" "With a world of choices rushing by like a music video," he says, "all a picker can do is grab this or that and hope for the best." Young people have grown up with masses of choice, says Dan O'Neil, a British life coach who helps people overcome indecision, "but they have never learned to make a choice and run with it. In adult life, they aren't equipped to cope."

Following the Crowd

Ever since the 19th century, when Levi Strauss began to stitch denim jeans for Americans and Abram Lyle started to sell tins of golden syrup to the English, brand managers have made it their business to offer shoppers an easier life. Brands simplify choices. They are a guarantee of quality or consistency in a confusing market, and a badge of trust. Companies spend heavily on marketing and legal advice to protect or reinvent their brands and keep customers loyal, exploiting customers' aversion to choice.

The more that options multiply, the more important brands become. Today, when paralysed by bewildering choice, a consumer will often turn to a brand that is cleverly marketed to appear to be one that others trust.

In Italo Calvino's novel "Mr Palomar," the eponymous hero is dazzled by the mouth-watering variety of cheese he comes across at a fine Parisian *fromagerie.* "Mr Palomar's spirit vacillates between contrasting urges: the one that aims at complete, exhaustive knowledge and could be satisfied only by tasting all the varieties; and the one that tends toward an absolute choice, the identification of the cheese that is his alone," writes Mr Calvino. In the end, "he stammers; he falls back on the most obvious, the most banal, the most advertised, as if the automatons of mass civilisation were waiting only for this moment of uncertainty on his part in order to seize him again and have him at their mercy."

The anti-globalisation and green movements have stirred a consumer backlash against a surfeit of choice

Despite the crisp flavourologists' best efforts, there is a limit to how many packs can be stacked on a supermarket shelf. What of stuff that is distributed digitally, however, where choice is almost limitless? Technology has cut media distribution costs and made available a vast new array of material that caters to specialised or obscure tastes, in music, video or the written word. In this universe of proliferating choice, demand is said to be shifting from a few mass products (at the head of the distribution curve) towards a great many niche interests (at the tail end), as argued by Chris Anderson in "The Long Tail."

It turns out, however, that despite the availability of all the extra stuff the hits are as important as ever. In 2009 there were 558 films released in America, up from 479 in 2000, not to mention the gigabytes of videos and film uploaded or shared online. Yet it was also the year in which one film, James Cameron's "Avatar," broke all box-office records to become the highest-grossing film ever, beating the director's own 1997 blockbuster, "Titanic." However many niches there are, in other words, filmgoers or TV viewers still want to watch what everybody else is watching, and musicians still manage to release mega-hits. Indeed, in a world that celebrates individualism and freedom, many people decide to watch, wear or listen to exactly the same things as everybody else.

When Less Is More

In small corners of the temples of consumption, business has begun to wake up to the perils of excess choice. Some firms employ "choice architects" to help guide consumers' decision-making and curb confusion. Tropicana's extra fruit-juice varieties boosted sales by 23% in Britain in 2009. But now the company puts colour-coded bottletops on sub-categories of juice to help customers "navigate what can be a difficult range," says Patrick Kalotis, its marketing director in Britain. In "Nudge," Richard Thaler and Cass Sunstein, two American academics, cite a study of company retirement plans. When a default option automatically selected an investment portfolio, saving employees the chore of picking their own mix of assets, participation shot up from 9% to 34%.

Some firms have pruned their ranges to avoid confusing shoppers. For example, Glidden, an American paint brand, decided in 2009 to reduce its palette of wall colours from an eye-dazzling 1,000 to a mere 282 because of a change in "Americans' priorities from 'more is better' to 'less is more.'" L'Astrance, a three-star Michelin restaurant in Paris's swanky 16th arrondissement, offers no choice at all on its menu: Pascal Barbot, the chef, concocts what he fancies from produce picked up in the market that day. And sometimes less really is more. When Procter & Gamble, an American consumer-products company, thinned its range of Head & Shoulders shampoos from 26 to 15, sales increased by 10%, according to Sheena Iyengar in "The Art of Choosing."

"Traditionally, companies said that it's all about the customer, and therefore give them everything they want," says Glen Williams of Bain, a consultancy. "In reality, this can make it difficult to identify which products the customer really wants, and can create problems for managing the business." Offering too many jazzy options for new cars, say, may not only confuse consumers but add to production costs and increase the potential for factory-floor bungles. A 2006 Bain study suggested that reducing complexity and narrowing choice can boost revenues by 5–40% and cut costs by 10–35%.

At the same time the anti-globalisation and green movements have stirred a consumer backlash against a surfeit of choice. Campaigns urge shoppers to buy locally grown fruit in season, and to shun cherries in winter or green beans flown in from Kenya. A "voluntary simplicity" movement calls on households to do away with excess consumer choice and lead a low-consumption, eco-friendly life. Courses promise to help people shed the distractions and stresses of the consumerist world and journey towards their inner wholeness. Short of turning the lawn over to organic vegetables and selling the car, books with such titles as "The Power of Less: The fine art of limiting yourself to the essential . . . in business and in life" or "Living Simply: Choosing less in a world of more" suggest practical ideas for cutting down on the effort of decision-making. The advice seems to boil down to shopping less often, keeping less stuff, watching less TV and sending fewer e-mails.

Life coaches offer to help with the perplexity of bigger choices. As recently as the early 1960s, in the world elegantly portrayed by a TV series, "Mad Men," society gave both women and men far fewer options. Dealing with the strains and expectations of choice is today's payback. "At a certain age, my clients have this sudden realisation that life hasn't gone quite the way they intended, and they feel stuck," says Mr O'Neil, who runs life-coaching classes. In the past they would have just got on with it. Today, he says, "they are paralysed by having too much choice."

Fifty years after the contraceptive pill was first licensed in America and 37 years after the Supreme Court legalised abortion, women seem to agonise more than ever about breeding. "We've grown up with a lot more choice than our mothers or grandmothers; for them, being child-free wasn't a choice, it was pitied," says Beth Follini, an American life coach who specialises in the "maybe baby" dilemma. "The anxiety comes from worrying about making the wrong choice." Having options seems to make people think they can have control over outcomes too. Sometimes, says Ms Follini, choosing is about learning to live without control.

Those in the business of helping people choose offer various tips. Mr O'Neil says the key is taking a decision: "The truth is that it doesn't matter what we choose, only that we do choose." Stick to the choices that matter and eliminate the rest, suggests one advocate of simple living, who supplies no fewer than 72 steps to choose from in order to simplify life. Another helpfully explains that "when you approach simple living, sometimes the decision is clear-cut. Sometimes it's not." The trouble with simplifying your life, it turns out, is that it involves too many choices.

Critical Thinking

1. With a small group of peers from your class, debate the following paragraph from the article: "As options multiply, there may be a point at which the effort required to obtain enough information to be able to distinguish sensibly between alternatives outweighs the benefit to the consumer of the extra choice. 'At this point . . . choice no longer liberates, but debilitates. . . . the fact that *some* choice is good doesn't necessarily mean that *more* choice is better.' "

2. Relate a personal choice (decision making) experience that either supports or negates the above statement.

A Shift in Meaning for 'Luxury'

More thought goes into purchases, markdowns sought—and tech reigns.

BRUCE HOROVITZ

Steve Hundley dumped his Jaguar convertible. He stopped taking Baltic cruises. And he stopped buying his wife pricey jewelry.

But last year, just as the recession raised its head, the San Diego resident paid $6,500 for an outdoor artisan pizza oven.

"We don't need the Jaguar or cruises to the Baltic," says Hundley, who at 56, is semiretired following a heart attack two years ago. "But cooking healthy food is a big priority."

> **"We don't need the Jaguar or cruises to the Baltic. But cooking healthy food is a big priority."**
>
> —Steve Hundley

Americans are dipping their toes back into the luxury pool—but with a mind-set smacked down and radically reshaped by the recession, the lure of new technologies and emerging lifestyle twists that are often as much personal as cultural.

"The luxury brands are all trying to reinvent themselves and deliver a better experience," says Milton Pedraza, CEO of the Luxury Institute, a research firm that consults for designer brands. "Apple is making all these companies rethink their business models."

It wasn't long ago that luxury primarily meant the accumulation of designer clothes, expensive jewelry and fancy cars. For some, it still does. But for many consumers, the new luxury is something seriously different.

For some, it's about owning top technology products. The four brands most admired by Americans with six-digit incomes in a recent survey by marketing specialist Affluence Collaborative were Apple, Microsoft, Best Buy and Sony.

For others, such as the Hundleys, the new luxury is about investing in a lifestyle experience that not only can help improve health but also escalate the experience of such mundane acts as baking a pizza at home.

Sales of outdoor artisan pizza ovens at Kalamazoo Outdoor Gourmet—similar to ovens used at pizza parlors—were up 48% last year and are up 74% this year.

"It creates an experience—and isn't consumable," says Pantelis "Pete" Georgiadis, president of Kalamazoo. "You can keep enjoying it for a long, long time."

For others, it's about buying luxury goods only when they're on sale—or at a steep discount.

Nearly three in four wealthy women say they'll only purchase luxuries if they can get a good deal, reports a recent survey by AgencySacks, a branding firm that consults for some of the nation's top luxury brands.

Slipping a Bit

Luxury spending slid 7.8% last year to $10.1 billion, says Spending Pulse, a consumer spending monitor from MasterCard. It's bounced back up for the first five months of 2010.

But even affluent customers continue to seek discounts, bargains and sales, says Tim Murphy, chief product officer at MasterCard. In a recent MasterCard poll, some 64% of all consumers said they were shopping sales.

"A few years ago, you'd just market access to the affluent. Now, you must market access with a discount," Murphy says.

All this was driven by the recession. "The recession made everyone stop and rethink luxury and value," Pedraza says. "Even though we're coming back, that realization has stuck."

The new world of luxury is less about designer labels and glitz and more about shopping savvy and an I-feel-good-owning-this mentality.

What luxury marketers want to know: Is this the "new normal"?

Pedraza certainly thinks so. He says that Apple and Sony are emerging as new luxury designer labels.

"With Apple, you get a better design, a better function and a better luxury experience than you do with most other luxury brands."

Pedraza recently asked the CEO of a European luxury apparel brand to name the company that the CEO sees as his toughest competitor. Without batting an eye, the CEO (whose company Pedraza won't name due to client confidentiality) said it was Apple. Apple declined to comment.

Not a Need, but a Want

But Yolanda Cummings, who works as a finance professional in Columbus, Ohio, says that to her, there are few things closer to luxury than her new Apple iPad. "I don't need it. I just wanted it because it's new, different and intriguing," she says. She paid about $699 for it. She already has a $300 Apple iPod touch and $1,600 Apple MacBook.

"I used to go overboard buying clothes," she says. "Now, I'm more inclined to purchase new technologies."

Andrew Sacks, president of AgencySacks, says he bought an iPad the first week it was introduced.

"Part of it is escapist luxury," he says. "We're living in a world where it's difficult to control a lot of things, so there's a feeling that owning new technology allows me to be more organized, more efficient and have more time."

The recession, he says, has helped to reset his own definition of luxury.

Recently, Sacks says, he reached into his closet and discovered a black leather John Varvatos jacket that he'd casually purchased several years ago for $1,500 at a New York boutique. He put the jacket in his closet—and forgot about it.

But when he recently rediscovered it—post-recession—his view of the jacket had changed entirely. "I was a little embarrassed that I could take something so expensive and put it away and not even have it on my mind," he says. "Today, I'd do a lot more research before even considering such a purchase."

For Don Contreras, luxury is the flat-screen Sony TV that he plans to buy and install in the gazebo in his backyard.

On weekends, the federal government physician from Albuquerque likes to do yard work and prune the fruit trees in his backyard. But he also likes to watch sports on TV. By placing the TV in his gazebo, he says, he'll be able to do both.

He only wants a Sony, he says, because that's the only electronics brand that he trusts. But he's waiting to buy it until he finds a really good deal.

"I'm not an impulsive buyer," he says. "I can wait."

Executives at Sony have concocted a new term to describe what their brand offers: "functional" luxury.

In a tough economy, says Stuart Redsun, marketing chief at Sony Electronics, "You don't have to worry about your product breaking down quickly."

Beyond that, he says, the functional luxury is from the product providing a new experience—such as the new Sony Cyber-shot camera, which lets folks shoot panoramic photos or new 3D TV sets that let folks experience home viewing of movies in a new way.

Another example: Sony soon will be the first consumer electronics maker with a Google feature built into its TV sets. Folks watching any show will be able to use a special remote to do a Google search on the same screen.

Sony also has pushed the value message hard. Over the holidays, for example, it bundled a new Sony TV, PlayStation gaming system, game and Blu-ray movie for $900 less than it would cost to buy the items separately.

"We sold out of all the units in that promotion," Redsun says. Sony recently rolled out a similar bundled deal that ends July 17.

Value and luxury have become synonymous.

At Neiman Marcus, "our customer's way of shopping has changed," says Karen Katz, CEO of Neiman Marcus Stores. "She is responding well to the opening and middle price points."

For example, many Manolo Blahnik designer shoes at Neiman Marcus typically sell for at least $500—and some for upwards of $900. But in the spring, Neiman Marcus had great success selling a Manolo Blahnik ballet flat for $395. "Our customer was very happy to have a Blahnik shoe for under $500," Katz says.

Bargain in the Bag

It's no accident that Coach, whose handbags used to start at about $250—and whose average retail price for a handbag hit close to $350 before the recession—launched a new line last year, Poppy, which starts at $198.

Beyond that, Coach has added more bags at lower price points—and made them more functional for women carrying devices from iPhones to iPads, says Michael Tucci, president of Coach's North American retail division. "The last thing I want you to get from this is that Coach got cheaper. We got more compelling from a value standpoint."

Consumers have responded. Coach sales are up 8% for the first nine months of its fiscal 2010.

Value, of course, is in the eye of the purchaser.

To Lori Wachs, a hedge fund partner from Philadelphia, nothing says luxury value like getting top-notch designer clothing at 40% to 70% off—simply by visiting a website.

Several times a week, she visits the luxury discount site Gilt.com, where shoppers have 36 hours or less to order luxury goods before someone else beats them to the limited number of items.

While Wachs won't say exactly what she's spent in the past 18 months, she says she's spent "thousands" of dollars on the 100 or so items she's purchased. Among them, a Chloé handbag, originally priced at $1,500, that she snatched for about $600.

"There's an adrenaline rush when there is a certain brand that you love," she says, "and after you click on it, you wait to see if it's been added to your basket—or to someone else's cart."

In two years, Gilt Groupe has amassed more than 2 million members, CEO Susan Lyne says.

"A lot of people feel like chumps if they pay full price," Lyne says. "When you get a deal on a luxury item, it makes you feel smart."

Critical Thinking

1. Define customer value. How does value play a role in post-recession consumer decision making?

2. According to this article, how has the meaning of luxury changed after the recent recession?

Logoland

Why Consumers Balk at Companies' Efforts to Rebrand Themselves

JOSEPH SCHUMPETER

One of last year's most interesting business books was Clay Shirky's "Cognitive Surplus: Creativity and Generosity in a Connected Age." The rise of the affluent society has left people with lots of time and talent to spare, Mr Shirky argues. For decades they squandered this cognitive surplus watching television. Today, thanks to the Internet, they can also channel it into more productive pursuits.

For a surprising number of people these productive pursuits involve worrying about companies' logos. Howard Schultz, the boss of Starbucks, recently announced that his company would mark its 40th anniversary this March by changing its logo a bit. The words "Starbucks" and "coffee" will disappear. And the mermaid, or siren, will be freed from her circle.

Starbucks wants to join the small club of companies that are so recognisable they can rely on nothing but a symbol: Nike and its swoosh; McDonald's and its golden arches; Playboy and its bunny; Apple and its apple. The danger is that it will join the much larger class of companies that have tried to change their logos only to be forced to backtrack by an electronic lynch mob.

As soon as the change was mooted, bloggers started blogging and tweeters began to tweet. Starbucks.com has been inundated with complaints, such as "focus on your core business and forget this foolishness." Fox News, not normally an authority on corporate marketing strategy, has likened the proposal to Prince's decision, in 1993, to swap his name for an unpronounceable symbol, an action he reversed seven years later. The protesters have plenty of success stories to inspire their efforts. Gap, a clothing retailer, abandoned a new logo in October after a week of concentrated online hazing. Tropicana (which tried to replace its straw-in-an-orange logo with a picture of a glass of orange juice) and Britain's Royal Mail (which renamed itself Consignia) held out a bit longer but eventually had to retreat.

Why do people get so upset about such changes? An obvious reason is that so many logos and names are either pig ugly or linguistically challenged. Think of BT's "piper" logo, which looked like someone drinking a yard of ale and disfigured all things BT-related for 12 years (admittedly, Britain's incumbent telecoms firm was not too popular to begin with); or the SciFi channel's decision to call itself SyFy—a name that raises the spectre of syphilis.

Moreover, the people who spend their lives creating new logos and brand names have a peculiar weakness for management drivel. Marka Hansen, Gap's president for North America, defended the firm's new logo (three letters and a little blue square) with a lot of guff about "our journey to make Gap more relevant to our customers." The Arnell Group explained its $1m redesign of Pepsi's logo with references to the "golden ratio" and "gravitational pull," arguing that "going back-to-the-roots moves the brand forward as it changes the trajectory of the future."

Ghastly stuff, to be sure. But why do aesthetically sensitive consumers harry companies to go back to old logos rather than simply shifting their loyalties elsewhere? One answer is that people have a passionate attachment to some brands. They do not merely buy clothes at Gap or coffee at Starbucks, but consider themselves to belong to "communities" defined by what they consume. A second reason is that the more choices people have, the more they seem to value the familiar. These days there are so many choices available to Western consumers—the average supermarket stocks 30,000 items and America's patent and trademark office issues some 200,000 patents a year—that they are in danger of being overwhelmed. *Homo economicus* may be capable of carefully considering all available products. But poor, fumbling *Homo sapiens* seizes on logos as a way of creating order in a confusing world.

The debate about logos reveals something interesting about power as well as passion. Much of the rage in the blogosphere is driven by a sense that "they" (the corporate stiffs) have changed something without consulting "us" (the people who really matter). This partly reflects a hunch that consumers have more power in an increasingly crowded market for goods. But it also reflects the sense that brands belong to everyone, not just to the corporations that nominally control them.

They Want Your Opinion, as Long as It's Positive

Companies have gone out of their way to encourage these attitudes. They not only work hard to create emotional bonds with consumers (Victoria's Secret is one of many firms, including *The Economist,* that encourage customers to "like" them on Facebook). They involve them in what used to be regarded as internal corporate operations. Snapple asks Snapple-drinkers to come up with ideas for new drinks. Threadless encourages people to compete to design T-shirts.

Starbucks has been in the forefront of this consumer revolution. It consults consumers on everything from the ambience of its stores to its environmental policies. It emphasises that it is not just in the business of selling coffee. It sells entry to a community of like-minded people (who are so very different from the types who get their coffee from Dunkin' Donuts or McDonald's) gathered in a "third place" that is neither home nor work.

The company's new logo hints at a big ambition. Mr Schultz wants to burst asunder the bonds created by Starbucks's humble origins as a coffee shop. Some of his cafés are to sell alcohol as well as coffee. Many more Starbucks-branded goods are to appear in supermarkets. Starbucks is to become a force in the emerging world as well as the emerged. Such changes would be difficult even for an old-fashioned corporate dictatorship. Mr Schultz is about to discover whether they are possible for a company that has made such a fuss about giving power to its customers.

Critical Thinking

1. In your opinion, why are consumers emotionally affected by changes in companies' logos?

2. Discuss the influence that bloggers and tweeters have on consumer perceptions, attitudes, and behaviors.

3. With a small group of peers from your class, develop a list of innovative ways that companies attempt to create emotional bonds with their consumers. **Economist.com/ blogs/schumpeter**

UNIT 3
Developing and Implementing Marketing Strategies

Unit Selections

Learning Outcomes

After reading this Unit, you should be able to:

- Most ethical questions seem to arise in regard to the promotional component of the marketing mix. How fair is the general public's criticism of some forms of personal selling and advertising? Give some examples.

- What role, if any, do you think the quality of a product plays in making a business competitive in consumer markets? What role does price play? Would you rather market a higher-priced, better-quality product or one that was the lowest priced? Why?

- What do you envision will be the major problems or challenges retailers will face in the next decade? Explain.

- Given the rapidly increasing costs of personal selling, what role do you think it will play as a strategy in the marketing mix in the future? What other promotion strategies will play increased or decreased roles in the next decade?

Student Website
www.mhhe.com/cls

Internet References

American Marketing Association Homepage
www.marketingpower.com

Consumer Buying Behavior
www.courses.psu.edu/mktg/mktg220_rso3/sls_cons.htm

"Strategy and timing are the Himalayas of marketing. Everything else is the Catskills."

—Al Ries

© Lars A. Niki

Marketing management objectives," the late Wroe Alderson once wrote, "are very simple in essence. The firm wants to expand its volume of sales, or it wants to handle the volume it has more efficiently." Although the essential objectives of marketing might be stated this simply, the development and implementation of strategies to accomplish them is considerably more complex. Many of these complexities are due to changes in the environment within which managers must operate. Strategies that fail to heed the social, political, and economic forces of society have little chance of success over the long run. The lead article in this section provides helpful insight suggesting a framework for developing a comprehensive marketing plan. The selections in this unit provide a wide-ranging discussion of how marketing professionals and U.S. companies interpret and employ various marketing strategies today. The readings also include specific examples from industry to illustrate their points. The articles are grouped in four sections, each dealing with one of the main strategy areas: product, pricing, distribution (place), and promotion. Because each selection discusses more than one of these areas, it is important that you read them broadly. For example, many of the articles covered in the distribution section discuss important aspects of personal selling and advertising.

Product Strategy. The essence of the marketing concept is to begin with what consumers want and need. After determining a need, an enterprise must respond by providing the product or service demanded. Successful marketing managers recognize the need for continuous product improvement and/or new product introduction.

The articles in this subsection focus on various facets of product strategy. The first article describes a methodology pinpointing how to conduct the right product market investigations in the right way. "Brand Integrity" reflects that excellence is achieved when the brand, the talent, and the customer experience are all in alignment. "Brand Apathy Calls for New Methods" argues that building market share requires a new set of tools and brand strategies designed to shift consumer preference away from competitive brands. In the next article, "Should You Launch a Fighter Brand?," Mark Ritson examines how recent economic strains are causing consumers to become more value-conscious and trade premium brands for low-priced rivals. "Everybody Loves Zappos" closes this subsection describing how Tony Hsieh uses relentless innovation, stellar service, and a staff of believers to make Zappos.com an e-commerce giant.

Pricing Strategy. Few elements of the total strategy of the "marketing mix" demand so much managerial and social attention as pricing. There is a good deal of public misunderstanding about the ability of marketing managers to control prices and even greater misunderstanding about how pricing policies are determined. New products present especially difficult problems in terms of both costs and pricing. The costs for developing a new product are usually very high, and if a product is truly new, it

cannot be priced competitively, for it has no competitors. "Rocket Plan" relates how companies can fuel success with a rigorous pricing approach. The *HBR* article, "Competing against Free," documents how free offerings are rapidly spreading beyond online markets to the physical, brick and mortar world. The authors give pointers on how incumbents can effectively fight back.

Distribution Strategy. For many enterprises, the largest marketing costs result from closing the gap in space and time between producer and consumer. In no other area of marketing is efficiency so eagerly sought after. Physical distribution seems to be the one area where significant cost savings can be achieved. The costs of physical distribution are tied closely with decisions made about the number, the size, and the diversity of marketing intermediaries between producer and consumer. The articles in this subsection scrutinize ways retailers can create value for their customers and be very competitive in the marketplace. "The Devolution of Marketing" is a thought-provoking article that argues that the current American marketing distribution model is dysfunctional, and small and medium-sized businesses operate under a misconceived ideology of producing and selling. "Retail Therapy" is an interesting narrative on how a Chinese superstar athlete and an American design firm join forces to build China's first truly global retail brand.

Promotion Strategy. The basic objectives of promotion are to inform, persuade, or remind the consumer to buy a firm's product or pay for the firm's service. Advertising is the most obvious promotional activity. However, in total dollars spent and in cost per person reached, advertising takes second place to personal selling. Sales promotion supports either personal selling and advertising, or both. Such media as point-of-purchase displays, catalogs, and direct mail place the sales promotion specialist closer to the advertising agency than to the salesperson. The articles in this final unit subsection cover such topics as noteworthy advertising campaigns, innovative guerrilla marketing techniques, the power of social networks, and the ubiquitous nature of infomercial products.

The Very Model of a Modern Marketing Plan

Successful companies are rewriting their strategies to reflect customer input and internal coordination.

SHELLY REESE

*I*t's 1996. Do you know where your marketing plan is? In a world where competitors can observe and rapidly imitate each other's advancements in product development, pricing, packaging, and distribution, communication is more important than ever as a way of differentiating your business from those of your competitors.

The most successful companies are the ones that understand that, and are revamping their marketing plans to emphasize two points:

1. Marketing is a dialog between customer and supplier.
2. Companies have to prove they're listening to their customers by acting on their input.

What Is a Marketing Plan?

At its most basic level, a marketing plan defines a business's niche, summarizes its objectives, and presents its strategies for attaining and monitoring those goals. It's a road map for getting from point A to point B.

But road maps need constant updating to reflect the addition of new routes. Likewise, in a decade in which technology, international relations, and the competitive landscape are constantly changing, the concept of a static marketing plan has to be reassessed.

Two of the hottest buzz words for the 1990s are "interactive" and "integrated." A successful marketing plan has to be both.

"Interactive" means your marketing plan should be a conversation between your business and your customers by acting on their input. It's your chance to tell customers about your business and to listen and act on their responses.

"Integrated" means the message in your marketing is consistently reinforced by every department within your company. Marketing is as much a function of the finance and manufacturing divisions as it is the advertising and public relations departments.

Integrated also means each time a company reaches out to its customers through an advertisement, direct mailing, or promotion, it is sending the same message and encouraging customers to learn more about the product.

Why Is It Important?

The interaction between a company and its customers is a relationship. Relationships can't be reproduced. They can, however, be replaced. That's where a good marketing plan comes into play.

Think of your business as a suitor, your customers as the object of your affection, and your competitors as rivals. A marketing plan is your strategy for wooing customers. It's based on listening and reacting to what they say.

Because customers' priorities are constantly changing, a marketing plan should change with them. For years, conventional wisdom was 'prepare a five year marketing plan and review it every year.' But change happens a lot faster than it did 20 or even 10 years ago.

For that reason, Bob Dawson of The Business Group, a consulting firm in Freemont, California, recommends that his clients prepare a three year plan and review it every quarter. Frequent reviews enable companies to identify potential problems and opportunities before their competition, he explains.

"Preventative maintenance for your company is as important as putting oil in your car," Dawson says. "You don't wait a whole year to do it. You can't change history but you can anticipate what's going to happen."

Essential Components

Most marketing plans consist of three sections. The first section should identify the organization's goals. The second section should establish a method for attaining them. The third section focuses on creating a system for implementing the strategy.

Although some plans identify as many as six or eight goals, many experts suggest a company whittle its list to one or two key objectives and focus on them.

"One of the toughest things is sticking to one message," observes Mark Bilfield, account director for integrated marketing of Nissan and Infiniti cars at TBWA Chiat/Day in Los Angeles, which handles national advertising, direct marketing, public relations, and promotions for the automaker. Bilfield argues that a

Illustration by Kelly Kennedy

focused, consistent message is easier to communicate to the market place and to different disciplines within the corporation than a broad, encompassing one. Therefore, he advises, "unless there is something drastically wrong with the idea, stick with it."

Section I: Goals

The goals component of your plan is the most fundamental. Consider it a kind of thinking out loud: Why are you writing this plan? What do you want to accomplish? What do you want to achieve in the next quarter? The next year? The next three years?

Like taping your New Year's resolution to the refrigerator, the goals section is a constant reminder of what you want to achieve. The key difference between a New Year's resolution and your marketing goals, however, is you can't achieve the latter alone.

To achieve your marketing goals you've got to convince your customers to behave in a certain way. If you're a soft drink manufacturer you may want them to try your company's latest wild berry flavor. If you're a new bank in town, you need to familiarize people with your name and convince them to give your institution a try. Or perhaps you're a family-owned retailer who needs to remind customers of the importance of reliability and a proven track record in the face of new competition.

The goals in each of these cases differ with the audiences. The soft drink manufacturer is asking an existing customer to try something new; the bank is trying to attract new customers; the retailer wants to retain existing customers.

Each company wants to influence its customers' behavior. The company that is most likely to succeed is the one that understands its customers the best.

There's no substitute for knowledge. You need to understand the demographic and psychographic makeup of the customers you are trying to reach, as well as the best methods for getting their attention.

Do your research. Learn as much as possible about your audience. Trade associations, trade journals and government statistics and surveys are excellent resources, but chances are you have a lot of data within your own business that you haven't tapped. Look at what you know about your customer already and find ways to bolster that information. Companies should constantly be asking clients what they want and how they would use a new product.

"If you're not asking people that use your end product, then everything you're doing is an assumption," argues Dawson.

In addition, firms should ask customers how they perceive the products and services they receive. Too often, companies have an image of themselves that they broadcast but fail to live up to. That frustrates consumers and makes them feel deceived.

Companies that claim to offer superior service often appear to renege on their promises because their definition of 'service' 'doesn't mesh with their customers,' says Bilfield.

"Airlines and banks are prime offenders," says Bilfield. "They tout service, and when the customers go into the airport or the bank, they have to wait in long lines."

The problem often lies in the company's assumptions about what customers really want. While an airline may feel it is living up to its claim of superior service because it distributes warm towels and mints after a meal, a business traveler will probably place a higher value on its competitor's on-time record and policy for returning lost luggage.

Section II: The Strategy

Unfortunately, after taking the time and conducting the research to determine who their audience is and what their message should be, companies often fail by zooming ahead with a plan. An attitude of, "OK, we know who we're after and we know what we want to say, so let's go!" seems to take over.

More often than not, that gung-ho way of thinking leads to disaster because companies have skipped a critical step: they haven't established and communicated an internal strategy for attaining their goals. They want to take their message to the public without pausing to get feedback from inside the company.

For a marketing plan to work, everyone within the company must understand the company's message and work cooperatively to establish a method for taking that message to the public.

For example, if you decide the goal of your plan is to promote the superior service your company offers, you'd better make sure all aspects of your business are on board. Your manufacturing process should meet the highest standards. Your financial department should develop credit and leasing programs that make it easier for customers to use your product. Finally, your customer relations personnel should be trained to respond to problems quickly and efficiently, and to use the contact as an opportunity to find out more about what customers want.

"I'm always amazed when I go into the shipping department of some company and say, 'What is your mission? What's the message you want to give to your end user?' and they say, 'I don't know. I just know I've got to get these shipments out on time,'" says Dawson.

Because the success of integrated marketing depends on a consistent, cohesive message, employees throughout the company need to understand the firm's marketing goals and their role in helping to fulfill them.

"It's very important to bring employees in on the process," says James Lowry, chairman of the marketing department at Ball State University. "Employees today are better than any we've had before. They want to know what's going on in the organization. They don't want to be left out."

Employees are ambassadors for your company. Every time they interact with a customer or vendor, they're marketing your company. The more knowledgeable and helpful they are, the better they reflect on your firm.

At Nordstrom, a Seattle-based retailer, sales associates are empowered to use their best judgment in all situations to make a customer happy.

"We think our sales associates are the best marketing department," said spokeswoman Amy Jones. "We think word of mouth is the best advertising you can have." As a result, although Nordstrom has stores in only 15 states, it has forged a national reputation.

If companies regard marketing as the exclusive province of the marketing department, they're destined to fail.

"Accounting and sales and other departments have to work together hand in hand," says Dawson. "If they don't, you're going to have a problem in the end."

For example, in devising an integrated marketing campaign for the Nissan 200SX, Chiat/Day marketers worked in strategic business units that included a variety of disciplines such as engineers, representatives from the parts and service department, and creative people. By taking a broad view of the business and building inter-related activities to support its goals, Chiat/Day was able to

Getting Started

A Nine-step Plan That Will Make the Difference Between Writing a Useful Plan and a Document That Gathers Dust On a Shelf

by Carole R. Hedden and the *Marketing Tools* editorial staff

In his 1986 book, *The Goal,* Eliyahu M. Goldratt writes that most of us forget the one true goal of our business. It's not to deliver products on time. It isn't even to manufacture the best widget in the world. The goal is to make money.

In the past, making money depended on selling a product or service. Today, that's changed as customers are, at times, willing to pay for what we stand for: better service, better support, more innovation, more partnership in developing new products.

This section of this article assumes that you believe a plan is needed, and that this plan should weave together your desires with those of your customers. We've reviewed a number of marketing plans and come up with a nine-step model. It is perhaps more than what your organization needs today, but none of the steps are unimportant.

Our model combines some of the basics of a conventional plan with some new threads that we believe will push your plan over the edge, from being satisfactory to being necessary. These include:

- Using and improving the former domain of public relations, image, as a marketing tool.
- Integrating all the business functions that touch your customers into a single, customer-focused strategic marketing plan.
- Borrowing from Total Quality theories to establish performance measures beyond the financial report to help you note customer trends.
- Making sure that the people needed to deliver your marketing objectives are part of your plan.
- "Selling" your plan to the people whose support is essential to its success.

Taking the Plan Off the Shelf

First, let's look at the model itself. Remember that one of the primary criticisms of any plan is that it becomes a binder on a shelf, never to be seen again until budget time next year. Planning should be an iterative process, feeding off itself and used to guide and measure.

Whether you're asked to create a marketing plan or write the marketing section of the strategic plan for your business, your document is going to include what the business is trying to achieve, a careful analysis of your market, the products and services you offer to that market, and how you will market and sell products or services to your customer.

1. Describe the Business

You are probably in one of two situations: either you need to write a description of your business or you can rely on an existing document found in your annual report, the strategic plan, or a capabilities brochure. The description should include, at minimum:

- Your company's purpose;
- Who you deliver products or services to; and
- What you deliver to those customers.

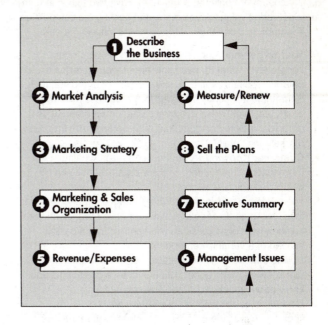

Too often, such descriptions omit a discussion about what you want your business to stand for—your image.

This is increasingly important as customers report they are looking for more than the product or service; they're in search of a partner. The only way to address image is to know who you want to be, who your customers think you are, and how you can bridge the gap between the two.

Part of defining your image is knowing where you are strong and where you are weak. For instance, if your current yield rate is 99.997 percent and customers rate you as the preferred supplier, then you might identify operations as a key to your company's image. Most companies tend to be their own worst critic, so start by listing all your strengths. Then identify weaknesses or the threats you face, either due to your own limitations or from the increased competency of a competitor.

The description also includes what your business delivers to its owners, be they shareholders, private owners, or employees. Usually this is stated in financial terms: revenue, return on investment or equity, economic value added, cash generated, operating margin or earnings per share. The other measures your organization uses to monitor its performance may be of interest to outsiders, but save them for the measurement section of your plan.

The result of all this describing and listing is that you should have a fairly good idea of where you are and where you want to be, which naturally leads to objectives for the coming 6, 12, or 18 months, if not longer.

2. Analyze the Market

This is the section you probably believe you own. *Marketing Tools* challenges you to look at this as a section jointly owned by most everyone working with you. In a smaller company, the lead managers may own various pieces of this section. In a larger organization, you may need to pull in the ideas and data available from

(continued)

other departments, such as logistics, competitor intelligence, research and development, and the function responsible for quality control or quality assurance. All have two things in common: delivering value to customers, and beating the competition. Together, you can thoroughly cover the following areas:

- **Your target markets.** What markets do you currently compete in? What do you know about them in terms of potential, dollars available, and your share of the market? Something frequently prepared for products is a life cycle chart; you might want to do the same for your market. Is it embryonic, developing, mature or in decline? Are there new markets to exploit?
- **Customer Knowledge.** Your colleagues in Quality, Distribution, Engineering, or other organizations can be helpful in finding what you need.

    The customer's objectives. What threats do your customers face? What goals does the customer have? Work with your customer to define these so you can become a partner instead of a variable component.

    How is the customer addressing her or his markets? Do you know as much about your customer's position as you know about your own? If not, find out.

    How big is each customer, really? You may find you're spending more time on a less important customer than on the customers who can break you. Is your customer growing or in decline? What plans does the customer have to expand or acquire growth? What innovations are in development?

    What does your customer value? Price, product quality, service, innovation, delivery? The better you know what's driving your customer's purchasing decision, the better you'll be able to respond.
- **Clearly identify the alternatives your customer** has. As one customer told employees at a major supplier, "While you've been figuring out how to get by, we've been figuring out how to get by without you." Is backward integration—a situation in which the customer develops the capability in-house—possible? Is there an abundance of other suppliers? What is your business doing to avoid having your customers looking for alternatives?
- **Know your competition.** Your competitors are the obvious alternative for your customer, and thus represent your biggest threat. You can find what you need to know about your competitors through newspaper reports, public records, at trade shows, and from your customers: the size of expansions, the strengths that competitor has, its latest innovations. Do you know how your competition approaches your customers?
- **Describe the Environment.** What changes have occurred in the last 18 months? In the past year? What could change in the near future and over a longer period of time? This should include any kinds of laws or regulations that might affect you, the entry or deletion of competitors, and shifts in technology. Also, keep in mind that internal change does affect your customers. For instance, is a key leader in your business planning to retire? If so, decision making, operations or management style may change—and your customer may have obvious concerns. You can add some depth to this section, too, by portraying several different scenarios:

- What happens if we do nothing beyond last year?
- What happens if we capitalize on our strengths?
- What might happen if our image slips?
- What happens if we do less this year than last?

3. The Marketing Strategy

The marketing strategy consists of what you offer customers and the price you charge. Start by providing a complete description of each product or service and what it provides to your customers. Life cycle, again, is an important part of this. Is your technology or product developing, mature or in decline? Depending on how your company is organized, a variety of people are responsible for this information, right down to whoever is figuring out how to package the product and how it will be delivered. Find out who needs to be included and make sure their knowledge is used.

The marketing strategy is driven by everything you've done up to this point. Strategies define the approaches you will use to market the company. For instance, if you are competing on the basis of service and support rather than price, your strategy may consist of emphasizing relationships. You will then develop tactics that support that strategy: market the company vs. the product; increase sales per client; assure customer responsiveness. Now, what action or programs will you use to make sure that happens?

Note: strategy leads. No program, regardless of how good it is, should make the cut if it doesn't link to your business strategies and your customer.

The messages you must craft to support the strategies often are overlooked. Messages are the consistent themes you want your customer to know, to remember, to feel when he or she hears, reads, or views anything about your company or products. The method by which you deliver your messages comes under the heading of actions or programs.

Finally, you need to determine how you'll measure your own success, beyond meeting the sales forecast. How will you know if your image takes a beating? How will you know whether the customer is satisfied, or has just given up complaining? If you don't know, you'll be caught reacting to events, instead of planning for them.

Remember, your customer's measure of your success may be quite different from what you may think. Your proposed measures must be defined by what your customer values, and they have to be quantifiable. You may be surprised at how willing the customer is to cooperate with you in completing surveys, participating in third-party interviews, or taking part in a full-scale analysis of your company as a supplier. Use caution in assuming that winning awards means you have a measurable indicator. Your measures should be stated in terms of strategies, not plaques or trophies.

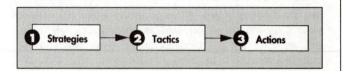

(continued)

4. The Marketing and Sales Organization

The most frequently overlooked element in business is something we usually relegate to the Personnel or Human Resources Office—people. They're what makes everything possible. Include them. Begin with a chart that shows the organization for both Marketing and Sales. You may wish to indicate any interdependent relationships that exist (for instance, with Quality).

Note which of the roles are critical, particularly in terms of customer contact. Just as important, include positions, capabilities, and numbers of people needed in the future. How will you gain these skills without impacting your cost per sale? Again, it's time to be creative and provide options.

5. Revenue and Expense

In this section, you're going to project the revenue your plan will produce. This is usually calculated by evaluating the value of your market(s) and determining the dollar value of your share of that market. You need to factor in any changes you believe will occur, and you'll need to identify the sources of revenue, by product or service. Use text to tell the story; use graphs to show the story.

After you've noted where the money is coming from, explain what money you need to deliver the projected return. This will include staff wages and benefits for your organization, as well as the cost for specific programs you plan to implement.

During this era of budget cuts, do yourself a favor by prioritizing these programs. For instance, if one of your key strategies is to expand to a new market via new technologies, products, or services, you will need to allocate appropriate dollars. What is the payback on the investment in marketing, and when will revenues fully pay back the investment? Also, provide an explanation of programs that will be deleted should a cut in funding be required. Again, combine text and spreadsheets to tell and to show.

6. Management Issues

This section represents your chance to let management know what keeps you awake at night. What might or could go wrong? What are the problems your company faces in customer relations? Are there technology needs that are going unattended? Again, this can be a collaborative effort that identifies your concerns. In addition, you may want to identify long-term issues, as well as those that are of immediate significance.

To keep this section as objective as possible, list the concerns and the business strategy or strategies they affect. What are the short-term and long-term risks? For instance, it is here that you might want to go into further detail about a customer's actions that look like the beginnings of backward integration.

7. Executive Summary

Since most senior leaders want a quick-look reference, it's best to include a one-page Executive Summary that covers these points:

- Your organization's objectives
- Budget requirements
- Revenue projections
- Critical management issues

When you're publishing the final plan document, you'll want the executive summary to be Page One.

8. Sell the Plan

This is one of the steps that often is overlooked. Selling your plan is as important as writing it. Otherwise, no one owns it, except you. The idea is to turn it into a rallying point that helps your company move forward. And to do that, you need to turn as many people as possible into ambassadors for your marketing efforts.

First, set up a time to present the plan to everyone who helped you with information and data. Make sure that they feel some sense of ownership, but that they also see how their piece ties into the whole. This is one of those instances where you need to say your plan, show your plan, discuss your plan. Only after all three steps are completed will they *hear* the plan.

After you've shared the information across the organization, reserve some time on the executive calendar. Have a couple of leaders review the plan first, giving you feedback on the parts where they have particular expertise. Then, present the plan at a staff meeting.

Is It Working?

You may think your job is finished. It's not. You need to convey the key parts of this plan to coworkers throughout the business. They need to know what the business is trying to achieve. Their livelihood, not just that of the owners, is at stake. From their phone-answering technique to the way they process an order, every step has meaning to the customer.

9. Measure/Renew

Once you've presented your plan and people understand it, you have to continuously work the plan and share information about it. The best way to help people see trends and respond appropriately is to have meaningful measures. In the language of Total Quality, these are the Key Result Indicators—the things that have importance to your customers and that are signals to your performance.

For instance, measure your ability to deliver on a customer request; the amount of time it takes to respond to a customer inquiry; your productivity per employee; cash flow; cycle time; yield rates. The idea is to identify a way to measure those things that are critical to you and to your customer.

Review those measurements. Share the information with the entire business and begin the process all over again. Seek new ideas and input to improve your performance. Go after more data and facts. And then renew your plan and share it with everyone—all over again.

It's an extensive process, but it's one that spreads the word—and spreads the ownership. It's the step that ensures that your plan will be constantly in use, and constantly at work for your business.

Carole Hedden is a writer and communication/planning consultant living in Elmira, New York.

create a seamless campaign for the 200SX that weaves advertising, in-store displays, and direct marketing together seamlessly.

"When everybody understands what the mission is, it's easier," asserts Bilfield. "It's easier to go upstream in the same direction than to go in different directions."

After bringing the different disciplines within your company on board, you're ready to design the external marketing program needed to support your goals. Again, the principle of integrated marketing comes into play: The message should be focused and consistent, and each step of the process should bring the consumer one step closer to buying your product.

In the case of Chiat/Day's campaign for the Nissan 200SX, the company used the same theme, graphics, type faces, and message to broadcast a consistent statement.

Introduced about the same time as the latest Batman movie, the campaign incorporates music and graphics from the television series. Magazine ads include an 800 number potential customers

can call if they want to receive an information kit. Kits are personalized and include the name of a local Nissan dealer, a certificate for a test drive, and a voucher entitling test drivers to a free gift.

By linking each step of the process, Chiat/Day can chart the number of calls, test drives, and sales a particular ad elicits. Like a good one-two punch, the direct marketing picks up where the national advertising leaves off, leveraging the broad exposure and targeting it at the most likely buyers.

While the elaborate 200SX campaign may seem foolproof, a failure to integrate the process at any step along the way could result in a lost sale.

For example, if a potential client were to test drive the car and encounter a dealer who knew nothing about the free gift accompanying the test drive, the customer would feel justifiably annoyed. Conversely, a well-informed sales associate who can explain the gift will be mailed to the test driver in a few weeks will engender a positive response.

Help Is on the Way

Three Software Packages That Will Help You Get Started

Writing a marketing plan may be daunting, but there is a variety of software tools out there to help you get started. Found in electronics and book stores, the tools are in many ways like a Marketing 101 textbook. The difference lies in how they help.

Software tools have a distinct advantage: They actually force you to write, and that's the toughest part of any marketing plan. Sometimes called "MBA In a Box," these systems guide you through a planning process. Some even provide wording that you can copy into your own document and edit to fit your own business. Presto! A boiler plate plan! Others provide a system of interviewing and questioning that creates a custom plan for your operation. The more complex tools demand an integrated approach to planning, one that brings together the full force of your organization, not just Sales or Advertising.

1. Crush

Crush, a modestly named new product from a modestly named new company, HOT, takes a multimedia approach. (HOT stands for Hands-On Technology; *Crush* apparently stands for *Crushing the Competition*.)

Just introduced a few months ago, *Crush* is a multimedia application for Macintosh or Windows PCs. It features the competitive analysis methods of Flegis McKenna, marketing guru to Apple, Intel and Genentech; and it features Mr. McKenna himself as your mentor, offering guidance via on-screen video. As you work through each section of a complete market analysis, McKenna provides germane comments; in addition, you can see video case studies of marketing success stories like Intuit software.

Crush provides worksheets and guidance for analyzing your products, customers, market trends and competitors, and helps you generate an action plan. The "mentor" approach makes it a

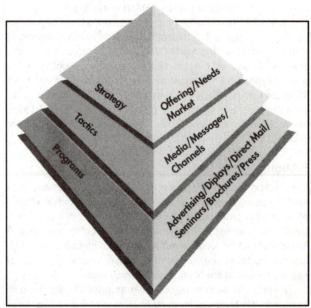

Pyramid Power: *Plan Write's* pyramid approach asks the user to define the messages for a business as part of the tactics.

useful tool for self-education; as you work through the examples and develop your company's marketing plan, you build your own expertise.

2. Marketing Plan Pro

Palo Alto's *Marketing Plan Pro* is a basic guide, useful for smaller businesses or ones in which the company leader wears

(continued)

a number of different hats, including marketing. It includes the standard spreadsheet capability, as well as the ability to chart numerical data. *Marketing Plan Pro* uses a pyramid process.

I liked the pyramid for a simple reason: It asks you to define messages for your business as part of your tactics. Without a message, it's easy to jump around, reacting to the marketplace instead of anticipating, leaving customers wondering what really is significant about your company or your product.

The step-by-step process is simple, and a sample plan shows how all the information works together. The customer-focus aspect of the plan seemed a little weak, demanding only sales potential and buying capacity of the customers. Targeted marketing is increasingly important, and the user may want to really expand how this section is used beyond what the software requires.

The package displays, at a glance, your strategy, the tactics you develop for each strategy, and the action plan or programs you choose to support the strategy. That could help when you're trying to prioritize creative ideas, eliminating those that really don't deliver what the strategy demands. Within each of three columns, you can click on a word and get help. Click on the heading program: a list of sample actions is displayed. They may not be what you're looking for, but if this is your first plan, they're lifesavers.

I also really liked *Marketing Plan Pro's* user's manual. It not only explains how the software works with your computer, it helps with business terms and provides a guide to planning, walking you through step-by-step.

3. Plan Write

Plan Write, created by Business Resource Software, Inc., is exponentially more powerful than *Marketing Plan Pro. Plan Write* brings together the breadth of the business, integrating information as far flung as distribution systems and image. And this software places your marketing strategy within the broader context of a business plan, the approach that tends to prove most effective.

As with *Marketing Plan Pro, Plan Write* provides a sample plan. The approach is traditional, incorporating a look at the business environment, the competition, the product or service mix you are offering, the way you will tell customers about that mix, pricing, delivery, and support.

Among the sections that were particularly strong was one on customer alternatives and people planning. Under the heading of customer alternatives, you're required to incorporate competitive information with customer information. If you don't meet the customer's needs, where could he or she go? Most often we look only at the competition, without trying to imagine how the customer is thinking. This exercise is particularly valuable to the company who leads the market.

The people part of planning too often is dumped on the personnel guy instead of being seen as a critical component of your organization's capabilities. *Plan Write* requires that you include how marketing is being handled, and how sales will be accomplished. In addition, it pushes you to define what skills will be needed in the future and where the gaps are between today and the future. People, in this plan, are viewed as a strategic component.

Plan Write offers a fully integrated spreadsheet that can import from or export to most of the popular spreadsheet programs you may already be using. Another neat feature allows you to enter numerical data and select from among 14 different graphing styles to display your information. You just click on the style you want to view, and the data is reconfigured.

Probably the biggest danger in dealing with software packages such as *Marketing Plan Pro* and *Plan Write* is to think the software is the answer. It's merely a guide.

—Carole Hedden

Section III: Execution

The final component of an integrated marketing plan is the implementation phase. This is where the budget comes in.

How much you'll need to spend depends on your goals. If a company wants to expand its market share or promote its products in a new region, it will probably have to spend more than it would to maintain its position in an existing market.

Again, you'll need to create a system for keeping your employees informed. You might consider adding an element to your company newsletter that features people from different departments talking about the marketing problems they encounter and how they overcome them. Or you might schedule a regular meeting for department heads to discuss marketing ideas so they can report back to their employees with news from around the company.

Finally, you'll need to devise a system for monitoring your marketing program. A database, similar to the one created from calls to the 200SX's 800 number, can be an invaluable tool for determining if your message is being well received.

It's important to establish time frames for achieving your goals early in the process. If you want to increase your market share, for instance, you should determine the rate at which you intend to add new customers. Failing to achieve that rate could signal a flaw in your plan or its execution, or an unrealistic goal.

"Remember, integrated marketing is a long-range way of thinking," warns Dawson. "Results are not going to be immediate."

Like any investment, marketing requires patience, perseverance, and commitment if it is to bear fruit. While not all companies are forward thinking enough to understand the manifold gains of integrated marketing, the ones that don't embrace it will ultimately pay a tremendous price.

Critical Thinking

1. What is the purpose of a marketing plan for a company?

2. Outline and briefly summarize the elements of the marketing plan.

SHELLY REESE is a freelance writer based in Cincinnati.

Surveyor of the Fittest

With the correct methodology, companies can effectively assess what market is viable and what market is not.

HONGJUN (HJ) LI

Industry research shows that 75% of new-product launches fail in the marketplace (visit www.microsoft .com to read its section about new-product development performance). That number does not even include product concepts that never successfully enter the market. There are many reasons for such failures, but lack of market demand for new products introduced is definitely the most important one.

According to an AMR Research Inc. report released in June 2005: Out of 20 large manufacturers polled about poor performance of product launches, 47% cited failing to understand and meet customer needs exactly—compared with 33% citing being late to market and 23% citing poor pricing.

No company will develop and introduce a new product if it knows beforehand that there will be no market demand. Unfortunately, most companies try to justify new-product development (NPD) expenditures by doing some market analysis—only to find out later that projected market demand has failed to materialize. Thus, a critical question to industry players is how they can become more effective in their market assessment efforts. This article offers a practical methodology that answers the question.

Defining "New Product"

For the purpose of this article, "new product" refers to one of the following:

- a product that creates or implements a new technology
- a product that implements an existing technology on a new platform
- a product that integrates multiple technologies or functions into a single product for the first time
- a product that provides significant enhancements to an existing product category

Executive Briefing

You might be surprised at how many new-product introductions fail every year. Unfortunately, such failure is not necessarily due to lack of market investigation. That is not to state, however, that market investigation is not relevant anymore. On the contrary: The industry's poor performance with new-product introductions pinpoints the importance of doing the right market investigation the right way. Here is a systematic, effective, and easy-to-follow methodology that illustrates exactly how to accomplish that.

The focus of our discussion is the overall market, not company-specific issues that can also lead to new-product introduction failures. There are many cases in which market demand for a new-product category exists but a particular company's product—falling into that category—fails in the market because of poor internal execution. Although internal execution is certainly critical, companies must first and foremost understand whether there will be a market for their new products being conceived or developed. Market investigation, in other words, remains highly relevant.

We will also assume that when a new product is introduced, it works—and its functionality conforms to original design requirements or intentions. Product failures attributed to unintended design flaws or quality problems are excluded from the scope of discussion. Again, such issues are internal and not market-related.

Common Pitfalls

Because so many new-product introduction failures can be attributed to lack of market demand, it is necessary to understand why companies fail to foresee them in the first place. Granted that market forecasting is sometimes a very difficult thing to do, companies can significantly reduce risks of new-product introduction failures if they do some basic market assessment homework the right way.

In general, the following are the common market assessment pitfalls into which companies fall:

- blind faith in one's capability to drive or create market demand
- looking at technological merits only
- selective use of incomplete, biased, or deceiving market data and feedback in line with product concepts or initial decisions
- taking input from direct customers only, without looking at demand from customers' customers (when applicable)
- relying on feedback or data of customer/consumer interest only, without looking at many other market factors that drive actual purchase decisions
- depending on third-party market forecasts only, without looking at or fully understanding the methodology used and assumptions made

Some companies might achieve market success even if they fall into one of these pitfalls, but such success requires really good luck and can hardly be duplicated in different settings.

Assessing the Market

Market assessment can be viewed as a science or an art. The challenge to market research professionals: Although some commonly used research techniques and tools exist, they might not be adequate to address the complete scope of market assessment required for sound business decision making. The challenge to senior executives is that they don't have the time to do detailed market investigations themselves. In addition, they might not have an effective framework for judging the quality and reliability of their subordinates' market assessments.

Both dedicated market research professionals and senior executives can use the methodology suggested here. The former can use it to investigate all the key aspects of a new product's market potential; the latter can use it to evaluate their subordinates' work. The methodology, if used the right way, can help companies avoid the aforementioned pitfalls.

The individual elements in the suggested market assessment framework are nothing new (see Figure 1). What might be new, however, are identification of all major market-related factors that affect demand for a new product, categorization of these factors within a systematic framework, and a step-by-step process that is easy to follow: (1) define target segment and needs, (2) analyze relative value, and (3) evaluate food-chain and ecosystem risks.

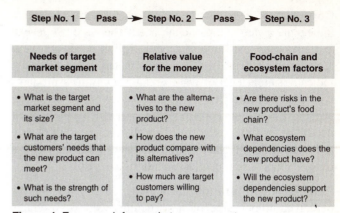

Figure 1 Framework for market assessment.

Note: Customers are those that make purchase decisions (in the case of business-to-business and business-to-consumer). Customers might be different from end users in the case of business-to-business-to-consumer.

Defining Target and Needs

With rare exceptions, a particular new product serves only a particular market segment or niche. This is especially true in the consumer-technology market. If a new product to be introduced simply targets "everybody," then it will most likely have a tough road ahead—because different segments and niches have different needs. There is a direct correlation between clarity of market-segment definition and ability to meet target customers' specific needs. Not surprisingly, the phenomenon of "shoot and aim" can explain why so many new products fail.

Defining the target market segment entails a detailed analysis of key segment characteristics such as size, demographics, and purchasing behavior. Without a clear understanding of the target segment, it will be difficult to identify the needs that a new product can meet.

Associating a generic need with a product is easy, and it can mislead companies into believing that their new product meets target customers' needs. To avoid that pitfall, companies can ask a simple question: What, exactly, is the problem that the new product solves?

Take the failed WebTV (a set-top box that consumers connect to their television sets, which allows dial-up Internet connection), for example. Consumers with a personal computer (PC) at home do not need it for Internet access. WebTV does allow non-PC households to access the Internet; unfortunately, the amount of non-PC households with such a need is very small. Moreover, WebTV cannot address that need well because of poor display of Web content on a standard-definition TV.

Even if the specific need for a new product is identified or defined, companies must assess the strength of that need, as different strength levels mean different market sizes. In general, two variables influence the relative strength of the need for a product: cognizance and perceived importance.

Cognizance. This determines to what extent target customers are aware of a particular need. There are two levels: explicit needs and implicit needs. Explicit needs are well-recognized and can be clearly articulated. They normally indicate a high level of need strength. Only new products with meaningful differentiation (to be discussed next) can turn these needs into corresponding market demand. Implicit needs, on the other hand, are not well-recognized or clearly articulated. They typically represent a new market that takes time, resources, and market education to develop.

Perceived importance. Depending on how strong the perceived importance of a particular need is, products meeting a particular need can fit into three categories: must-have, nice-to-have, and can-live-without. Must-have products meet the needs with the highest level of perceived importance and have the broadest market reach. Nice-to-have products address less-important needs and therefore have lower market demand. Can-live-without products generally have the lowest market-penetration rate.

Although measuring need strength can be difficult and subjective, it is a critical element of market analysis. A common method of need-strength assessment is conducting a quantitative survey to ask consumers their interest level in a particular new product or service. The challenge, however, is that different survey designs can yield significantly different results even if the same topic is addressed. Thus, as mentioned, understanding methodologies used and assumptions made is vital to appropriate interpretation of survey results.

One example of different survey results on the same topic is a study on consumers' interest in watching video on mobile devices. A survey by RBC Capital Markets shows that only 24% are interested, whereas a study by The Diffusion Group shows that 32% are interested. The delta can be attributed to differences in measurement scales (true/false versus a 7-point scale) and age groups of survey respondents (ages 21–65 versus ages 15–50). (Read "The Appeal of Mobile Video: Reading Between the Lines" under the TDG Opinions section at www.tdgresearch.com.)

Regardless of which is right (or closer to being correct), consumer interest is only one variable; other factors also drive market demand for a new product. This is why completing the following second step is essential, too.

Analyzing Relative Value

In today's environment, in which new technologies are rapidly emerging, consumers are having more and more choices that meet the same needs. For a new product to succeed in the marketplace, it will need to deliver a more compelling value proposition than alternative solutions by accomplishing at least one of the following: being a better product for a similar price and/or having a better price for a similar product. It is noteworthy that the higher market penetration alternatives have already achieved, the more important it is for new products to have strong differentiation in features/performance or cost.

The main reason voice over Internet protocol (VoIP) has been able to gain traction in both business and consumer markets is that it can deliver the same service as traditional wireline voice but at a lower cost. VoIP also enables certain features not available from "plain old telephone service" (POTS), but lower cost is the main driver of market adoption.

On the other hand, independent VoIP-over-broadband operators (at least those in the United States) have had difficulties quickly penetrating the consumer market without spending tons of marketing dollars. That is because of the availability of four primary alternatives: existing POTS, mobile phone service, Skype-type (a peer-to-peer Internet telephony network) services, and inexpensive VoIP phone cards. Those services either make voice communications an already fulfilled need or deliver cost savings similar to VoIP-over-broadband.

The same thing can be said of telcos' Internet protocol television (IPTV) service. In many markets, especially the United States, cable and satellite television have already made home-video entertainment a fulfilled need. If telcos' IPTV offers only me-too video services, then the most effective way for it to gain market share from cable and satellite television companies is to offer a lower price—as part of a discounted service bundle or a lower cost, stand-alone service. Alternatively, telcos can develop new applications: true video on demand and other innovative, compelling services that leverage the Internet protocol network.

Alternative solutions are not limited to similar products from direct competitors. They also include various other substitutes that address the same need. For example, the use of hands to turn lights on or off is an alternative to a lighting-control home-automation solution that requires a purchase—even though the former is less convenient. As taught in any Economics 101 course, substitutes create a negative impact on demand for a particular product.

Even if a cool new product has no or few existing alternatives and addresses a specific need, affordability or customers' price elasticity will determine its market penetration. A good example is high-end home-control (also called home-automation) systems. Of course they are not truly new products today, as a category, but they were when introduced about three decades ago. Those systems address consumers' need for comfort, convenience, safety, and prestige. However, because of high price tags (typically tens of thousands of dollars), high-end home-control systems have found success only in the custom-installed electronics market. And today's household penetration rate in the United States is still less than 2%, according to Parks Associates (an industry analyst firm).

Evaluating Risks

Suppose a new-product concept passes the test of the previous two steps; there is still no guarantee of market success. This third step prompts companies to identify market risks from a new product's food chain and its ecosystem. In this article, "ecosystem" refers to the interdependency of a certain set of infrastructure elements, platforms, devices, and other components that function as a whole to meet a particular need of customers.

From a market perspective, food-chain risks arise from direct customers' business model issues or uncertainty of demand from customers' customers. Although food-chain risks do not apply to everybody, they can be significant in certain sectors. For example, food-chain issues can explain the failure of some telecommunications equipment companies—and their products—that specifically targeted competitive local exchange carriers (CLECs) in the 1990s in the United States. Various newly developed products for CLECs, at that time, could certainly pass the test of the previous two steps. But they failed eventually because their CLEC customers did not have a sustainable business model after capital market bubbles burst.

Food-chain risks can also apply to a company in the business-to-business-to-consumer market. Assume that a service provider has just approached a vendor of videophones for the deployment of a new service. To assess how many units the vendor can actually sell, it will need to carefully assess consumers' potential take rate, partially based on the service provider's marketing and pricing plans. If the service provider cannot sign up many subscribers to the service that involves the use of a videophone, then the vendor will not be able to sell many units either—no matter how rosy the service provider's deployment plan appears to be.

A new product might also face significant market risks if it has too much dependency on certain ecosystem elements beyond the product developer's control. Products that enable delivery of online video to the television represent a good example. The main device that has such capability is the digital media adapter (DMA), a special set-top box that connects to both the television and a home network. For DMA to succeed as a product category, it will need support from at least the following ecosystem elements:

- wide availability of high-quality online video content, which is subject to Hollywood's receptivity to digital-content distribution and compatible digital-rights management solutions
- attractive pricing from content owners
- high penetration of robust, no-new-wire home networking solutions for multimedia distribution (beyond Ethernet and 802.11b/g, a wireless LAN standard)
- wide deployment of higher-bandwidth broadband access networks beyond ADSL1 or DOCSIS1.0 (Asymmetric Digital Subscriber Line, Data Over Cable Service Interface Specification)

DMA devices first appeared on the consumer market around 2003. Over the past few years, however, very few units have been sold (according to research from Parks Associates and NPD). The poor showing of DMA as a product category can be attributed to not only factors illustrated in the previous two steps but also poor ecosystem support (e.g., very limited availability of quality online video content, various home networking issues). Going forward, though, the DMA market is expected to gain stronger momentum—this time driven by positive developments of the ecosystem.

Implementing the Process

The person or team responsible for market intelligence should (1) develop detailed output based on the key questions in the three aforementioned steps and then (2) provide an overall assessment (see Figure 2). The market intelligence function should present to executives not only the overall assessment but also a summary of the detailed output—so they can see how conclusions are reached.

To judge the quality and reliability of the market intelligence function's work, executives can ask themselves three simple questions:

- Is there clear definition of the target market segment, the specific needs of target customers, and the strength of their needs?
- Is there adequate assessment of the impact from alternatives and customers' price elasticity?
- Are food-chain and ecosystem risks clearly identified and evaluated?

Steps	Detailed output
Step No. 1: Needs of target market segment	• definition of the target market segment and estimate of the total size of the target segment • definition of the specific needs that the new product can address • categorization of the strength of the identified needs: level of cognizance and importance
Step No. 2: Relative value for the money	• list of alternatives to the new product and their market penetration rate • feature and price comparison between alternatives and the new product • target customers' price elasticity and estimated market adoption rate at specific price points
Step No. 3: Food-chain and ecosystem factors	• analysis of viability of target customers' business model specific to the new product • list of ecosystem elements that the new product depends on • the current status and projected future developments of the identified ecosystem elements
Overall assessment	• qualitative assessment of the viability of the new product's market • quantitative projections of the total available market in terms of units and revenues (if feasible and needed)

Figure 2 The market intelligence function's implementation.

Note: Certain items of the output list can be omitted only if relevant facts (1) are already common knowledge to everybody or (2) do not apply to a particular new product.

Market assessment results		Yellow light	Red light
Needs of target market segment	Difficult-to-define target market segment		X
	Difficult-to-define specific needs of target customers		X
	Implicit needs	X	
	Nice-to-have product	X	
	Can-live-without product		X
Relative value for the money	Presence of alternatives with a high market penetration rate	X	
	High price elasticity of target customers	X	
Food-chain and ecosystem factors	Questionable business model of target customers		X
	Too much ecosystem dependency	X	
	Lack of ecosystem support		X

Figure 3 New-product development risk assessment.

Yellow light: Market demand is limited or has substantial uncertainties.
Red light: Market demand is very limited or has very high uncertainties.

A tool for executive decision making. How should the three-step market assessment process be used for NPD decision-making purposes? As different companies have different business models, financial objectives, market power, and so forth, perhaps there is no clear-cut answer that applies to everybody. However, executives might find Figure 3's risk-assessment framework (based on the three-step process) a useful tool for distilling output from the market intelligence function and making decisions on NPD projects.

If yellow lights are associated with a new-product concept, then executives will need careful assessment of the new product's value proposition and market positioning before making a "go" decision on product development. If a new-product concept faces one or more red lights, then there will be high risks of market failure—and executives might be better off allocating development resources to an alternative new product that addresses a more viable market.

How often should the process be used? In fast-changing industries or markets, it is probably necessary for that market assessment framework to be used more than once for the entire NPD process. That will allow companies to not only reduce new-product introduction failure risks but also identify new market opportunities in a timely fashion.

Other participants in the market assessment process. Although the market intelligence function and executives are the most direct users of the recommended market assessment framework, a few other functions should be included: product management, sales, marketing, strategic planning, and engineering managers. Their inclusion can take the form of providing input, reviewing output, and communicating relevant findings to individual team members. The more synchronized the internal communication, the more capabilities companies will have for developing and selling new products that meet market needs.

Avoiding the Trap

There have been too many cases in which companies developed new technologies or products looking for problems to solve. To avoid falling into such a trap, companies can complete the aforementioned three simple steps. Afterward, they will be in a much better position to assess the market viability of a new-product concept and whether product development resources should be committed to it.

Critical Thinking

1. In your opinion, what are some possible reasons for the failure of new-product introductions?

2. You have been assigned as a consultant for a business that is looking to develop a new product. Prepare a list of DOs and DON'Ts to help it design a new product development process and a successful market introduction.

HONGJUN (HJ) LI is director of product marketing at the Plano, Texas, office of Kodiak Networks, a startup specializing in advanced mobile-communication applications headquartered in San Ramon, Calif. He may be reached at hli@kodiaknetworks.com or hongjunli888@ yahoo.com. To join the discussion about this article, please visit www.marketingpower.com/marketingmanagementblog.

From *Marketing Management*, September/October 2007, pp. 39–44. Copyright © 2007 by American Marketing Association. Reprinted by permission.

Brand Integrity

It starts with internal focus.

TOM PETERS AND VALARIE WILLIS

After the layoffs and budget cuts, now what do you do? Are you living up to your brand promises, or are you falling short on customer experiences? How can you sustain your brand and the power of your values? When you focus only on the bottom line and ignore people, your brand suffers—as your customers lose sight of what you stand for, and they no longer trust what you can deliver.

What about Your Brand?

The news is full of stories about downsizing, job evaporations, and budgets being slashed to shreds. So, what happens to your brand? Does it survive? Or is it bruised and battered? As a leader, you are responsible for the integrity of your brand. You need to pull your head out of the financial data long enough to assess the current state of your brand and of your talent.

When you experience a strong economic shift, your brand can easily become diluted, especially if no one is asking, "What about the brand?"

In the hub of your organization is your talent, and your talent is your brand. It is the talent that brings your brand to life. If your people (talent) are no longer happy, if they are concerned about their own welfare, or they are hunkered down to stay out of sight, your brand may be on its last breath as well. And when the brand is struggling, the customer experience is compromised. Talent can become non-caring and cynical, and these attitudes permeate into how customers experience the brand.

Whenever you experience a strong shift, you must recalibrate and set the organization back on course. As a leader, you can best do this by taking these five steps: 1) revisit the ambition or goal of the organization and connect people to it; 2) spend time on the front lines talking to people and getting a handle on the issues; 3) re-state the brand promise and ensure that everyone knows how his or her job affects the promise; 4) look at the changes and assess the impact on the brand and the impact on the customer experience; and 5) design a course of action to put the brand back on track.

If your brand is bruised and battered, your customers may be headed to the competition—the exact opposite of your aims. In tough economic times, focus on keeping your current loyal customers and clients. Now is the time to re-think how to make the brand truly distinctive in the marketplace.

Excellence is achieved when the brand, the talent, and the customer experience are all in alignment.

Excellence Audit

To learn how your organization is doing, and if it needs recalibration, take our *Excellence Audit*. The 50 characteristics in the *Excellence Audit* describe the seven elements that interact in the *Future Shape of the Winner* model. As a mini-audit, answer these five questions:

- How can you keep focused on excellence in these tough economic times?
- Have you modified your ambitions in light of today's operating context?
- Are your team members fully committed to pursuing the agreed direction?
- Are your people totally focused on creating value for their customers?
- Is everyone on the payroll making their optimum contribution?

The *Excellence Audit* demystifies *excellence* for you by generating quantitative data on excellence. It identifies the most promising places to target improvement; reveals whether people agree about the priorities for improvement; exposes barriers to progress; helps you compile optimum improvement agendas that fit your context; generates joint agendas for management and professional teams determined to pursue excellence locally; helps you get your area focused and moving forward; and provides clarity and focus amid baffling complexity and conflicting demands.

Brand Inside's Effect on Brand

A cornerstone of our message about brand is that *your employees are also your customers.* We call this *Brand Inside*. We stirred up controversy over this notion by posting a PPT entitled *The Customer Comes Second*. The message is this: Since the customers in the firm serve the customers in the marketplace, put your employees first.

Matthew Kelly states: "Your employees are your first customers, and your most important customers."

Let me, Tom, get personal about all this. I *love* great customer or "end user" feedback! I am competitive to a fault in that regard and a slave to the market—after all these years.

At a higher level of marketplace engagement, I *love* a hearty business backlog, especially if it's based on repeat business—and I carefully measure it against the year-to-date of previous years. And I *love* a fee-per-event yield that exceeds last year, the year before, and so on. And yet, in an important way, I put the customer or end user second or third to employees.

It's simple and crystal clear to me: To give a high-impact, well-regarded, occasionally life-changing speech "to customers," I first, second, and third have to focus all my restless energy on "satisfying" *myself.* I must be physically, emotionally, and intellectually agitated and excited and desperate beyond measure to communicate, connect, compel, and grab people by the collar and say my piece about a few things, often contentious and not "crowd-pleasers," that, at the moment, are literally a matter of personal *life and death.*

I crave great customer feedback—but in no way, shape, or form am I trying to "satisfy my customer." I am, instead, trying to satisfy *me*—my own deep need to reach out and grab my customer and connect with my customer over ideas that consume me.

Hence, my "Job One" is purely *selfish and internally focused*—to be completely captivated by the subject matter at hand. That is Job One: *self-motivation.*

Warren Bennis, my primo mentor, said, "No leader sets out to be a leader *per se,* but rather to express him- or herself freely and fully. That is, leaders have no interest in proving themselves, but an abiding interest in expressing themselves."

So I'm back to my somewhat disingenuous message: To put the marketplace customer first, I must put the person serving the customer "more first." Excitement and self-stimulation first. Customer service second. That's my cause-and-effect scheme.

My message is that in order to *put the marketplace customer first, I must put the person serving the customer "more first."*

There is no great external focus unless a great internal focus is in place. I contend that finding and keeping and co-creating with great folks is not about clever tools to induce prospective "thems" to "shop with us," but a 99 percent internal effort to create such an exciting, spirited, entrepreneurial, diverse, humane "professional home" that people will line up by the gazillions (physically or electronically) to try and get a chance to come and live in our house and become what they'd never imagined they could become!

If you are serious about developing leaders, I suggest that you construct small leadership opportunities for people within days of their start on the job. *Everybody a leader* is entirely possible. So give you folks leadership responsibility from the outset, if not day #1 then within the first month. Hence, leadership development becomes a theme activity from stem to stern.

Boost Your Brand

Take this quick quiz (only 10 questions) for assessing your organization. Ask team members to rate themselves and the team against each question.

1. I know what my organization does to provide value to our customers.
2. I understand our products and services well enough to explain them.
3. I see how my job contributes to the value our organization creates.
4. I understand what a brand is.
5. I can tell the story of our brand.
6. I believe our brand is valuable.
7. We continually improve how we deliver products/services to customers.
8. I understand how my job brings our brand promise to life.
9. I can develop my talent while contributing to this organization's success.
10. I'm passionate about my work.

These questions investigate how connected you and your team feel to your *Purpose* and *Brand Promise.* The consolidated results can be used in a team discussion to identify the most promising targets for development.

Critical Thinking

1. In your perspective, what do the authors mean by "excellence is achieved when the brand, the talent, and the customer experience are all in alignment"?
2. Do you agree with the following statement: "Your employees are your first customers, and your most important customers"? Justify your answer.

Tom Peters is CEO of The Tom Peters Company, and **Valarie Willis** is a Keynote Speaker, Facilitator, and Consultant. Visit www.tompeters.com.

Brand Apathy Calls for New Methods

Turn Customer Preference from "No Brand" to "Some Brand"

DON E. SCHULTZ

Brand managers are accustomed to seeing challenging numbers. Faltering economies around the world guarantee that. Yet management plows ahead—setting double-digit internal sales objectives, increasing market share and expanding retail shelf space—doing all the things that mollify shareholders and prop up stock prices.

There's increasing evidence that organic sales improvement, line extensions and acquisitions just don't do it today.

Some brands have tried more focused sales efforts on specific segments, expanded their online and interactive promotional tools, and adjusted prices through coupons and other promotions. Still, major national brands are challenged as never before.

Unfortunately, the news I have to deliver in this column isn't very encouraging. However, if brand managers understand the new competitive landscape and refocus their efforts on differentiated initiatives while adjusting their competitive mindset, all is not lost. A rainbow and pot of gold may not be just around the corner, but there may be an improved opportunity for national brands.

Brand managers historically have focused on the general marketplace (i.e., sales volume compared with a year ago, incremental distribution increases and the like). While paying attention to competitive brands, they've often been willing to give up short-term share points to generate sales volume. The result has been more market knowledge than competitive knowledge. Share has been important, just not that important, primarily because they've been incented to grow volume.

That game is changing. Following four quarters of profit declines, Procter & Gamble (P&G) has declared "no more market share losses." Moving from valuing sales volume (in the case of P&G, the base was organic sales growth) to market share doesn't sound like a big deal—but it is. Brand managers cut their teeth driving short-term, quarter-to-quarter sales increases.

Building share is a different ball game, requiring a new set of tools and techniques. Finely tuned brand strategies designed to shift ongoing consumer preference and purchase from competitive brands to yours on an ongoing basis are the orders of the day—long-term, not short-term, returns.

Not so difficult, one would think—only it is. Getting consumers to change brands and maintain that change through ongoing preference is much more difficult than simply getting short-term sales volume from in-and-out, deal-prone consumers.

Most fast-moving consumer goods markets consist of (a) a limited number of brand loyal buyers, (b) a large group of brand switchers and (c) a growing bunch of unknowns or in-and-out buyers. That is, they only purchase when the price or promotion or communication is right. Promote to the switchers and sales often go up.

Observing this new emphasis on brand share growth, a Northwestern colleague and I decided to take a fresh look at brands, brand preferences and brand shares. That's where we found the scary numbers.

> **A rainbow and pot of gold may not be just around the corner, but there may be an improved opportunity for national brands.**

While one could argue that preference doesn't really reflect actual purchases, a person must be favorably inclined if a brand purchase is to be made. In addition, brand preference is forward-looking, while actual measured brand shares are historical. Thus, we believe preference is a relevant measure for most brands and their managers.

Using monthly online consumer reported preference information from the BIGresearch Consumer Intentions and Actions (CIA) panel, the consumer reported brand preferences were calculated for two product categories: breakfast products and salty snacks. (The data used was for August 2010 with a base of 8,000-plus U.S. respondents. See www.bigresearch.com for details.) Consumers also reported their retail grocery/mass merchandiser preferences. This dual retailer/brand combination is important. From previous research, we've found consumer retail store loyalty impacts national brand sales. If the preferred retailer doesn't stock the national brand, sales don't occur.

From the CIA data, a modified "Net Promoter" calculation, similar to the one Fredrick Reichheld of Boston-based Bain & Company developed, was calculated. Using a scale of 1 to 10 (1 being detractors or non-recommenders and 10 being promoters or people who favorably recommend), a Net Promoter Score was calculated first for the retail food store.

The store chain with the top Net Promoter Score was Publix, followed by Aldi and then HEB. Far down the list were some of the retailing giants, such as Wal-Mart and Safeway.

While these retail calculations were interesting, the brand results were even more so. For this, the brand preference rating in two product categories (using the same 1-to-10 system) was determined. That was then combined with the retail chain preference.

In the breakfast product category, when the chain and brand were indexed, the top brand was Cheerios, followed by Special K. The only brand with an index greater than 100 was Kashi. This simply means that Kashi brand preference is stronger than the retail store preference.

In the salty snack category, Frito-Lay (no specific product name) was the top indexing brand, followed by Tostitos. None of the national brands indexed more than 100, signifying to us that the retail chain store choice was stronger than the brand choice.

The really scary numbers in both categories, however, were the large numbers of "no preference" consumers. In the breakfast product category, 30 percent reported no preference. In salty snacks, 36.7 percent had no preference. Store brands (private label) registered a 4.1 share in breakfast products and a 6.8 share in salty snacks.

These scary figures seem to indicate that the share battle going forward isn't going to be getting consumers to prefer General Mills products over Kellogg's. The challenge is getting them to prefer "some brand" over "no brand." The national brand battle isn't between the leading national brands—or even the national brands against store brands or private label. It's against brand apathy.

Preference apathy is a tough task for a brand manager. If consumers don't care about the brand or don't perceive that it is even worth their time to learn about the category or the brand, most traditional marketing tools and concepts go right out the window.

When 30 percent or more of your product category consumers say their top choice is no preference, major rethinking needs to be done. Maybe P&G is right in shifting its performance evaluation to share-of-peer brand market, but how relevant is that when there is such a preponderance of customers who just don't care?

Critical Thinking

1. In your perspective, has the competitive landscape changed for businesses operating today? If yes, then discuss these changes.

2. With a small group of peers from your class, develop a list of DOs and DON'Ts to help businesses compete more effectively and enhance their market shares.

DON E. SCHULTZ is professor emeritus-in-service of integrated marketing communications at The Medill School, Northwestern University. He also is president of the Agora Inc. consulting firm in Evanston, Ill. He may be reached at dschultz@northwestern.edu.

Should You Launch a Fighter Brand?

Customers are suddenly hyperconscious of value, and new low-price competitors are nipping at your heels.

MARK RITSON

Managers contemplating a new product launch during the prosperous early years of the twenty-first century typically looked only in one direction: up. Thanks to consumers' rising incomes and apparently insatiable desire for superior quality, the era began with a focus on "premiumization," "trading up," and "luxury for the masses."

But times change. Economic strains are now causing consumers to trade down, and many midtier and premium brands are losing share to low-price rivals. Their managers face a classic strategic conundrum: Should they tackle the threat head-on by reducing prices, knowing that will destroy profits in the short term and brand equity in the long term? Or should they hold the line, hope for better times to return, and in the meantime lose customers who might never come back? Given how unpalatable both those alternatives can be, many companies are now considering a third option: launching a fighter brand.

A fighter brand is designed to combat, and ideally eliminate, low-price competitors while protecting an organization's premium-price offerings. Philip Morris used the strategy in 1998, when a sudden devaluation of the ruble quadrupled the price of its internationally produced Marlboro cigarettes in Russia, rendering them unaffordable to many smokers there. Rather than lose share to local competitors, the company concentrated its efforts on its locally made fighter brand Bond Street. When the ruble's value returned to normal, consumers came back to Marlboro, which had retained its premium pricing and brand equity.

In its best applications, a fighter brand strategy can have even more impressive results. In such cases—like that of Busch beer (see the sidebar "The One to Beat")—the fighter brand not only eliminates competitors but also opens up a new, lower-end market for the organization to pursue. Such triumphs, however, usually turn out to be the exception. For the most part, the history of fighter brands is a discouraging roll call of campaigns that inflicted very little damage on the targeted competitors and resulted instead in significant collateral losses for the companies that initiated them. What tripped them up? Five major strategic hazards that a manager must negotiate carefully in order to enjoy fighter brand success.

Hazard 1: Cannibalization

Most fighter brands are created explicitly to win back customers that have switched to a low-price rival. Unfortunately, once deployed, many have an annoying tendency to also acquire customers from a company's own premium offering. This was Kodak's experience when it attempted to beat back its Japanese rival, Fuji, in 1994.

Idea in Brief

In eras of belt tightening, marketers are often tempted to launch fighter brands. Properly executed, a fighter brand fends off low-cost rivals while allowing a company's premium brand to stay above the fray. Busch beer, for example, helped Anheuser-Busch hold on to value-conscious customers that would otherwise have defected to Budweiser's cheaper competitors. But the long list of failed fighter brands shows how hard they are to pull off. To be sure launching a fighter brand makes sense, ask five tough questions:

- Will it cannibalize our premium offering?
- Will it fail to bury the competition?
- Will it lose money?
- Will it miss the mark with customers?
- Will it consume too much management attention?

Over the previous decade, Kodak's market share had dropped as many of its customers switched to Fujicolor Super G film, which was priced 20 percent lower than Kodak's best-selling Gold Plus film. Faced with continuing losses in share, Kodak launched a fighter brand called Funtime, which sold at the same price as Fuji's offering. In an attempt to avoid cannibalization, Kodak manufactured Funtime using an older, less effective formula emulsion that made it significantly inferior to Gold Plus. But what appeared, from a corporate standpoint, to represent a genuine product distinction was lost in the subjective world of consumer interpretation. Already a low-involvement purchase, film had increasingly become a commodity, and most consumers were unaware of the differences in product quality. They simply saw Funtime as Kodak film at a lower price, and the fighter brand ate into Gold Plus sales more than it damaged Fuji's. Kodak withdrew Funtime from the market after only two years and began to experiment with other alternatives.

Positioning a fighter brand presents a manager with a dual challenge: You must ensure that it appeals to the price-conscious segment you want to attract while guaranteeing that it falls short for current consumers of your premium brand. That means you must match your fighter brand's low price with equally low perceived quality. Kodak got it right in theory but in practice failed to see to it that consumers considered Funtime inferior to the premium brand it was meant to protect.

The One to Beat

When company president August "Gussie" Busch, Jr., addressed the board of Anheuser-Busch in 1954, he admitted he'd made "the biggest mistake in the company's history." A year earlier, Anheuser-Busch had followed other national brewers in raising wholesale prices. That move proved disastrous: Regional brewers had recently gained a stronger foothold in the market, thanks to labor strikes that cut into the supplies from national breweries, and they now used their lower operating costs and cheaper prices to expand their share at Anheuser-Busch's expense.

With his reputation on the line, Busch went on to propose a solution: Busch Bavarian—the company's first new brand since Prohibition. Promoted as being "yours at popular prices," the beer was priced at the same level as regional competitors and almost half the wholesale price of its sister brands, Budweiser and Michelob. As well as advertising support, the fighter brand was given a separate sales force and distinct distribution trucks to distance it from the other two brands and reduce potential cannibalization.

The rest is business school legend. Busch successfully won back millions in sales, opened up the lower end of the market, and helped force many regional breweries to close. To this day, it's still priced at the same discount from its premium sister brands, Budweiser and Michelob.

Luvs

Company: Procter & Gamble

P&G slashed prices on Luvs by 16 percent to fend off private-label diapers—and managed to keep Pampers, its premium brand, above the fray.

As with the launch of any new brand, it's crucial to have a keen grasp of consumers' coordinates of value, but with a fighter brand, you must use those coordinates to deliberately miss one target segment while hitting the other.

Contrast Kodak's story with that of Procter & Gamble, which used a fighter brand to fend off private-label competitors. In the 1980s, P&G, which sold the leading diaper brand, Pampers, and the number three brand, Luvs, was responsible for half of all diaper sales in the United States. But as the market share of private labels in the category grew to 20 percent and the profit pool available to marketers like P&G shrank, the idea of operating two premium diaper brands made less and less sense. In 1993 P&G responded by adjusting its brand portfolio: It repositioned Luvs as a fighter brand and slashed its price by 16 percent. To avoid cannibalizing Pampers' sales, P&G also ensured that Luvs offered considerably less relative value. R&D and product innovation on Luvs were cut back, as were TV advertising and promotional support. Existing features, like handles on Luvs' packaging, were even removed to emphasize that the brand offered consumers less than Pampers.

Call it "un–brand management." To prevent cannibalization, a company must deliberately lessen the value, appeal, and accessibility of its fighter brand to its premium brand's target segments. It may even need to actively disable existing product features and withhold standard marketing support from the fighter brand. The good news, for those managers who find value destruction a difficult concept to contemplate, is that the other way to ensure that a fighter brand offers a sufficiently differentiated proposition is to innovate around the premium brand and strengthen its brand equity. Indeed, this proved central to P&G's strategy when, despite all the company's efforts, the repositioned Luvs still initially stole its sister brand's sales. It was only when

P&G focused greater managerial and financial resources on marketing and improving the features of Pampers that the two brands began to enjoy separate but equally successful roles within the portfolio.

Managers need to weigh the effects of cannibalization before rolling out fighter brands. Because these brands are explicitly oriented toward the rivals that have stolen share from a company, the initial break-even calculations used to justify their launch often are oversimplistically derived from an estimate of the lost sales that can be recouped. An accurate break-even analysis must account for cannibalization as well. How can you predict whether excessive cannibalization will occur? Test-marketing is the best way to ensure that a fighter brand can compete with low-price offerings without robbing significant sales from its higher-price, more profitable sister brand.

Hazard 2: Failure to Bury the Competition

Cannibalization might be the most obvious hazard, but it's certainly not the only one you need to navigate. Indeed, in many cases organizations actually overprotect their premium brands from cannibalization at the expense of the combative potential of their fighter brand. Merck made exactly this mistake in 2003 when it tried to prepare for the loss of patent protection on its blockbuster drug Zocor in Germany. Zocor—a statin used to treat high cholesterol—had been a major cash cow, but once the patent expired, generic drugs offering identical efficacy would enter the market for as little as 30 percent of its price.

The obvious strategic response was a price reduction, but for Merck that was not an option, because it would have encouraged parallel exports of Zocor from Germany to EU markets where patent protection still existed. Instead, Merck decided to launch a fighter brand called Zocor MSD. It rolled out the fighter brand four months before the patent expiration to give it some time to cannibalize Zocor's customers, who would then, Merck hoped, remain loyal when generics invaded the market. Because Merck was competing with only itself during this initial stage of Zocor MSD's launch, the fighter brand was priced just slightly less than the original premium brand. Once generics entered the market, the new brand's price dropped to 90 percent of Zocor's.

Within three months of its launch, Zocor MSD had missed its modest sales goals by 50 percent. More than 30 generics would divide the lion's share of the category among themselves. Merck's desire to protect its profits for as long as possible had prevented it from launching a brand priced low enough to seriously compete with the generics. Even when Merck realized it had set the wrong initial price, it was incapable of quick course correction. As a blue-chip multinational, it lacked the competencies to win the kind of price war it was entering. Merck was used to maintaining prices for long periods of time and altering them only after much consultation and reflection. Its generic competitors, accustomed to competing on price, could turn on a dime. With losses mounting fast, Merck withdrew all marketing support from Zocor MSD and admitted defeat.

Celeron

Company: Intel

After being derided as a "decapitated" Pentium, Celeron came back for round two with a better product and thwarted AMD's encroachment.

Intel offers another instructive example of the perils of overprotecting a premium brand. In the late 1990s, personal computers had matured to the point that much of the market growth was in "good enough" home PCs that were priced under $1,000. Intel's chips had been designed for much more expensive machines; a Pentium processor alone could cost as much as $800. Archrival AMD recognized that Intel was not well positioned to serve this growing segment of the market and launched a fighter brand of its own. Priced at around $260, AMD's new processor chip was dubbed the K6 in honor of kryptonite, the only substance that could defeat Superman—a cryptic reference to its anti-Intel mission.

Not surprisingly, Intel was keen to stop AMD before it got a foothold in the low-end market. At the same time, it hated the thought of eroding Pentium's profits and brand equity by dropping its price. So Intel decided to create a brand called Celeron and price it under $200 a chip. The news that Intel was offering a new chip that significantly undercut AMD generated tremendous buzz in the market when Celeron was launched, in April 1998. But while Celeron's price was aggressive, the same could not be said for the product itself. The first Celerons were little more than early series Pentium chips with features disabled and a lower cache memory. Initial customer excitement soon turned to disgust as chip buyers took to referring to Celeron as a "decapitated" Pentium.

In contrast with Zocor MSD, however, Celeron was able to go back for a round two. Chastened by the negative reaction, Intel rushed out a new version called Celeron A only a few months later. The new chip retained its low price but now offered much of the memory cache and processing performance of the more expensive, but soon to be replaced, Pentium II chip. It proved a success in the lower-end PC market, and Intel has continued to augment and improve Celeron's offer, just behind its premium brand, ever since.

Why such different outcomes? Intel, with its history of frequent product launches, upgrades, and deletions, was better equipped than Merck to learn from its first foray into the good-enough segment. For companies that don't enjoy such rapid turnover of products, the lessons should be underscored: Market-test your fighter brand, and be prepared to recalibrate its price and performance to ensure it finds the sweet spot between cannibalizing overperformance and uncompetitive underperformance. Intel's 80 percent share of the processor market is testament to both the power of fighter brands to open up lower-tier market opportunities and their unequaled ability to keep competitors at bay. Intel also achieved something with Celeron that even the Man of Steel has never managed—it found a cure for kryptonite.

Hazard 3: Financial Losses

In the pantheon of fighter brands, none offer more salutary lessons than Saturn from General Motors. Its 25-year history provides unparalleled insights into, first, the strategic attractions of a fighter brand and, then, the eviscerating damage that such a brand can inflict on its organization if it fails.

Saturn was conceived by GM in 1982 as a direct response to the growing threat from the fuel-efficient and affordable cars being launched into America from Japan. Concerned that its reputation for making midprice and midsize cars might damage Saturn's effectiveness against Honda and Toyota, GM went to great lengths to distinguish Saturn from its existing stable of brands and position it as "a different kind of car company." The new brand was given its own dedicated plant in Tennessee, and its cars were built very differently from those in Detroit. When the first Saturns hit the market in 1990, they proved an immediate success and quickly achieved the highest repurchase rates and customer satisfaction scores in the industry. Saturn's unique dealership network with its transparent, no-haggling approach to pricing further emphasized the products' differentiation. By 1996 orders actually exceeded Saturn's production capacity, and the brand's fighting prowess was resoundingly confirmed when dealer research revealed that 50 percent of these orders were from individuals who would otherwise have bought a Japanese import. When Professor David Aaker of the Haas Business School concluded in 1994 that "Saturn has built from scratch one of the strongest brands in the U.S.," he was correct in every aspect except one.

For all its brand success, Saturn was proving to be a financial disaster. It made an annual operating profit just once, and that's before even considering GM's initial setup costs of $5 billion. By 1997 the brand was looking for a major new investment of funds to develop new models, but GM was now balking at Saturn's huge operating costs. Saturn's plant had been five times more expensive to build than the usual GM production line and had double the employees of a typical plant. Saturn cars also cost more to produce because they used virtually no shared GM parts. The brand had a separate marketing and branding budget and its own dedicated dealership network as well. Overhead, in short, was huge and had to be covered by a brand exclusively focused on the low-price, low-margin small-car business. In creating a very different kind of car company and a supereffective fighter brand, GM had also burdened Saturn with an overwhelmingly unprofitable business model. By 2000, despite continuing sales success, Saturn was losing $3,000 for every car it sold.

GM began to rethink things. It delayed or canceled expensive new features like passenger air bags and plastic body panels and dissolved the unique operating systems and labor agreements at Saturn's plant. Saturn's "new" generation of cars did eventually arrive, but they consisted of rebadged versions of other GM models. Saturn's original small cars evolved into the midsize cars, SUVs, and minivans more traditional of GM. Saturn's dealers were also reined in and, despite an initial pledge to avoid all price promotions, were now included in GM-wide dealership offers like 0 percent financing. If the first chapter of Saturn's existence was characterized by fighter brand success hampered by unprofitability, its second chapter centered on lowering costs at the expense of Saturn's brand equity and ultimately its fighter brand effectiveness. Shared platforms, rebadged models, and GM promotions spelled the end of Saturn's differentiation and led to increasing cannibalization of sister brands like Pontiac and Chevy. Meanwhile, the Asian competitors Saturn had been designed to fight steadily gained market share in the United States. GM vice chairman Bob Lutz summarized the Saturn story in 2009, telling *Automotive News:* "We spent a huge bundle of money in giving Saturn an absolutely no-excuses product lineup, top to bottom. They had a better and fresher lineup than any GM division, and the sales just never materialized." Not quite true. Sales did materialize, but when profits did not follow GM was forced to look for synergies and savings—and then sales dropped off. Because of its financial woes, Saturn will ultimately be remembered as one of the most cautionary case studies of fighter brand failure.

Saturn

Company: General Motors

Launched by GM in 1990, Saturn was everything a fighter brand should be—except a money maker. It made an annual operating profit just once.

Ted

Company: United

Ted wasn't much of a match for rivals Frontier and Southwest. The airline's employees joked blackly that its name stood for "the end of United."

Fighter brand success depends on more than initially matching the price and value of your intended enemy; you must also achieve those goals while attaining a sustainable level of profits. Unfortunately, such profits can prove elusive for organizations accustomed to higher price points and more generous operating models. Suddenly, they find themselves competing in the low-price sector against brands that probably originated there and that have evolved an operating model well suited to it. To meet that challenge a premium organization may have to strip back a fighter brand's cost structure and alter its traditional definition of what constitutes strategic success.

For managers at 3M who set about creating a lower-price version of Post-it Notes called Highland, this meant using a lower-grade adhesive, offering the new product in limited formats, and completely forgoing trade promotions. As one 3M executive put it, the overriding objective for the fighter brand was to ensure that "if consumers did use Highland, none would have a complaint." Highland's basic quality and timid goal of avoiding disappointment may seem surprisingly at odds with 3M's reputation for innovation but achieved two key objectives. First, they ensured that Highland did not cannibalize Post-it Notes' sales. Second, they enabled Highland to be profitable despite its much lower price, which has allowed 3M to keep the product in the company's portfolio long after seeing off its cheaper rivals.

Hazard 4: Missing the Mark with Customers

Normally, a successful brand has its genesis in the recognition of an unmet consumer need. The subsequent development and marketing of the product stay focused on its target consumer segment. But the provenance of a fighter brand is very different. It originates with a competitor and the strategic success it has achieved, or threatens to achieve, against your organization. The DNA of a fighter brand is therefore potentially flawed from the very outset because it is derived from company deficiencies and competitor strengths, not a focus on consumers.

When United launched its fighter brand Ted to combat discount airlines Frontier and Southwest, the skewed orientation of the new brand was evident from the start. During the 2004 launch John Tague, United's executive vice president (who was appointed president in 2009), set the tone: "We think Ted can do things that United can't." He and his team made the mistake of benchmarking Ted just against their own premium brand. Although they celebrated Ted's points of difference, such as easygoing service, guerrilla marketing, and using only a single crew member for check-in, those features differentiated Ted only from its parent brand. A market-oriented strategist would have recognized that they were long-established features of Ted's low-price rivals and therefore nothing more than points of parity. Nowhere was this internal orientation more obvious than in pricing. Compared with United, Ted was a discount airline. But external analysis confirmed that Ted's fares were around 15 percent higher than those of its budget

competition. In the face of rising fuel costs and increasing losses, Ted ceased operations in 2009.

While Ted was a victim of internal benchmarking, it's more common for fighter brands to focus excessively on rivals at the expense of consumers. Consider the situation at British supermarket Tesco. Aside from offering the traditional selection of manufacturer brands, Tesco pioneered a three-tiered private-label strategy all under the Tesco brand. In 2008, however, shoppers were confronted by yet a fourth form of private label. Alarmed by the growing threat of the German retailer Aldi, Tesco launched 350 new Discount Brands priced between its lowest- and mid-tier private-label brands and imitating Aldi's "house of brands" architecture. Its new fighter brand in ketchup, for example, did not feature the Tesco name; it was called Oak Lane and mimicked Aldi's private-label ketchup offering, Bramwell. Tesco even went so far as to cite Aldi's equivalent product price on its shelf labeling to assure customers they could not do better across the street. Unfortunately, the strategy complicated Tesco's formerly simple pricing structures and confused many of its customers.

Though a fighter brand inevitably originates from the recognition of a competitor and the limitations of an organization's existing premium brand, management's focus should immediately switch to the consumer segments that the new brand is targeting. Only then will it achieve the kind of consumer orientation necessary to avoid a potentially fatal focus on competitors.

When Qantas decided to strike back after the successful launch of Virgin Blue into Australia (see the sidebar " How Qantas Launched the Perfect Fighter Brand"), its planning process began not with internal benchmarking or an assessment of Virgin Blue's operating model but rather with a series of focus groups. The groups, run all over Australia, were attended by the senior managers, including newly hired chief executive Alan Joyce. "What we found were a few characteristics they wanted from an airline," Joyce told the *Sydney Morning Herald.* "They also wanted an airline to project an Australian image—they wanted an open, accessible, and egalitarian airline." Those insights helped guide Qantas's fighter brand, Jetstar, to unprecedented success. Rather than striving to match the strengths of the competitor it was designed to attack, Jetstar concentrated on meeting the needs of the consumers it would one day serve.

Hazard 5: Management Distraction

Launching a fighter brand while selling a premium brand is like fighting a war on two fronts. An organization must divide its resources at the very time when it should perhaps concentrate its efforts on the business at hand. Rather than going off to war with a fighter brand, should a manager stay and defend the homeland?

A number of the companies that have recently launched and then retracted fighter brands have also experienced bankruptcy: United (Ted) in 2002, Delta (Song) in 2005, GM (Saturn) in 2009. Granted,

How Qantas Launched the Perfect Fighter Brand

After dominating the Australian airspace for decades, Qantas was threatened in 2000 by low-fare entrant Virgin Blue. In 2003 Qantas's management discussed launching a fighter brand. The strategy that emerged provides a first-class example of the steps to achieving fighter brand success:

1. **Determine whether another brand is truly necessary.** Like any company, and especially one with just a single brand, Qantas did not want to create a new brand unless it had to. Exhaustive strategic sessions confirmed, however, that the Qantas brand was simply not in a position to combat Virgin Blue's explosive growth. A fighter brand was the only option.

2. **Run the numbers.** Fortunately for Qantas, Virgin Blue had entered Australia with a low-frills, rather than no-frills, airline. Qantas's detailed projections showed that by offering no frills, its new airline could achieve a 20 percent cost advantage over its rival; thus allowing it to undercut Virgin Blue's prices while sustaining a profit.

3. **Listen to customers, early and often.** Well before any key decisions had been made, the new brand's executive team attended secret focus groups across Australia—a crucial step to avoiding excessive internal benchmarking or competitor orientation.

4. **Move fast.** In 2004 Jetstar was launched with 14 planes flying to 14 destinations. The speed at which Jetstar attacked took Virgin Blue by surprise and knocked it off balance. It also meant that Jetstar entered a market that was still growing—a major consideration for a fighter brand intent on reducing the cannibalization of its premium brand.

5. **Control for cannibalization.** Jetstar took over the tourist routes that Qantas had lost money on. Because Jetstar proved profitable on those routes, it cannibalized only revenues, not profits. The fighter brand also opted for a shadow endorsement from Qantas. This approach aided Jetstar's initial launch while distancing it from the premium brand and further reducing cannibalization.

6. **Reinvest in your premium offering and calibrate between the two brands.** Thanks to Jetstar, Qantas was able to refocus on its more profitable business routes and increase the frequency of its flights on those legs. The subsequent boost in profits, along with Jetstar's growing contribution, were reinvested in overhauls of Qantas's business lounges and business class cabins—strengthening the Qantas brand and the distinction between it and Jetstar.

Five years on, Jetstar has proved a dramatic success. It enjoys a 22 percent share of the domestic market and consistently impressive annual profits. Qantas estimates that Jetstar has added more than $300 million to the company's bottom line since its introduction. Equally important, Jetstar has stopped the growth of Virgin Blue, and Qantas is now using the brand to fight other competitors in Asia and New Zealand.

---

their fighter brands were created to respond to serious competitive threats that had already caused sizable business losses. But instead of alleviating the situation, the financial investment wasted on unsuccessful fighter brands further contributed to the dire straits that these organizations found themselves in. According to *Fortune*, GM lost more than $15 billion on Saturn—an enormous sum even by its standards. Similarly, Song wreaked havoc with Delta's finances as the costs of the launch, marketing communications, and hiring and training of new staff piled up to an estimated $65 million. Then there were the operating costs. Industry analysts estimated that Song was losing around $16 million a month in 2005. Add to that the expense of decommissioning 48 planes and refitting them back to Delta standards and severance pay for fired staff, and you have a devastating mountain of costs at a time when Delta was already desperately short of cash.

The opportunity costs of launching, managing, and then withdrawing an unsuccessful fighter brand can be even bigger than the financial impact. Significant managerial resources that could have been invested in a company's premium brand are instead wasted on what is often a loss-making venture that only distracts the organization from its core business. That premium brand might also face challenges other than low-price entrants in the market. Fighter brands do nothing to abate those other competitive threats. In fact, by siphoning away vital funds and management attention, they may actually render the premium brand more vulnerable. While Tesco worked on its Discount Brand line, for example, its main rival, Sainsbury's, grew at a much greater rate. While P&G executed its new fighter brand strategy for Luvs, Pampers lost considerable market share to premium brand competitor Huggies. Employees are often quick to recognize the detrimental impact that a fighter brand can have on their organization. United staff, for example, blackly joked that the name Ted was derived from "the end of United," while former Delta CEO Gerald Grinstein openly referred to his fighter brand with the damning sobriquet of "Swan Song"—a comment he later apologized for.

A manager will probably never encounter a strategy as tempting or potentially ruinous as a fighter brand.

But the greatest cost of a fighter brand may be its propensity to cause managers to delay essential strategic decisions on their existing portfolio of brands. In many cases, when a leadership team finally decommissions a failed fighter brand, its next action is a strategic review of its premium brand. United, Delta, and Kodak, for example, all embarked on major cost cutting and repricing strategies for their premium brands after acknowledging that their respective fighter brands had failed. In each instance, however, those crucial strategic moves had been delayed for years while the organizations focused on their fighter brands. Nowhere were these repercussions more damaging than at GM. Back in 1983, when then-chairman Roger Smith unveiled the first Saturn prototype, he had proudly declared: "In Saturn we have GM's answer—the American answer—to the Japanese challenge." In hindsight, the greatest cost of Saturn was the time it took GM executives to realize that Saturn was not the "answer" to its Japanese rivals at all. By the time GM's executives acknowledged this, a quarter century of missed opportunities had passed them by. What would GM now give to be able to go back to 1983 and review its original portfolio of brands and strategic response to Asian imports all over again?

A manager will probably never encounter a strategy as tempting or as potentially ruinous as a fighter brand. When it works, as in the case of Busch beer or Intel Celeron, it is the stuff of marketing brilliance. Troubling competitors are destroyed or seriously limited in scope. New market segments, often exhibiting high growth potential, are suddenly opened up. And the combination of a premium and a value brand in the market allows a company to calibrate those two offerings to its own strategic advantage.

Now forget those glittering outcomes and concentrate first on avoiding the hazards that render most fighter brands failures. Think about how thoroughly a fighter brand might cannibalize premium brand sales, and make sure that the value equation between your two brands is suitably distinct in the mind of the customer. Check that you will be able to launch a fighter brand that is competitive enough to damage your enemy and profitable enough to continue to do so over the long haul. Consider carefully the strategic implications of dividing your organization's resources during a period when focus and investment are critical.

And then make your decision because, as the Greek playwright Euripides pointed out more than 2,000 years ago, the god of war hates those who hesitate.

Critical Thinking

1. Define the term *fighter brand*.
2. Summarize the five major strategic hazards associated with launching a fighter brand.
3. Discuss Qantas Airlines' successful strategy to launch a fighter brand.

MARK RITSON *(m.ritson@mbs.edu)* is an associate professor at Melbourne Business School in Australia.

Everybody Loves Zappos

Get Happy: How Tony Hsieh uses relentless innovation, stellar customer service, and a staff of believers to make Zappos.com an e-commerce juggernaut—and one of the most blissed-out businesses in America.

Max Chafkin

"**What would make you happier in your life?**" Tony Hsieh asks me this question as we sit at a booth with half a dozen young people in one of those absurdly lavish lounges that can be found only in Las Vegas. It's called Lavo, setting of recent Paris Hilton and Nelly sightings and the city's newest hot spot. The theme is an ancient Roman bathhouse, and so, in addition to the normal nightclub features—thumping bass, low tables, dim lighting—there's the distracting aspect of two scantily clad women performing a risqué bathing routine, complete with damp sponges and music.

It's a strange setting for an interview—especially for an interview with Hsieh (pronounced *Shay*). He's a thoughtful, low-key fellow who seems out of place in such a louche setting. Indeed, he seems oddly oblivious to his surroundings, which makes sense, given that he runs what is arguably the decade's most innovative start-up, Zappos.com. Hsieh helped start Zappos in 1999 as an online shoe store, and the company has since expanded to all manner of goods. Zappos booked $1 billion in gross sales in 2008, 20 percent better than the year before. It has been profitable since 2006.

At a time when most business leaders are retrenching, Hsieh is thinking big. In late 2006, he launched an outsourcing program to handle selling, customer service, and shipping for other companies, and last December, he started an educational website for small businesses that charges them $39.95 a month to tap Zappos executives for advice. Hsieh has said Zappos will eventually move beyond retail to businesses such as hotels and banking—anything where customer service is paramount. "I wouldn't rule out a Zappos airline that's just about the best customer service," he announced at the Web 2.0 conference last fall.

But Hsieh, 35, isn't interested in talking about any of this right now. He's still on the happiness thing. "On a scale of 1 to 10, how happy are you right now?" he asks, informing me that, right now, he's at about an 8.

I think for a second and then respond, "Maybe a 7?"

This isn't polite conversation for Hsieh. "I've been doing a lot of research into the science of happiness," he says. In addition to asking everyone he meets what makes him or her happy, he has also been studying books on the subject, especially Jonathan Haidt's *The Happiness Hypothesis,* which uses social psychology experiments to evaluate the world's great religions and philosophies and concludes that ancient wisdom and science are both useful tools in the quest for contentment. Hsieh is working on a system to supersede both. "I've been trying to come up with a unified theory for happiness," he says.

Unlike the world's great religions, the Tony Hsieh Unified Happiness Theory is not entirely settled. It involves establishing balance among four basic human needs: perceived progress, perceived control, relatedness, and a connection to a larger vision. And because Hsieh's life is his company, the test subjects are Zappos employees. "I've got a few different frameworks, and I'm just figuring out how to combine them," he says without irony or even a smile. "I think I'm pretty close."

Hsieh is widely regarded as one of the most innovative Internet marketers of all time. The Web entrepreneur and marketing guru Seth Godin has likened Hsieh's ability to use technology to connect with his customers to the Beatles' ability to animate their teenage fans. The blog Search Engine Land calls Zappos "the poster child for how to connect with customers online." And Hsieh's mastery isn't limited to marketing. Zappos's warehouse boasts a fleet of 70 brand-new robots that allows it to ship a pair of shoes in as little as eight minutes, earning reams of praise from logistics-industry trade publications.

But Hsieh has a hard time getting excited about any of this. What he really cares about is making Zappos's employees and customers feel really, really good. This is not because Hsieh is a nice guy (though he is a very nice guy), but because he has decided that his entire business revolves around one thing: happiness. Everything at Zappos serves that single end. Other business innovators work with software code or circuit boards or molecular formulas. Hsieh prefers to work with something altogether more complex and volatile: human beings themselves.

That single-minded focus on happiness has led to plenty of accolades for the company, which routinely scores high on lists of the best places to work. But Zappos's approach to workplace bliss differs significantly from that of other employee-friendly businesses. For one thing, Zappos pays salaries that are often below market rates—the average hourly worker makes just over $23,000 a year. Though the company covers 100 percent of health care costs, employees are not offered perks found at many companies, such as on-site child care, tuition reimbursement, and a 401(k) match. Zappos does offer free food to its employees, but the pile of cold cuts in the small cafeteria loses its allure faster than you can say *Googleplex*. Instead of buying his employees' loyalty, Hsieh has managed to design a corporate culture that challenges our conception of that tired phrase.

Hsieh's accomplishments are all the more impressive when you consider Zappos's origins. The idea of selling shoes on the Web may seem merely unoriginal today, but it seemed truly wrong-headed in 1999. "There wasn't an ounce of evidence to suggest it would work," says Michael Moritz, a partner with Sequoia Capital and the guy who backed Yahoo, Google—and, after initially passing on the company in 2001, Zappos. And yet, as Hsieh turned that daft idea into a business, his company transformed. Zappos now boasts systems that are breathlessly praised by academics, entrepreneurs, and, of course, the customers who seem eternally tickled by the company's free shipping and unbelievably responsive service. At many companies, talk of corporate culture dulls the luster, inducing cynicism among employees and creating hours of busywork for managers. At Zappos, the culture is the luster. And Hsieh—soft-spoken, deliberate, awkward—has emerged as a most unlikely business guru.

I first met Hsieh three years ago at a cocktail hour at the Inc. 500 conference. (Zappos had landed at No. 23, with revenue of $135 million.) We spoke for 10 minutes or so, and I remember being struck by the scope of his achievement. But I was even more impressed by the oddness of Hsieh's mannerisms.

Hsieh is hard to know and even harder to read. He's generous and smart, but so subdued in one-on-one conversation that it's easy to mistake his reticence for rudeness. When he does speak, it's in full paragraphs that sound as if they have been formulated in advance. He sometimes smiles—as he does when he's explaining the clever way Zappos manages its call center—but he doesn't laugh at other people's jokes and seldom tells his own.

And yet, this mild-mannered fellow leads a company that is entirely uninhibited. Interviews are held over vodka shots, bathrooms are plastered with "urine color" charts (ostensibly to ensure that employees are hydrated but also just to be weird and funny), and managers are encouraged to goof off with the people they manage. Zappos's 1,300 employees talk about the place with a religious fervor. The phrase *core values* can prompt emotional soliloquies, and the CEO is held with a regard typically afforded rock stars and cult leaders.

Hsieh tries his best to keep up with the goofy, libertine culture. Every day, he blasts a steady stream of playful messages to 350,000 people on Twitter. (Before taking the stage at a conference earlier this year, he posted this missive: "Spilled Coke on left leg of jeans, so poured some water on right leg so looks like the denim fade.") He has also become an accomplished public speaker who spends a good chunk of his time on the road giving talks, which are delivered without notes.

What most of Hsieh's admirers—and even some Zappos employees—don't know is that this openness doesn't come naturally. Hsieh has been exceptionally shy all his life and finds meeting strangers exhausting. (His trick to get over his shyness is to pretend he's interviewing you for a job.) Those seemingly off-the-cuff Twitter missives? He spends 10 minutes or so carefully composing each one. He takes his employees out to restaurants and bars not because he loves nightlife but because he thinks it sets a good example. "I just want to have a company where people can hang out together," he says, "and then come in to work the next day and not worry about whether they've done something stupid." Most CEOs make their companies in their own image; Hsieh seems to have designed his company to behave the way he wishes he could.

Hsieh has always been a little different. He grew up in San Rafael, California, and excelled from an almost creepily young age. In first grade, he taught himself to program, playing with a Radio Shack microcomputer that his father, Richard—a Chinese-born chemical engineer with a Ph.D., an M.B.A., and 29 patents to his name—brought home. The next year, Richard blew a month's salary and bought his son an IBM XT personal computer. By third grade, Hsieh's bedroom was littered with pages of software code for a bulletin board system—a precursor to today's Internet message boards, accessed by dial-up modem—that he ran for several years, tying up the household phone line and mystifying his parents. "He stayed in his room for hours at a time," says Richard Hsieh.

Hsieh started his first company, LinkExchange, shortly after graduating from Harvard with a degree in computer science. The company allowed amateur Web publishers to barter for advertising by agreeing to publish one another's ads. "It was just something to keep busy," he says. "But within a week, we knew we were onto something." In three months, Hsieh signed up 20,000 websites; he decided that the site could make money by selling ads as well as trading them. Though LinkExchange was unprofitable, the idea had enough steam to pick up a $3 million investment from Sequoia Capital—Moritz led the investment. By 1998, the company, which had revenue of about $10 million, would be sold to Microsoft for a staggering $265 million. Hsieh was just 24 years old.

And yet, despite this success, Hsieh found himself depressed. "The easiest way to explain it was that going into the office started to feel like work," he says. He felt increasingly that the people he had hired were not committed to the venture's long-term growth. "The Silicon Valley culture is, 'I'm going to work hard for four years and make millions of dollars and then retire,'" he says. Work, which once had felt liberating, had become a chore. He resolved that his next company would not be about a short-term payday. It would be about long-term growth, about creating a place to which he and his employees would want to come every day.

When you visit Zappos's headquarters in Henderson, Nevada, it's easy to miss Hsieh's desk. Not only is it tucked into a row of cubicles in the middle of the floor, but it's also smaller and more cluttered than any CEO's desk I have ever seen. There are stacks of unopened mail, empty Styrofoam cups, several unopened liquor bottles, and a sizable collection of self-help books—titles include *Mastering the Rockefeller Habits, The Time Paradox: The New Psychology of Time That Will Change Your Life,* and *14,000 Things to Be Happy About.* There are a few science titles—part of Hsieh's quest for a happiness framework—a few on food and wine, and one on marathon running, which he recently took up.

Hsieh is a relentless self-improver, which may help explain why, after selling LinkExchange, he didn't start a new company. Instead, he started 27. In 1999, he and Alfred Lin, a Harvard classmate, launched something called Venture Frogs. Though structured as a venture capital fund, it was more ambitious. Hsieh and Lin leased 15,000 square feet of office space in the same San Francisco building in which they both owned lofts, and they gave the space to the start-ups in which they invested.

Hsieh's involvement in Zappos started with a voice mail from a young man named Nick Swinmurn, who said he wanted to start an online shoe company. Hsieh had never been particularly taken with the idea of online retail, but when Swinmurn mentioned that catalog companies sold $2 billion a year worth of shoes, Hsieh got interested. In 1999, Venture Frogs agreed to invest $500,000, if Zappos—the name is a play on *zapatos,* the Spanish word for *shoes*—could recruit someone with shoe experience. Swinmurn found Fred Mossler, then a Nordstrom buyer.

Six months later, Swinmurn was out of money, and the site offered only three shoe brands. (Most orders were initially filled by a few local retailers.) "We were down to the last day, essentially," says Mossler. "And Tony called." Hsieh said he would keep the company afloat and offered to help. By the summer of 2000, Hsieh and Swinmurn were co-CEOs, and Zappos was operating out of Hsieh's living room. Says Hsieh: "It was the most interesting opportunity, and the people were the most fun."

This is also a delicate way of saying that Hsieh was not especially happy as an investor. A few of Venture Frogs' investments succeeded—notably the search engine Ask.com and the restaurant reservation system OpenTable—but as the dot-com bubble burst, most struggled to survive, and some were shuttered. Hsieh had been attracted to investing because it seemed to bring all the fun of start-ups on a larger scale; instead, it became a treadmill of meetings full of bad news. "I think it was much harder than he first imagined," says Moritz. What Hsieh wanted, he realized, was the unstructured fun of a new company. As he puts it, "I wanted to be involved in building something."

Zappos's early years were a scramble. Footwear brands, which associated the Web with heavy discounting, resisted putting their merchandise on Zappos. Still, Mossler succeeded in signing up about 50 companies in the first year and a half. Hsieh wrote software code and focused on financing—he bankrolled the company until he secured a line of credit with Wells Fargo in 2003. Nobody had set jobs, nobody cared about titles, and everybody hung out with everybody else after work. The economy was falling apart around them, but somehow, even the struggle was fun.

The defining aspect of the Zappos customer experience—free shipping and free returns—was concocted out of necessity.

Hsieh figured that there was no other way to get people to try the site. He also added a prominently displayed toll-free customer support number, a personal buying service, free socks—anything to help put skeptical customers at ease. Because the company could not afford to spend money on marketing, the sales strategy involved making customers so happy that they bought again or told their friends or both.

Though shoemakers were initially reluctant to sell to Zappos—Nike held out for more than seven years—by 2002, Mossler had lined up more than 100 brands, including Steve Madden and Converse, and the company was beginning to do a brisk business. Sales hit $32 million in 2002, up from $8.6 million the previous year. At the time, 25 percent of orders were shipped from manufacturers' warehouses; these orders were often delayed for days. Hsieh decided to stop listing these items on Zappos and opened a warehouse outside of Louisville.

A few months later, Hsieh moved the company from San Francisco to Las Vegas—70 of the company's 100 employees made the trip. The move made sense for lots of reasons, chief among them lower taxes and a lower cost of living. Hsieh also wanted to be in a city where restaurants and stores are open 24 hours a day, to accommodate call center reps who work the graveyard shift. The move corresponded with yet another jump in sales and helped put an end to any financial worries. In late 2004, the company, which sold $184 million worth of goods that year, landed $20 million from Sequoia Capital.

Such rapid growth was exciting. But it also led Hsieh to wonder how he could preserve Zappos's radical dedication to customer service and its fun, loose work environment. "We always hired for culture fit," he says. "But we were growing so quickly that managers who hadn't been around for very long might not know what our culture was." He wrote an e-mail to the entire company asking for help, and he distilled the responses into a list of 10 core values, including "Be humble," "Create fun and a little weirdness," and "Deliver WOW through service." Then he assigned and collected short essays from every employee on the subject of the company's culture and published them, unedited, in a book that he distributed to the staff.

Every year, all employees, both new and old, contribute a fresh essay to the book, which has grown to 480 pages. Hsieh uses it as a way not only to get employees thinking about the meaning of their work but also to show the outside world what he has built. Talk to Hsieh for five minutes, and he will inevitably try to get your address so he can mail you a copy. The book is painfully earnest and yet affecting nonetheless. There are all the clichés one might expect—acronyms, ridiculous overstatement (one call center rep compared Zappos to China's Ming Dynasty), and a fondness for the word *Zapponians.* It often goes way over the top. "Could you imagine if Zappos was more than an online retailer, or the job that pays the bills, but actually became a way of life?" wrote Donavon Roberson, a pastor who left the ministry before joining Zappos.

Most Zappos employees are familiar with all this history. In fact, despite all the research I did before heading to Las Vegas, I didn't know that Nike had spurned Zappos until I sat in on a two-hour Zappos history class—part of a four-week course on the subject—and watched as employees called out various milestones: 2002, $32 million in gross sales! 2006, the year the company recorded its first $3 million day! 2007, the year Nike joined Zappos!

This mastery isn't accidental. It's required. All new Zappos employees receive two weeks of classroom training. Then they spend two weeks learning how to answer customer calls. At the conclusion of the program, trainees are famously offered $2,000, plus time worked, to quit. The practice, Hsieh's idea, began in 2005, with a $100 offer. "Our training team had gotten good at figuring out who wasn't going to make it, and we were thinking, How do you get rid of those people?" says Hsieh. Paying them to quit saves the company money by weeding out people who would jump ship anyway and allows those who remain to make a public statement of commitment to their new employer.

All employees receive four weeks of training. Then they are offered $2,000 to quit.

More recently, Hsieh has overseen the development of an even more comprehensive curriculum. The first course, intended for employees who have worked at Zappos for two years or less, involves more than 200 hours of class time (during work hours) and mandates that students read nine business books. Topics include Sarbanes-Oxley compliance and Twitter use. Advanced students can take classes in public speaking and financial planning. "The vision is that three years from now, almost all our hires will be entry-level people," Hsieh says. "We'll provide them with training and mentorship, so that within five to seven years, they can become senior leaders within the company."

The Zappos headquarters takes up three modest buildings in a nondescript office park about a 20-minute drive from the Las Vegas Strip. Walk in, and it becomes immediately clear why for some entrepreneurs, visiting Zappos is of a piece with the buffet at the Bellagio or a trip to the top of the (replica) Eiffel Tower. In fact, Zappos hosts a tour of its headquarters every couple of hours, an operation that is staffed by 12 people and includes two SUVs and a bus with custom Zappos paint jobs. Call the company from your hotel, and someone will pick you up and ferry you to Henderson.

Zappos hosts a tour of its headquarters every couple of hours. Call the company from your hotel, and someone will pick you up.

My tour is led by Roberson, the former pastor, who wears jeans and a maroon polo shirt and carries a giant Zappos flag. We are joined by four consultants from Deloitte. In the lobby, Roberson points out the Reply to All Hat—a sort of dunce cap for employees who commit that venial office sin of the inadvertent mass e-mail—and takes us past the nap room, where three employees are stretched out on couches. At the office of the company's staff life coach, who also happens to be Hsieh's former chiropractor, we are each photographed while sitting on a throne.

But the most striking thing about the tour is the extent to which the company's long-term plan is on display. A sales chart in the lobby informs everyone in the building that the day before—March 4, 2009—Zappos sold $2.5 million worth of merchandise. A computer printout in the hallway notes that there are currently 4.1 million items, mostly shoes, in stock in the warehouse in Kentucky. At the conclusion of the tour, we are invited to peruse the company library, which is filled with multiple copies of two dozen business and self-help books. We are urged to take whatever grabs our fancy, a policy that applies to employees as well. Roberson explains that one of Zappos's core values is personal growthand that books are given out to help employees grow with the company.

When I tell Hsieh that Zappos strikes me as not unlike a religious cult, he doesn't disagree. "I think there's a lot you can learn from religion," he says. "This is not just a company. It's like a way of life."

---

10 Questions for Tony Hsieh

What's your favorite part of a typical day?
Anytime I'm building something new.

What's the least glamorous thing you do in the line of duty?
Going through airport security.

What skill would you most like to improve?
Humor. I've been researching the science of humor, and I think it can be learned like any skill.

What's the simplest thing you never learned to do?
To whistle.

What accomplishment are you most proud of?
Being involved in building the Zappos culture.

What keeps you up at night?
Trying to figure out how to make the company culture stronger as we get bigger.

Who is the smartest person you know?
I believe that people are smart in different ways. With everyone I meet, I try to figure out what they're smart about and learn from them.

If you could go back and do one thing differently, what would it be?
I would try to do everything faster.

What was the happiest day of your career?
Our company milestones—like when we signed Nike after trying to get them for eight years.

On a scale from 1 to 10, how happy are you right now?
8.5.

Of course, nobody except Hsieh works at Zappos to save his or her soul. It's a job—and not a particularly glamorous one. Customer service reps start at $11 an hour, warehouse workers at $8.25. But even in its hiring process, Zappos creates wildly different expectations than do most companies. Prospective hires must pass an hourlong "culture interview" before being handed off to whatever department they are applying to. Questions include, "On a scale of 1–10, how weird are you?" and "What was your last position called? Was that an appropriate title?" (The first question makes sure that employees are sufficiently weird; the second, in which the interviewer is trying to goad the applicant into grumbling about his or her title, tests for humility.)

If there is a disagreement between HR and the manager doing the hiring, Hsieh personally interviews the candidate and makes the final call. His strategy is to get the applicant into a social situation to see if they can connect emotionally. Alcohol often figures in the hiring process. "I had three vodka shots with Tony during my interview," says Rebecca Ratner, Zappos's head of human resources. "And I'm not atypical." I asked Hsieh if this wasn't exposing the company to unnecessary risks. "It's a risk," he says. "But if we're building a culture where everyone is friends with everyone else, it's worth the risk."

After my tour, I spend a few minutes sitting in the Zappos call center with Grace Hale, a bubbly young woman with dyed black hair and a lip piercing. Unlike most call center operators, Zappos does not keep track of call times or require operators to read from scripts. Hale has a penchant for offering unsolicited commentary on customers' shoe selections—"They *are* beautiful," she coos during one call, as she pulls up a picture of a pair of Dr. Scholl's Asana heels that a customer found uncomfortable. Not only are reps encouraged to make decisions on their own—for instance, offering a refund on a defective item—they are supposed to send a dozen or so personal notes to customers every day. "It's all about P-E-C," Hale explains to me. "Personal Emotional Connection with the customer." (After a few hours at Zappos, you actually stop noticing this argot.)

Zappos does not track call times or require operators to read from scripts. "It's all about P-E-C: Personal Emotional Connection with the customer," says one rep.

All of this is designed to impress customers—or as Hale would have it, "wow them." Last year, Zappos stopped promising free overnight shipping on its website, but not because of the cost. In fact, the company *still* ships almost every order overnight, but Hsieh wanted customers to be surprised when they got the item the next day. According to Patti Freeman Evans, an analyst with Forrester Research, this has helped Zappos fend off challenges from copycat sites such as Amazon's Endless.com and IAC's Shoebuy.com, which offer similar perks and even lower prices. "A lot of companies talk about service. Zappos really does it," Evans says.

During Zappos's early days, long workdays would often spill into late-night socializing. Hsieh enjoyed this so much that he formalized it at Zappos: Managers are now required to spend 10 percent to 20 percent of their time goofing off with the people they manage. "It's just kind of a random number we made up," Hsieh concedes. "But part of the way you build company culture is hanging out outside of the office."

On my last night in Las Vegas, Hsieh offers to take me out and show me what he is talking about. We are joined by a couple of his friends and six Zappos employees and bounce from a bar to a lounge to a nightclub. By the time I beg out, at 2 A.M., Hsieh and a few others are heading to a dive bar to grab a late-night bite to eat. Though Hsieh seems to enjoy himself—and though he does indulge in a few shots of Grey Goose—he never really lets loose. For the first half of the evening, we chat seriously about happiness. Then he withdraws, eventually sitting down, playing with his BlackBerry, and watching the party with what looks like a smile.

In his speeches, Hsieh likes to point out that Zappos does not have specific policies for dealing with each customer service situation. He claims that the company's culture allows it to do extraordinary things. I saw him make this point earlier this year in New York City, when he told a story about a woman whose husband died in a car accident after she had ordered boots for him from Zappos. The day after she called to ask for help with the return, she received a flower delivery. The call center rep had ordered the flowers without checking with a supervisor and billed them to the company. "At the funeral, the widow told her friends and family about the experience," Hsieh said, his voice cracking and his eyes tearing up ever so slightly. "Not only was she a customer for life, but so were those 30 or 40 people at the funeral."

Hsieh paused to compose himself. "Stories like these are being created every single day, thousands and thousands of times," he said. "It's just an example that if you get the culture right, then most of the other stuff follows."

Critical Thinking

1. Visit Zappos' website and discuss why it has been called "the poster child for how to connect with customers online."
2. Define corporate culture. According to the article, what makes Zappos' corporate culture distinct?

Max Chafkin is Inc.'s senior writer.

From *Inc. Magazine*, May 2009, pp. 66–73. Copyright © 2009 by Mansueto Ventures LLC. Reprinted by permission.

Rocket Plan

**Companies can fuel success with a rigorous pricing approach—
one that measures customer value, the innovation's nature,
and the product category life cycle stage.**

MARK BURTON AND STEVE HAGGETT

Innovation is the fuel that drives growth. Any good sales
executive can tell you that the quickest path to revenue
growth is through new product innovation rather than
fighting for share in existing markets. Innovation offers
immediate differentiation and the chance to command a premium price. Yet the risks of failure are high. Consider this
statement from Eric von Hippel, a professor of the Massachusetts Institute of Technology (*Harvard Business Review,*
January 2007): "Recent research shows that the 70% to 80%
of new product development that fails does so not for lack of
advanced technology but because of a failure to understand
users' needs."

A new-product launch enjoys many proud parents: the development team that followed a rigorous staged development process, the manufacturing organization that trained Six Sigma black
belts, the marketing team that developed creative promotions and
toured with industry trade shows, the public relations team that
built a compelling publicity campaign, and the sales team that
enthusiastically extolled the product's virtues to customers. So
why are there high failure rates?

Many companies' innovation efforts are inwardly focused.
The results are billions of dollars wasted developing offerings that have little to no appeal to customers. In business-to-
business markets there are three principal reasons for that:

**Failure to connect customer needs to value: financial,
competitive, and strategic benefits to the customer.**
PictureTel was an early innovator in the videoconferencing
industry 20 years ago, developing a breakthrough technology
enabling live videoconferences. Its product launch focused on
its leading performance and truly impressive technical capabilities. Yet after PictureTel's great investment and product differentiation, the market did not beat a path to its door. The early
value propositions failed to translate the cost of the system into
clear value for customers: revenue benefits of reaching more
customers or cost savings from travel. In 2000, PictureTel lost
$100 million; in 2001, a smaller and more profitable rival pur-
chased it.

Executive Briefing

The majority of new-product launches fail. However, it is
seldom the technology itself that's to blame. A rigorous
pricing approach can improve customer adoption rates,
grow profitability, and increase return on investment. A
strategy that quantitatively measures customer value,
evaluates the nature of the innovation (whether minor,
major, or disruptive), and assesses the stage of the product life cycle can be the difference between success and
failure. The authors describe an effective approach.

**Use of product-based value propositions centering
on technical ability over market needs.** Iridium was a
triumph of rocket science. In 1987, the wife of a senior Motorola technology leader fumed because she couldn't call home
from a boat in the Bahamas. Eleven years and more than
$2 billion later, Motorola had successfully launched a necklace of
66 satellites linking $3,000 phone sets for $7-a-minute calls.
However, cell phone customers wanted increasingly small units,
not 1-pound "shoe phones," and the market for people who
needed a dedicated satellite system for $7 a minute was tiny.
In 2000, the network was sold for around $25 million—about a
penny on the dollar for Motorola's investment.

**Overemphasis on the role of pricing in driving cus-
tomer adoption.** Petrocosm launched as an oil industry transaction platform with a $100 million investment from Chevron
and top leadership from the oil equipment industry. It offered
a cheap source of high-technology drilling equipment. But in
an industry requiring billion-dollar offshore platforms poised
over explosive hydrocarbon reservoirs, replacing the trust and
experience that trained sales and service representatives offer
with a low-cost transaction failed to gain a customer base. The
customer base didn't want cheap; it wanted cost-effective. Petrocosm faded away.

The good news is that the pricing process is straightforward and will improve the returns on investment in innovations. Most successful innovators follow a few simple rules:

- Define the financial benefits that customers receive from adopting the new solution.
- Align price levels with financial and psychological drivers of customer value.
- Align pricing strategy with the specific nature of the innovation and the product category life cycle status.
- Create outstanding launch programs—taking the emphasis off price by mitigating perceived risks for customers.

Companies that adhere to those principles enjoy significant benefits over their competitors, including (1) a more effective screening process that enables them to focus resources only on those innovations that provide significant value to the customer, (2) compelling launch programs that communicate the business value of innovations, and (3) a coherent pricing strategy that prevents panic discounting to drive sales. Taken together, those benefits translate to greater success rates for new offerings and better pricing for those that make it to market.

The Value-on-Innovation Paradox

In B-to-B markets, technological possibility often drives innovation, not defined customer needs. Living on the uncertain edge of technology, it should be less risky to focus on what's possible rather than invest money in less-certain research based on customer wish lists—trusting in Moore's Law rather than Murphy's Law. (Moore's Law is the observation that the number of transistors on an integrated circuit for minimum component cost doubles every 24 months, described by Intel cofounder Gordon Moore. Murphy's Law states that anything that can go wrong, will.) But the results show the drawbacks of a technology-driven approach.

Often, market research is focused on projections of market size and growth based on customer intent-to-purchase studies. Although this information can be important, it overlooks the most fundamental issue of whether an innovation will be successful: Is there a compelling business reason for customers to go through the upheaval of changing how they do things—to get the potential benefits of adopting your innovation? In short, what value does the customer expect to get, and how does value compare with the costs of switching? That question sets a much higher standard for research. To address it, companies need to focus on the six areas in Figure 1.

Great innovators use the answers to those questions to draw a map of where innovation will have the greatest impact—at both the market and individual customer level. Not until they understand (1) the customer value their innovations create, (2) the barriers, and (3) enablers of adoption do they finalize specifications. These same insights are used to define high-impact value propositions and to establish pricing models and price levels.

Define customer objectives	• How do customers make money? • How do they plan to grow? • How do they differentiate their offerings? • What are their greatest challenges?
Define current solution	• Which business processes support critical customer objectives? • What is the current work flow? • Who are the process owners and what are their priorities?
Define problem solved	• How does our innovation improve performance against key customer objectives and performance of critical business processes? • What is the impact of solving the problem defined? Is it significant enough to go forward?
Define financial impact	• How does our innovation affect revenues and costs relative to current solutions?
Define barriers to adoption	• What and whom in the customer buying group would our innovation affect? • What are the switching costs? • Is our innovation compatible with customer processes and supporting technology? • What is the organizational or political impact of our innovation?
Define likely adopters	• Who will benefit most from a change to our solution? • Who has the power to push for the change?

Figure 1 Customer value.

Defining barriers to adoption and identifying likely adopters are critical. Companies commonly misread how their innovations change the buying center dynamics. Existing customer contacts might not be the right targets for an innovation when relationships with new decision makers and influencers need to be cultivated. Companies often call on the same old contacts and fail to anticipate that those contacts will not have the power to drive change and/or are very much invested in the status quo. When that happens, they find that those relationships actually impede their ability to sell innovations to their current customers.

The smartest road to profitable returns on innovations starts with an understanding of the customer; technology comes second.

Using Value Insights

Translating the results of customer value research into effective pricing for innovations requires answering some challenging questions about value to the customer. Importantly, it is not

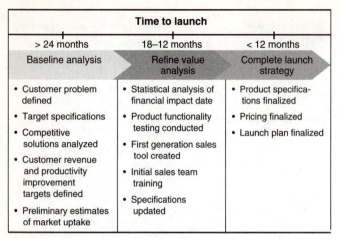

Figure 2 Preparing for effective launch pricing.

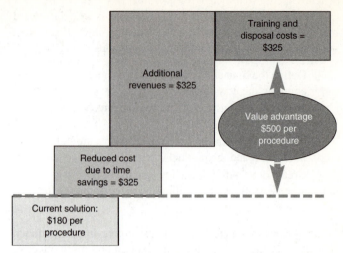

Figure 3 Use customer value data to determine your price.

necessary to exhaustively answer these questions at the start of your customer research and innovation development processes. In fact, one defining characteristic of many leading innovators is that they are comfortable with a certain amount of ambiguity to start. The key is that they continue to (1) ask hard questions about customers and value and (2) refine their views on offering specifications, value positioning, and pricing. They do it early and they do it often.

A leading manufacturer of dental equipment (disguised), which has built its business by entering new markets with innovative offerings, does exactly this. Figure 2 shows a summary of its process.

It is tempting to look at the timeline and say "Our product life cycles are too short for this to be practical." But the fact is that all windows of innovative advantage are shortening. For all companies, it is critical to do value homework and get launch pricing right. Although your business might require far more compressed timelines, the process of establishing and refining your view of value to the customer is the foundational element for successful introduction, pricing, and positioning of innovations.

When the manufacturer was able to employ new technologies, to replace reusable dental instruments with disposable ones, it knew it had a potentially valuable innovation to bring to market. Through direct customer interviews and operational studies, it determined that such a device would improve procedure-room utilization by reducing cleanup time. The device also provided a market opportunity for oral surgeons seeking to differentiate themselves by advertising that they use the safest and most advanced equipment.

Using this information to establish a range for pricing is a three-step process: Determine the total costs to the customer of his current solution options, define the financial benefits that your innovation delivers over and above current alternatives, and identify the switching costs for customers who want to move to your solution.

In the case of our dental equipment manufacturer, that meant determining the following:

- the cost per procedure of current solutions—by amortizing the total lifetime costs of current and reusable equipment over the number of procedures performed
- the cost savings due to greater procedure-room utilization
- the increases in revenues from patients brought in through oral surgeons advertising use of the new equipment
- switching costs (in this instance, disposal and training costs)

Its findings are summarized in Figure 3.

The results of customer value research yield a band of customer value and establish upper and lower boundaries for price range. Using that information about financial value, the manufacturer was then able to set an initial price that captured a fair share of the value created for customers. To do that, it first defined its value advantage over existing solutions: in this case, $500 per procedure. Next, it added the cost of the current solution to define the maximum range of price options available: $180–$680 (the $180 cost of the current solution plus the $500 value advantage).

To narrow down the range, the manufacturer analyzed the psychological elements of value from the customer's perspective. That included negative perceptions (e.g., risk from adopting the new technology, concerns about moving from the comfortable old solution to something new) and psychological benefits (e.g., pride in being on the cutting edge). Finally, the manufacturer needed to set a price that offered some incentive to purchase. At the end of the process, it decided on $400 per instrument. Although that was at the lower end of the possible range, it ensured a significant profit and gave customers a reasonable incentive to switch.

How do companies best select the right price within the range of customer value? Let's turn to that by looking more closely at pricing strategy.

Pricing Strategy Selection

To really refine the pricing decision, evaluate price ranges against a defined pricing strategy for your innovation. This is an iterative process of checking (1) pricing strategy against market research data and (2) possible price points against your pricing strategy. The best way to get your arms around the pricing strategy element is to think about the following two variables.

What is the nature of the innovation? Is it a minor improvement, such as an interim software update? Is it a major one, such as the introduction of flat-panel TV sets? Or is it disruptive, such as the current move to solid-state flash memory for applications previously covered by high-speed disk drives?

Understanding the nature of the innovation defines the degrees of freedom that the innovator has in selecting a pricing strategy. Minor innovations (e.g., line extensions) are often necessary, but they do little to create advantage over the competition. As such, they provide little to increase pricing power. Innovations that are recognized as major breakthroughs present much greater flexibility in choosing a pricing strategy. This is because companies can keep prices high to skim value until the market develops—and then bring prices down to drive growth.

With disruptive innovations, the decision is a bit trickier. In the groundbreaking article "Disruptive Technologies: Catching the Wave" (*Harvard Business Review,* January 2005), Clayton M. Christensen points out that such innovations fall into one of two categories.

Some, such as flash memory, offer significant performance advantages for niche markets (e.g., aerospace applications) but are too expensive for mainstream applications (e.g., laptop computers). The best approach for these products is to go upmarket and use a skim pricing strategy—until costs and complementary technologies make it possible to enter main-stream markets.

Alternately, some offer inferior performance on many key attributes but offer clear benefits in one or two areas for some customers. That was the case with 3.5-inch disk drives when they were introduced. In that instance, the best approach is to go down-market and use a penetration pricing strategy with prices set below established alternatives.

In what stage of the life cycle is the product category? This element is critical but often overlooked. Failure to consider the life cycle dimension can result in disastrous financial consequences. That happened with flat-panel TVs. Early entrants initially played the game well. Prices for the early sets were high, reflecting both costs and the value that enthusiasts placed on them. As process technologies improved, prices dropped precipitously and customer adoption took off. Unfortunately, as the market started to show signs of maturity, most manufacturers were slow to take their feet off the pricing gas. The result has been terrible margin pressures due to low prices and overcapacity—at exactly the time that consumers are becoming sophisticated enough to value and actively seek out differentiation.

Taken together, those two variables point to default pricing strategies for each combination type and stage of the product category life cycle.

Driving Customer Adoption

In addition to doing their homework on value to frame initial prices as fair and reasonable, great marketers take the focus off price by targeting the right customers, working to mitigate

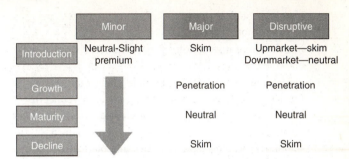

Figure 4 Pricing strategies change with market conditions.

the risks of adopting a new technology, and making it easy for customers to see the value for themselves (as Figure 4 shows).

When rolling out a true innovation, marketers are often focused on identifying and converting early adopters. Those customers are desirable because they become references for later adopters. The motivations for early adopters run the gamut from (1) exploiting the latest technologies to get ahead of the competition to (2) desiring to satisfy the emotional need to be on the cutting edge. Regardless of the specific motivation, early adopters are traditionally less price-sensitive. However, they are still concerned about the potential challenges in adopting an innovation; even the most motivated aren't completely careless about how much risk they will take on. And if the price is too high for an unknown product and its unproven benefits, then the product might never get off the ground.

To address those concerns, marketers should build their launches on what does drive adoption of new technologies. And they should use that knowledge to support sales. Key drivers of customer adoption include the following:

- compelling advantages over existing technology
- the ability to observe and measure the impact of those advantages
- the complexity of the new solution
- compatibility with existing processes and technologies
- the ability to try out an innovation before making a full commitment

Note that price is not on the list. What the list represents is customer desire to mitigate the risks inherent in adopting an innovative new technology. Too often, companies fail to take into account these drivers of adoption when launching an innovative new offering. Instead, the approach is: "Our specifications are set. Our product is so innovative that it's hard to prove value or understand risk until we get it into customers' hands. Once they have it, they'll see the genius of what we have created."

Consider how Azul Systems addressed adoption drivers in the launch of an entirely new server for handling Java applications. In addition to being a new player in the business, Azul's product did not replace any existing customer equipment—further squeezing already tight information technology budgets. Yet it enjoyed a successful launch. Here's how:

- an economic advantage program: "A free, private consulting engagement helps customers quantify the financial gains their organization will realize through a

computer pool deployment." (See www.azulsystems
.com for more information.)

- integration of its technology that required changing only one line of code
- a relationship with IBM to provide global support, services, and spare parts to address customer concerns about ongoing support and maintenance
- documented adherence to widely accepted industry standards for interfacing with existing platforms
- a no-cost 45-day evaluation program for qualified accounts

Successful introduction of new products is challenging, but some simple things can be done to greatly improve your chances. More than anything, companies need to understand what ease of adoption will mean to their customers.

An alternative method of enlightening customers is often absurdly low introductory price deals. That compounds the perception of risk by leading customers to think: "If this technology is so good, then why do they seem so desperate for customers?" Price dealing to get those early "reference accounts" can also dramatically affect future revenues. Once low prices are out on the street, it is very difficult to raise them.

Pricing for Success

Price strategy can be the lever that maximizes return on the risky investment or the velvet rope that bars customers from your service. Get it right and your company enjoys a commanding market position, increased profits, and well-earned confidence across the team. Get it wrong and your company limits both sales and profitability and suffers from a weakened market position, financial performance, and team capabilities.

Lessons from successful new-product launches demonstrate an effective process for innovation price strategy.

First, implement a customer-value measurement process as rigorous as the technology development process. Answers to the questions posed in Figure 1's six customer value areas will enable the company to (1) offer a quantified value message as compelling as the technology and (2) estimate a price range corresponding to customer value. Without a solid understanding of quantified customer value, the launch process is unnecessarily risky.

Second, within that range of customer value, set prices based on the interaction of the innovation's nature (minor, major, or disruptive) and the stage of product life cycle (introduction, maturity, growth, or decline). This simple matrix allows companies to plot a price point that maximizes both adoption and profitability.

The rules laid out here offer a guideline of where to set a price for a product or service innovation. That process can help companies overcome the long odds of new-product success—and fuel growth in both revenues and profitability.

Critical Thinking

1. How is price related to customer value?
2. How should pricing strategies vary as a product moves through the stages of the product life cycle?

MARK BURTON is vice president of Holden Advisors in Concord, Mass., and may be reached at mburton@holdenadvisors.com. **STEVE HAGGETT** is a client manager for Holden Advisors and may be reached at shaggett@holdenadvisors.com. To join the discussion about this article, please visit www.marketingpower.com/marketingmanagementblog.

Authors' note—*Pricing with Confidence: Ten Ways to Stop Leaving Money on the Table* (John Wiley & Sons), Mark Burton's book with co-author Reed Holden, will be published in February 2008.

Competing against Free

Free offerings are rapidly spreading beyond online markets to the physical world. Here's how incumbents can fight back.

DAVID J. BRYCE, JEFFREY H. DYER, AND NILE W. HATCH

A new competitor enters your market and offers a product very similar to yours but with one key difference: It's free. Do you ignore it, hoping that your customers won't defect or the free product won't last? Or do you rapidly introduce a free product of your own in an attempt to quash the threat? These are questions faced by an increasing number of companies—and not just in the digital realm. The "free" business models popularized by companies such as Google, Adobe, and Mozilla are spreading to markets in the physical world, from pharmaceuticals to airlines to automobiles.

How should established companies respond? Clearly, managers are having difficulty figuring this out. For the past five years, we have been studying how incumbents have dealt with competitors employing free business models in a variety of product markets. (See the sidebar "About the Research.") We have found no examples of companies in the non-digital realm that have prevailed against rivals with free offerings. In fact, in two-thirds of the battles that have progressed far enough to be judged, incumbents (both digital and physical) made the wrong choice. In a handful of instances, companies that should not have taken action did so immediately by introducing their own free offering—hurting their revenues and profitability. They should have either waited and allowed the attacker to self-destruct or recognized that the two could peacefully coexist.

More commonly, companies that should have taken action didn't do so quickly enough or at all. Surprisingly, these included incumbents that had identified a genuine threat from a new entrant and had all the weapons they needed to win a head-to-head battle: an established customer base, superior product features, a strong reputation, and abundant financial resources.

Even companies with formidable assets are slow to fend off free-product competitors. The reason: the ubiquity of the profit-center structure and mind-set.

Why didn't these companies use their formidable assets to fend off free-product competitors? The answer is so obvious that you've probably guessed it: Managers were reluctant to abandon an existing business model that was generating healthy revenues and profits. But if the answer is obvious, why did managers make this mistake? The reason is the ubiquity of the profit-center structure and mind-set. Drawing from our research on free offerings in online and physical markets, we explore in this article how to assess whether the introduction of a free product or service in your market is a threat and how to overcome the profit-center challenge.

Assessing the Threat

The seriousness of the threat posed by a new entrant hinges on three factors: the entrant's ability to cover its costs quickly enough, the rate at which the number of users of the free offering is growing, and the speed with which your paying customers are defecting.

Some new competitors self-destruct because they can't convert nonpaying customers into paying ones fast enough to cover costs or because they can't find a third party that will pay for access to their users. So it's crucial to determine if the competitor's free offering is generating revenue in some way. Of course, some companies may have enough funding to wait a year or more before they need to monetize their user base. (For example, Skype offered its free phone service for a year before it introduced SkypeOut, a paid service for calling landlines from a computer.) But this scenario can actually benefit an incumbent by giving it time to assess the potential of the model and decide whether to launch its own free product.

We learned that an entrant will usually find a way to turn users into revenue-generating customers if its user base is growing rapidly or if the incumbent's paying customers are defecting to the free offering at a high rate. What rates signal danger? Our examination of the dynamics in a number of markets suggests that if the free offering's user base is growing by 40 percent or more a year (meaning that it will at least double every two years) or your customer defection rate is 5 percent or

Idea in Brief

Business models that involve offering a product or service for free and making money in other ways are spreading beyond the digital realm. But managers of threatened companies are having difficulty figuring out how to respond: An ongoing study has found that some companies respond too quickly but most don't do so quickly enough—even when they have sufficient resources.

To assess the threat, incumbents should consider the entrant's ability to cover its costs quickly enough, the rate at which the number of users of the free offering is growing, and the speed with which paying customers are defecting.

A bigger challenge is overcoming the ubiquitous profit-center structure, which discourages managers from giving away offerings. The remedy is to move P&L responsibility to a senior management group and to assign revenue stream and cost management oversight to separate lower-level groups.

more a year (meaning that you stand to lose at least 25 percent of your customers within five years), serious trouble may be looming. As the matrix "How Big a Threat Is 'Free' Competition?" shows, assessing those rates (or reasonable estimates of them) helps a company determine the level of threat from the free product and respond accordingly.

Choosing Whether and When to Respond

When both rates mentioned above are high, the entrant represents a *business model* threat. Most established companies must not only respond with a free offering but also radically change their business model to survive. And they need to do so pretty quickly—within two or three years. Many newspapers competing against online rivals that offer free classified advertising or editorial content are in this quadrant. They will continue to deteriorate sharply without a fundamental rethinking of their business model.

Fortunately for incumbents, most threats wind up in one of the other quadrants, which means there may be more time to respond. When the entrant's users are multiplying rapidly but the established firm's customers are defecting slowly, the entrant represents a *delayed* threat. This means the free product or service is attracting either customers from other established competitors or brand-new users. In such cases, your offering can coexist with the free one for at least a few years—especially if yours is targeting premium segments. This is the situation that Microsoft finds itself in with its Office software: Because of the high switching costs, most current enterprise users aren't defecting, but new users—college students, small businesses, and educational institutions—are increasingly using Google Docs and Oracle's Open Office, both of which are free. (See the sidebar "Why Microsoft Should Take Its 'Free' Competition More Seriously.")

The trick for incumbents facing delayed threats is figuring out exactly when to respond with either a free version of the existing offering or a new free product that appeals to new users. Responding sooner rather than later allows an incumbent to beat back the entrant and probably won't significantly hurt existing sales (because established customers are switching slowly). As soon as the entrant's users are in the millions, however, the incumbent must respond—as Intuit did when it acquired upstart Mint.com for $170 million in 2009, eliminating a threat to its Quicken personal finance software and gaining a free online product. (Mint.com had attracted more than 2 million users in just three years.)

When the defection rate among your paying customers is high and the growth rate of the entrant's users is low, the threat is obviously *immediate* because your revenues are rapidly eroding. Even though the free offering has not yet attracted a large following, it's a problem for you and demands a prompt response. It also suggests that you are overserving your customers and thereby inviting disruption. You must quickly figure out a way to launch a free offering.

Finally, when both rates are low, the threat is *minor*. In these cases, the incumbent should continue to monitor the situation.

Offer a Better Free

If you've established that free offerings are a threat to your business and have considered the timing of your response, the next step is to figure out *how* to respond. Most incumbents can successfully counterattack by unleashing their arsenal of weapons, which typically includes a large base of users or customers who have made investments in learning how to use the product, advanced technical know-how, substantial brand equity, significant financial resources, knowledge of the market, and access to important distribution and marketing channels. Incumbents can use those assets to introduce a better free product and to employ some tried-and-true sales and pricing strategies to generate revenues and profits: up-selling, cross-selling, selling access to customers, and bundling the free product with paid offerings. (See the sidebar "Four Tried-and-True Strategies.")

Yet, as we mentioned above, incumbents often fail to counterattack. A widely known case in point is the reluctance of almost all major newspapers in the United States to embrace a free business model when Craigslist attacked their profitable classified-ads business. According to our research, Salt Lake City is the only top 50 U.S. metropolitan market for classified ads that is not dominated by Craigslist. The reason? Deseret Media (which includes the *Deseret News,* KSL TV, and KSL NewsRadio) responded quickly to the business model threat by launching its own free classifieds site and making other significant changes. The site, ksl.com, is better developed and easier to navigate than Craigslist, and it leveraged the established KSL brand to attract classified ads.

Deseret Media quickly benefited from network effects: More buyers went to ksl.com than to Craigslist because more sellers were posting there. The site generates revenue by charging

How Big a Threat Is "Free" Competition?

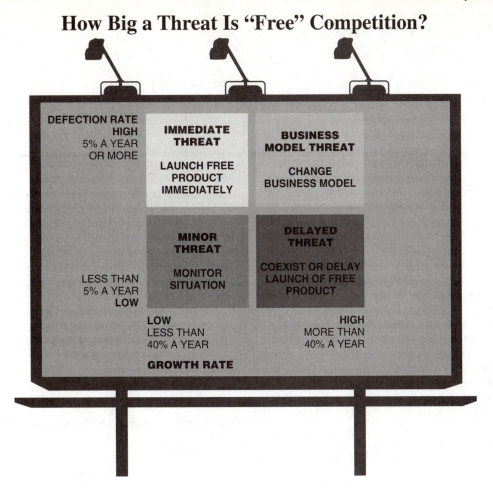

DEFECTION RATE		
HIGH 5% A YEAR OR MORE	**IMMEDIATE THREAT** LAUNCH FREE PRODUCT IMMEDIATELY	**BUSINESS MODEL THREAT** CHANGE BUSINESS MODEL
LESS THAN 5% A YEAR LOW	**MINOR THREAT** MONITOR SITUATION	**DELAYED THREAT** COEXIST OR DELAY LAUNCH OF FREE PRODUCT
	LOW LESS THAN 40% A YEAR	**HIGH** MORE THAN 40% A YEAR
	GROWTH RATE	

Companies That Prevailed

Personal finance software company **Intuit** responded to the threat from free rival Mint.com by purchasing the company. Mint.com, which makes money by selling access to its user base, lets Intuit maintain a free offering separate from its popular Quicken product.

Yahoo, the leading provider of free e-mail, responded to Google's entry by matching, and then exceeding, Gmail's free storage offer.

Companies That Ignored the Threat

The major airlines in Europe have been slow to respond to **Ryanair,** which offers free or deeply discounted tickets and charges for other services. Ryanair has made impressive gains in Europe; its share now exceeds that of Air France.

Satellite radio company **SiriusXM,** which offers subscription packages for its more than 180 channels, has done nothing to stem the loss of share to Pandora, which provides free radio over the internet and generates revenue by charging for ad-free service and selling access to its user base to third parties.

---

advertisers that want to post regular ads as well as classified sellers who want preferred positions. The site's profits now exceed those of the traditional businesses, including the newspaper.

Meanwhile, Deseret Media has changed the newspaper's business model by cutting nearly half its staff and crowdsourcing some of its content. In 2010, the paper increased its print and online audience by 15 percent, the second-highest growth rate in the industry. Overall, Deseret Media is thriving.

Yahoo is another example of an incumbent that prevailed by introducing a better free product. In 2004, Google launched its free Gmail service, which provided 10 times more storage than Yahoo, the leading provider of free e-mail at the time. As a new

entrant, Google could afford to offer significantly more storage because it had relatively few users. A Google executive told us, "We don't do something unless it is an order of magnitude better—maybe five to 10 times better—than what others are offering, particularly if we have to get users to switch from another free product to ours."

Google's entry created a dilemma for Yahoo, which generated some revenue from up-selling (persuading users to pay for more storage or other add-ons) but much more from advertisers

Four Tried-and-True Strategies

1. Up-Sell

Introduce a free basic offering to gain widespread use and then charge for a premium version.

Requirements

- A free product that appeals to a very large user base so that even a low conversion rate of users to paying customers will generate substantial revenues **or**
- A high percentage of users willing to pay for the premium version

Examples

Virtually every iPhone app uses this strategy. One tactic is to offer a free version of the product to consumers and a premium version to the business market, as Adobe does with its Reader software.

Skype, which offers free computer-to-computer calls and charges for add-ons, succeeds with up-selling because it has more than 400 million users, many of whom become paying customers. Flickr, the free photo-sharing site, has a much smaller user base and a low conversion rate. That explains why eBay paid $2.6 billion for Skype, and Yahoo paid less than $30 million for Flickr.

2. Cross-Sell

Sell other products that are not directly tied to the free product.

Requirements

- A broad product line—preferably one that complements the free product—**or**
- The ability through partnerships to sell a broad line of products to users of the free product

Examples

Ryanair offers roughly 25 percent of its airline seats free but cross-sells a variety of add-on services, such as seat reservations and priority boarding. Once on the plane, the customer is sold food, scratch-card games, perfume, digital cameras, MP3 players, and other products. (Ryanair employs a second strategy: charging third parties for in-flight advertisements.) Specialty pharmaceuticals company Galderma rebates out-of-pocket costs for Epiduo, a prescription acne gel, and cross-sells other skin care products.

3. Charge Third Parties

Provide a free product to users and then charge a third party for access to them.

Requirements

- A free offering that attracts either many users who can be segmented for advertisers or a targeted group that makes up a customer segment **and**
- Third parties willing to pay to reach these users

Examples

Google, which charges companies to advertise to its millions of users, is the poster child for this strategy. Another example is Finnish telecommunications company Blyk, which offers 200 free cell-phone minutes a month to 16-to-24-year-olds who fill out a survey and agree to receive ads. Blyk then sells access to and information about them. Blyk was recently acquired by Orange, the largest brand of France Telecom.

Generating users does not guarantee success. Xmarks offered web-browser add-on tools that attracted more than 2 million users—and plenty of venture capital. But the company recently shut down because it couldn't deliver a clear segment to advertisers.

4. Bundle

Offer a free product or service with a paid offering.

Requirements

- Products or services that can be bundled with the free offering **or**
- A free product that needs regular maintenance or a complementary offering

Examples

Here the "free" effect is largely psychological—the customer must buy the bundle to get the free product. Think of Hewlett-Packard, which often gives away a printer with the purchase of a computer.

Better Place plans to lease electric cars in Israel by bundling a free lease with a service contract. Customers would pay to swap out their battery packs.

Banks are increasingly bundling free services, such as accounts and stock trades, with paid services, such as investment accounts that require minimum balances. But the bundled product doesn't have to be related to the free one. Banks also give away iPods, iPads, and other products to customers opening accounts.

(its real customers). To match Google's offer, Yahoo would have had to buy warehouses of servers to provide storage for its 125 million e-mail users—an investment that would have generated no additional revenues.

Yahoo decided to respond in a way that sent a message to Google and to its own e-mail users and advertisers: It immediately announced that it would match Google's offer of one gigabyte of free storage. A couple of years later, it began to offer unlimited storage. Those moves left Yahoo users with no reason to switch to Google—and left Google with few options for offering a better free product. Although the increased costs hurt Yahoo's profits in the short term, the company's share of the e-mail market continues to be several times larger than Google's. But Google has not given up: Gmail now serves as a platform for the company's other free products, such as Google Docs and Calendar. In the long run, this could make Gmail the better free product.

The most important lesson from these cases? If your user base is vital to your revenue stream, you must quickly offer a free product that is comparable or superior to the new competitor's. If you can, you should try to crush that competitor or at least prevent it from becoming powerful enough to mount a serious challenge.

Rethink Profit Centers

Two obstacles prevent managers at established companies from making the leap to free strategies. The first is the deeply rooted belief that products must generate a respectable level of revenues and profits on their own. The second is the profit-center structure and the accounting system it employs, which both reflect and reinforce this mind-set.

In stable competitive environments, profit centers are a godsend: They push P&L accountability down, usually to the product level; they place revenue and cost streams in the hands of an individual, clearly identifying where the buck stops; and they provide a career ladder for those hoping to oversee units with larger budgets. But profit centers have a dark side: They make it impossible for an organization to consider a product's revenues and costs separately—a perspective that's essential for conceiving and implementing a free-product strategy.

To fix this problem, profit responsibility must be pushed up to a management group that oversees revenue and cost streams from a much wider variety of sources than traditional profit centers do. Clearly, a company that relies primarily on free-product strategies, such as Google, will place this responsibility much higher in the organization than one that uses free offerings as a small part of a more comprehensive strategy.

In addition to moving profit responsibility higher, companies with free business models generally place responsibility for revenue streams and cost management at lower levels, and in separate hands. *Revenue managers* in these companies pursue all possible ways to increase revenues—except product price. Clearly, the job requires creativity, but revenue is typically generated in the four ways mentioned up-selling, cross-selling, selling access to users, and bundling.

A separate set of *product development managers* is responsible for overseeing costs and building in product features that will expand the user base as rapidly as possible. On the basis of conversations with current executives at Google, we estimate that only the CEO and three or four senior vice presidents have P&L responsibility there.

Clearly, tensions can arise between the revenue group and the product development group, and it pays to spell out how they will be resolved. For example, Google's product development group can nix revenue models it believes would damage the user experience. When the two groups can't resolve disagreements, the senior managers with P&L responsibility—and sometimes even the CEO—arbitrate.

Why Microsoft Should Take Its "Free" Competition More Seriously

For the past four years, Microsoft's Office software has been under attack from free alternatives: Google Docs and Oracle's Open Office. Although Microsoft finally responded in 2010 with Microsoft Live, a free "cloud" version of Office, it waited too long and was not forceful enough to contain what could become a serious threat.

Microsoft's reluctance to embrace a free-product strategy is not surprising. Its office applications business has long enjoyed a near monopoly and has been highly profitable. And except for price-sensitive users such as college students and public entities, its customers have not flocked to the free products. Indeed, concerns about file incompatibility, the lack of functions in competing products, and the need to teach employees how to use new applications have kept the vast majority of Microsoft's target corporate customers in the fold.

But in our view, Microsoft has erred in not taking the defection among price-sensitive customers more seriously. Our survey of college students suggests that nearly 20 percent now exclusively use free alternatives, up from about 4 percent five years ago. According to a competitor, the number of students in the United States using Google Apps has increased from 7 million to 10 million in the past two years, and about 3 million small-business users and some large institutions (including Brown, the California State University system, Gonzaga, the University of Minnesota, the University of Virginia, Vanderbilt, Villanova, and William & Mary) have adopted it as well. This is a big problem for Microsoft: Open Office and Google Docs will continue to improve, becoming more attractive to younger and newer users as well as price-sensitive institutions—especially those overserved by the function-laden Office suite.

So far, Microsoft Live doesn't seem to be effective in countering the free offerings of its competitors. There are several possible reasons. One is that Microsoft, unlike Open Office, doesn't offer a version that can be downloaded to and operated from an individual computer. Another is that Microsoft has not promoted its free product aggressively enough, and, as a result, it is not as well-known as Google Docs.

Judging from Microsoft's half-hearted response to date, the company doesn't want customers switching to its free product. This is a mistake. By sacrificing a portion of revenues from price-sensitive or overserved customers, Microsoft could prevent free-product competitors from expanding their foothold and give itself a better shot at retaining its most valuable customers: the business and power home users who are loyal today but could ultimately defect.

Another culprit that undermines many companies' ability to offer free products is the cost accounting system, which is excellent for averaging costs across large numbers of products and then allocating overhead but not for identifying the *actual* cost of the last product or service sold. The distinction between average cost (what some call variable cost or total cost) and actual cost (what some call marginal cost) is important because the latter is almost always lower than the former, often dramatically so. Think of what it costs an airline to fly an empty seat on an otherwise full or mostly full airplane: essentially nothing. This principle applies in nearly every industry. Once an operation is up and running and costs are largely incurred, generating additional products or services adds very little to total costs. Company leaders can use this notion to their advantage as they consider alternative pricing approaches, such as free offerings. By stepping back from the cost accounting system, they may find flexibility they didn't realize they had.

An example from the pharmaceutical industry illustrates how the profit-center structure and mind-set and the cost accounting system make it difficult for established companies to react when rivals offer free products or services. In 2008, specialty pharmaceuticals manufacturer Galderma (a joint venture of Nestlé and L'Oréal) launched Epiduo, a prescription acne lotion, in the United States. Because Benzac, its other acne product, was about to lose U.S. patent protection, Galderma felt tremendous pressure to build Epiduo's U.S. market share as quickly as possible. But in Europe, the product had met stiff competition from Duac, an acne gel made by GlaxoSmithKline (GSK). Expecting more of the same in the United States, Galderma decided to implement a program to reimburse a patient's out-of-pocket costs for the product for as long as a year. In exchange for rebate coupons, customers gave the company their e-mail addresses. Galderma then sent them skin care tips, acne information, and special offers for its non-prescription products, such as cleansing bars.

Heavily rebating new drugs in the early days to build market share is a common strategy in the pharmaceutical industry. The hope is that once the company has won a substantial share, health insurance companies will agree to cover the drug, allowing the company to offset its development costs and make a profit before its patents expire.

But incumbents selling established drugs are generally unwilling to take risks with pricing. Their cost accounting systems and P&L structures make them feel that they must cover their substantial product costs—which explains why GSK and other incumbents seemed paralyzed when Galderma launched the rebate program for Epiduo. One GSK executive told us, "We can't afford to match them, and we can scarcely afford to discount. So we're losing share."

In reality, the marginal cost—the material and labor—of a tube of lotion or gel is small (from a few pennies to a few dollars). Therefore, in the short run incumbents would have lost almost nothing if they had deeply discounted their products or matched Galderma's rebate. Moreover, like Galderma,

About the Research

For five years, we have been studying companies that face competition from rivals offering free products and services. The 34 incumbents we've been following are in 26 product markets representing the digital and physical realms as well as the intersection of the two. The markets include airlines, automobiles, classified advertising, dermatology pharmaceuticals, internet services, music, office applications, operating systems, personal finance software, radio, and telecommunications. Twenty-four of the battles between incumbents and free-product rivals have progressed far enough for us to judge the incumbents' actions. In two-thirds of those cases, the incumbents made the wrong choice: They introduced their own free offering too quickly, responded too slowly, or did nothing at all.

they could have cross-sold products and, by breaking down the walls around P&L centers, used profits from other highly successful products to subsidize short-term losses in dermatology. This would have forced Galderma into the untenable position of giving away its product without growing share. The battle is ongoing, but so far Galderma's strategy has allowed it to gain customers and profitably cross-sell products.

Because free-product strategies entail experimentation and, admittedly, some risk taking, embracing them may require a cultural shift. Strong executive leadership will be needed to build the case for mounting a competitive response, revamping organizational structures, and questioning cost accounting information. When a free offering is a threat, few strategies are available besides meeting free with free. Incumbents that spend too much time looking for some other killer strategy often only defer the inevitable. By taking decisive action as soon as the threat is clear, incumbents can survive and thrive.

Critical Thinking

1. Discuss how consumer defection rate and growth rate impact the seriousness of the threat posed by a new market entrant.

2. In your opinion, what do the authors mean by a "better free"? Do you agree with their recommended strategies?

DAVID J. BRYCE (dbryce@byu.edu) is an associate professor of strategy, **JEFFREY H. DYER** (jdyer@byu.edu) is the Horace Beesley Professor of Strategy, and **NILE W. HATCH** (nile@byu.edu) is an associate professor of entrepreneurship at Brigham Young University's Marriott School of Management. Dyer is also an adjunct professor at the University of Pennsylvania's Wharton School.

From *Harvard Business Review*, June 2011, pp. 104–111. Copyright © 2011 by Harvard Business School Publishing. Reprinted by permission.

The Devolution of Marketing

Is America's Marketing Model Fighting Hard Enough to Keep Up?

Andrew R. Thomas and Timothy J. Wilkinson

The American marketing model is dysfunctional. Small and medium-sized companies, as well as large multinational firms, have been lured into a misconceived form of producing and selling. It goes like this:

- Invest blood, sweat, tears and money to innovate a new product or service.
- Sell it through the largest distributor possible.
- Maximize the volume of sales through that distributor.
- Deal with the inevitable cost-cutting demands.
- Compromise brand integrity.
- Export capital, jobs, quality control and pollution to developing markets.
- Watch the innovation become a commodity.
- Lose money.
- Begin to develop new innovations.
- And then, start all over again . . .

A large portion of what drove us into the Great Recession is rooted in this dysfunctional pattern of distribution. Sell more and more through a mega-distributor—with much of the profit split by distributors and overseas manufacturers. Earnings obtained by the latter are reinvested into the United States, and then are lent to consumers so they can continue to spend beyond their means—thereby propping up the global economy.

Discussions are abundant about out-of-control lending, consumer spending, the impact of outsourcing and the lack of sustainability. But little attention is paid to the harmful impact that the distribution strategies employed by mega-distributors have played—not only on innovators, but on the overall economy. As we talk to business leaders around the world, it is clear that many of them realize a fundamental shift has occurred: Power has transferred from those who create innovative products and services to mega-distributors, who are increasingly in control of the global marketplace.

Mistakenly, many marketing departments see deals with mega-distributors as the way to boost sales and market share. In reality, the Megas live by high volume and low prices. They use their powerful leverage to demand price cuts and other concessions from suppliers. Companies end up with razor thin or non-existent profit margins, even as their innovative products and services are treated like commodities by both the Megas and the buying public. Surprisingly, this transformation of the business landscape has occurred with little fanfare or real analysis.

The Blame Game

Before you think that this is merely another attempt to blame Wal-Mart Stores, Inc., GE Capital, AutoNation, The Home Depot and others for the ills of the world, let us be clear: We do not blame the Megas for the distribution trap and what it has caused. As far as we know, no one has ever been forced to sell their products or services to someone else. Megas rarely, if ever, travel to visit potential suppliers. They wait for would-be vendors to show up. And boy, do they—in great numbers, each hoping to strike it rich!

Beginning in the early 1980s, innovative firms permitted, either consciously or subconsciously, outsiders into their companies. They allowed these outsiders to gain increasing control over sales and distribution activities. Innovative firms and the people who led them were responding to what management theorists were saying at that time. The "business gurus" talked about organizational transformation—emphasizing things like resources, capabilities, innovation, technology and operational effectiveness. "Total quality management," "lean manufacturing" and "zero defects" were just a few of the solutions preached by business elites to companies of all sizes.

Drinking this elixir, thousands of companies that once had been in control of all aspects of their innovative development began to lose interest in sales and distribution, preferring instead that other companies take over this "business function." The concept of "core competencies" was provided as the justification for letting loose of control after the producing firm had exercised its unique set of value-adding activities. Why manage a string of dealers if your core competency—your basis of differentiation—is in research and development or manufacturing? Taking this advice, companies divested themselves of activities that were not perceived as value added. Sales and distribution were pushed aside.

One of the people who understood the ramifications of the new transformational thinking was Sam Walton. He and a raft of imitators stepped in to fill the power vacuum that the strategy gurus had helped create. The result was the evolution of massive distributors, which ultimately drove the sales and distribution of innovative products and services in the United States.

The Distribution Trap

Numerous manufacturers have seen their profit margins squeezed and their brands eroded because they decided to sell through the Megas. Rubbermaid, Levi Strauss, Goodyear and many lesser-known companies have been literally trashed by the relentless pressure from the Megas to cut prices. Remember Jones Soda Co.? In 2006, this company showed profits of $39 million on $406 million in revenue. A distribution strategy initially based on selling through tattoo parlors and snowboarding shops morphed into one focused on Panera Bread, Barnes & Noble and Starbucks. But in 2007, Jones Soda began to sell to the Megas (including selling a limited selection to Wal-Mart), and ended up posting an $11.6 million loss for the year.

One website summed it up: "And just exactly what is Jones Soda doing for sale at Wal-Mart? Is Jones Soda now going to market itself as a value-priced soda, except with weird flavors?" (Source: www.bloggingstocks.com/2007/06/14/jones-soda-loses-its-fizz.) In September 2010, after suffering from years of quarterly losses, the company went all-out in marketing to the Bentonville, Ark., giant, agreeing to sell 6-packs of its most popular sodas to the Mega's 3,800 stores. This served to only further debase what had at one time been a popular, upstart brand.

The scope and magnitude of a Mega can quickly consume the brand equity of individual products and services. Private labels, discounting, lack of service and mass-market presentation have diluted the value of American brands. The distribution trap has squeezed margins by making products that were once viewed with respect easily substituted with either store brands or inexpensive knock-offs. In fact, the Megas can be viewed as instruments of brand dilution. The very act of discounting, which is the business model of the Megas, undermines the entire idea behind a manufacturer's brand.

In 1993, Rubbermaid, the long-time producer of high-quality storage products was named America's Most Admired Company by *Fortune* magazine. Rubbermaid offered 5,000 different items, producing nearly 400 new, innovative products each year. Most the company's history was defined by strong relationships with end-users through a network of independent distributors and dealers. However, beginning in the early 1990s, a new leadership team entered and committed to expanding sales through the Megas.

The CEO at the time, Wolfgang Schmitt, explained: "It's typically the bigger suppliers that can form the sort of close partnerships that retailing's behemoths are increasingly demanding. The goal is to boost sales and reduce costs for both sides by slashing inventories, shortening lead times and eliminating error: There is a healthy interdependence between us and people like Wal-Mart. We need them; they need us." Wal-Mart accounted for about 14 percent of Rubbermaid's business when, in 1994, disaster struck.

The key components of Rubbermaid products are polymer-based resins, which make up about one-third of the cost of any given product. The price of resins had been stable for years, but costs shot up in spring 1994 because of new global demand and a supply shortage resulting from problems at key refineries. Within 18 months, the price of resins nearly doubled—adding $200 million to Rubbermaid's costs. Focused as always on earnings growth, the company increased its prices. The price increases were met with derision by the Megas. The giant retailers objected to monthly price increases, and complained that Rubbermaid was unresponsive to the realities of the market. Wal-Mart, frustrated with the price increases, emptied shelves of Rubbermaid's "Little Tikes" line of toys, and turned the space over to Fisher-Price.

Left with no other real option, Rubbermaid felt compelled to change gears. In 1994, it began to compete aggressively on the basis of price, offering steep discounts to the Megas. Its margins quickly eroded, and cost-cutting measures were enacted, including the elimination of its dealer network, thousands of American jobs and the closure of nine plants. The company purged 6,000 color and size variations and cut the total number of products by 45 percent. These efforts produced only temporary relief. Rubbermaid was acquired by the Newell Corporation in 1998 for a mere $6 billion in stock.

The Outsourcing Compulsion

Another consequence of the distribution trap is outsourcing and offshoring. While the academic literature is replete with theories about foreign direct investment (FDI), the real motivator for much of the 23 percent FDI that is "contracted-out" has been entirely ignored. Producers are being literally forced to invest in overseas manufacturing by their mega-distribution partners. Outsourcing is a coping mechanism in response to relentless price pressures from the Megas. Companies locked into the distribution trap can substantially lower costs by shuttering domestic manufacturing operations.

Lakewood Engineering & Manufacturing Co. is a case in point. For years, this electric fan manufacturer sold its 20-inch box fan for $20. Responding to Wal-Mart's downward price pressure, the company opened a factory in Shenzhen, China in 2000, where labor costs averaged $0.25 per hour compared with $13 per hour in Chicago. By 2003, the fan was sold at the Mega for $10. In 2008, Lakewood employees, alongside local labor organizations, protested the company's decision to close its electric heater operations and move production to China. Wal-Mart buys 80 to 90 percent of the company's heaters.

Lakewood claimed that its hands were tied because it was heavily mortgaged to Wells Fargo Bank, which refused to lend it more money. The company's relationship with the Mega resulted in the layoff of 220 workers and the outsourcing of production. All too often, the compulsive embrace of offshoring by U.S. firms is not a function of internally generated goals and objectives, but is instead driven by the sheer demands of corporate survival.

One of the consequences of the outsourcing compulsion is environmental degradation in the developing countries where distributor-forced outsourcing takes place. In many emerging markets, environmental laws are lax or simply go un-enforced. These countries may be viewed favorably by multinationals, because they constitute "pollution havens"—with the cost of pollution absorbed by the people living in those countries, not by the multinational corporations or their customers. For example, China's industrial cities are so full of air pollution that their occupants rarely see the sun. The heavy reliance on coal has polluted the air with suspended particles of liquid or solids that float in the air. These particulates—and China has lots of them floating around—are associated with respiratory problems and heart disease. In the U.S., the growth of municipal waste has grown in tandem with the contribution of retail trade to the gross domestic product. According to the Environmental Protection Agency, 55 to 65 percent of municipal waste is classified as "residential waste": It is the product of the buying habits of individuals and families. This has taken place because during the last 25 years, as consumer prices have dropped and as consumption has increased, people have purchased increasing amounts of cheap stuff from the Megas—which quickly wears out and is then discarded.

The rush to the cheapest possible price has not yet factored in these costs of environmental degradation. When that inevitably happens, prices will have to rise. In short, the offshoring of production, driven by the mega-distributors, is not sustainable. China and other emerging

---

Briefly

- Partnering with mega-distributors holds an irresistible lure for many companies.
- The Megas' business model depends on mass marketing, low price and volume.
- Avoiding the Megas may mean less volume, but can have other advantages.

economies have traded extremely high economic growth for polluted air, water and land. No country can pursue such a strategy indefinitely. In the coming decades, as emerging markets grow up, environmental concerns will outweigh the appetite for runaway growth, and the unreasonably low prices that Americans have come to expect as they make purchases from the Megas will end.

The Independent Solution

Falling into the distribution trap is not an inevitable outcome of American business practice. But companies like Red Ants Pants have prospered by avoiding the big-box stores and other mass-market retailers. Thirty-year-old company founder Sarah Calhoun became so frustrated with ill-fitting work pants, designed without the female figure in mind, that she started her own company. There are now 70 different sizes of the double-knee, double-seat work pants with their lower-rise front and higher-rise backs. By importing 12-ounce cotton canvas from India, and having it cut and sewn by a factory in Seattle, Calhoun is free to sell the premium priced pants ($119 a pair) to her target market: women who work for a living in the construction trades. A 1964 Airstream trailer decorated with red ants is the marketing vehicle of this small firm. Calhoun's Tour de Pants road trips allow her to make direct sales to groups of women at homes across the country. Personal contacts made through trade shows and conferences further extend her direct marketing approach.

Another example is STIHL Inc., a manufacturer of outdoor power equipment that has never sold its products through mass merchants. Instead, the company sells its innovative products through thousands of independently owned servicing dealers across America and throughout the world. An industry global leader in both market share and profitability, STIHL continues to embrace its founding principle of only selling the company's products through servicing dealers.

The Current Landscape

The rise of the Megas has created a groundswell of community-based efforts to help local independent businesses compete effectively and prevent chains and online giants from displacing local entrepreneurs. More than 100 such groups have organized in North America since 2000, including 70 affiliated with the American Independent Business Alliance (AMIBA), a non-profit dedicated to supporting these community efforts.

AMIBA facilitates group purchasing, cooperative promotions and advertising and other activities to help local businesses gain economies of scale. It also wages sophisticated "buy local" campaigns to promote the greater overall value local businesses often can provide to customers, as well as the vital economic, social and cultural role they play in communities. Lastly, these alliances are advocates for the interests of local entrepreneurs in their local government and media. As their ranks grow, AMIBA aims to shift state and national policies that favor larger corporations at the expense of smaller community enterprise. Another effort to support local business is Independent We Stand, sponsored in part by STIHL. Independent We Stand focuses on the money spent at locally owned companies and how it re-circulates throughout the community. Whether it is the taxes that are paid, the payroll of the workers or the businesses' own spending, the impact of local-driven commerce makes a community a far better place to live.

The battle lines are being drawn for a new showdown between locally focused groups like AMIBA and Independent We Stand and Wal-Mart. The mega-retailer recently announced that it is targeting urban areas with the idea of introducing smaller stores like the ones it already operates across Latin America. In a recent *Wall Street Journal* article, Bill Simon, head of Wal-Mart's U.S. stores business, said that Wal-Mart hopes to open many of its "Neighborhood Markets" across the country. These stores will be like the smaller "bodegas" the company has set up across Latin America. According to Simon, Wal-Mart believes that the opportunity exists for "hundreds" of the smaller-sized outlets, which will offer customer staples and produce.

The Reality Check

For many companies, the lure of partnering with a megadistributor is irresistible. These giants can put products in front of hundreds of millions of customers—and potentially bring in huge gains in sales and market share. But behind these high hopes may be a faulty premise that can lead to disaster. Whether out of naiveté, arrogance or greed, innovative companies expect that the Megas will care about the success of their products and services as much as they do.

What companies forget, or ignore, is that the Megas' business model depends on mass marketing, low price and volume. Naturally, the Megas use their tremendous leverage to dictate tough terms to innovators. They insist on ever-greater price reductions and force companies to redesign products and services to better suit their needs. In the end, many producers discover that all the blood, sweat, tears and money they have poured into their products and services has been wasted: Their hard-won creations have been turned into commodities with razor-thin profit margins. From this perspective, the outcomes for the innovator are not surprising: the abandonment of brand integrity, the acceleration of the innovation into a commodity and the inevitable cost cuts that result from offshoring and outsourcing.

Having created the process and product, and invested time and money, why would companies turn the final stage of the operation over to a third party? Business leaders do it all the time. It is their choice, and they must bear responsibility for what happens.

To avoid the negative outcomes described, companies must control their own distribution. This may mean selling directly to customers online or through company-owned retail stores. Or, it may mean striking strong deals with distributors and avoiding partners who will not agree to stringent terms. Of course, avoiding the Megas may mean less volume, but the advantages of doing so are likely to make up for it. Companies that keep a tight rein on distribution have a greater ability to control pricing, customer service and after-sales service. They can also build stronger, longer-lasting relationships with their customers. And isn't that what every company ultimately needs?

Critical Thinking

1. Explain the lure for manufacturers to partner with and sell their products through mega-distributors.

2. In your opinion, do small businesses that control their own distribution and avoid partnerships with mass-market retailers stand a chance at success?

ANDREW R. THOMAS is assistant professor of international business at the University of Akron in Ohio, TIMOTHY J. WILKINSON is professor of marketing and Interim Dean of the College of Business at Montana State University Billings. They co-authored "The Distribution Trap: Keeping Your Innovations from Becoming Commodities" (Praeger, 2009), winner of the Berry-AMA Book Award for the best marketing book of 2010. They may be reached at art@uakron.edu and timothy.wilkinson@msubillings.edu, respectively.

In Lean Times, Retailers Shop for Survival Strategies

They're cutting costs, listening to customers.

JAYNE O'DONNELL

An economic slowdown tends to spook the retail industry. When the economy sputters, people close their wallets and delay purchases, and stores suffer. Store chains, after all, can't survive very long without robust consumer spending.

But retailers don't just stand there and take a beating. They slim down, shut stores, trim inventory, slice payroll and take other strategic steps they hope will help them endure the pain. Some stores even thrive in recession even as others struggle.

With fears that the coming months could be the toughest for them since the 1991 recession, retailers are fighting to gain any edge they can over their rivals and to cushion themselves from the slide in customer spending. Many of them are redeploying staff and revising promotions; some are putting a new stress on low prices. In the end, they know, some of them will be winners, others losers.

"I see clients being more aggressive about promotion and reviewing the strategy by which they promote and how often they do it," says Madison Riley, a retail strategist with consulting firm Kurt Salmon Associates, whose clients include most major retailers.

The stores' strategies vary. So do their prospects for success. Much depends on how vulnerable they are in the first place.

Retailers that specialize in furnishing or refurbishing homes have been among the hardest hit. Specialty stores with highly discretionary products, such as the high- and low-end tchotchkes sold by Sharper Image and Lillian Vernon, respectively, may be worst off of all. Both retailers filed for Chapter 11 bankruptcy protection last week.

Retail chains know survival isn't in the bag, so they work even harder.

Specialty apparel stores are struggling, too. Even though some clothing, especially for growing kids or for career women, is regarded as essential, sales figures suggest that many of those purchases are being postponed.

Home Depot has slashed 500 jobs at its headquarters. Jewelry store chain Zales has announced plans to close 60 stores, and Ann Taylor plans to slash 180 jobs and close 117 stores within two years.

"The retailers accept that we're in a recession—smack in the middle of it," Riley says.

Among the most visible ways that stores are trying to ease their pain from the spending slowdown:

- **Merchandise.** Retailers must take care not to stock too little of the latest hot fashion or product—or showcase it too late. Many stores, Riley says, are working more closely with overseas suppliers to settle quickly on designs and shorten the development process.
- **Pricing.** Even retailers that try to avoid across-the-board price slashing are embracing the deep discounting trend, which Wal-Mart capitalized on so successfully last fall and holiday season.
- **More consumer input.** Retailers can't afford to wait until the end of a season to determine which trends will prove most popular. Riley says stores are stepping up consumer research and using their websites to gather real-time opinions from shoppers.

Thanks to luck, foresight or a bit of both, some retailers are better positioned to manage a downturn. Those with low, low prices—think Wal-Mart and off-price retailers including T.J. Maxx—and those that cater to the wealthy are tending to outperform those in the middle.

But opportunities exist for midlevel retailers, too. If shoppers are trading down to Wal-Mart, as its sales suggest, then more affluent people may be ready to cut back on their Bloomingdale's trips in favor of Kohl's. Tough economic times tend to diminish loyalty to stores across the spectrum.

"In this type of economy, the super shoppers get coupons out and check things online; they're going to be loyal to themselves first," says Phil Rist of the consumer insights firm BIGresearch. "Everyone's trying to find ways to make their money

	Target	Neiman Marcus and Saks	Macy's	J.C. Penney
Optimistic about the economy in next 6 months	33%	35%	36%	33%
Shopping closer to home	38%	26%	36%	44%
Shopping for sales more often	42%	22%	39%	45%
Spending less on clothing	39%	28%	35%	42%
Taking fewer shopping trips	39%	11%	34%	44%

How the Views of These Stores' Regular Shoppers Compare

Source: BIGresearch survey using national sample; responses are percentages of 2,434 people who said they regularly shopped at Target, 1,632 at Macy's, 2,723 at J.C. Penney and 32 at Neiman Marcus or Saks.

Here is how these retailers' shoppers compare with the U.S. population as a whole. Depending on who the store is targeting, they want to have close to or a higher composition of shoppers than the U.S. average. An index of 100 is considered average.

	Target	Neiman Marcus	Macy's	J.C. Penney
Age 18–34	104	99	92	89
Age 35–64	110	112	110	105
Age 65 and older	69	70	82	97
Education—high school	82	71	78	92
Education—college	112	115	113	105
Household size two or fewer	88	91	91	95
Income less than $40,000	63	55	56	75
Income $40,000–$99,000	121	96	116	120
Income $100,000 and more	155	240	186	122

Stores and Their Shoppers

Source: Claritas, a Nielsen company.

go as far as they can so there's something left for things they really want."

Christopher Maddox of Washington, D.C., says he's not giving up on Macy's, one of his favorite retailers, but is being far more cautious about his purchases this year.

"I'm only buying essentials due to the economy," Maddox says. "Luxury and big-ticket items are not in my budget due to increased costs of gas, food and utilities."

What follows is a look at the strategies of four retailers—Target, J.C. Penney, Macy's and Neiman Marcus—that draw from often-overlapping segments of shoppers.

As they brace for a possible recession, these stores are re-examining, in particular, four areas that will be most evident to shoppers: inventory, staffing, store openings and promotions.

Macy's
Frequent Big Sales and Discount Offers Won't Be Ending Anytime Soon

The nation's largest department store chain concedes that the economic slowdown has forced it to put off plans to scale back its sales and promotions.

"We still believe the strategy is a good one, but the timing is not necessarily good," says CEO Terry Lundgren.

In 2006, Macy's said it was trying to wean customers off frequent sales in favor of its "Every Day Value" pricing. Though

Lundgren says there were slightly fewer promotions in 2007 than in 2006, he says Macy's won't reduce the timing or the number of sales until consumer spending starts to bounce back.

All the great deals now in stores are one benefit of the depressing economic news, says Marietta Landon of Cambridge, Mass. She finds sales everywhere she goes. "Especially Macy's—they make every weekend a sale with saving passes and advertising galore," Landon says.

Macy's says its plan, announced earlier this month, to eliminate 2,300 management jobs in the company's central office and create 250 new ones in its local markets wasn't necessarily driven by the economy. But saving about $100 million a year sure doesn't hurt. The plan to localize decision-making "was conceived long before there was talk of a credit crunch or mortgage crisis, but executing it now in the face of a possible recession does have its benefits," says Macy's spokesman Jim Sluzewski.

The addition of Tommy-Hilfiger-branded men's and women's apparel this fall, which will make Macy's the only place to buy the brand in the USA outside of Hilfiger stores, should further boost sales, he says.

Macy's has also announced plans to close nine poor-performing stores this year. Though struggling with some of the same issues that its rival J.C. Penney faces in catering to the middle class, Macy's holds an advantageous position, says Phil Rist of BIGresearch. That's because Macy's enjoys the image of being something of a novelty in many areas since it renamed the former May department stores in the fall of 2006.

Its clientele is generally more affluent than Penney's, notes analyst Bill Dreher. Still, in times like this, even a Macy's will likely be hurt by the tendency of customers to cut back on non-essentials.

"All the department stores are vulnerable because they are about 80% apparel and 20% home goods," Dreher says. "After years of strong apparel sales, customers have full closets, and with a weak fashion cycle, there's nothing fashionistas have to run out and buy."

Neiman Marcus
Despite the Times, Life Is Still Sweet at the High End of the Retail Spectrum

Neiman Marcus is preparing for a possible sales slowdown, recognizing that while affluent customers might not trade down to lower-quality stores, they might buy less even if they remain loyal.

The luxury retailer may adjust the amount of merchandise in stores, but otherwise is "just continuing business as usual," says spokeswoman Ginger Reeder.

Neiman "knows how to react," to economic troubles, Reeder says. That means preserving its customer service and high-quality merchandise but adjusting its inventories to concede the reality that its customers may be tightening their snakeskin belts.

"We've found our customers are very resilient," says Reeder, referring to Neiman's history during past economic slowdowns. "They're not trading down but might potentially buy less."

As at other luxury retailers with strong presences in California and Florida, Neiman's sales have suffered along with their customers' finances during the housing recession, says Craig Johnson of retail consulting and research company Customer Growth Partners. But for the "premier luxury retailer in the U.S.," in Johnson's words, suffering means merely moderate sales growth—down from double-digit increases in recent years. "As the economy stabilizes and spring returns, we look for improving results," Johnson says.

Neimans focuses its promotions on two major sales a year, which Reeder says won't change.

In this economy, sales figures show, the safest demographic spot for retailers to occupy is either the low end or the very high end. "Middle-market department stores continue to bleed market share to discounters such as Wal-Mart and TJX, to high-end players like Saks and Neiman Marcus and to hot specialty stores such as Anthropologie," Johnson says.

As Reeder suggests, those who remain loyal to Neimans through economic turmoil are typically those who prize quality over price.

"I still shop at Neiman's and will continue to," says Amy Cavers, of Skillman, N.J. "If things worsen or my budget gets tighter, I may cut back on my volume if anything, but not where I shop. I still want the same quality in my purchases. . . . I would rather have fewer shoes and dresses but with the same uniqueness and flair or style that I expect."

Jennifer Stillman of Atlanta says that rather than cutting designer labels out of her apparel budget, she's buying groceries at Wal-Mart and Costco over pricier markets such as Whole Foods.

J.C. Penney
Growth Plan with Swanky Fashion Lines Calls for Full Steam Ahead

Damn the economic naysayers, J.C. Penney is designing its most ambitious five-year plan for store openings in its history and last week oversaw its largest-ever merchandise launch. Still, facing a persistent drop in consumer spending, CEO Mike Ullman says the chain is scaling back those store openings from 50 to 36 this year and will adjust its inventories to reduce the need for hefty markdowns.

Ullman hopes that Ralph Lauren's new American Living fashion, home and footwear line for men, women and kids will further invigorate the Penney brand, which has drawn more and younger customers with the addition of the Sephora makeup line and two private-label lingerie lines designed, in part, to compete with Victoria's Secret. The American Living line will be found in 600 of the chain's 1,000 stores, often with its own in-store shops.

Deutsche Bank senior retail analyst Bill Dreher questions whether now is a good time for Penney to launch a line that's about 25% higher-priced than similar merchandise already in its stores.

Under the deal, Ralph Lauren's name won't appear anywhere on the new merchandise or displays, Dreher notes. Kohl's, by contrast, was able to connect the Lauren name with its Chaps line for many years, which helped keep customers aware of the connection. The new line is "no panacea," he says.

Still, Dreher notes, Penney has successfully reinvented itself over the past decade from a chain known for "dowdy, older-lady-type fashions to one that's very much hip, on-trend and cool." More recently, Penney has recognized that its catalog business is less important now than its website, he says.

About six months ago, Penney decided to merge its store, catalog and online marketing operations; the change will result in 100 to 200 job losses. Ullman insists it's "not a cost-driven exercise," but rather one that'll give shoppers "one view of our merchandise."

"People expected us to have cost-cutting, but that's not how you grow a business," Ullman says.

Ullman says Penney benefits by serving the "middle third" of the country, where people aren't "living paycheck to paycheck." Still, all bets are off if a weak economy grows really sick.

Nick Birchfield of Garden City, Mich., is still shopping at Penney, but that could change. If the economy gets much worse and gas prices rise higher, he says, "I will not be shopping at J.C. Penney unless they are giving their merchandise away."

Target
Upscale Discounter Starts to Spotlight Low-Priced Goods in Addition to Style

"Hello goodbuy."

Couldn't that be a Wal-Mart slogan?

As the economy struggles, Target, long known as the purveyor of the well-designed product, is increasingly spotlighting its low-priced goods. "Hello goodbuy" is the tag line for ads that now focus as much on the price of its products as they do on their style. After all, in a down economy, hand-painted toilet-bowl-brush covers that cost several bucks more than the next one are seldom a major consumer priority.

That leaves Target more vulnerable in this economy than, say, Wal-Mart, says Deutsche Bank senior retail analyst Bill Dreher. It may be a discounter, but it's hard for it to compete with Wal-Mart on price, Dreher says.

"Target has historically focused more on being fashion-forward and having value-added design," Dreher says. "The problem is, consumers don't want that now. They're not redecorating or refurbishing their homes. They're looking for everyday life staples."

At the same time, Dreher says, Target is better positioned than department stores these days.

Target has been trying for years to get its low-price message across, says spokeswoman Lena Michaud. And she says its business plan will carry it through hard times: "We are very confident in our strategy going forward."

That includes trying to rein in costs in a way that customers won't notice. That may be difficult given that a key target is hourly payroll expenses. Michaud says Target is investing in technology to make sure workers are scheduled at the right times. Unlike some of its competitors, Target is sticking to its plan to open stores, about 100 of them, which Michaud says is consistent with the number it has opened in recent years.

The chain is also preparing for the departure this year of designer Isaac Mizrahi, who has a line of popular private-label apparel at Target but is leaving to join Liz Claiborne. Spokeswoman Susan Giesen says Target will still offer apparel from trendy designers, which, along with the new Converse All-Star apparel and footwear line, should fill any gaps in its clothing lines.

That might not be enough to keep clothing customers loyal. Based on BIGresearch's survey data on people who shop at Target primarily for at least one category of merchandise, these consumers are shopping around. "The folks who shop at Target for health and beauty aids—a lot of them go to Kohl's, Macy's and Penney's first for clothing," says Phil Rist of BIGresearch. "There's a lot of cross-shopping."

Critical Thinking

1. With a small group of peers from your class, conduct a comparative analysis of the four retailers discussed in the case on the dimensions of inventory, staffing, store openings, and promotion.

2. In your opinion, is it more challenging for retailers to maintain customer loyalty during tough economic times? Justify your answer.

Contributing: Erin Kutz.

Retail Therapy

A Chinese superstar athlete and an American design firm join forces, looking to build China's first truly global brand.

ARIC CHEN

You may think you've never heard of Li Ning. But assuming you were one of the 4 billion or so people watching the opening ceremony of last year's Beijing Olympics, you've seen him. Remember the guy who lit the Olympic flame? The one who, as if by some superhuman power, levitated more than 100 feet and ran that mesmerizing aerial lap around the Bird's Nest stadium before setting the Olympic cauldron ablaze? That was Li Ning. And if he has his way, you won't be forgetting him again.

Li Ning, the man, is a hero in China—the gymnast who snagged six medals, including three gold, at the 1984 Los Angeles Olympics and thus helped launch a national surge that reached its height last summer when China won more gold than any other country. (Before Li's Olympic debut, China hadn't appeared at a summer Games since Helsinki in 1952, when it failed to take home a single medal.)

Li Ning, the company, is China's biggest domestic maker of athletic footwear and sports apparel. This year, it's set to rake in over $1 billion from more than 6,300 stores across the country. In the next four years, it plans to add 3,000 more. And to top it off, the company is now undergoing a major overhaul that, with the help of the American consultancy Ziba Design, just might prime it for its ultimate goal: becoming an international name. "We want Li Ning to be a globally recognized brand," says Li, who founded the company in 1990 because he wanted Chinese athletes to be able to wear a Chinese label. "This is our real asset, and building it up is our long-term commitment."

That's where Ziba comes in. Based in Portland, Oregon, the spiritual home of sneakers, Ziba is the 110-person firm behind such innovation milestones as HP's first flat-panel PC monitor and Microsoft's first ergonomic keyboard. And for the past two years, it's been hard at work helping Li Ning remake itself. Everything from the company's product line and store interiors to its visual identity and even its logo are going under the knife. But Ziba is also helping Li Ning learn to think of itself as a global company, which is no small thing for an operation that's been almost exclusively focused on the domestic market. "Defining the problem is more important than solving the problem," says Ziba founder Sohrab Vossoughi. And for Li Ning, "The problem, and goal, was to create a world-class design competency."

In China, the problem is not just Li Ning's, and the current economic downturn has only underscored the urgency of addressing it. To become a true superpower, China knows its manufacturing-based economy needs an upgrade. On the one hand, the country has to continue to fuel domestic consumption that will reduce reliance on exports; on the other, it needs to grow domestic brands that can compete worldwide. So far, the latter effort has yielded little. The Chinese computer giant Lenovo, for example, has struggled to maintain momentum since its much-ballyhooed purchase of IBM's PC division in 2005. And remember TCL? Exactly. (It took over RCA in 2003, but has hardly returned it to its glory days.) True, China's corporate leaders are beginning to understand the value of design in broadening their reach. But the words "Haler appliance" have yet to make Americans swoon.

Li Ning wanted to avoid repeating the mistakes of others by not expanding abroad too hastily. More important, before it could become a global player, it had to reclaim its home turf: In 2002, despite Li Ning's double-digit growth, both Nike and Adidas surpassed the company in Chinese market share. And they've been gaining since. "When that happened," says Zhang Zhiyong, Li Ning's youthful 41-year-old CEO, "we realized that revenue is not the most important thing for a company. It's product and brand innovation—a design strategy, not just designs."

Or as Ziba creative director Jeremy Kaye tells it: "Li Ning had been the leading Chinese brand for 15, 16 years by essentially competing with itself." But with fierce foreign rivals capturing the prestige, and lower-end brands undercutting them in price, "it couldn't continue by just putting product on the shelves."

Rolling across 25 acres in the outskirts of Beijing, Li Ning's gleaming corporate campus is a manifestation of the company's newfound self-awareness. Completed in 2007, its sleek, low-slung buildings are ringed by red granite walkways evoking running tracks and hexagonal concrete benches that could have been peeled off a giant soccer ball. In the soaring visitor's center, school groups snap photos with life-size cutouts of China's Olympic gymnastics team and Houston Rockets forward (and Yao Ming teammate) Chuck Hayes. There are basketball and badminton courts. An eight-lane swimming pool. An outdoor soccer field. A rock-climbing wall.

The message is clear: This company lives and breathes sports. But it also looks and sounds a mite familiar. "There's a perception that what Nike does, Li Ning follows," says Charley Kan, the Beijing-based creative director of MEC China, a leading communications consultancy, echoing many others.

Indeed, when Abel Wu first arrived at Li Ning as its marketing VP in 2004, he found a brand afflicted with a fuzzy identity. Even worse, "the majority of customers were middle-aged; they didn't look fashionable and neither did the product," says Wu, who now oversees Li Ning's Lotto division. (The company owns the Chinese rights for both that Italian sportswear label and its French counterpart, Aigle.) "It was like a typical Chinese brand." He doesn't mean it as a compliment.

Under Wu, tactics such as sponsoring athletes (the Spanish national basketball team, Shaquille O'Neal) helped Li Ning woo a younger audience by burnishing its international cachet. But from a design standpoint, the company was still foundering. Its stores looked tired. Its logo bore an unfortunate resemblance to Nike's swoosh. Its products were mishmashes of motifs and styles—the mentality was to "just put everything on one shoe," Kaye recalls—and were being churned out without much thought for overall coherence. Li Ning needed a better strategy.

As it happened, the Chinese company's quest for authenticity began with hiring an American design firm that had worked with Nike in the past. But Li Ning had a not-so-secret weapon that neither Nike nor Adidas could ever claim: Li himself. "They have a heritage to be uniquely differentiated in the industry," says Ziba account director Lili Yeo. They also have a ready market. "Although they have many choices, deep in their hearts, we think Chinese consumers are looking for a Chinese brand they can be proud of," says Li. As a credible national icon—at his insistence, the company did little to exploit his Olympic torch-lighting moment—Li's DNA can really resonate with the Chinese.

This may be especially true of the balinghou—literally "post-80s"—generation, that savvier-than-ever, outward-looking cohort of young Chinese born in the post-economic reform years. The object of every marketing exec's lust, the balinghou came of age during China's ascendancy and are increasingly sure of themselves and their country. Ziba knew that simply waving a Chinese flag in front of them wouldn't be enough. So to reach them, it conducted an exhaustive yearlong study, including interviews in eight cities, to produce a design strategy that would get their attention.

Ziba found a subtle yet profound difference in the way these Chinese and their Western peers view the role of sports in their lives. "The Chinese don't categorize themselves by the sports they play; you seldom hear people saying 'I'm a bowler,' or 'I'm a football player,'" says Kaye, the Ziba creative director, adding that Li Ning had been working under the opposite paradigm, or "the Nike model." The reality, Ziba determined, was that the Chinese see sports as movement and movement as part of their day-to-day lives. "It's the kid who bikes to school, plays a quick game of pickup, does his homework, and sees a movie with his girlfriend," says Kaye. "All in the same outfit." At the same time, Ziba saw an emphasis on "appropriateness," as Kaye puts it—a desire among young Chinese to find what's right for them based on who they are right now, versus who they aspire to be or might later become.

Placed under the rubric "Sport for my modern Chinese life," these and other findings are helping Ziba remake Li Ning's product line in some fundamental ways. For starters, what was once an ad hoc approach will be replaced by an overarching design language with multiple translations. Two of those will target, respectively, hard-core sports buffs (for example, with performance-oriented gear) and the style-conscious crowd (skater graphics and the like). The third will reach for that larger group for whom sports are simply an integral part of their daily routine—those kids playing pickup games after school. Think the sneaker equivalents of jeans and pocket tees.

Meanwhile, Ziba has come up with design templates, now being tested, for Li Ning's 6,000-plus stores. "In some ways, this is the holy grail, to get the retail right," says Kaye. The new look will include ring-shaped lights that recall the company's gymnastic roots and chalkboard walls where the staff can, for example, list its top picks. Throughout, concrete floors and splashes of red will provide the bold strokes of a more contemporary Chinese look. The goal, of course, is to deepen Li Ning's connection with its customers; to drive home the point, changing graphics will evoke a "hero in all of us" ideal.

In the end, however, Li Ning's overhaul goes beyond redesigning stores and sneakers for the Chinese market. Instead, it aims to steer the company away from China's reigning culture of imitation and toward one of authentically creative, original ideas and products. If Ziba and Li Ning can manage to translate that message into a language that can be understood across the Pacific, the new company could become the global force it hopes to be. And to prove it's serious, Li Ning is currently instituting multilingual IT platforms and making a few significant, if cautious, moves overseas. While it has yet to reveal its plans for launching in the United States, in 2007, the company opened a now 20-member design studio in Portland—just around the corner from Ziba—where the first things you see are the Chinese and American flags hanging, stadium-style, side by side.

Of course, the challenges ahead are not lost on anyone, and they run deeper than the usual implementation, logistics, and corporate-culture banalities. It's unclear, for example, whether Ziba's product design guidelines will be enough to produce the blockbusters the industry demands; any protocol will be only as good as the ability of Li Ning's designers to interpret it—and results won't start to hit shelves until next year. Moreover, in preparing itself for an international move, Li Ning is in many ways banking on the idea that a Chinese trademark might one day have the luster to capture the hearts and minds of consumers abroad. Yet as everyone knows, Brand China rarely gets the benefit of the doubt these days. Even many Chinese assume that Li Ning's "Anything is possible" slogan is a rip-off of Adidas's "Impossible is nothing"—despite the fact that the former predates the latter by two years.

Still, let's not forget that "Made in Japan" once also implied "cheap knockoff." And don't underestimate Li Ning's determination to become an international presence. In some ways, it has no choice. "Li Ning users expect us to become an international brand," says Zhang, the CEO. In other words, the company had better go global if it wants to stay competitive at home, and it even has a time frame for accomplishing that. "We have a vision," Zhang says. Within the next decade, "we want to be one of the top five sports brands worldwide." To borrow a phrase from this side of the ocean, they might just do it.

Critical Thinking

1. What is a 'global' brand?

2. Discuss the steps and tactics taken by Abel Wu, Li Ning's marketing VP, to reposition the company and the brand.

3. What is the role of the American design company, Ziba, in this repositioning effort?

Williams-Sonoma's *Secret Sauce*

The retailer's recipe for growth required two entrepreneurs. Until now, Howard Lester was the hidden ingredient.

Jessica Shambora

Professional managers like Howard Lester aren't supposed to be entrepreneurs. You know the type: the seasoned exec who takes the wheel from the founder when it's time to drive growth, layering on necessary infrastructure. He's the "suit" or the "gray-hair" whose arrival signals an end to the fun, scrappy days before people had to consult policy manuals. At San Francisco's Williams-Sonoma Inc., Lester succeeded founder Chuck Williams, who stayed on as chairman. But even Williams, 94, concedes that the home-furnishings retailer wouldn't have become a $3 billion juggernaut without Lester.

Lester, 74, who capped 32 years at the company when he retired in May, is an entrepreneur in his own right. Not only did he successfully found (and sell) a company before buying Williams-Sonoma in 1978, but his stewardship could hardly have been more entrepreneurial: He pushed for growth, took risks, made mistakes. (Laura Alber, CEO since May, is his third successor; two others flamed out.) Lester transformed Williams-Sonoma into a kitchen and home-furnishings empire, with brands like Pottery Barn and West Elm (see table). "He made a lot of bold decisions about growing this business and had real vision about the opportunity to expand a very high-taste concept in a really scaled way," says Matt Fassler, a Goldman Sachs analyst.

> **"He made a lot of bold decisions about growing this business and had real vision about the opportunity to expand a very high-taste concept."**
> —Matt Fassler, Goldman Sachs

Unlike other nonfounder entrepreneurs, Lester focused on making the brand, and not himself, a household name. Williams-Sonoma was begun in 1956, an outgrowth of its founder's passion for French culinary traditions. But Lester's zeal is what has really gotten Williams-Sonoma cooking. His passion? Business.

"I had no interest in making quiches," says Lester. Here's a taste of his recipe for growth:

Opportunity Doesn't Knock, It Taps

In 1976, at age 40, Lester's only plans were to putter around. He sold Centurex, a software business he'd founded, and spent six months playing golf. He was poking around for a business to buy when a buddy suggested he look into a struggling cookware retailer and cataloguer that was for sale.

Lester ended up spending weeks "looking at every detail and talking to every employee" at Williams-Sonoma. What he saw was a financially shaky business with $4 million in revenue and $700,000 in debt. "It had no systems, no idea of inventory, and that was something I did know about," he says. Along with a partner, who never assumed an operating role, Lester bought the company for $100,000. His only previous retail experience was as a shopper.

Learn What You Don't Know

Lester found direction by hitting the road. He went on buying trips to Europe with Williams, and also traveled across the U.S. visiting kitchen stores, noting that "they were run more as a hobby than a business," he says.

Although he sniffed a big opportunity, he didn't act on it right away. Rather than jump into the capital-intensive business of building stores, he focused on growing catalogue sales by hiring a direct-marketing expert. When the company went public in 1983, catalogues represented 75% of revenue—compared with 50% five years earlier. In turn, the addresses of catalogue customers became a road map for where to locate new outlets.

Lester hired experts to teach him about real estate too. Soon he was cherry-picking locations as fastidiously as a chef lines up knives. When mall owners tried to put the newfangled "kitchen" shop by the food court, he refused. Williams-Sonoma belonged with the luxury brands.

Williams-Sonoma through the Years

Brand	What Do They Sell?	The Skinny
Williams-Sonoma	Fancy kitchen gadgets and appliances	From four stores to 259 in 32 years.
Pottery Barn	Home furnishings to fantasize about	PB's 199 stores produce the largest share of the company's revenue today.
Pottery Barn Kids	Furniture for little sprouts	Current CEO's pet project, launched in 1999, is now an 85-store empire.
PBteen	Furniture for teens	Catalogue-only brand started in 2003 after success of kids line.
West Elm	Modern home goods for hip urban dwellers	First catalogue mailed in 2002; today 37 stores and building momentum.
Williams-Sonoma Home	Classic, high-end home furnishings	Debuted in 2004; "future potential of this brand is limited," W-S says.
Hold Everything	Organization and storage products	Founded in 1983; closed in 2006; lost the edge to the Container Store.
Gardener's Eden	Outdoor tools and decorative doodads	Catalogue-only brand bought in 1982; sold in 1999 to Brookstone.

Big Bets Come from Small Insights

Williams-Sonoma pushed the boundaries of retailing, offering cooking classes, table-setting demonstrations, and tastings. A company philosophy, "Think like a shopkeeper," originated with Lester, who read every customer letter and comment card. He emphasized not inventory levels or, later, website clicks, but rather such customer metrics as this: "How many did we fail to satisfy yesterday?"

Even as the company was adding roughly five stores every year (starting in 1982), Lester could recite the revenue numbers for each store, as well as the name of its manager. That skill didn't come naturally to his successor, a 15-year veteran of the company who served as president for four years. Alber, 41, devised her own photo flash cards to replicate his total recall.

By 1986, Williams-Sonoma had grown from four shops in California when Lester had bought it eight years earlier, to 27 stores in 14 states with sales of $68 million. That year another San Francisco–based retailer, Gap, was seeking a buyer for its troubled 25-store Pottery Barn unit. Lester scooped it up for $6 million, planning to use the prime real estate to expand Williams-Sonoma.

But first he tried an experiment, applying his company's catalogue know-how to the brand by displaying the merchandise as part of a broader lifestyle. The results: double-digit same-store gains. "It was a real eye-opener for us," says Lester.

Not everything has worked. A gardening catalogue the company bought in 1982 languished and was sold in 1999. Hold Everything, which sold storage products, folded in 2006. And the company recently abandoned its high-end Williams-Sonoma Home brand.

Companies Don't Crush Innovation, CEOs Do

Alber credits Lester for attracting—and protecting—the creative minds the company needed to expand: "A feeling lives within all of us today, which is, What can we build that isn't there yet? How do you push it further?"

Alber should know: In 1997 she was among a group of women who pitched the idea for Pottery Barn Kids. After working on the project nights and weekends, they set up the store format in the garage at headquarters to show Lester. While wary, he let them test it in a catalogue. Pottery Barn Kids now operates 85 stores. And when the notion for Pottery Barn Teen came along six years later? "I didn't argue," says Lester.

It's a difficult time to be in the top spot at almost any retailer. Williams-Sonoma's revenue hit $3.1 billion in fiscal 2009, a 21% drop from its 2007 peak. But the company, which now operates 610 stores in 44 states, is showing some resilience, and the stock price has more than doubled in the past year.

Meanwhile, Lester, who was retired when he bought the business, says he's ready to go through with it this time. After all, what is it they say about the perils of having too many cooks in the kitchen? Lester, undoubtedly, knows.

Critical Thinking

1. What makes the combination of Lester and Williams such a success for Williams-Sonoma?
2. What external environmental factors pose possible opportunities or threats for Williams-Sonoma's various brands?

Fellow Graduates, before We Greet the Future, a Word from My Sponsor

Marketers Get School's Valedictorian to Plug Movie in Her Speech, but the Flick Still Flops.

ETHAN SMITH AND SABRINA SHANKMAN

Last month, 18-year-old Kenya Mejia closed her valedictory address at Los Angeles's Alexander Hamilton High School on a startling note: publicly professing a secret passion for a classmate.

"I cannot let this opportunity just pass by," said Ms. Mejia, who is to enroll at the Massachusetts Institute of Technology in the fall. "I love you, Jake Minor!"

The crowd roared. Mr. Minor stood and pumped his fists in the air. A few days later, Ms. Mejia cashed a check for $1,800.

The commotion Ms. Mejia created was actually part of a ploy cooked up by marketing executives and consultants for Twentieth Century Fox, the Hollywood studio whose headquarters is less than two miles from Hamilton High.

The goal of the plot, which included a marketing company called the Intelligence Group and at least one other contractor, was to create a "viral" buzz online for the romantic comedy "I Love You, Beth Cooper." The movie opens with an unassuming valedictorian using his graduation speech to proclaim his feelings for the most popular girl in school. Fox and its consultants hatched the ruse to recreate the scene at a real high school before the film's July 10 opening, say people familiar with the matter, in hopes of creating online chatter about the way the movie supposedly inspired copycats.

The incident represents an increasingly common Hollywood tactic: staging events that look spontaneous to inspire online buzz.

"Brüno," a Universal Pictures comedy that opened the same day as "Beth Cooper," relied on similar methods. At the MTV Movie Awards in May, the movie's star, Sacha Baron Cohen, was lowered abruptly by wires onto rapper Eminem in an apparent technical malfunction that tangled the two men in a suggestive position. After days of speculation about whether the episode was really an accident, the rapper acknowledged it had been staged by the filmmakers.

In 2007, Walt Disney Co.'s Hollywood Records helped singer Marié Digby produce several homemade-looking music videos that were posted online. Only after the videos began to attract millions of viewers did the record label send out a news release announcing it had signed the "breakthrough YouTube phenomenon"—even though her record deal dated to 2005. Ms. Digby's career still hasn't taken off, though.

A few weeks before the June graduation season, an employee of the Intelligence Group asked members of a focus group to help find valedictorians. The company, a unit of Creative Artists Agency, regularly polls thousands of teens to identify consumer trends. One panelist was a friend of Ms. Mejia and approached her with the company's proposition: It would pay her $1,000 to $1,500 if she would mention the movie by name and say its trailer inspired her to make her own confession of love.

Ms. Mejia, who describes herself as "like, the biggest introvert ever," says she still can't quite believe she participated in the stunt. "I really don't know what I was thinking," she says by telephone from Cambridge, Mass., where she's already taking summer classes at MIT in physics, chemistry, calculus and humanities in preparation for her freshman year.

Fox hired another firm to videotape the episode in a style that emulated a home movie. The company then posted it on YouTube—a tactic employed by a growing number of marketers seeking to create seemingly amateur videos that appear more authentic than conventional ads.

Unfortunately for the studio, lightning didn't strike. "I Love You, Beth Cooper" has been a bomb in an otherwise buoyant summer movie season. The movie, which cost an estimated $19 million to make, took in $13.4 million domestically its first three weeks in release, according to Hollywood.com. Even Ms. Mejia hasn't seen it.

Nor has the 67-second YouTube clip become the blockbuster Fox hoped for. More than a month after it was posted, the clip had garnered fewer than 2,000 views. That is a far cry from the millions of views attracted by successful viral ruses like "Lonelygirl15"—the supposedly amateur video series that became wildly popular online in 2006 before being revealed as a production of professional filmmakers with Hollywood connections; it continued to be popular after that revelation.

The stunt did succeed in outraging officials at Hamilton High and the Los Angeles Unified School District, who were horrified when informed by a reporter that a movie company had essentially planted a paid advertisement in the midst of a graduation ceremony.

Hamilton High Assistant Principal Roberta Mailman says neither she nor anyone from the school was contacted for permission—either for the stunt itself or for filming it. Before learning of the payment, she says, "I thought it was a great speech."

School District spokeswoman Gayle Pollard-Terry says she is unsure whether the episode violated any policy, but adds that Ms. Mejia's diploma is safe. In a statement, Local District Superintendent Michelle King wrote: "Obviously, this is not condoned by the District. It's unfortunate."

A spokesman for Fox, a unit of News Corp., which also owns Dow Jones & Co., publisher of *The Wall Street Journal*, said: "We hired an outside company to look for viral opportunities for this movie, and this is one of the opportunities they found." A spokeswoman for CAA declined to comment.

Ms. Mejia says she essentially fell into the plot when she was contacted by the friend who was in the focus group. He couldn't be reached for comment. A few days later, Ms. Mejia received another call, this time from an Intelligence Group employee whose name she doesn't recall.

"First they were just saying that I had to share a secret," Ms. Mejia recalls. "But then the next day they said it had to be about my crush. I was like, 'Oh that changes things a bit!'"

Ms. Mejia says she plans to put the $1,800 she earned toward expenses at MIT. People familiar with the transaction confirmed the amount, but it isn't clear why she was paid more than the initial offer.

She ran the plan past her boyfriend—not Jake Minor—who endorsed it. The strongest opposition came from her parents. "They were shocked that I was willing to do it," she recalls. "I don't really know why I agreed. It was just the thrill of the moment." Her parents, Luis and Maura Mejia, didn't respond to a message seeking comment.

The prospect of making a public declaration for a boy other than her boyfriend still gave Ms. Mejia jitters. "I was like, 'Wow, I'm crazy,'" she recalls. "But it wasn't too bad after I did it." Ms. Mejia was also able to work in the requisite plug for "Beth Cooper."

Though it was less spontaneous than it appeared, Ms. Mejia's "confession" contained a grain of truth. She says she really had a crush on Mr. Minor for at least part of her senior year, but kept it to herself.

She did give Mr. Minor, who is headed to the University of California, Berkeley, an oblique heads-up just before the graduation ceremony began, asking that he pay attention to what she was going to say. "She came up to me and said, 'Will you please listen to my speech?'" he recalls. "So I figured something was up."

Ms. Mejia and Mr. Minor agree the episode didn't spark a new romance. Nonetheless, he says that he—along with his girlfriend at the time—was taken by surprise when Ms. Mejia delivered her message.

"I had no idea that she liked me," Mr. Minor says. "She's pretty quiet."

Critical Thinking

1. What makes a "viral" online buzz promotion a successful strategy?

2. With a small group of peers from your class, discuss the ethical implications of the case stated in the article from the perspectives of the movie studio (and its agent), as well as the student who accepted payment.

What's Your Social Media Strategy?

A new study shows four ways companies are using technology to form connections.

H. James Wilson et al

A global bank executive recently described to us a challenge for our times. It turns out that a customer who normally would qualify for the lowest level of service has an impressive 100,000 followers on Twitter. The bank isn't doing much yet with social media and has no formula for adapting it to particular customers, but the executive still wondered whether the customer's "influence" might merit special treatment.

It's the kind of perplexing question many companies face as they formulate their thinking about social media. To understand how businesses are approaching the challenge, we analyzed strategies and practices at more than 1,100 companies across several industries and continents, and conducted in-depth interviews with 70 executives who were leading social media initiatives. Our research revealed four distinct social media strategies, which depend on a company's tolerance for uncertain outcomes and the level of results sought.

The "predictive practitioner." This approach confines usage to a specific area, such as customer service. It works well for businesses seeking to avoid uncertainty and to deliver results that can be measured with established tools.

To increase Clorox's virtual R&D capabilities, the social media team created Clorox Connects—a website that enables brainstorming with customers and suppliers. A typical query posted there: "We're working on X product idea. What features would you like to see included?" To encourage participation, Clorox uses incentives borrowed from gaming. For example, people who post answers or add rating comments are awarded points. The site features different levels of difficulty, and contributors who demonstrate expertise can advance to problems requiring greater creativity, knowledge, and involvement. The sharpest contributors gain visibility, making participation rewarding and sticky. One early success came after Clorox posted a question about a specific compound for its salad dressings. Five responses quickly came in. The company decided on a solution within a day and brought the problem solver into the product development process.

The "creative experimenter." Companies taking this approach embrace uncertainty, using small-scale tests to find ways to improve discrete functions and practices. They aim to learn by listening to customers and employees on platforms such as Twitter and Facebook. Sometimes they use proprietary technologies to conduct internal tests.

The IT services giant EMC is a creative experimenter. It pays particular attention to how its 40,000 global employees use internal social media to locate needed expertise within the company. In an effort to reduce the use of outside contractors, it created a test platform, called EMC/ONE, that helped employees (many of whom were new because of recent acquisitions) network and connect on projects. "We were very clear that in two months we might unplug this and try a completely different approach," says Len Devanna, the director of social strategy. "This was the reason we were inside the firewall: To be free to make mistakes and learn our lessons before exposing ourselves to the outside." Within a year EMC/ONE was delivering substantial benefits. For instance, a division that needed to produce a sales video connected with an in-house production group, saving $10,000 as a result. The company estimates that EMC/ONE has generated more than $40 million in savings overall.

The "social media champion." This involves large initiatives designed for predictable results. It may depend on close collaboration across multiple functions and levels and include external parties.

Consider Ford's 2009 Fiesta Movement campaign, used to prepare for the car's reintroduction in the U.S. It required joint efforts among marketing, communications, and the C-suite. Ford decided to lend 100 Fiestas for six months to recipients who would use social media to discuss their experiences with the cars in an authentic, direct way. It held an online contest to select candidates, carefully choosing drivers with large social media followings. To further reduce uncertainty, it required them to regularly produce content on themed "missions" (for example, volunteerism) and designed a schedule for postings. Within six months the drivers had posted more than 60,000 items, which garnered millions of clicks, including more than 4.3 million YouTube views. The $5 million campaign created a prelaunch brand awareness rate of 37% among Millennials, generated 50,000 sales leads to new customers, and prompted 35,000 test-drives—a level of results that might be expected from a traditional campaign costing tens of millions of dollars.

Understanding Your Current Social Media Strategy: A Quiz

A company's social media strategy is generally oriented toward one of four types. This quiz can help you identify your dominant approach (the category with the highest total). Then consider whether you're using the strategy that best suits your resources and goals, or perhaps diffusing your efforts over multiple approaches when you would be better served by focusing on one.

	Don't Agree			Strongly Agree
Predictive Practitioner				
Each of our social media projects is owned by a specific functional group or department.	0	1	2	3
There is little or no cross-functional coordination among projects.	0	1	2	3
Each project has a clear business objective.	0	1	2	3
We can measure each project's impact with existing metrics.	0	1	2	3
			TOTAL	
Creative Experimenter				
Our overall objective is to learn from our social media projects.	0	1	2	3
In particular, we aim to enable engagement and to listen and learn from resulting conversations.	0	1	2	3
We position our projects as experiments within discrete functions or departments.	0	1	2	3
We are not overly concerned with predefining outcomes.	0	1	2	3
			TOTAL	
Social Media Champion				
We have a centralized group and specific leaders dedicated to coordinating and managing social media projects across departments and functions.	0	1	2	3
This centralized group develops policies and guidelines for social media use.	0	1	2	3
We enlist executive champions and other evangelists, including external influencers, to promote and participate in our projects.	0	1	2	3
We share best practices and lessons learned from various projects throughout the organization.	0	1	2	3
			TOTAL	
Social Media Transformer				
Our portfolio of social media projects involves both internal employees and external stakeholders, such as customers and business partners.	0	1	2	3
Our social media technologies are tightly integrated with how we learn and work.	0	1	2	3
Our projects typically encompass multiple functions and departments.	0	1	2	3
We have centralized groups tasked with thinking about how social media can inform our business strategy and culture in light of surprises and emerging trends.	0	1	2	3
			TOTAL	

What Happens When Companies Lack a Social Media Strategy?

Here's what often occurs when companies encounter a new technology: One group begins a small experiment. So does another . . . and another. The various groups' efforts are typically ad hoc; there's little coordination and no effective way to share lessons learned. One manager summed up the social media experiments in progress at his company this way: "It's a free-for-all."

Sometimes companies start out with a clear strategy but lose focus as the effort expands. One professional services firm gave its marketing department a limited mandate to use Twitter and other social networks to try to increase its lead generation. The group began well enough, devising specific policies, practices, and metrics for increasing conversations with potential clients—behavior that placed it firmly on the predictive practitioner track. Made heady by early successes, however, it pushed to increase the scale of the initiative and ended up haphazardly pursuing elements of both the social champion and creative experimenter strategies. It struggled to recruit executive champions for an internal community and also urged all employees to blog and tweet about the company's services. Lacking a strategic mandate or clear learning objectives, and without much buy-in outside the department, it tried to drum up support by offering prizes for participation and asking HR to make blogging a job requirement. Today it's hard to say what this company's social media strategy is; it's as if the firm has been using a shotgun to try to hit its target.

Companies that are still taking a small-scale, experimental approach to social media need to be strategic about ramping up. Long-term success is rarely found in a free-for-all.

The "social media transformer." This approach enables large-scale interactions that extend to external stakeholders, allowing companies to use the unexpected to improve the way they do business.

In 2010 Cisco launched Integrated Workforce Experience (IWE), a social business platform designed to facilitate internal and external collaboration and decentralize decision making. It functions much like a Facebook "wall": A real-time news feed provides updates on employees' status and activities as well as information about relevant communities, business projects, and customer and partner interactions. One manager likens it to Amazon. "It makes recommendations based on what you are doing, the role you are in, and the choices of other people like you. We are taking that to the enterprise level and basically allowing appropriate information to find you," he says.

Cisco also makes extensive use of video. It conducts most of its training and meetings virtually, through video streamed to desktops and available via video-on-demand. Like Facebook, the system lets users tag and comment on videos. These technologies have accelerated "time to trust" among Cisco's stakeholders, quickly establishing collegiality and knowledge sharing among new geographically dispersed teams.

Putting Strategy into Practice

The strategies are temporal, and many organizations will progress from one to another. Companies with clear objectives for using and measuring social technologies in a specific part of the organization should begin as predictive practitioners. They should look for a group (marketing, for instance) that wants to become more social in its business.

Creative experimenters are driven in part by small budgets; labeling a project "experimental" can exempt it from ROI constraints. Both the predictive practitioner and creative experimenter strategies can quickly create significant results and learning and serve as a training ground for larger efforts.

Other companies should use—or migrate toward—a larger-scale strategy if they want significant results. A social champion strategy can help companies identify and enlist enthusiasts to expand initiatives inside and outside the organization. As Ford's Fiesta Movement showed, carefully engaging those who have a sizable influence in social networks can reduce risk.

With all else being equal, the social transformer strategy can have the largest impact on an enterprise, affecting everything from R&D and operations to channel partners and customers. However, moving from a champion to a transformer strategy requires major, companywide changes to such things as incentive systems, business processes, resource management, and leadership styles. The social transformers we've seen often have broader social business objectives and view social technologies as a key enabler of—but not the final answer to—those objectives.

It's worth remembering that despite their ubiquity, Twitter and Facebook are only five and seven years old, respectively. Who knows what new technologies lie ahead? Understanding how company strategies are evolving to use existing social media not only will be of use today but also should guide managers as they adapt to platforms developed in the years to come.

Critical Thinking

1. List and summarize the four social media strategies proposed in this article.
2. With a small group of peers from your class, brainstorm some alternative social media strategies that companies could pursue to better target the college students segment.

H. JAMES WILSON is a senior researcher at Babson Executive Education. PJ GUINAN and SALVATORE PARISE are associate professors of information systems at Babson College. BRUCE D. WEINBERG is the chair of the marketing department at Bentley University.

From *Harvard Business Review*, July/August 2011, pp. 23–25. Copyright © 2011 by Harvard Business School Publishing. Reprinted by permission.

20 Highlights in 20 Years
Making Super Bowl Ad History Is No Easy Feat

As Ad Meter hits the two-decade mark, USA TODAY takes a look back.

BRUCE HOROVITZ

Watching Super Bowl advertising has become a pop-culture ritual. But the ads are not just being scrutinized by about 90 million TV viewers.

For 20 years, they've also come under the magnifying glass of USA TODAY's Super Bowl Ad Meter, an exclusive, real-time consumer rating of all the game's ads. Focus groups in multiple cities use handheld devices to register their second-by-second reactions to the commercials. It's been quite a ride.

Who can forget the beer-pitching Bud Bowl ads of the late 1980s? And celebrity-laden Pepsi spots of the 1990s? And the wacky dot-com commercials that filled the 2000 game?

Through the perspective of Ad Meter, USA TODAY is spotlighting here 20 of the high points, low points and turning points in Super Bowl ads over these two decades.

Each year, Super Bowl ads mirror American culture. Most years, they aim no higher than a superficial reflection. But, once in a while, they offer a peek at something deeper.

All in 30 seconds.

This Sunday, 37 advertisers, who paid an average $2.7 million per 30 seconds, will air about 55 ads aimed at winning Super Bowl ad immortality. Odds are none will get there.

"Everyone we work with says, 'Do the next '1984'," says ad guru Jeff Goodby, a reference to Apple's famous Super Bowl spot of the woman who shatters Big Brother's image. "But that's easier said than done."

That won't stop folks such as Goodby, whose agency is a Super Bowl ad veteran, from trying. He knows the impact of Ad Meter intimately. It has forced many advertisers to work overtime trying to win the top prize—and the acclaim that comes with it. But, in the process, he only half-jokes, "It has ruined the Christmas vacations of advertising and production people worldwide."

Alex Bogusky, co-chairman of Crispin Porter + Bogusky, tries to avoid that. Because there is only one Ad Meter winner, it makes "losers" out of most Super Bowl advertisers. "I counsel clients against doing Super Bowl advertising."

In Ad Meter's history, there've been vintage years, full of highs and lows, and others best forgotten. Here are 20 indelible Super Bowl ad moments:

1 "You-Per" Bowl (2007)

Madison Avenue's biggest showcase became Main Street's newest stomping ground last year when a few cutting-edge marketers got real people—not ad agencies—to create memorable ads.

Tops among them: Doritos' consumer-generated ad contest winner in which a chip-eating driver crashes his car while ogling a Doritos-munching woman. The ad made the top five in Ad Meter alongside four pro ads from Anheuser-Busch.

Many Super Bowl ads cost upwards of $1 million to film. This one cost $12, for four bags of Doritos. That's punch for the crunch.

2 Now You See Me (2007)

Last year's Super Bowl will be best-remembered by some as the year that two ads quickly were dispatched to the commercial graveyard by special-interest groups.

A Snickers ad featured two car mechanics who pulled out chest hair to assert their manliness after sharing a Snickers bar led to an accidental smooch. Gay-advocacy groups made the ad disappear the next day.

A General Motors ad with a robot fantasizing about suicide while dreaming of losing its assembly-line job got the heave after a suicide-prevention group balked.

3 Too Tight for Comfort (2005)

How tight can a model's strappy top be before network censors squirm? That's a question for which GoDaddy.com's first Super Bowl ad got free PR galore.

In the ad, Go Daddy's buxom spokesmodel wiggles and giggles before a faux censorship committee. When an overstretched strap snaps, one elderly committee member needs oxygen. The Fox network got so many angry calls after it aired the spot that it shelved plans to run it again later in the game.

Even then, the ad was a dud with consumers rating it for Ad Meter: They relegated it to the bottom five of all the game's ads.

But the ad got gazillions to go online to see it again. And again.

4 Tasteless Bowl (2004)

It wasn't just Janet Jackson's infamous "wardrobe malfunction" that torpedoed good taste that year. Some ads helped, particularly two for Bud Light.

In one, a romantic sleigh ride goes south after the horse passes explosive gas. In another, a guy surrenders his Bud Light only after a dog bites his crotch.

Not that Ad Meter's consumers took offense. They rated the crotch commercial best of the game.

"We hope the humor didn't offend anybody," Anheuser-Busch CEO August Busch IV said after the game. At an ad conference later, he said good taste would be a criterion for A-B ads, not just for its beer.

5 Clydesdales Bow to 9/11 (2002)

Anheuser-Busch is mostly famous for its Super Bowl commercials that make viewers laugh. This one, however, made many cry.

Airing less than five months after the Sept.11 terrorist attacks, it struck a national chord. The Budweiser Clydesdales pull the beer wagon across the country before coming to a stop with a view of the World Trade Center site. The lead horse bows in respect to the 9/11 victims, and the team follows.

"That touched a nerve in this country," says Linda Kaplan Thaler, regarded as one of Madison Avenue's top ad chiefs. "During a contest that pits one team against another, this ad showed that, ultimately, we're all on the same team." But the bow may have been too subtle. Some Ad Meter panelists didn't get it and ranked the ad just outside the top 10. But it still tugs the heart today, and A-B can take a bow for this one.

6 Dot-Com Bowl (2000)

At the height of the Internet bubble, a dozen dot-coms spent more than $40 million on Super Bowl ads to get noticed.

The hard part now is remembering many of the ads, except two:

Pets.com's singing Sock Puppet crooned *If You Leave Me Now.* The ad broke into Ad Meter's top five. And E-Trade's monkey clapped along with two men in an ad that ends with the message: "We just wasted 2 million bucks. What are you doing with your money?"

Not a total waste, however: The ad ranked just outside of Ad Meter's top 10, and the company is one of the few of those dot-coms still in business.

7 Superman Walks (2000)

Sometimes special effects make an ad memorable, like it or not. Such was the case with the eerie image of paralyzed actor Christopher Reeve walking in this commercial for Nuveen.

In the spot, Reeve gets an ovation as he leaves his wheelchair to present an award for spinal injury research. The ad took criticism because it was fakery: The late actor never walked after he was paralyzed.

Because the ad got so much pregame PR, the image did not surprise Ad Meter panelists, and it finished in the middle of the pack. After this, many advertisers kept their climax secret until game day.

8 Ego Bowl (2000)

Phil Sokolof is hardly a household name. But the retired steel industry millionaire, who had his first heart attack at age 43, wrote, starred in and bought $2 million in ad time for his cautionary health ad.

In the ad, Sokolof, who died of heart failure in 2004, waxed unpoetically on the use of cholesterol-producing drugs to prevent heart disease.

The ad bombed: next-to-last on Ad Meter. "I can't say I'm proud of that," he later conceded to USA TODAY. "It was a downer."

9 Sexy Fashion Show (1999)

Victoria's Secret was among the first to use a Super Bowl spot as a glorified promotion to lure viewers to its website.

The ad featured lingerie-clad models pitching an online fashion show. While Ad Meter men loved the ad, women mostly hated it. Perhaps that's why the ad finished in the middle of the pack.

But it worked. The live, 17-minute online fashion show later that week attracted then-record Web traffic, and the site crashed. The retailer is in the game this year for the first time since then, with supermodel Adriana Lima pitching Valentine's Day sales.

10 When I Grow Up (1999)

A Super Bowl ad full of bright-eyed, optimistic kids would surprise no one.

Which is precisely why job site Monster.com's artsy black-and-white ad showed cute kids looking ahead to career doom. One says: "I want to be forced into early retirement." Another: "I want to claw my way up to middle management."

Goodby, whose agency was named Agency of the Year by *Advertising Age* and *Adweek,* calls this the best Super Bowl spot of the past 20 years. But Ad Meter panelists ranked it right in the middle. So much for artful angst.

11 Exploding Mosquito (1999)

Why does a sweaty guy, pouring Tabasco sauce onto his pizza, just sit on his porch and watch a mosquito bite his leg?

The punch line: After biting the Tabasco eater, the mosquito explodes in midair.

This hot, hot, hot ad for McIlhenny Tabasco made Ad Meter's top five, the only outsider that year to challenge a Pepsi/Anheuser-Busch ad juggernaut.

12 Cindy's Bowl (1997)

It's rare that a celebrity appears in two ads in one Super Bowl, but Cindy Crawford did in this one.

In a Pepsi spot, she and fellow supermodel Tyra Banks blow kisses at a newborn who winks and blows back a smooch. Then, in a Cadillac Catera spot, Crawford plays a princess with a plunging neckline. It was later pulled by General Motors after complaints about its portrayal of women.

Crawford did not appear again in a Super Bowl ad until 2005. That Diet Pepsi ad, where she checks out a hot guy, was a huge hit online afterward. Say this three times fast: Cindy certainly sells soda.

13 Clydesdales Play Ball (1996)

What if horses played football? Budweiser showed just that in this classic spot pitting two teams of Clydesdales. As two cowboys watch, one horse even kicks a field goal.

The ad rated in Ad Meter's top five, and Bud updated it for the 2004 Super Bowl with a parody of the NFL's video review policy—with a real zebra checking the instant replay while the horses wait.

14 Special Effects Bowl (1995)

Great Super Bowl ads require great ideas, and sometimes great special effects. Two had both in this game.

In a Pepsi spot, the Ad Meter winner, a boy at the beach sucks himself into a Pepsi bottle.

And kicking off in this game were the famous Budweiser frogs: "Bud," "Weis" and "Er." In the swamp, the three croak their names to form "Budweiser."

They earned a long series of ads. And that led to lizards. Which led to, well, Cedric the Entertainer.

15 Hopper's Rant (1995)

This may be the Super Bowl's oddest ad. For one, it was 90 seconds. For another, it starred Dennis Hopper, in an odd bow to Gen. George Patton, as an obsessed football fan.

Hopper rants about his love for football, at one point referring to football as the "ballet of bulldozers."

Some critics charged that the ad poked fun at the mentally ill. Years later, Hopper said he regretted the campaign. "It was a career move—backwards."

16 Bud Bowl Finale (1995)

Anheuser-Busch's Bud Bowls were Super Bowl staples from the first one in 1989 that featured animated Bud Light and Budweiser bottles facing off on the gridiron.

Over the years, the formula got more complex. But the laughs kept coming up shorter, ending with this one in which Bud Light "spokescharacters" Iggy, Frank and Biff, watch the game from a desert island.

A running joke during Super Bowl blowouts was that the Bud Bowl was better than the game. For sheer endurance, score one for A-B.

17 Nothing but Net (1993)

McDonald's paired Michael Jordan and Larry Bird for a Super Bowl spot that remains an All-Star. With a Big Mac on the line, Jordan and Bird match shots in an extreme version of playing H-O-R-S-E.

What makes the ad sing isn't just the crazy shots each nails, but the stars' comic timing: Jordan's gee-whiz smirks and Bird's aw-shucks shrugs.

The spot was a slam-dunk Ad Meter winner.

18 Subaru's Meltdown (1993)

Subaru not only aired Ad Meter's last-place ad this year, it aired five of the bottom seven in the panelists' rating. No advertiser has matched that feat.

The ads were for its all-new Impreza and were just 15 seconds each. In a bid to attract women, they were narrated by an unseen Kirstie Alley.

The problem wasn't Alley or the content—it was the notion you could get a coherent Super Bowl message across in a bunch of 15-second sound bites. Call it Subaru's 15 seconds of shame.

19 McDonald's Bold Move (1991)

The chain broke new ground by addressing the issue of Down syndrome on the Super stage.

McDonald's introduced the world to Mike Sewell, who has the condition. Mike, in turn, introduces viewers to his family and friends.

The ad finished second in Ad Meter and earned McDonald's a burst of positive PR. Bravo, Ronald!

20 Coke Goes 3-D (1989)

The buildup was big. Coca-Cola distributed 20 million cardboard 3-D glasses so folks could watch its Diet Coke ad in 3-D. The ad, about a runaway Diet Coke machine, finished a laudable fifth in Ad Meter. It also was beaten by two spots for Pepsi.

Still, Coke garnered spin galore for the 3-D gimmick. Word of a run on 3-D glasses kept Coke in the news for weeks before the game. But most viewers ended up watching the overhyped ad, and related halftime show, without the special specs. After that, 3-D got the Super Bowl boot.

Critical Thinking

1. In your opinion, what is the significance of securing Super Bowl ad immortality?
2. Look over the 20 ads described in the article and develop a list of elements or features that make an ad memorable.

UNIT 4

Global Marketing

Unit Selections

Learning Outcomes

After reading this Unit, you should be able to:

- What economic, cultural, and political obstacles must an organization that seeks to become global in its markets consider?

- Do you believe that an adherence to the "marketing concept" is the right way to approach international markets? Why, or why not?

- What trends are taking place today that would suggest whether particular global markets would grow or decline?

- Which countries do you believe will see the most growth in the next decade? Why?

- In what ways can the Internet be used to extend a market outside the United States?

Student Website
www.mhhe.com/cls

Internet References

International Trade Administration
    www.ita.doc.gov
World Chambers Network
    www.worldchambers.net
World Trade Center Association OnLine
    www.iserve.wtca.org

It is certain that marketing with a global perspective will continue to be a strategic element of U.S. business well into the next decade. The United States is both the world's largest exporter and largest importer. In 1987, U.S. exports totaled just over $250 billion—about 10 percent of total world exports. During the same period, U.S. imports were nearly $450 billion—just under 10 percent of total world imports. By 2010, exports had risen to $5131.3 trillion and imports to $6641.6 trillion—roughly the same percentage of total world trade.

Regardless of whether they wish to be, all marketers are now part of the international marketing system. For some, the end of the era of domestic markets may have come too soon, but that era is over. Today, it is necessary to recognize the strengths and weaknesses of our own marketing practices as compared to those abroad. The multinational corporations have long recognized this need, but now all marketers must acknowledge it. International marketing differs from domestic marketing in that the parties to its transactions live in different political and cultural units. It is the "international" element of international marketing that distinguishes it from domestic marketing—not differences in managerial techniques. The growth of global business among multinational corporations has raised new questions about the role of their headquarters. It has even caused some to speculate whether marketing operations should be performed abroad rather than in the United States.

The key to applying the marketing concept is understanding the consumer. Increasing levels of consumer sophistication are evident in all of the world's most profitable markets. Managers are required to adopt new points of view in order to accommodate increasingly complex consumer wants and needs. The markets in the new millennium will show further integration on a worldwide scale. In these emerging markets, conventional textbook approaches can cause numerous problems. The new marketing perspective called for by the circumstances of the years ahead will require a long-range view that looks from the basics of exchange and their applications in new settings.

© Dr. Parvinder Sethi

The selections presented here serve two purposes. The first three articles in this unit were chosen to provide an overview of world economic factors, competitive positioning, and increasing globalization of markets—issues to which each and every marketer must become sensitive. "Emerging Lessons" describes how understanding the needs of poorer consumers can be both profitable and socially responsible for multinational companies. "Three Dimensional" shows how the markets of Japan, Korea, and China are far from homogeneous. The remaining two articles in this unit are intended to spark a discussion about today's growth markets, namely China and—less intuitively—Africa. "Cracking the Next Growth Market: Africa" provides guidance on how companies can seize emerging opportunities in Africa. In "What the West Doesn't Get about China," the authors present readers with some insight on how to adapt to the shift in China's economy from an export-focused one to a consumer-driven market.

Emerging Lessons

For multinational companies, understanding the needs of poorer consumers can be profitable and socially responsible.

MADHUBALAN VISWANATHAN, JOSÉ ANTONIO ROSA, AND JULIE A. RUTH

Businesses, take note: An underserved and poorly understood consumer group is poised to become a driving force in economic and business development, by virtue of sheer numbers and rising globalization.

They are subsistence consumers—people in developing nations like India who earn just a few dollars a day and lack access to basics such as education, health care and sanitation.

As these consumers gain access to income and information over the next decade, their combined purchasing power, already in the trillions of dollars, likely will grow at higher rates than that of consumers in industrialized nations. The lesson for multinational companies: Understanding and addressing the needs of the world's poorest consumers is likely to become a profitable, as well as a socially responsible, strategy.

A characteristic associated with low-income consumers, and one that has major implications for doing business with them, is that many struggle with reading and math. Like the 14% of Americans estimated to be functionally illiterate in a U.S. government survey, subsistence consumers have difficulty reading package labels, store signs or product-use instructions, or subtracting the purchase price of an item from cash on hand—all of which hampers their ability to put their limited incomes to best use.

Our research shows that low-literacy consumers process market information and approach purchasing decisions differently than other groups of shoppers. As a result, companies may have to alter marketing practices such as packaging, advertising, pricing, store signage and the training of retail-store employees in order to communicate with them more effectively and win their business.

Here is what we learned from our studies on low-literacy, low-income consumers in the U.S. and subsistence consumers in developing markets, and our recommendations on how marketers can improve the value these groups get from product purchase and use.

Concrete Thinking

One of the key observations we made is that low-literacy consumers have difficulty with abstract thinking. These individuals tend to group objects by visualizing concrete and practical situations they have experienced.

They exhibited what science would call a low grasp of abstract categories—tools, cooking utensils or protein-rich foods, for example—which suggests low-literacy consumers may have difficulty understanding advertising and store signs that position products that way. Their natural inclination is to organize merchandise according to the ingredients needed to make a particular dish or the products needed to complete a specific task, such as doing laundry or cleaning the bathroom, and that is often what they are envisioning as they navigate store aisles, deciding what to buy.

This is reminiscent of research on low-literacy peasants in Central Asia in the early 20th century, who, when presented with a set of objects such as hammer-saw-log-hatchet and asked to select the three that could be placed in one group or be described by one word, didn't derive abstract categories such as "tools" even when prompted. Instead, they grouped the objects primarily around envisioned tasks such as chopping firewood.

Being anchored in the perceptual "here and now" also interferes with the ability of low-literacy consumers to perform mathematical computations, especially those framed in abstract terms. For example, when we asked low-literacy shoppers in the U.S. to estimate whether they had enough cash to pay for the groceries in their cart, many needed to physically handle cash and envision additional piles of currency or coins to accurately estimate the cost of goods in their cart; when the sensorial experience of counting cash was taken away, they often were at a loss.

Because handling cash while walking store aisles isn't advisable, many low-literacy consumers arrive at checkout counters not knowing whether they have enough money to cover their purchases. All too often, they hand all of their cash to the register attendant and hope for an honest transaction.

One of the most potentially detrimental results of concrete thinking, however, is the difficulty that low-literacy consumers have with performing price/volume calculations. They tend to choose products based solely on the lowest posted price or smallest package size, even when they have sufficient resources for a larger purchase, because they have difficulty estimating

For Further Reading

See these related articles from MIT Sloan Management Review.

Strategic Innovation at the Base of the Pyramid

Jamie Anderson and Costas Markides (Fall 2007)
   Strategic innovation in developing markets is fundamentally different from what occurs in developed economies.
   http://sloanreview.mit.edu/smr/issue/2007/fall/16/

The Great Leap: Driving Innovation From the Base of the Pyramid

Stuart L. Hart and Clayton M. Christensen (Fall 2002)
   Companies can generate growth and satisfy social and environmental stakeholders through a "great leap" to the base of the economic pyramid.
   http://sloanreview.mit.edu/smr/issue/2002/fall/5/

Has Strategy Changed?

Kathleen M. Eisenhardt (Winter 2002)
   Globalization has quietly transformed the economic playing field.
   http://sloanreview.mit.edu/smr/issue/2002/winter/10/

The Need for a Corporate Global Mind-Set

Thomas M. Begley and David P. Boyd (Winter 2003)
   Many international business leaders consider a global mind-set desirable, but few know how to embed it companywide.
   http://sloanreview.mit.edu/smr/issue/2003/winter/3/

The Dynamic Synchronization of Strategy and Information Technology

C.K. Prahalad and M.S. Krishnan (Summer 2002)
   The authors' work with 500 executives revealed that few managers believed their information infrastructure was able to handle the pressures from deregulation, globalization, ubiquitous connectivity and the convergence of industries and technologies.
   http://sloanreview.mit.edu/smr/issue/2002/summer/2/

the longevity and savings that come from buying in larger volumes. Some base purchase decisions on physical package size, instead of reported volume content, or on the quantity of a particular ingredient—such as fat, sodium or sugar—but without allowing for the fact that acceptable levels of an ingredient can vary across product categories or package size.

Misspent Energy

We found that low-literacy consumers spend so much time and mental energy on what many of us can do quickly and with little thought that they have little time to base purchase decisions on anything other than surface attributes such as size, color or weight.

They tend to think in pictures, so any change in visual cues such as sign fonts, brand logos or store layouts can leave them struggling to locate a desired product category or brand. Price displays can cause confusion because of the many numbers presented, such as original prices, discounted percentages and discounted prices. Even estimating the price of two gallons of milk if the price of one is known may require a pencil-and-paper calculation unless the price is set in whole or half-unit increments, such as $3 or $3.50.

Because so much shopping time is devoted to deciphering product labels and locating products, we found that low-literacy consumers are less able than other groups to assess the value of products based on subsurface attributes—this computer has more memory and will do what I need more effectively, for example.

When shopping in unfamiliar stores, some low-literacy consumers will choose products at random, buying the first brand they see once they locate a desired product category or aisle. Others simply walk through the store, choosing items that look attractive based on factors such as packaging colors or label illustrations, without regard to whether they even need the product.

When shopping in familiar stores, many low-literacy consumers buy only the brands they recognize by appearance or have purchased previously. While this approach reduces the incidence of product purchases for which the consumer has no use, it precludes the adoption of new and improved products as a category evolves and improves over time.

The pitfalls and uncertainty that come from choosing products at random, based on surface attributes or out of habit provoke anxiety in many low-literacy consumers, leading us to another finding: Shopping takes a heavy emotional toll on this group.

Buying the wrong items, running short of cash at the register or having to ask for help in the aisle to locate products are recurring worries, even cause for despair. The anticipation of such stressful experiences prompts some low-literacy consumers to avoid new, large or what they perceive to be threatening shopping venues or to delay shopping until family or friends can assist, even if waiting means doing without essentials. Although low-literacy consumers tend to be passive in public settings, they will remember episodes of poor treatment by service personnel and won't patronize stores or brands they associate with disrespectful treatment.

Despite the significant constraints that low-literacy consumers face, their ingenuity in coping and positive outlook are a testament to human adaptiveness. For instance, subsistence consumers overcome many of the challenges that come from not being able to read or do math problems by relying on their interpersonal networks—family and friends who may have complementary skills and knowledge. In many situations, the network includes the owners of neighborhood stores who offer very limited product assortments and high prices, but who can answer questions and offer advice to consumers unable to read the labels and determine the value of products on their own.

Subsistence consumers are resource-poor but likely to be relationship-rich, and this must be taken into account by businesses seeking to serve them.

Drawing Them In

To win and enhance customer loyalty in developing markets, manufacturers and retailers need to understand the difficulties faced by low-literacy consumers and create shopping environments that make them feel less vulnerable. Here are a few ways that companies can help customers make better purchases and avoid embarrassment:

- Display prices and price reductions graphically—a half-circle to indicate a 50% markdown, for example, or a picture of three one-dollar bills to indicate a purchase price of $3. Price products in whole and half numbers to make it easier for low-literacy consumers to calculate the price of, say, two bags of rice. These pricing practices are critically important in marketplaces where general stores and kiosks are being replaced by self-service stores, where there is less interaction between customer and store owner.

- Clearly post unit prices in common formats across stores, brands and product categories to make it easier for low-literacy consumers to perform price/volume calculations.

- Include illustrations of product categories on store signs to make it easier for low-literacy consumers to navigate new or refurbished stores. Similarly, use graphical representations of sizes, ingredients, instructions and other information to communicate product information more effectively in shelf and other in-store displays.

- Put the ingredients required for the preparation of popular local dishes in the same section of the store. This would be helpful to low-literacy consumers who often envision the sequence of activities involved in fixing specific dishes to identify the ingredients and quantities they need to purchase. The same can be done for other domestic tasks.

- Incorporate familiar visual elements—such as color schemes or font types—into new store concepts or redesigned brand logos to minimize confusion and anxiety among low-literacy shoppers and increase the likelihood that they will try new products and stores.

- Create a friendly store environment by training store personnel to be sensitive to the needs of low-literacy shoppers and by verbally disclosing and consistently applying store policies. In addition, allow employees to form relationships with consumers by learning their names and offering small amounts of individualized assistance. This is particularly important for global brands and companies entering markets where foreigners are mistrusted or have accrued a history of mistreating people.

As subsistence markets become more attractive, additional opportunities to serve low-literacy consumers will probably become available. Because literacy deficiencies are likely to be addressed at a slower pace than the pace at which poor consumers gain discretionary income and the ability to spend it on products and services, the companies that respond to this group's needs early on will have an advantage. Low-literacy consumers can be a profitable and loyal customer group if treated properly.

Critical Thinking

1. According to the articles what are some of the challenges associated with marketing to subsistence consumers?

2. You have been assigned as a consultant for a business that is looking to target subsistence consumers. Prepare a list of DOs and DON'Ts to help it attract and retain this target market.

DR. VISWANATHAN is an associate professor of marketing at the University of Illinois at Urbana-Champaign in Champaign, Ill. **DR. ROSA** is a professor of marketing and sustainable business practices at the University of Wyoming in Laramie, Wyo. **DR. RUTH** is an associate professor of marketing at Rutgers University in Camden, N.J. They can be reached at reports@wsj.com.

Three Dimensional

The markets of Japan, Korea, and China are far from homogeneous.

MASAAKI KOTABE AND CRYSTAL JIANG

Asia is one of the world's most dynamic regions, and offers multiple opportunities for businesses and investors. In terms of its nominal gross domestic product (GDP) in 2005, Japan has the largest economy ($4.80 trillion), followed by China ($1.84 trillion) and Korea ($.72 trillion). China's real purchasing power exceeds $7 trillion, Japan's is estimated at $4 trillion, and Korea's is estimated at $1 trillion. These giants' combined purchasing power is comparable to the $12 trillion U.S. economy.

One of the challenges faced by American and other Western multinational companies is a tendency to lump together these markets and assume that Asian consumers have similar tastes and preferences, moderated by different income levels. This is not only a very shortsighted view, but also a risky assumption when entering these markets.

Asian countries have distinct cultural, social, and economic characteristics that affect consumer behavior, with consumers in Japan, Korea, and China differing in brand orientations, attitudes toward domestic and foreign products, quality and price perceptions, and technology feature preferences. A comparative analysis of consumer behaviors can help companies identify effective marketing strategies, and enable them to successfully tackle these Asian markets (see Table 1).

Brand Orientation

Japan. Of all the developed countries, this is the most brand-conscious and status-conscious. It is also intensely style-conscious: Consumers love high-end luxury goods (especially from France and Italy), purchasing items such as designer handbags, shoes, and jewelry. Since 2001, Hermes, Louis Vuitton (commonly referred to as LVMH), and Coach have opened glitzy flagship stores in Tokyo and enjoyed double-digit sales growth. And the country represents 20% of Gucci's worldwide revenue, 15% of LVMH's, and 12% of Chanel's. It seems that a slumping economy has not inhibited its consumers.

Eager to "know who they are," they prefer brands that contribute to their senses of identity and self-expression. These highly group-oriented consumers are apt to select prestigious merchandise based on social class standards, and prefer products that enhance their status. Accordingly, they attach more

Executive Briefing

Globalizing markets might not mean that markets have become similar. Although multinational companies tend to believe that all Asian markets are the same, a comparative analysis proves that consumers in Japan, Korea, and China differ in their brand orientations, attitudes toward domestic and foreign products, quality and price perceptions, and product feature preferences. To ensure success, companies must set aside narrow and risky assumptions, and tailor country-specific strategies to target these consumers.

importance to the reputation of the merchandise than to their personal social classes.

Noticeably, the country's consumer markets have expanded to China and Korea. In Shanghai or Seoul, you can see the influence of Japan's fashion trends and products. There's even a Chinese word for this phenomenon: ha-ri, which means the adoration of Japanese style.

Korea. Consumers have very sophisticated tastes, show immense passion for new experiences, and favor premium and expensive imported products. In 2004, the Korean Retail Index showed continuous growth of premium brands in certain product categories, such as whiskey, shampoo, and cosmetics. Consumers also demonstrate great interest in generational fads (expressions of their generations and cultures, not just of their economics or regions), thereby selecting products that follow their generations' judgments and preferences.

China. Roughly 10 million–13 million Chinese consumers prefer luxury goods. The majority of them are entrepreneurs or young professionals working for foreign multinational firms. Recent studies found that 24% of the population, mostly in their 20s and 30s, prefers new products and considers technology an important part of life. (Those in their 40s and 50s are price-conscious, brand loyal, and less sensitive to technology.) With higher education and purchasing power, this generation is brand- and status-conscious. It considers luxury goods to be personal achievements, bringing higher social status.

Table 1 Market Characteristics of the Three Largest Asian Economies

	Japan	Korea	China
Population (2005)	127 million	48 million	1,306 million
Nominal GDP (2005)	$4.80 trillion	$ .72 trillion	$1.84 trillion
GDP purchasing power parity (2004)	$3.7 trillion	$ .92 trillion	$7.3 trillion
GDP per capita purchasing power parity (2004)	$29,400	$19,200	$5,600
GDP real growth rate of country (2004)	2.9%	4.6%	9.1%
Degree of luxury brand consciousness	Very strong	Strong	Varied
Preference for foreign products	Strong (particularly for European products)	Weak	Very strong
Price/quality perception	Extremely quality demanding	Polarization of consumption	Very price conscious
Importance of high-tech features on new products	Very high	Very high	Varied

Sources: Central Intelligence Agency, *World Factbook,* and *Index Mundi.*

Purchasing behavior tends to vary regionally. Consumers in metropolitan areas follow fashions/trends/styles, prefer novelty items, and are aware of brand image and product quality. These consumers live on the eastern coast—in major cities such as Shanghai, Beijing, Shenzhen, and Dalian. There, luxury brands such as Armani, Prada, and LVMH are considered prominent logos for high-income clientele.

According to LVMH, this country is its fourth-largest market in terms of worldwide sales. It's no wonder that many high-end firms label these consumers "the new Japanese": a group of increasingly wealthy people hungry for brands and fanatical about spending.

Domestic vs. Foreign

Japan. Although consumers are extremely demanding and have different perceptions of products made in other countries, they are generally accepting of quality foreign products. However, Japan is mostly dominated by well-established companies such as Canon, Sony, and Toyota. Many globally successful firms experience great difficulty gaining footholds.

In this market, Häagen-Dazs Japan Inc. succeeded the exit of competitor Ben & Jerry's, dominating the premium ice cream market with a 90% market share. It successfully delivered the message of a "lifestyle-enhancement product" with word-of-mouth advertising, garnering a flood of free publicity. The company flourished by promoting high quality with local appeal.

Korea. These consumers hold negative attitudes toward foreign businesses; the majority believes that these businesses transfer local wealth to other countries, and crowd out small establishments. Consumers are very proud, and demonstrate a complicated love-hate relationship with foreign brands.

Very few consumers understand or speak English, let alone the languages of their closest trading partners: Japan and China. Often, Korean campaigns require significant rebranding—use of localized brands—to influence local perceptions. According to an official at Carrefour (the world's second-largest retailer), the company has difficulty expanding its investments into other provinces because of excessive regulations, and hasn't done enough research to keep up with Korean consumers' needs.

Nevertheless, the country is increasingly comfortable with the presence of foreign companies in previously closed industries. (In fact, the society is much too uncritical and passive in the acceptance of foreign—especially American—products.) And consumers are far less brand-conscious than before, and will embrace new products from unknown companies.

China. Attitudes toward foreign products differ, depending on consumers' age groups. Companies can no longer view this country's youth through the lens of traditional cultural values; this generation considers international taste a key factor in making decisions. Conversely, the mature generation (55 years and older) expresses a definite preference for locally made products. In general, consumers believe imported products under foreign brand names are more dependable.

Many foreign companies (e.g., Nike, Nokia, Sony, McDonald's) have replaced unknown local brands. The country retains more than 300 licensed Starbucks outlets, and chairman Howard Schultz says of this market: "In addition to the 200 million middle-to-upper-class segments of the population that are typically customers for upscale brands, there is a growing affinity from the younger, affluent consumer for Western brands."

However, some foreign companies—with an increased focus on local appeal—have lost their prominent brands' images to domestic rivals, ultimately forfeiting their market share. After all, when this country's consumers are inspired by design and function, they prefer domestic brands because of their good value for the money.

Quality and Price

Japan. These consumers are the world's strictest when it comes to demand for product quality, and they clearly articulate their needs/desires about a product or packaging operation. They view information other than price (e.g., brand, packaging, advertising) as important variables in assessing quality and making decisions. Compared with Chinese and Korean consumers, they have much higher expectations for products—and are willing to pay premium prices for them. In agricultural produce, for example, they are less tolerant of skin blemishes, small size, and nonuniformity.

Foreign companies that don't fully understand and meet consumers' needs/expectations struggle with their investments. Although Wal-Mart dwarfs the competition (with $285 billion in 2004 global sales) and owns 42% of all Japanese supermarket chains, it faces losses there. Its "everyday low prices" philosophy doesn't seem to attract Japanese consumers, because they often associate low price with low quality: yasu-karou, warukarou—cheap price, cheap product.

To cater to these consumers, manufacturers have adopted a total quality approach. To survive fierce local competition, Procter & Gamble sought the best available materials for product formulations and packaging. In the process, it learned some invaluable lessons on how to improve operations, and obtained new product ideas from consumers. (Interestingly, the company took this education on the Japanese way of interacting with consumers and applied it globally.) Today, the country serves as Procter & Gamble's major technical center in Asia, where it develops certain global technologies.

And McDonald's opened its first store in Tokyo's Ginza district, which is identified with luxury brand-name goods. It purchased expensive land—not justified by the limited profits of a hamburger establishment—to boost the quality image of its product. Today, McDonald's Japan has grown to become the country's largest fast-food chain.

In terms of cost, the younger generation prefers low-priced products—everything priced at 100 yen (similar to U.S. dollar stores). The "two extreme price markets" segmentation model explains how consumers value lower prices for their practical use while paying premium prices for self-satisfaction, social status, and the quality of products—especially those from Europe. As a result, anything that falls in the middle of the price range—such as the country's designer brands—generates petty profits.

Korea. Consumption has been sluggish since the Asian financial crisis of 1997–1999. However, the younger generation is at the forefront of a new and emerging pattern; it holds opposing expectations of/preferences for low-priced and high-priced goods. When purchasing high-tech or fashion-related items, these consumers prefer well-known brands, and tend to purchase expensive goods to attain psychological satisfaction. Yet they are willing to purchase unbranded goods with low prices, as long as the basic features are guaranteed. It has taken several decades for discount stores to surpass the retail market.

China. Most consumers are price sensitive, and try to safeguard part of their income for investment. In 2005, many global automakers readjusted their strategies in this country, based on demand predictions that most consumers would purchase cars priced less than $12,000. One popular Chinese automaker, Chery, priced its QQ model between $5,500 and $7,500; another aggressive domestic automaker, Xiali, priced its cars at similarly affordable prices.

Although this market is lucrative with growing demand, foreign brands (e.g., Honda, General Motors, Volkswagen Group) cannot compete with Chinese automakers' competitive prices. And when the younger generation worships Western and luxury brands—in eagerness to establish its social identity—it might prefer pirated versions to domestic ones, making anticounterfeiting control a major issue for companies.

Technology Features

Japan. Because of the country's harmonic convergence of the domestic market and the industrial sector, consumers have always preferred high-tech gadgets. According to an estimate by The World Bank Group, the country possesses 410,000 of the world's 720,000 working robots (which perform useful chores and provide companionship). Its electronics companies create gizmos by borrowing new concepts from the computer industry, such as personal video recorders, interactive pagers, and Internet radios.

Instead of looking for cost or value, consumers are willing to pay for better and cooler features and technological sophistication. Largely because of Japan's small living quarters, manufacturers have become experts at miniaturizing and creating multifunction devices. For instance, Sony's PlayStation Portable compacts the power of the original PlayStation into a palm-sized package. According to the company, it can deliver music and MPEG-4 video, can display photos, and even offers a Wi-Fi connection for wireless gaming and messaging. It's also no wonder that the country welcomed Baroke, the first company to successfully produce quality sparkling and still wine in a can.

Korea. The most wired country in the world is a leader in Internet usage and high-tech industries such as mobile phones, liquid crystal displays, and semiconductors. It also has widespread broadband, and high volumes of personal computer ownership. While mobile phone sales have cooled in Japan, these consumers continue to trade in phones for newer models about every six months.

> **Largely because of Japan's small living quarters, manufacturers have become experts at miniaturizing and creating multifunction devices.**

According to a Samsung Research Institute survey, consumers prefer to express themselves without following social conventions. The Cyworld virtual community website, for instance, provides a subscriber with a private room, a circle of friends, and an endless range of "home" decoration possibilities and cool music. Ever-widening cyberspace reaches more than one-fourth of the population. The younger generation in particular enjoys virtual shopping malls and e-commerce.

China. It is imperative for companies to understand the major differences in consumer behavior between generations. Young Chinese consumers (typically affluent segments in the prosperous cities) are passionate about the latest developments. Recent studies found that 24% of the population—most with ages in the early 20s or 30s—prefer new products and consider technology an important part of life. Those in their 40s–50s, on the other hand, are price conscious, brand loyal, and less sensitive to technology.

Advice and Recommendations

Marketers need to tailor country-specific strategies to target consumers in Japan, Korea, and China. The existence of strategically equivalent segments (e.g., the younger generation, with its propensity to purchase high-quality, innovative, and foreign products) suggests a geocentric approach to global markets. These similarities allow for standardized strategies across national boundaries.

By aggregating such segments, companies not only preserve consumer orientation, but also reduce the number of marketing mixes they have to offer—without losing market share, marketing, advertising, research and development, and production throughout Asia.

Moreover, because product design, function, and quality determine consumers' experiences, companies must simultaneously incorporate all areas—such as product development and marketing—to establish commanding positions in mature markets. Once they create positive images in these countries, success will be forthcoming.

Japan:

- This is the most profitable market for luxury goods companies. The key to success is promotion of high quality, local appeal, and a sense of extravagance.
- As one of the most volatile markets, it requires a steady flow of new stimuli with an improved rhythm of innovations. To survive, companies must continuously develop new products and establish prestigious brand value. If they can succeed there, then they can do so anywhere.
- Picky Japanese consumers clearly articulate their requirements about products or packaging operations. As a result, companies can use the country as their technical center—to gain firsthand experience in satisfying consumers in the region.
- These consumers are willing to pay for better and cooler features and technological sophistication. Companies can win their hearts by introducing gizmos.
- Because significant differences exist among generations, and those differences will translate into diverse consumer behaviors, segmentation marketing (identifying variations based on age, region, and gender) is best. Companies must be aware of these differences, and understand what kinds of products/services can meet the market segment's needs. For example: Coca-Cola has introduced more products here than anywhere else, including coffee and green tea beverages that appeal to Japanese tastes. As a result, its net operating revenue represents more than 60% of the total Asian segment (20% of its worldwide revenue).

Korea:

- A consumer-oriented approach is crucial for identifying tastes and blending in, rather than being viewed as foreign. Careful market, brand, and advertising testing is imperative.
- It can be difficult to enter this market alone; strategic alliances with domestic companies are a practical way to understand local preferences when introducing a global brand.
- If foreign companies make greater efforts to intensify their involvements with—and long-term commitments to—the country's economic development, then consumers' perceptions of an "invasion" will dissipate over time.
- Product design directly affects a company's competitiveness. This and brand power can overcome

product quality, and even product functions. To present the best product design to its consumers, Samsung Electronics hired an influential British industrial designer. According to the company's Economic Research Institute, a good design "provides a good experience for consumers"; it looks different, feels good, is easy to use, and has an identity.

China:

- Foreign companies can no longer wait; the market for consumer goods is growing rapidly, stimulated by a strong economy.
- Its diversity and the vastness of its consumer base make it critical for companies to segment consumers based on demographic, geographic, and psychographic/lifestyle variations.
- Because of the younger generation's brand orientation, promoting symbolic value is imperative for conspicuous and inconspicuous foreign products.
- Multinational companies can't assume that their first-mover advantages will be rewarded for brand recognition and established distribution channels.
- Cost-conscious consumers are quite unpredictable, so companies should avoid a too-high premium price strategy. Instead, they should research quantitatively acceptable price/value trade-offs by category.
- Because local brands are on the rise, foreign companies must work harder to localize research and development and the contents of their products. They must also better evaluate the market and the potential for long-term growth. Without competitive pricing and world-class product design/quality, companies will have a tough time surviving.

Company executives must remember that not all countries are created equally. By understanding and learning to appreciate the differences and similarities between these three Asian purchasing giants, companies from other countries can immerse their organizations seamlessly.

Critical Thinking

1. With a small group of peers from your class, conduct a comparative analysis of Japan, Korea, and China.

2. Are consumers from these three Asian nations different from American consumers? If so, describe some major differences.

MASAAKI KOTABE is the Washburn Chair of International Business and Marketing and director of research at the Institute of Global Management Studies at Temple University's Fox School of Business and Management in Philadelphia. He may be reached at mkotabe@temple.edu. CRYSTAL JIANG is a PhD candidate in strategy and international business at the Fox School of Business and Management. She may be reached at crystalj@temple.edu. To join the discussion on this article, please visit www.marketingpower.com/marketingmanagementblog.

From *Marketing Management*, March/April 2006, pp. 39–43. Copyright © 2006 by American Marketing Association. Reprinted by permission.

Cracking the Next Growth Market: Africa

The continent is home to many of the world's biggest opportunities. The trick is deciding where and how to seize them.

MUTSA CHIRONGA ET AL.

A year ago, when South Africa hosted the World Cup of football, a Tswanian phrase, *Ke Nako* ("It's Time"), reverberated across the world like the cacophony of a million vuvuzelas, announcing that Africa's moment had come. Economists, consultants, and executives all suggested that the African economy, which had languished during the last two decades of the 20th century, was finally stirring.

Nevertheless, most companies have been slow to enter Africa. Many assumed that the flutter of attention was the reflection of a global boom in commodity prices, and therefore of relevance primarily to oil and mining companies. The recent political turmoil in such countries as Algeria, Egypt, Libya, Morocco, and Tunisia and the civil war in Ivory Coast have dramatically reminded executives of the enormous uncertainty that businesses must cope with in Africa. With prodemocracy movements breaking out in some of Africa's fastest-growing economies, multinational companies face a double bind: Some of the most promising countries present the highest risks.

That's not all. In Africa the infrastructure is still poor; talent is scarce; and poverty, famine, and disease afflict many nations. Most Western executives, unsure of the size of Africa's consumer markets, prefer to invest in Asia's dragon and tiger economies rather than in Africa's economic lions. "Is it truly Africa's time?" they wonder.

So often were we asked the question that last year McKinsey & Company decided to analyze Africa's economies and conduct a microlevel study of its consumer markets. Our goal was to identify Africa's sources of growth, determine if it would continue over time, and size opportunities in key sectors. (For the full analysis, see *Lions on the Move: The Progress and Potential of African Economies* at www.mckinsey.com/mgi.)

The findings surprised us. Over the past decade, Africa's real GDP grew by 4.7 percent a year, on average—twice the pace of its growth in the 1980s and 1990s. The surge cut across nations and sectors. By 2009, Africa's collective GDP of $1.6 trillion was roughly equal to Brazil's or Russia's. The continent is among the fastest-expanding economic regions today. In fact, Africa and Asia (excluding Japan) were the only continents that grew during the recent global recession. Though Africa's growth rate slowed to 2 percent in 2009, it bounced back to nearly 5 percent in 2010, and in 2011 it is likely to touch 5.2 percent.

While political troubles, wars, natural disasters, and poor policies could slow Africa down, the prospects for consumer-facing companies are bright. Africans spent $860 billion on goods and services in 2008—35 percent more than the $635 billion that Indians spent, and slightly more than the $821 billion of consumer expenditures in Russia. If Africa maintains its current growth trajectory, consumers will buy $1.4 trillion worth of goods and services in 2020, which will be a little less than India's projected $1.7 trillion but more than Russia's $960 billion.

In 2008, Africans spent $860 billion on goods and services—35 percent more than Indians spent.

As Africa's economies progress, opportunities are opening in sectors such as retailing, telecommunications, banking, infrastructure-related industries, resource-related businesses, and all along the agricultural value chain. Consider that telecom companies in Africa have added 316 million subscribers—more than the entire U.S. population—since 2000. According to UN data, Africa offers a higher return on investment than any other emerging market. For several reasons: Competition is less intense and few foreign companies have a presence there, and pent-up consumer demand is strong. Companies that desire revenues and profits, we believe, can no longer ignore Africa.

Smart multinational companies are busy planting their stakes in the ground. Nokia and Coca-Cola have distribution networks in nearly every African country; Unilever has a presence in 20 African nations, Nestlé in 19, Standard Chartered Bank in

14, Barclays in 12, and Société Générale in 15. Homegrown giants are expanding: Ecobank and South African Breweries each operate in over 30 African countries, while MTN and Shoprite are in 16 African countries each. Companies that enter Africa now, we believe, can shape industry structures, segment markets, and establish brands.

The Growth Ahead

Busy executives may wonder whether the African economy's recent growth is just a flash in the pan. After all, the economy had picked up during the 1970s oil boom, but when oil prices fell, it began to slow. In our opinion, Africa's long-term prospects are strong, because both internal and external trends are propelling its growth.

To be sure, Africa is benefitting from the increases in commodity prices. Oil prices have shot up since 1999, when they were less than $20 a barrel, reaching more than $145 a barrel in 2008, and prices for minerals, grains, and other raw materials have also soared. Yet that trend explains only part of the African story. Natural resources directly accounted for just about a quarter (24 percent) of GDP growth from 2000 through 2008, according to our calculations. Other industries, such as wholesale and retail trade, transportation, telecommunications, and manufacturing, contributed the rest. In fact, countries that export commodities grew just a tad faster, at 5.4 percent a year, than nonexporters, which on average grew 4.6 percent from 2000 through 2008.

Three factors are responsible. One, several African countries, such as Angola and Mozambique, halted deadly hostilities, creating the political stability necessary for growth. The number of serious conflicts in Africa—those in which deaths exceed 1,000 people a year—declined from an average of 4.8 a year in the 1990s to 2.6 in the 2000s. Two, economies became healthier as governments shrank budget deficits, trimmed foreign debt, and brought down inflation. Since 2000, African countries have cut their combined foreign debt from 82 percent of GDP to 59 percent and reduced budget deficits from 4.6 percent of GDP to 1.8 percent, which sent inflation rates tumbling from 22 percent to 8 percent.

Three, several governments adopted market-friendly policies. They privatized state-owned enterprises, reduced trade barriers, cut corporate taxes, and strengthened regulatory and legal systems. Nigeria, for example, privatized more than 116 enterprises between 1999 and 2006; Morocco and Egypt struck free-trade agreements with their main export partners; and Rwanda established courts to settle business disputes. These and other steps helped local companies invest more, achieve greater economies of scale, and become more competitive.

Africa will continue to profit from the rising global demand for oil, natural gas, minerals, food, and other natural resources. The continent has an abundance of riches, including 10 percent of the world's oil reserves, 40 percent of its gold ore, and 80 percent to 90 percent of its deposits of chromium and platinum group metals. To exploit them, African governments are forging new types of partnerships in which buyers from countries such as China and India provide up-front payments, invest in infrastructure, and share management skills and technology.

Long-term growth will get a boost from Africa's demographic and social trends. The population is young, growing, and migrating to the metropolitan centers. In 1980, 28 percent of Africans lived in cities; today 40 percent do—a proportion close to China's and larger than India's. Workers in cities earn higher pay than those in rural areas and can afford to buy products and services beyond the necessities of food and shelter. That expands demand, which leads to a virtuous cycle of growth and job creation.

Many people picture Africans as subsistence farmers, but there's a sizable middle class on the continent. By 2008, 16 million African households had incomes above $20,000 a year—a level that enabled them to buy houses, cars, appliances, and branded products. Another 27 million households earned $10,000 to $20,000. In addition, 41 million households reported incomes of $5,000 to $10,000—the level at which families start spending more than half their income on nonfood items. By 2020 the total number of households in all three segments will reach 128 million, which should make Africa one of the fastest-growing consumer markets of this decade.

Categorizing the Opportunities

Corporations must start developing their strategies by recognizing that Africa isn't one economy. It's home to 50-plus nations, each with its own policies and attitudes toward multinational companies, as well as its own languages, currency, and traditions. Successful companies use filters to decide which countries to enter and tailor their entry strategies to specific sectors. They focus their efforts on key markets, but those that think broadly benefit from greater scale and diversified risks.

Economists usually group countries by income level or geography, but we organized them according to their economic diversification and level of exports. As economies develop, agriculture and natural resources account for a smaller and smaller share of GDP, while the share of manufacturing and services grows. That boosts per capita income, with a 15 percent increase in manufacturing and services as a share of GDP usually resulting in a doubling of per capita income. Exports are the means by which emerging economies earn hard currency to pay for imports of capital goods. In most African countries, capital goods imports account for roughly half of investment, making exports a critical enabler of growth.

Classified by these two parameters, which together provide a snapshot of how developed markets are, African countries fall into four broad clusters. This framework can guide executives as they assess which markets to enter and how.

The diversified economies. Africa's four most advanced economies—Egypt, Morocco, South Africa, and Tunisia—have well-developed manufacturing and service industries. They have relatively high per capita incomes and more stable GDP growth than most of the other economies, despite the political risks that have come to the fore in North Africa. Services, such as banking, telecom, and retailing, have accounted for more than 70 percent of GDP growth in these countries over the past decade.

Readying for Takeoff

Africa's growth accelerated rapidly after 2000 and continued even during the global recession.

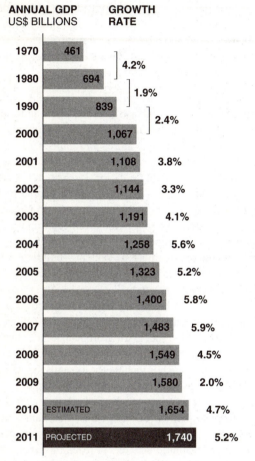

	ANNUAL GDP US$ BILLIONS	GROWTH RATE
1970	461	
		4.2%
1980	694	
		1.9%
1990	839	
		2.4%
2000	1,067	
2001	1,108	3.8%
2002	1,144	3.3%
2003	1,191	4.1%
2004	1,258	5.6%
2005	1,323	5.2%
2006	1,400	5.8%
2007	1,483	5.9%
2008	1,549	4.5%
2009	1,580	2.0%
2010 ESTIMATED	1,654	4.7%
2011 PROJECTED	1,740	5.2%

Note: Growth rates for the 1970s, 1980, and 1990s are compound annual rates.

Since 2000, the continent has been the world's third-fastest growing region, outpacing Eastern Europe and Latin America.

COMPOUND ANNUAL REAL GDP GROWTH, 2000–2010

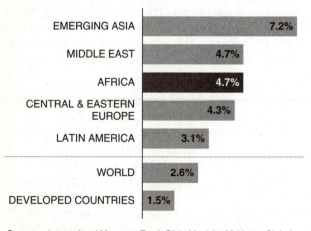

EMERGING ASIA	7.2%
MIDDLE EAST	4.7%
AFRICA	4.7%
CENTRAL & EASTERN EUROPE	4.3%
LATIN AMERICA	3.1%
WORLD	2.6%
DEVELOPED COUNTRIES	1.5%

Sources: International Monetary Fund, Global Insight, Mckinsey Global Institute.

These countries are also Africa's largest consumer markets; 90 percent of households there have some discretionary income. That makes them ideal places for consumer-facing businesses to anchor their operations. Walmart, for example, recently struck a $2.4 billion deal to pick up a 51 percent stake in one of South Africa's largest retailers, Massmart, which has stores in 13 other African countries.

However, these economies have higher labor costs than China or India and struggle to compete even in low-value manufacturing industries. They need to expand exports, improve education to create a skilled workforce, and build infrastructure.

The oil exporters. Africa's oil and gas exporters have the continent's highest per capita incomes but are the least diversified economies. Three of the largest—Algeria, Angola, and Nigeria—have already attracted the world's petroleum majors and have rapidly growing consumer markets. In Angola, for instance, retail banking is expected to grow by 6.8 percent a year through 2020, telecommunication services by 5.2 percent a year, and nonfood consumer goods by 4.4 percent a year. Because of their income levels, the oil exporters are attractive markets for high-end goods and services.

Africa's oil exporters face the same challenges as many resource-rich nations: maintaining political stability; resisting the temptation to overinvest, which would make them vulnerable if commodity prices decline; and creating a diversified economy. Nigeria has already begun the transition to a diversified economy. While resources have accounted for 35 percent of the country's GDP growth since 2000, services have accounted for 37 percent. The number of telecommunications subscribers there increased from practically zero in 2000 to 63 million by 2008, and banking assets grew fivefold.

The transition economies. Africa's transition economies—such as Ghana, Kenya, Uganda, and Senegal—have lower per capita incomes than the countries in the first two groups but are growing rapidly. Though their agriculture and resource sectors together account for as much as 35 percent of GDP and two-thirds of exports, these countries increasingly export manufactured goods to other African countries. The penetration of banking, telecom, and modern retailing is much lower than it is in the diversified economies, but that offers attractive opportunities.

Companies targeting these markets must tailor products to poorer customers. Still, early entrants will find less competition here, and the rapid growth is expected to continue. Several transition economies are likely to increase their commodity exports in the coming years, which could turbocharge growth. In Ghana and Uganda, for instance, recent oil discoveries will boost tax revenues, making it easier for them to diversify their economies.

The pretransition economies. These economies are poor, with annual per capita GDP of just $353 on average. But some of them are expanding rapidly. The three largest—the Democratic Republic of the Congo, Ethiopia, and Mali—have grown, on average, 7 percent a year since 2000. However, their growth has been erratic in the past.

These pretransition economies differ greatly, but all of them lack the basics, such as stable governments, strong public institutions, and sustainable agricultural development. Multinational companies must track these economies, but only those that can handle the risks should enter them.

The economies of the Democratic Republic of the Congo, Ethiopia, and Mali have grown 7 percent a year since 2000.

Four Keys to Success

Winning in Africa requires executives to understand the business environment in each country they enter and to tailor their plans accordingly. It demands innovation; the winners are often companies that tackle complex challenges creatively. In our work, we have found four other elements critical to success in Africa.

1. **Pick the right entry strategy.** Once a company has identified the countries and industries in which it would like to have a presence, it must choose an approach. Should it start from scratch and grow on its own? Should it build a presence by acquiring small local players? Should it take a stake in a Pan-African player?

The answer will depend on the industry. In relatively well developed sectors such as retail banking and telecom, it's probably too late to deploy only an organic strategy using traditional business models. African banks, such as Ecobank and Standard Bank, as well as foreign banks like Standard Chartered and Barclays, have already spent decades establishing operations in many countries. More recently, some have grown their footprints by buying up local banks.

New entrants will increasingly have to use M&A as an entry strategy. One option is to knit together a Pan-African operation by acquiring regional players. Another is to buy a stake in a big African company. That's what China's ICBC did, purchasing 20 percent of Standard Bank in 2008. The alliance gave ICBC immediate access to the 17 African countries in which Standard Bank operates and enabled it to finance the activities of Chinese companies all over Africa.

Organic growth strategies are possible in sectors such as retailing. Formal retailing is limited in most African countries, and that allows global players to move in. Zara, the Spanish retailer, has opened 12 stores across North Africa in the past five years. Shoprite had just one store outside its home country of South Africa in 1995 but has since become the continent's largest food retailer, opening 71 stores in other African nations. Organic growth is also possible in industries where disruptive technologies create new products and services. Consider Safaricom's mobile-phone-based money-transfer service, M-Pesa, which enables customers to deposit and withdraw money from a network of agents. Launched in Kenya in 2007, M-Pesa captured 6.5 million customers in just two years' time, and it has since been launched in Tanzania and South Africa as well.

2. **Get—and get to—customers.** Consumer preferences vary enormously across Africa, so companies must invest in market intelligence. Brand-conscious consumers will save up to buy premium items, but most people have low incomes and lack access to credit. Using imaginative strategies—selling products in small quantities; offering credit, hire purchase, and layaway plans; and educating consumers—is essential. Developing innovative, low-priced consumer products and services is often critical. For example, Nokia focuses on phone models priced from $20 to $50 and adjusts profit targets to reflect the lower prices instead of adopting a global benchmark.

Reaching customers is arguably as tough as understanding their needs. Africa's infrastructure is poor, and more sales occur through informal channels, such as vendors and family-run businesses, than through stores and malls. Companies can overcome these challenges only by being flexible. Some foreign companies have a single national distributor; others over half a dozen. But all find they need more people to manage distributors in Africa than they do elsewhere. In Nigeria, P&G appointed exclusive distributors for seven geographic areas and hired employees to support each one, which it doesn't do in any other country. You must be patient—building a logistics network in Africa takes time. P&G spent 10 years building its Nigerian network.

Multinationals can hasten the expansion of formal retailing channels by co-investing in mall development or selling through multibrand stores. One successful European retailer has become a mall developer in Africa, which ensures strategic locations for its stores as well as anchor tenants for its malls. Shoprite is taking a similar tack as it expands across the continent.

In many African countries informal retail channels account for more than 80 percent of retail sales. Companies must find innovative ways to work with them. Coke has created a network of micro distribution centers to reach informal retailers in both rural and urban areas. It comprises 2,800 small businesses that use bicycles and manual pushcarts to deliver products over unpaved roads.

Infrastructure gaps demand creative solutions from service providers, too. For example, to ensure that it has continuous electrical power, Africa's largest cellular services operator, MTN, has built generators into each of its 5,000-plus towers in Nigeria. It uses a fleet of trucks to feed them diesel. By providing better service, MTN has acquired 31 million subscribers and built a $4.5 billion business in the country. Despite the added costs, its profit margins in Nigeria are routinely above 50 percent.

3. **Fill the skills gap.** High-skilled workers in Africa are similar to those in other emerging economies. The best-educated attend top universities, often overseas. Each year 200,000 students from sub-Saharan Africa study abroad. At the other end of the spectrum, there's also little difference between Africans and workers from other developing economies. One study found that factory workers in Kenya are as productive as those in China and India, but the overall production costs in Kenya are higher because of poor regulation and infrastructure—problems that are likely to go away.

What's missing is a cadre of midlevel managers—a shortage that reflects the weaknesses in Africa's secondary and tertiary education systems. To fill the gaps as their operations grow, multinational companies use several strategies:

Bringing in midlevel expatriates. Particularly in the early years, foreign companies import managers to start operations and groom local talent. Successful organizations create clear expectations about talent development; draw up targets; and monitor progress. One multinational company has reinforced its middle management in Nigeria with expatriate managers from other emerging markets, such as India, who have the skills and experience needed to deal with the Nigerian environment.

Setting up extensive training programs. Multinationals usually find that employees at all levels in Africa need training. Some invest in the local education system to develop people with the skills they require. Such programs may also help them win support from governments; companies can leverage them to obtain permits to enter markets, get tax credits, or gain access to land and other resources. A major oil company in Angola has created a program to train 14- to 16-year-olds as upstream specialists. It also works with a local university to increase the number of engineers and scientists graduating every year and funds a law program in oil and gas that produced its first class, of 28 graduates, in 2008.

Insisting on global rotations. Other corporations rotate senior executives and emerging leaders recruited in Africa through positions abroad so that they can bring home an array of skills to share. A case in point is the financial services firm Old Mutual, which maintains a constant flow of talent between its offices in Africa and those overseas.

Buying talent. Entry strategies that rely on M&A have one key advantage: the talent that comes with acquisitions. Mobile Telecommunications Company, for example, inherited a slew of senior and midlevel executives when it bought Celtel, then Africa's leading mobile player, six years ago.

4. **Manage risks.** Political instability is one of the two biggest risks foreign companies face on the continent, as the world is witnessing in North Africa. The other is adverse actions by governments, such as reneging on contracts or passing legislation that hampers operations—which some resource companies have experienced in West Africa. Abrupt changes in import tariffs and quotas can also affect operations.

Diversifying across geographic markets mitigates these risks. In addition, companies can create coalitions of stakeholders that help them detect potential problems early so that they can head them off or draw up contingency plans. Companies can do this in three ways:

Building partnerships. Local businesspeople and politicians usually know the political landscape and learn of changes long before they hit the news. Such partners can help foreign companies navigate bureaucracies and foster relationships with official and unofficial powers.

Wooing the influentials. Smart companies identify key influencers, such as congressional representatives, regulators, and mayors, in each country. They take the time to figure out, say, who among the top 50 influencers are their strong supporters; who's indifferent but can be turned into a supporter; and who'll never support them. They actively cultivate the first two groups.

Putting key stakeholders on their boards. Inviting key public and private sector stakeholders to join a country board aligns their incentives with the company's. It gives the locals a stake in the company's success.

In many ways Africa holds the same potential that China did 20 years ago. A large rural population is moving to the cities, landing jobs with higher incomes, and starting to enjoy discretionary spending. Demand is growing, and foreign direct investment has soared: from $9.4 billion in 2000 to $46.4 billion in 2009. Just as investing in China embodies some political risk, so too does doing business in Africa. Companies must think carefully about the approaches they adopt, but it will be worthwhile. Above all, first movers will have the opportunity to forge strong local partnerships and capture market share before everyone wakes up to the buzz around the Bright Continent.

Critical Thinking

1. According to this article, what are some of the internal and external strengths propelling Africa's long-term prospects and growth?

2. List the four types of African economies resulting from the authors' classification scheme. Do you agree with the choice of diversification and level of exports as classification parameters? Why or why not?

Mutsa Chironga is a consultant in Johannesburg, **Acha Leke** is a senior partner in Lagos, and **Arend van Wamelen** is a partner in Johannesburg at McKinsey & Company. **Susan Lund** is a research director of the McKinsey Global Institute, based in Washington, DC.

What the West Doesn't Get about China

Its export-focused economy is giving way to a consumer-driven market more quickly than most companies think. Here's how to adapt.

GEORGE STALK AND DAVID MICHAEL

When many managers think about China, they imagine a container ship whose hold and deck are brimming with cartons of toys, clothing, iPhones, and other goods bound for the world's consumer markets, whose populations power China's economic engine.

That view couldn't be more wrong.

Despite the Chinese government's well-publicized program to encourage domestic consumption, few Westerners grasp just how much progress the country is making on this front. Although millions of peasants live on subsistence wages, millions more Chinese are moving to urban centers and achieving a recognizably middle-class lifestyle. Consider just a few data points that give evidence of China's unexpectedly fast-paced move toward a more balanced, consumer-driven economy:

- In a variety of consumer categories—including such items as shoes, consumer electronics, and jewelry—China already ranks as the number one or number two market in the world. (See the list in the box "An 'Emerging' Market?")
- The combined flow of shipping containers between Asia and North America and Asia and Europe is already less than the flow among Asian nations—with much of the latter consisting of goods imported to China.
- Domestic demand accounts for most sales of Chinese-produced air conditioners, motorcycles, trucks, and steel.
- Adoption rates of new technologies among the rising middle class exceed those of nearly every other developing country. China has 400 million internet users, most with broadband access. Mobile telephony is ubiquitous in urban areas, and most of its consumers have leapfrogged landlines.
- China's cities are growing so quickly that the country now has more urban centers than most Western nations do. For instance, China has about 90 cities with a middle-class population of 250,000 or more; the U.S. and Canada together have fewer than 70. According to projections, by 2020 China will have 400 cities with at least 250,000 middle-class inhabitants—and 50 of those cities will have more than 1 million middle-class

inhabitants. And by then it is expected to have 800 cities whose residents' real disposable incomes are greater, on average, than those of Shanghai's residents today.
- Looking beyond consumer markets, we find that Chinese companies are already recognized as among the world leaders in numerous B2B technologies, including wind-turbine blades, solar panels, highspeed rail equipment, steam boilers, port terminal cranes, and electric-transmission equipment.

Few Western managers who visit China get a realistic picture of its economic development. They typically go to Beijing or Shanghai. They stay in five-star hotels—often Hiltons and Hyatts. There's apt to be a Starbucks in the lobby. The familiar atmosphere leads them to think that China's market will someday resemble a typical Western economy, full of Western-made products. But in fact, cities far from Beijing and Shanghai are teeming with goods and services from domestic companies—and if Western companies don't get to those cities soon, they'll be left out.

To be sure, despite its rapid progress China is still far from self-sufficient in a number of areas. It remains dependent on foreign multinationals for market access—many Chinese companies lack the ability to generate significant export trade on their own. The country can provide a college education for a growing share of the population but still relies largely on foreign universities for top-flight graduate education. Its only traditional energy resource is coal, and its demand for imported oil has been a major factor in rising prices over the past decade. China is also a net importer of food. Finally, it lacks the innovative pharmaceutical and health care sectors of Western economies, and as its consumers become increasingly upscale, they will demand more of the pills and procedures that Westerners take for granted.

How MNCs Should Navigate the Emerging China

Although every multinational has a China strategy, most companies aren't moving quickly enough for their strategies to succeed. To better position themselves, they need to be aware of these trends:

An "Emerging" Market?

Not in These Categories

China is already the world's largest or second-largest consumer of a variety of products:

Global Ranking: 1

Bikes and motorcycles (7 percent)*
Shoes (12 percent)
Automobiles (22 percent)
Mobile phones (22 percent)
Luxury goods (19 percent)

Global Ranking: 2

Home appliances (12 percent)
Consumer electronics (15 percent)
Jewelry (13 percent)
Internet use (63 percent)

*Compound annual growth, 2005–2009.

How Five Multinationals Figured China Out

Volkswagen

The German multinational was the first Western automaker to enter China, establishing its initial joint venture there in the 1980s, when other car manufacturers considered the country too risky. By the 1990s it had captured up to 90 percent of the market for passenger cars. Though it has since lost share to other overseas companies, it sold 1.9 million vehicles in 2010.

Yum Brands

The parent company of KFC, the first fast-food chain to open in China, Yum is the largest and fastest-growing restaurant chain in the country. It currently operates nearly 3,800 restaurants (more than 500 of which opened in 2010) in 700 cities across China.

Procter & Gamble

The consumer-goods giant has several brands that hold the top spot in the Chinese market, including Rejoice, Safeguard, Olay, Pampers, Tide, and Gillette. Fully 98 percent of its employees are Chinese, including many in top management positions. P&G recently opened the Beijing Innovation Center, which will provide global R&D support, and plans to invest at least $1 billion in China over the next 5 years.

Nokia

Having initially entered China as a network equipment supplier, Nokia is now the largest mobile-phone manufacturer in China, and China is its largest market.

General Electric

GE has operated in China for many decades in sectors including energy, aviation, health care, and transportation. It plans to extend its Chinese operations even further and recently announced five new deals expected to generate $2 billion in revenue.

Source: Company websites.

First, the rise of domestic competitors will happen faster than most MNCs expect. Local companies in some high-growth markets—for example, Xizi in elevators, 7 Days Inn in budget hotels, and Midea in consumer appliances—have already become leaders. Multinationals that hope to have strong market share a few years down the road need to establish themselves now.

Second, whether or not they are currently selling in China, companies looking to capitalize on the opportunities there need to be ready to do business in hundreds of locations, not just in a handful of the current megacities. This has dramatic implications for organizational structure, distribution infrastructure, choice of business partners, and the amount of capital needed.

Third, companies must prepare for extraordinary growth in demand. Some Western companies today are struggling to handle 35 percent annual sales growth in China—but the markets they're playing in are growing at 60 percent. Despite their enormous investments in human and capital resources, these companies are already ceding share to competitors—and their competitors will increasingly be Chinese companies. In a market growing this quickly, it can be worthwhile to build excess capacity, and it's smart to take a hard look at whether your present forecasts may be overly conservative.

Fourth, Western companies need to understand that Chinese consumers have very different needs than consumers in their home markets. Chinese households don't want cappuccino machines; they want water filters, air filters, and soy milk makers (at the moment, one of the hotter consumer categories in China—and one with no foreign competition). The classic example involves automakers, which had to learn that many Chinese who can afford cars like to employ drivers—so backseat features are very important to them.

The rise of local competitors will happen faster than most multinationals expect. MNCs that hope to have strong market share in China in a few years need to establish themselves now.

Fifth, MNCs must realize that product adoption rates will be higher in China than in most markets they've experienced, meaning that in some categories, the competitive landscape will be settled quickly. Companies that don't strive to be number one at the outset won't have the luxury of entering and being competitive later.

Sixth, as Chinese companies gain prowess in their home market, more will expand abroad. They are likely to move into Africa and South America before they enter North America and Europe. Whether they realize it or not, Western companies aren't fighting just for a position in the Chinese market—they're also fighting to forestall potential competitors in other emerging markets and eventually on their own turf. MNCs may not be inclined to pay much attention to small local companies in China today, but they should.

Last, Western companies will increasingly be on their own when dealing with many of the politically based difficulties of doing business in China. The power of Western governments to impose their will on the Chinese is diminishing rapidly—if it was ever really there at all—as the rise of China's own markets makes the country less dependent on Western companies. Competing in China will have less to do with government policy and more to do with offering the right products and services to the right customers at the right price.

Some Western companies are showing adroitness in exploiting the new opportunities in China. Among them are General Motors, General Electric, Honeywell, Phillips, Emerson, and Yum Brands. But these are exceptions. Most Western companies underestimate how quickly the Chinese market is developing and how little time they have to establish a competitive foothold—particularly in cities other than Beijing and Shanghai.

In many ways China today is what the United States was to Great Britain in the late 1800s. British managers couldn't imagine or execute the strategies necessary to do business in a geographical landscape far vaster than their home market. The same challenges now face Western managers in China, but on an even greater scale: Never before have businesses had to deal with market opportunities spread across such a wide geography, with so many different languages and ethnic populations. These are challenges that require aggressive action—and ones few companies are currently prepared to meet.

Critical Thinking

1. In your opinion, to what factors can you attribute the shift in the Chinese economy from an export-based one to a consumer-driven market?

2. Do Chinese consumers have different needs than Western consumers? If so, provide detailed examples to illustrate how their needs differ.

GEORGE STALK is a senior adviser and fellow at Boston Consulting Group. DAVID MICHAEL is a senior partner at BCG and heads the firm's globalization practice.

Glossary

This glossary of marketing terms is included to provide you with a convenient and ready reference as you encounter general terms in your study of marketing that are unfamiliar or require a review. It is not intended to be comprehensive, but taken together with the many definitions included in the articles themselves, it should prove to be quite useful.

A

acceptable price range The range of prices that buyers are willing to pay for a product; prices that are above the range may be judged unfair, while prices below the range may generate concerns about quality.

adaptive selling A salesperson's adjustment of his or her behavior between and during sales calls, to respond appropriately to issues that are important to the customer.

advertising Marketing communication elements designed to stimulate sales through the use of mass media displays, direct individual appeals, public displays, give-aways, and the like.

advertorial A special advertising section in magazines that includes some editorial (nonadvertising) content.

Americans with Disabilities Act (ADA) Passed in 1990, this U.S. law prohibits discrimination against consumers with disabilities.

automatic number identification A telephone system that identifies incoming phone numbers at the beginning of the call, without the caller's knowledge.

B

bait and switch Advertising a product at an attractively low price to get customers into the store, but making the product unavailable so that the customers must trade up to a more expensive version.

bar coding A computer-coded bar pattern that identifies a product. *See also* universal product code.

barter The practice of exchanging goods and services without the use of money.

benefit segmentation Organizing the market according to the attributes or benefits consumers need or desire, such as quality, service, or unique features.

brand A name, term, sign, design, symbol, or combination used to differentiate the products of one company from those of its competition.

brand image The quality and reliability of a product as perceived by consumers on the basis of its brand reputation or familiarity.

brand name The element of a brand that can be vocalized.

break-even analysis The calculation of the number of units that must be sold at a certain price to cover costs (break even); revenues earned past the break-even point contribute to profits.

bundling Marketing two or more products in a single package at one price.

business analysis The stage of new product development where initial marketing plans are prepared (including tentative marketing strategy and estimates of sales, costs, and profitability).

business strategic plan A plan for how each business unit in a corporation intends to compete in the marketplace, based upon the vision, objectives, and growth strategies of the corporate strategic plan.

C

capital products Expensive items that are used in business operations but do not become part of any finished product (such as office buildings, copy machines).

cash-and-carry wholesaler A limited-function wholesaler that does not extend credit for or deliver the products it sells.

caveat emptor A Latin term that means "let the buyer beware." A principle of law meaning that the purchase of a product is at the buyer's risk with regard to its quality, usefulness, and the like. The laws do, however, provide certain minimum protection against fraud and other schemes.

channel of distribution *See* marketing channel.

Child Protection Act U.S. law passed in 1990 to regulate advertising on children's TV programs.

Child Safety Act Passed in 1966, this U.S. law prohibits the marketing of dangerous products to children.

Clayton Act Anticompetitive activities are prohibited by this 1914 U.S. law.

co-branding When two brand names appear on the same product (such as a credit card with a school's name).

comparative advertising Advertising that compares one brand against a competitive brand on at least one product attribute.

competitive pricing strategies Pricing strategies that are based on an organization's position in relation to its competition.

consignment An arrangement in which a seller of goods does not take title to the goods until they are sold. The seller thus has the option of returning them to the supplier or principal if unable to execute the sale.

consolidated metropolitan statistical area (CMSA) Based on census data, the largest designation of geographic areas. *See also* primary metropolitan statistical area.

consumer behavior The way in which buyers, individually or collectively, react to marketplace stimuli.

Consumer Credit Protection Act A 1968 U.S. law that requires full disclosure of the financial charges of loans.

consumer decision process This four-step process includes recognizing a need or problem, searching for information, evaluating alternative products or brands, and purchasing a product.

Consumer Product Safety Commission (CPSC) A U.S. government agency that protects consumers from unsafe products.

consumerism A social movement in which consumers demand better information about the service, prices, dependability, and quality of the products they buy.

convenience products Consumer goods that are purchased at frequent intervals with little regard for price. Such goods are relatively standard in nature and consumers tend to select the most convenient source when shopping for them.

cooperative advertising Advertising of a product by a retailer, dealer, distributor, or the like, with part of the advertising cost paid by the product's manufacturer.

corporate strategic plan A plan that addresses what a company is and wants to become, and then guides strategic planning at all organizational levels.

Glossary

countersegmentation A concept that combines market segments to appeal to a broad range of consumers, assuming that there will be an increasing consumer willingness to accept fewer product and service choices for lower prices.

customer loyalty concept To focus beyond customer satisfaction toward customer retention as a way to generate sales and profit growth.

D

demand curve A relationship that shows how many units a market will purchase at a given price in a given period of time.

demographic environment The study of human population densities, distributions, and movements that relate to buying behavior.

derived demand The demand for business-to-business products that is dependent upon a demand for other products in the market.

differentiated strategy Using innovation and points of difference in product offerings, advanced technology, superior service, or higher quality in wide areas of market segments.

direct mail promotion Marketing goods to consumers by mailing unsolicited promotional material to them.

direct marketing The sale of products to carefully targeted consumers who interact with various advertising media without salesperson contact.

discount A reduction from list price that is given to a buyer as a reward for a favorable activity to the seller.

discretionary income The money that remains after taxes and necessities have been paid for.

disposable income That portion of income that remains after payment of taxes to use for food, clothing, and shelter.

dual distribution The selling of products to two or more competing distribution networks, or the selling of two brands of nearly identical products through competing distribution networks.

dumping The act of selling a product in a foreign country at a price lower than its domestic price.

durable goods Products that continue in service for an appreciable length of time.

E

economy The income, expenditures, and resources that affect business and household costs.

electronic data interchange (EDI) A computerized system that links two different firms to allow transmittal of documents; a quick-response inventory control system.

entry strategy An approach used to begin marketing products internationally.

environmental scanning Obtaining information on relevant factors and trends outside a company and interpreting their potential impact on the company's markets and marketing activities.

European Union (EU) The world's largest consumer market, consisting of 16 European nations: Austria, Belgium, Britain, Denmark, Finland, France, Germany, Greece, Italy, Ireland, Luxembourg, the Netherlands, Norway, Portugal, Spain, and Sweden.

exclusive distribution Marketing a product or service in only one retail outlet in a specific geographic marketplace.

exporting Selling goods to international markets.

F

Fair Packaging and Labeling Act of 1966 This law requires manufacturers to state ingredients, volume, and manufacturer's name on a package.

family life cycle The progress of a family through a number of distinct phases, each of which is associated with identifiable purchasing behaviors.

Federal Trade Commission (FTC) The U.S. government agency that regulates business practices; established in 1914.

five C's of pricing Five influences on pricing decisions: customers, costs, channels of distribution, competition, and compatibility.

FOB (free on board) The point at which the seller stops paying transportation costs.

four I's of service Four elements to services: intangibility, inconsistency, inseparability, and inventory.

four P's *See* marketing mix.

franchise The right to distribute a company's products or render services under its name, and to retain the resulting profit in exchange for a fee or percentage of sales.

freight absorption Payment of transportation costs by the manufacturer or seller, often resulting in a uniform pricing structure.

functional groupings Groupings in an organization in which a unit is subdivided according to different business activities, such as manufacturing, finance, and marketing.

G

General Agreement on Tariffs and Trade (GATT) An international agreement that is intended to limit trade barriers and to promote world trade through reduced tariffs; represents over 80 percent of global trade.

geodemographics A combination of geographic data and demographic characteristics; used to segment and target specific markets.

green marketing The implementation of an ecological perspective in marketing; the promotion of a product as environmentally safe.

gross domestic product (GDP) The total monetary value of all goods and services produced within a country during one year.

growth stage The second stage of a product life cycle that is characterized by a rapid increase in sales and profits.

H

hierarchy of effects The stages a prospective buyer goes through when purchasing a product, including awareness, interest, evaluation, trial, and adoption.

I

idea generation An initial stage of the new product development process; requires creativity and innovation to generate ideas for potential new products.

implied warranties Warranties that assign responsibility for a product's deficiencies to a manufacturer, even though the product was sold by a retailer.

imports Purchased goods or services that are manufactured or produced in some other country.

integrated marketing communications A strategic integration of marketing communications programs that coordinate all promotional activities—advertising, personal selling, sales promotion, and public relations.

internal reference prices The comparison price standards that consumers remember and use to judge the fairness of prices.

introduction stage The first product life cycle stage; when a new product is launched into the marketplace.

ISO 9000 International Standards Organization's standards for registration and certification of manufacturer's quality management and quality assurance systems.

J

joint venture An arrangement in which two or more organizations market products internationally.

just-in-time (JIT) inventory control system An inventory supply system that operates with very low inventories and fast, ontime delivery.

L

Lanham Trademark Act A 1946 U.S. law that was passed to protect trademarks and brand names.

late majority The fourth group to adopt a new product; representing about 34 percent of a market.

lifestyle research Research on a person's pattern of living, as displayed in activities, interests, and opinions.

limit pricing This competitive pricing strategy involves setting prices low to discourage new competition.

limited-coverage warranty The manufacturer's statement regarding the limits of coverage and noncoverage for any product deficiencies.

logistics management The planning, implementing, and moving of raw materials and products from the point of origin to the point of consumption.

loss-leader pricing The pricing of a product below its customary price in order to attract attention to it.

M

Magnuson-Moss Act Passed in 1975, this U.S. law regulates warranties.

management by exception Used by a marketing manager to identify results that deviate from plans, diagnose their cause, make appropriate new plans, and implement new actions.

manufacturers' agent A merchant wholesaler that sells related but noncompeting product lines for a number of manufacturers; also called manufacturers' representatives.

market The potential buyers for a company's product or service; or to sell a product or service to actual buyers. The place where goods and services are exchanged.

market penetration strategy The goal of achieving corporate growth objectives with existing products within existing markets by persuading current customers to purchase more of the product or by capturing new customers.

marketing channel Organizations and people that are involved in the process of making a product or service available for use by consumers or industrial users.

marketing communications planning A six-step process that includes marketing plan review; situation analysis; communications process analysis; budget development; program development integration and implementation of a plan; and monitoring, evaluating, and controlling the marketing communications program.

marketing concept The idea that a company should seek to satisfy the needs of consumers while also trying to achieve the organization's goals.

marketing mix The elements of marketing: product, brand, package, price, channels of distribution, advertising and promotion, personal selling, and the like.

marketing research The process of identifying a marketing problem and opportunity, collecting and analyzing information systematically, and recommending actions to improve an organization's marketing activities.

marketing research process A six-step sequence that includes problem definition, determination of research design, determination of data collection methods, development of data collection forms, sample design, and analysis and interpretation.

mission statement A part of the strategic planning process that expresses the company's basic values and specifies the operation boundaries within marketing, business units, and other areas.

motivation research A group of techniques developed by behavioral scientists that are used by marketing researchers to discover factors influencing marketing behavior.

N

nonprice competition Competition between brands based on factors other than price, such as quality, service, or product features.

nondurable goods Products that do not last or continue in service for any appreciable length of time.

North American Free Trade Agreement (NAFTA) A trade agreement among the United States, Canada, and Mexico that essentially removes the vast majority of trade barriers between the countries.

North American Industry Classification System (NAICS) A system used to classify organizations on the basis of major activity or the major good or service provided by the three NAFTA countries—Canada, Mexico, and the United States; replaced the Standard Industrial Classification (SIC) system in 1997.

O

observational data Market research data obtained by watching, either mechanically or in person, how people actually behave.

odd-even pricing Setting prices at just below an even number, such as $1.99 instead of $2.00.

opinion leaders Individuals who influence consumer behavior based on their interest in or expertise with particular products.

organizational goals The specific objectives used by a business or nonprofit unit to achieve and measure its performance.

outbound telemarketing Using the telephone rather than personal visits to contact customers.

outsourcing A company's decision to purchase products and services from other firms rather than using in-house employees.

P

parallel development In new product development, an approach that involves the development of the product and production process simultaneously.

penetration pricing Pricing a product low to discourage competition.

personal selling process The six stages of sales activities that occur before and after the sale itself: prospecting, preapproach, approach, presentation, close, and follow-up.

point-of-purchase display A sales promotion display located in high-traffic areas in retail stores.

posttesting Tests that are conducted to determine if an advertisement has accomplished its intended purpose.

predatory pricing The practice of selling products at low prices to drive competition from the market and then raising prices once a monopoly has been established.

prestige pricing Maintaining high prices to create an image of product quality and appeal to buyers who associate premium prices with high quality.

pretesting Evaluating consumer reactions to proposed advertisements through the use of focus groups and direct questions.

price elasticity of demand An economic concept that attempts to measure the sensitivity of demand for any product to changes in its price.

price fixing The illegal attempt by one or several companies to maintain the prices of their products above those that would result from open competition.

Glossary

price promotion mix The basic product price plus additional components such as sales prices, temporary discounts, coupons, favorable payment, and credit terms.

price skimming Setting prices high initially to appeal to consumers who are not price-sensitive and then lowering prices to appeal to the next market segments.

primary metropolitan statistical area (PMSA) Major urban area, often located within a CMSA, that has at least one million inhabitants.

PRIZM A potential rating index by ZIP code markets that divides every U.S. neighborhood into 1 of 40 distinct cluster types that reveal consumer data.

product An idea, good, service, or any combination that is an element of exchange to satisfy a consumer.

product differentiation The ability or tendency of manufacturers, marketers, or consumers to distinguish between seemingly similar products.

product expansion strategy A plan to market new products to the same customer base.

product life cycle (PLC) A product's advancement through the introduction, growth, maturity, and decline stages.

product line pricing Setting the prices for all product line items.

product marketing plans Business units' plans to focus on specific target markets and marketing mixes for each product, which include both strategic and execution decisions.

product mix The composite of products offered for sale by a firm or a business unit.

promotional mix Combining one or more of the promotional elements that a firm uses to communicate with consumers.

proprietary secondary data The data that is provided by commercial marketing research firms to other firms.

psychographic research Measurable characteristics of given market segments in respect to lifestyles, interests, opinions, needs, values, attitudes, personality traits, and the like.

publicity Nonpersonal presentation of a product, service, or business unit.

pull strategy A marketing strategy whose main thrust is to strongly influence the final consumer, so that the demand for a product "pulls" it through the various channels of distribution.

push strategy A marketing strategy whose main thrust is to provide sufficient economic incentives to members of the channels of distribution, so as to "push" the product through to the consumer.

Q

qualitative data The responses obtained from in-depth interviews, focus groups, and observation studies.

quality function deployment (QFD) The data collected from structured response formats that can be easily analyzed and projected to larger populations.

quotas In international marketing, they are restrictions placed on the amount of a product that is allowed to leave or enter a country; the total outcomes used to assess sales representatives' performance and effectiveness.

R

regional marketing A form of geographic division that develops marketing plans that reflect differences in taste preferences, perceived needs, or interests in other areas.

relationship marketing The development, maintenance, and enhancement of long-term, profitable customer relationships.

repositioning The development of new marketing programs that will shift consumer beliefs and opinions about an existing brand.

resale price maintenance Control by a supplier of the selling prices of his branded goods at subsequent stages of distribution, by means of contractual agreement under fair trade laws or other devices.

reservation price The highest price a consumer will pay for a product; a form of internal reference price.

restraint of trade In general, activities that interfere with competitive marketing. Restraint of trade usually refers to illegal activities.

retail strategy mix Controllable variables that include location, products and services, pricing, and marketing communications.

return on investment (ROI) A ratio of income before taxes to total operating assets associated with a product, such as inventory, plant, and equipment.

S

sales effectiveness evaluations A test of advertising efficiency to determine if it resulted in increased sales.

sales forecast An estimate of sales under controllable and uncontrollable conditions.

sales management The planning, direction, and control of the personal selling activities of a business unit.

sales promotion An element of the marketing communications mix that provides incentives or extra value to stimulate product interest.

samples A small size of a product given to prospective purchasers to demonstrate a product's value or use and to encourage future purchase; some elements that are taken from the population or universe.

scanner data Proprietary data that is derived from UPC bar codes.

scrambled merchandising Offering several unrelated product lines within a single retail store.

selected controlled markets Sites where market tests for a new product are conducted by an outside agency and retailers are paid to display that product; also referred to as forced distribution markets.

selective distribution This involves selling a product in only some of the available outlets; commonly used when after-the-sale service is necessary, such as in the case of home appliances.

seller's market A condition within any market in which the demand for an item is greater than its supply.

selling philosophy An emphasis on an organization's selling function to the exclusion of other marketing activities.

selling strategy A salesperson's overall plan of action, which is developed at three levels: sales territory, customer, and individual sales calls.

services Nonphysical products that a company provides to consumers in exchange for money or something else of value.

share points Percentage points of market share; often used as the common comparison basis to allocate marketing resources effectively.

Sherman Anti-Trust Act Passed in 1890, this U.S. law prohibits contracts, combinations, or conspiracies in restraint of trade and actual monopolies or attempts to monopolize any part of trade or commerce.

shopping products Consumer goods that are purchased only after comparisons are made concerning price, quality, style, suitability, and the like.

single-channel strategy Marketing strategy using only one means to reach customers; providing one sales source for a product.

single-zone pricing A pricing policy in which all buyers pay the same delivered product price, regardless of location; also known as uniform delivered pricing or postage stamp pricing.

slotting fees High fees manufacturers pay to place a new product on a retailer's or wholesaler's shelf.

social responsibility Reducing social costs, such as environmental damage, and increasing the positive impact of a marketing decision on society.

societal marketing concept The use of marketing strategies to increase the acceptability of an idea (smoking causes cancer); cause (environmental protection); or practice (birth control) within a target market.

specialty products Consumer goods, usually appealing only to a limited market, for which consumers will make a special purchasing effort. Such items include, for example, stereo components, fancy foods, and prestige brand clothes.

Standard Industrial Classification (SIC) system Replaced by NAICS, this federal government numerical scheme categorized businesses.

standardized marketing Enforcing similar product, price, distribution, and communications programs in all international markets.

stimulus-response presentation A selling format that assumes that a customer will buy if given the appropriate stimulus by a salesperson.

strategic business unit (SBU) A decentralized profit center of a company that operates as a separate, independent business.

strategic marketing process Marketing activities in which a firm allocates its marketing mix resources to reach a target market.

strategy mix A way for retailers to differentiate themselves from others through location, product, services, pricing, and marketing mixes.

subliminal perception When a person hears or sees messages without being aware of them.

SWOT analysis An acronym that describes a firm's appraisal of its internal strengths and weaknesses and its external opportunities and threats.

synergy An increased customer value that is achieved through more efficient organizational function performances.

systems-designer strategy A selling strategy that allows knowledgeable sales reps to determine solutions to a customer's problems or to anticipate opportunities to enhance a customer's business through new or modified business systems.

T

target market A defined group of consumers or organizations toward which a firm directs its marketing program.

team selling A sales strategy that assigns accounts to specialized sales teams according to a customer's purchase-information needs.

telemarketing An interactive direct marketing approach that uses the telephone to develop relationships with customers.

test marketing The process of testing a prototype of a new product to gain consumer reaction and to examine its commercial viability and marketing strategy.

TIGER (Topologically Integrated Geographic Encoding and Reference) A minutely detailed U.S. Census Bureau computerized map of the United States that can be combined with a company's own database to analyze customer sales.

total quality management (TQM) Programs that emphasize long-term relationships with selected suppliers instead of short-term transactions with many suppliers.

total revenue The total of sales, or unit price, multiplied by the quantity of the product sold.

trade allowance An amount a manufacturer contributes to a local dealer's or retailer's advertising expenses.

trade (functional) discounts Price reductions that are granted to wholesalers or retailers that are based on future marketing functions that they will perform for a manufacturer.

trademark The legal identification of a company's exclusive rights to use a brand name or trade name.

truck jobber A small merchant wholesaler who delivers limited assortments of fast-moving or perishable items within a small geographic area.

two-way stretch strategy Adding products at both the low and high end of a product line.

U

undifferentiated strategy Using a single promotional mix to market a single product for the entire market; frequently used early in the life of a product.

uniform delivered price The same average freight amount that is charged to all customers, no matter where they are located.

universal product code (UPC) An assigned number to identify a product, which is represented by a series of bars of varying widths for optical scanning.

usage rate The quantity consumed or patronage during a specific period, which can vary significantly among different customer groups.

utilitarian influence To comply with the expectations of others to achieve rewards or avoid punishments.

V

value added In retail strategy decisions, a dimension of the retail positioning matrix that refers to the service level and method of operation of the retailer.

vertical marketing systems Centrally coordinated and professionally managed marketing channels that are designed to achieve channel economies and maximum marketing impact.

vertical price fixing Requiring that sellers not sell products below a minimum retail price; sometimes called resale price maintenance.

W

weighted-point system The method of establishing screening criteria, assigning them weights, and using them to evaluate new product lines.

wholesaler One who makes quantity purchases from manufacturers (or other wholesalers) and sells in smaller quantities to retailers (or other wholesalers).

Z

zone pricing A form of geographic pricing whereby a seller divides its market into broad geographic zones and then sets a uniform delivered price for each zone.

Test-Your-Knowledge Form

We encourage you to photocopy and use this page as a tool to assess how the articles in *Annual Editions* expand on the information in your textbook. By reflecting on the articles you will gain enhanced text information. You can also access this useful form on a product's book support website at www.mhhe.com/cls

NAME: DATE:

_____

TITLE AND NUMBER OF ARTICLE:

_____

BRIEFLY STATE THE MAIN IDEA OF THIS ARTICLE:

_____

LIST THREE IMPORTANT FACTS THAT THE AUTHOR USES TO SUPPORT THE MAIN IDEA:

_____

WHAT INFORMATION OR IDEAS DISCUSSED IN THIS ARTICLE ARE ALSO DISCUSSED IN YOUR TEXTBOOK OR OTHER READINGS THAT YOU HAVE DONE? LIST THE TEXTBOOK CHAPTERS AND PAGE NUMBERS:

_____

LIST ANY EXAMPLES OF BIAS OR FAULTY REASONING THAT YOU FOUND IN THE ARTICLE:

_____

LIST ANY NEW TERMS/CONCEPTS THAT WERE DISCUSSED IN THE ARTICLE, AND WRITE A SHORT DEFINITION: